Edited with Commentary by

WILLIAM J. BENNETT

Simon & Schuster

OUR SACRED HONOR

❧

Words of Advice from the

Founders in Stories, Letters,

Poems, and Speeches

SIMON & SCHUSTER
Rockefeller Center
1230 Avenue of the Americas
New York, NY 10020

Designed by Karolina Harris

Manufactured in the United States of America

1 3 5 7 9 10 8 6 4 2

Library of Congress Cataloging-in-Publication Data

ISBN 978-1-4516-1355-1

ACKNOWLEDGMENTS

It was Matthew L. Jacobson, formerly of Broadman & Holman Publishers and now of Questar Publishing, who suggested I write a "virtues book" about the Founders. I am grateful to him for the idea—one that has led to so much pleasure and learning for me in the preparation of *Our Sacred Honor.*

I would like to thank Walter Berns of the American Enterprise Institute, Philip Hamburger of George Washington University Law School, Charles Kesler of Claremont McKenna College, and Matthew Spalding of the Heritage Foundation, for their reviews, assessments, and recommendations on early drafts. I would also like to thank my friend Rush Limbaugh, Jr., for bringing to my attention (through a wonderful speech by his father) the deeds of the lesser-known signers of the Declaration of Independence, such as Richard Stockton and Abraham Clark.

Bob Barnett, my agent, did his usual excellent work, this time working with the demands of two publishing houses. His counsel is always sound. I would like to thank Simon & Schuster and Broadman & Holman for their interest in and sponsorship of this work. Bill Rosen is an outstanding editor—wise, learned, and responsible. This book is better because of his efforts. Dorothea Israel Wolfson was central to this project. She researched, drafted, consulted, chased down reliable and unreliable leads both, and brought good sense, good judgment, and good taste to our deliberations. I am enormously grateful to her. She is a fine young scholar, and we will all benefit from reading her work in the future.

Finally, as always, I thank my wife, Elayne, and my sons, John and Joseph, for their understanding, support, and encouragement. They are my "Dearest Friend[s]" who have "softened and warmed my Heart."

CONTENTS

"And for support of this Declaration, with a firm reliance on Divine Providence we mutually pledge to each other our Lives, our Fortunes, & our sacred Honor."

THOMAS JEFFERSON
DECLARATION OF INDEPENDENCE
1776

INTRODUCTION

This is a book of advice. It is a collection of the thoughts of our Founders, some of the most thoughtful men and women who ever walked our nation. Their learning, their passion, and their sense of honor shine through this collection. In their advice for our nation, there is a vision of greatness and dedication to high purpose. Their words aim high—they instruct and inspire. In this book, we—all Americans—can see both our patrimony and our basic civic obligations: to keep our country safe and to hold its purpose high.

But how are we to do so? It is famously recorded that upon the conclusion of the Constitutional Convention of 1787 a Mrs. Powel of Philadelphia "asked Dr. Franklin, 'Well Doctor what have we got a republic or a monarchy?' 'A republic,' replied the Doctor, 'if you can keep it.' " Unfortunately, Franklin's challenge is little pondered today. And to the extent that it is, we answer that our political system is a machine that will go of itself, powered by such mechanisms as the separation of powers, federalism, institutional checks and balances, clashing political factions, free elections, pluralism, interest groups, and so on and so forth.

To some extent it does work this way, which was part of the Founders' plan. They believed that institutional arrangements would be central to the success of a modern republic, and Americans are rightfully proud to possess the world's longest-lasting and most imitated written political document—the Constitution. Yet even with such extraordinary political instruments and institutions, the Founders were aware that the American republic would not, over the long haul, be so easily maintained.

From their study of history, the Founders had learned of the travails of republics before this one—how the republics of old had, in time, been destroyed by convulsions and upheavals, by vice and decadence. And from their study of human nature, they became acutely aware of man's self-interestedness and his selfishness, designing America's political institutions to take these into account. They concluded that while such institutional supports were absolutely necessary and could do much to rechannel and curb individual selfishness and discourage political convulsions, something more would be needed if the republic was to survive. As John Adams put it, "Human passions unbridled by morality and religion . . . would break the strongest cords of our Constitution as a whale goes through a net."

The gritty and noble work of securing the republic would, in the final analysis, have to be done by individuals of sturdy character. Only a people possessing the right dispositions and mores, and strong but tempered religious beliefs, would be able to keep what the Founders had bequeathed to them in 1776. In other words, the arduous task of sustaining the American republic would fall upon us, upon you and me, upon the "millions yet unborn," as Washington then put it. The question of how to secure the republic is then the question of what sort of people we must be.

This is why I have chosen to offer to the American public a book on the Founders' vision of the virtues that they believed necessary for sustaining the American experiment. As the poet Robert Frost observed, the "vision" of the Founders was "to occupy the land with character . . . with people in self control."* That vision is not as systematically presented as is their analysis of political institutions—for example, there is no *Federalist Papers* for the virtues—but it is there for those who look. And it is necessary for each generation of Americans to look, since, as Lincoln warned, the great deeds and virtues of the founding generation "grow more and more dim by the lapse of time." How can Americans fully know this country and themselves without knowing at least a little about the men and women who pledged and risked their "lives," "fortunes," and "sacred honor" for the blessings of liberty we enjoy today? Thus, in preparing this book, I reviewed the private letters, public addresses, and pamphlets of the Founders to bring to light once again their answers. My aim was to share with a new generation of Americans the private and public reflections of the founding generation on what we must do to make America great.

I should note that this is the third time I have tackled the virtues. In my previous books *The Book of Virtues* and *The Moral Compass,* I collected stories, tales, addresses, poems, etc., that were meant to rekindle an art, lost in some places, the art of the moral education of the young (and adults as well). As wide-ranging as those books were, I began to realize that their very breadth left out something valuable. This book too

---

* Robert Frost, "A Talk for Students," *Fund for the Republic Publications* (New York, 1956), cited in Robert Rutland, *James Madison: The Founding Father,* p. 252.

is about the lost art of moral education. But this time, I was guided by Madison's observation in *The Federalist Papers* that our form of government "presupposes" virtue "in a higher degree than any other form" of government. What were the virtues that *he* had in mind? This book is then about *our virtues*—the virtues the Founders thought essential for the success of the American experiment.

The virtues I've chosen to highlight in this collection are, of course, not the exclusive property of the American people. Other cultures and peoples share them or might aspire to embrace them. But having said that, I would emphasize that there is something very American about these virtues. As John Hancock marveled, the Lord gave this country

a name and a standing among the nations of the world . . . I hope and pray that the gratitude of their hearts may be expressed by proper use of those inestimable blessings, by the greatest exertions of patriotism, by forming and supporting institutions for cultivating the human understanding, & for the greatest progress of the Arts and Sciences, by establishing laws for the support of piety, religion, and morality . . . and by exhibiting on the great theater of the world those social, public and private virtues which give more dignity to a people, possessing their own sovereignty than the crowns and diadems afford to sovereign princes.*

America would dazzle "the great theater of the world" not by its regal splendor but by adopting the virtues peculiar to a free people. The Founders sensed that America would chart a new course in world history; that Americans would show the "eyes of mankind," in the words of Samuel Adams, that their republic "will be productive of more Virtue, moral and political." The capacious vision of the Founders—their bold ambitions for themselves and for this nation—has made America truly exceptional. If it were asked wherein lies the spirit of America, I would say it is here in our capacity to govern ourselves, to excel in private and public virtue.

But lately Americans have become worried about the state of the culture and, in my opinion, rightly so. I have argued for years that it is not the economy that is the source of our present discontent. And most Americans now agree, citing moral decline as our chief malady. We have fallen way short of our duties and aspirations, and I do not except myself

* Speech in the Council Chamber, February 27, 1788, from *John Hancock's Life and Speeches: A Personalized Vision of the American Revolution 1763–1793*, ed. Paul D. Brandes, pp. 332–33.

in this regard. We need to engage in a relearning—to borrow novelist Tom Wolfe's phrase, "a great relearning." We also need to restore this nation's sense of greatness, to learn once again about the great deeds and the great men and women of our past so that we might move forward.

As we approach the twenty-first century, however, many will demand to know, what can we possibly learn about virtue from men and women of the eighteenth century? What could they possibly teach us moderns or even "post-moderns?" Others will point to the signs of cultural decay all about us—skyrocketing rates of divorce, drug use, premarital sex, children born out of wedlock, crime, etc.—and conclude that modern solutions are needed for modern problems. I would never suggest that reading this book will solve these problems. But I insist that it could be the first step in a long journey toward moral reform and cultural renascence in America. For the Founders were quite simply extraordinary men and women with extraordinary insights into the ways of humankind. Their advice is worthy; we would benefit, I think, from heeding it. They aspired to greatness in their public lives and to virtue in their private lives. And we, all of us, could do more of the same. We could more often aspire to excellence and aspire for greatness in our nation too.

Let me be frank: I admire without stint the lives the Founders lived as well as the sharp insight they bring to bear on the matter of vice and virtue, love and marriage, work and leisure, piety and justice—questions that were as much theirs as ours. This possibly presents a problem. Is the standard of reflection and conduct set by the Founders too high? Is it an unattainable goal? They were, after all, *founders,* driven by a love of fame and glory: Their ambitions aimed at founding a great nation and performing great deeds on the greatest of all stages, the theater of politics. They were given a special time and place in history.

If it is the case that most of us cannot reach as high as the Founders, we can at least learn from them. We can learn to raise our sights a bit. For as Abigail Adams warned, if we are surrounded by the trivial and the vicious, it is all too easy to make our peace with it. Human beings can adjust to anything. (I call this getting used to decadence.) So, though the Founders set standards that many of us, most of us, cannot hope to meet, their thoughts on patriotism and national greatness, on the proper relationship between God and man, men and women, work and leisure, and friends and strangers might help us to do better.

The Founders certainly were no angels—often they did not live by their own advice. They themselves acknowledged that if men were angels there would be no need for government. Most tragically, some of our Founders, such as Thomas Jefferson, James Madison, and George Washington, owned slaves, a gross violation of the very principles of human equality which they espoused. Most of the Founders, even the slaveholders, struggled with the evil of slavery, knowing that it violated the cause for which they were fighting.

Some of our greatest Founding Fathers had the most substantial flaws: John Adams admitted to being off-putting and vain; Alexander Hamilton had a very public extramarital affair; George Washington was known to have had a violent temper; Benjamin Franklin early in life had many "intrigues," as he put it, with various women and fathered an illegitimate son, beginning a long line of illegitimate sons which would continue through three generations of Franklins; Thomas Jefferson, while encouraging his children to industry and frugality, himself died over $100,000 in debt (today's equivalent of several million dollars); Lafayette, an early and great ally of the American cause, was said to have had a "canine appetite" for popularity.

So they were not perfect. But their flaws, whether great or small, hardly disqualify them as guides to use today. Their struggles should remind us only that the perfect is the enemy of the good. If we fall short, there is no reason to despair, only more reason to try harder. Thus, as John Adams urged the Americans of his time to "read and recollect and impress upon our souls the views and ends of our own immediate forefathers" and "recollect their amazing fortitude," so I urge the same recollection today. In many ways, living lives of virtue (though often falling short of it), the Founders knew of what they wrote. "Sacred honor" was not just a flourish of rhetoric that Jefferson inserted into the Declaration of Independence but a way of life for most of the Founders.

The book is divided into seven chapters, each one devoted to a specific virtue. What I have included is a sampling—space imposed its own constraints. My goal was to include selections on the virtues most important to the future vitality of the country. I have selected what I believed to be the best that the Founders wrote on these virtues. There is much here that is moving, memorable, worthy, and perhaps unfamiliar to most Americans. Ready-made answers, however, are not to be found. Instead, the reader will look on as different Founders struggle with the timeless questions of love, friendship, piety, and so on. Some of the selections might at first seem to make the same point or argument. The reader will discover that the Founders were not willing to state a proposition about virtue or patriotism once and leave it at that. They constantly revisited these matters, reworking their thoughts, deepening their understanding, and wrestling with unresolved questions. My hope is that the reader will join them in their struggles. This book is then neither history nor homily; it is a book of my favorite words and deeds and struggles of the Founders, reproduced in most (though not all) cases in a manner faithful to eighteenth-century grammar and spelling. Those seeking for a comprehensive and definitive portrait of the Founding generation will have to seek elsewhere.

A brief word about the time period: This book deals with the men and women involved in the events of 1776 through 1787. I decided not to include material relating to matters that arose later, such as the War of 1812, because I wanted to focus on the remarkable period of Founding. There is something *sui generis* about the Founding generation. Thus, I have included only the men and women who were the principal actors during that time period. (Though I have not hesitated to record their later reflections on these crucial years.) Even so, I have not hobbled this book with a blind obedience to this rule. Some works that celebrate the Founding, but were written long after it, are also included.

The book begins with patriotism and courage, the most public virtues. Chapters two and three explore the relations that make for a satisfying and healthy private sphere, namely love and courtship, and civility and friendship. The next two chapters focus on the virtues that form not only good citizens but self-sufficient ones: education, particularly the shaping of the minds and hearts of a free people, and industry and frugality. The last two chapters are in many ways the most important. They take up the question of justice and what Madison held to be our "first" duty—our obligation to God.

Sometimes a chapter is dominated by one or two Founders. For example, Jefferson makes many appearances in the civility and friendship chapter; John and Abigail Adams in the love and courtship chapter; Benjamin Franklin in the industry and frugality chapter; Madison and Jefferson in the justice chapter; and Washington in the piety chapter. This is in each case a reflection of their individual strengths and interests: Jefferson's capacity for friendship was unrivaled; Abigail and John Adams had one of the happiest and most famous marriages; Franklin's example of industry and frugality has become the model for all Americans to follow; Jefferson and Madison were the two men most responsible for America's two most important founding documents, the Declaration of Independence and the Constitution, respectively; Washington believed that the success of America depended most on religion and morality.

It seemed important to me that there be a book on the Founders, one that is accessible to people of all ages. Indeed, I have designed this collection with America's families especially in mind. In many ways, the selections can be interpreted as the Founders' advice to the young, for much of the material collected here was written originally by the Founders to their children, grandchildren, and other young relations. I hope this collection will serve as a way to enter into their world, which is our world too. Like Jefferson's grandson, who was eager to meet as many living Founders as possible, perhaps the readers of this book will be moved "to recount to those around" what we have "heard and learnt of the Heroic age preceding" our birth.* Finally, I hope that this book might rekindle in Americans the desire for another heroic age—an age not behind but before us.

---

* Jefferson to Adams, March 25, 1826.

I

PATRIOTISM AND COURAGE

"Our obligations to our country never cease but with our lives."

JOHN ADAMS TO BENJAMIN RUSH, APRIL 18, 1808

As every American knows, the first part of the Declaration of Independence establishes the rights to life, liberty, and the pursuit of happiness. Nothing, it seems, could be more fundamental to Americans than the protection of these rights. We are all well aware of them, and these days not shy about asserting them. However, few Americans pay enough attention to the last line of the Declaration of Independence. There Jefferson wrote: "we mutually pledge to each other our lives, our fortunes, and our sacred honor." These are not empty words; they are as important as the opening paragraphs of the Declaration. Rights are important. But just as we have a fair claim on our rights, so America's honor —our sacred honor—has a fair claim on us. The fifty-six men who signed the Declaration of Independence and the other leaders of the American Revolutionary War would either become glorious Founders of a new nation or they would swing from the gallows. As Benjamin Rush said, his fellow signers knew they were signing their own "death warrants."

Most of the signers of the Declaration as well as other Americans at the time suffered for their devotion to the cause of independence— many had to flee their homes; some lost their property and their fortunes, which they and their families never recovered. A few joined the Continental army. One of the sentiments that moved them to make these sacrifices was patriotism.

Patriotism means love of country, and it can call for great sacrifices and courage, perhaps even for the sacrifice of one's own life. Most of us don't have as keen a sense of that now as did the Founders. Though the word patriotism, from the Latin *pater* for "father," implies a familial connection, love of country is in fact different from all other attachments.

We have natural ties to our families, and sacrificing for loved ones is something each of us does every day. But sacrificing for our country requires a commitment to something more abstract and distant. It requires that we sacrifice our self-interest and private attachments for the sake of the common interest and public good for people we have never seen, for those who have gone before and for those who will come after us. And in America, what brings forth our patriotism—our greatest sacrifices—is our steadfast devotion to the ideals of freedom and equality. American patriotism, in short, is not based on tribe or family, but on principle, law, and liberty.

What makes the patriots of 1776 and 1787 so remarkable is that they were devoting themselves to something quite new—a new nation conceived in a new way and dedicated to a self-evident truth that all men are created equal. It was of course not easy, they wrote in the Declaration of Independence, to ignore the "ties of our common kindred"—their "British brethren." The bonds of "consanguinity" are strong, and most nations are held together by the ties of blood or common ethnicity alone. But these patriots had a new idea—a country tied together in loyalty to a principle. The universality of this principle caught fire and inspired a diverse group of men, women, Northerners, Southerners, even European nobility to make great sacrifices for the cause.

The founding was the product of "reflection" and "choice," as Alexander Hamilton would later put it. But it also took a long and grueling war to make independence a reality, a war led by the father of our country, George Washington. Our most prominent patriot, Washington once wrote that "when my country demands the sacrifice, personal ease must always be a secondary consideration." And he meant it and continued to serve his country despite his preference for private life. This chapter includes many accounts of Washington's unparalleled example of love of country and courage. It also includes accounts of some of our soldiers in action, such as Nathan Hale and Israel Putnam.

But other patriots, like James Madison, John Adams, or Thomas Jefferson, fought their battles with the pen, not the sword. These men, as has been said, were our Solon and Lycurgus—that is, our lawgivers. Madison himself saw the parallels—in *Federalist 38* he wrote that the Constitution provides the possibility for "immortality, as Lycurgus gave to that of Sparta." They seized the opportunity to found a nation on a humane and just foundation. As John Adams put it in his *Thoughts on Government:*

> You and I, my dear friend, have been sent into life at a time when the greatest lawgivers of antiquity would have wished to live. How few of the human race have ever enjoyed an opportunity of making an election of

government, more than of air, soil, or climate, for themselves or their children! When, before the present epoch, had three millions of people full power and a fair opportunity to form and establish the wisest and happiest government that human wisdom can contrive?

It must be said that the patriots of 1776 and 1787 were not acting completely out of a sense of disinterestedness. Their love of country, as the late historian Douglass Adair has shown, was buttressed, among other things, by what some may say is a more selfish passion—the love of fame and glory. This passion for fame or glory, in addition to their love of country, motivated the exertions of our patriots. In the *Federalist 72* Hamilton wrote that "the love of fame, the ruling passion of the noblest minds . . . prompt[s] a man to plan and undertake extensive and arduous enterprises for the public benefit." These men acted with their eyes toward posterity, concerned with how they would be remembered and immortalized. These concerns and passions may have been selfish in origin, but they elevated and strengthened the Founders' sense of public duty and gave rise to the "noblest" actions as well. Their love of glory stirred great, not petty, ambitions—ambitions which shaped their character and directed them to the political and national stage.

Adams endured long separations from his wife and family to participate in the Second Continental Congress, where he successfully urged his fellow delegates to adopt the resolution for independence. In Congress, Adams worked fifteen-hour days; as he told Mercy Warren, his schedule was to work "from seven to ten in the morning in the committee; from ten to four in Congress, and from six to ten again in committee." Like Adams, Thomas Jefferson left behind his beloved wife, who was often in frail health, to serve in Congress, where he wrote the Declaration of Independence, the "sheet anchor" of our liberties as Lincoln would later put it. Adams and Jefferson were family men—Jefferson was practically a newlywed when he served in Congress—yet they balanced their love of the private with a noble love of the *res publica*—"public things." James Madison worked day and night to restructure America's political institutions on a more lasting foundation than the republics of old. Madison later confided to a friend that his efforts at the Constitutional Convention "nearly killed me."

Abigail Adams noted the particularly difficult requirements patriotism exacted from women. And she observed that the sacrifices of women are no less than the most heroic of men. She was a woman of courage, who held down a farm by herself and took care of four children through the roar of nearby gunfire and a plague of dysentery.

Times of war and crisis reveal the character of patriotism in high relief.

But patriotism is an everyday virtue as well—a virtue that cannot be neglected or taken for granted. It requires education; it must be taught; and it must be, as Washington once said, supplemented by our self-interest. How is it that sacrifice becomes mixed with self-interest? According to Washington, once we appreciate how our own well-being, prosperity, and liberties are all the products of living in *this* country, as opposed to any other, we will become natural patriots. Our defense of principle becomes a defense of hearth and home.

Let me close with the reflections of Washington to Jefferson, a decade after American independence was declared, recalling the veterans of 1776 who had recently died: "Thus some of the pillars of the revolution fall. Others are mouldering by insensible degrees. May our Country never want props to support the glorious fabrick!" That is not a bad fate for each of us to contemplate—to spend at least a little of our lives as a "prop" for the greatest country the world has ever seen.

∞

"Our Lives, Our Fortunes, and Our Sacred Honor" Declaration of Independence

. . . *Prudence,* indeed, will dictate that governments long established should not be changed for light and transient causes; and accordingly all experience hath shown, that mankind are more disposed to suffer, while evils are sufferable, than to right themselves by abolishing the forms to which they are accustomed. But when a long train of abuses and usurpations, pursuing invariably the same object, evinces a design to reduce them under absolute despotism, it is their right, it is their duty, to throw off such government, and to provide new guards for their future security. Such has been the patient sufferance of these colonies; and such is now the necessity which constrains them to alter their former systems of government. . . .

We, therefore, the representatives of the United States of America, in General Congress Assembled, appealing to the Supreme Judge of the world for the rectitude of our intentions, do, in the name and by authority of the good People of these colonies, solemnly publish and declare, That these United Colonies are, and of Right, ought to be, FREE AND INDEPENDENT STATES; that they are Absolved from all Allegiance to the British Crown, and that all political connection between them and the State of Great Britain is, and ought to be, totally dissolved; and that as Free and Independent States they have full Power to levy War, conclude Peace, contract Alliances, establish Commerce, and to do all other Acts and Things which Independent States may of right do. And for the support of this Declaration, with a firm reliance on the protection of Divine Providence, we mutually pledge to each other our Lives, our Fortunes, and our sacred Honor.

∞

Benjamin Rush to John Adams, July 20, 1811

I DON'T know how many of us appreciate the grave risk taken by the signers to the Declaration of Independence. This might be because some of the signers bravely laughed in the face of danger: While writing his bold and now famous signature, John Hancock, the first to sign, reportedly said: "There! His Majesty can now read my name without glasses. And he can double the reward on my head!" To encourage solidarity, Hancock later told the delegates who were preparing to sign the document, that they must all hang together. To which Benjamin Franklin supposedly quipped: "We must all hang together, or we most assuredly will hang separately."

In this letter, Benjamin Rush shares another humorous exchange about hanging among the signers but also recalls the "pensive and awful silence" that filled the room as these patriots of '76 signed away their lives.

DEAR OLD FRIEND,

The 4th of July has been celebrated in Philadelphia in the manner I expected. The military men, and particularly one of them, ran away with all the glory of the day. Scarcely a word was said of the solicitude and labors and fears and sorrows and sleepless nights of the men who projected, proposed, defended, and subscribed the Declaration of Independence. Do you recollect your memorable speech upon the day on which the vote was taken? Do you recollect the pensive and awful silence which pervaded the house when we were called up, one after another, to the table of the President of Congress to subscribe what was believed by many at that time to be our own death warrants? The silence and the gloom of the morning were interrupted, I well recollect, only for a moment by Colonel Harrison of Virginia, who said to Mr. Gerry at the table: "I shall have a great advantage over you, Mr. Gerry, when we are all hung for what we are now doing. From the size and weight of my body I shall die in a few minutes, but from the lightness of your body you will dance in the air an hour or two before you are dead." This speech procured a transient smile, but it was soon succeeded by the solemnity with which the whole business was conducted.

∞

Richard Stockton, Delegate from New Jersey, Signer of the Declaration of Independence

MANY OF the signers of the Declaration of Independence suffered reprisals from the British. Most of them lost their fortunes as the British looted or destroyed their property and estates. Some of the signers and their families had to flee their homes and go into hiding. Others further risked their lives on the battlefield. However, through all their trials, the signers of the Declaration of Independence never abandoned their sacred honor—they stood firm for the cause of independence.

Consider the delegates from New Jersey—Francis Hopkinson, John Witherspoon, Abraham Clark, John Hart, and Richard Stockton. Hopkinson and his family fled their home shortly before British soldiers came and destroyed it. Witherspoon, who was also the president of the College of New Jersey (now Princeton) and James Madison's teacher, had to flee his home with his family, as the British raided the college, occupied its buildings as well as nearby homes, and burned its library, which contained many of Witherspoon's prized books from Europe. The Hessian soldiers aggressively pursued Hart, who had to leave his wife at her sickbed and go into hiding. He finally returned to his farm, now destroyed, to find his wife had died from the trauma, his children scattered. He died a despondent man a few years later. And Clark's son, who was a captain in the American army and a prisoner of war on a British prison ship, was singled out for his father's deeds and tortured and nearly starved to death.

In the following, I share a retelling of the ordeal Richard Stockton went through—an ordeal that eventually killed him. Who could have blamed any of these men if they had renounced the cause of independence to avoid persecution to themselves and their families? But none did—their sacred honor was at stake, and that sustained them.

. . . *His* duty to his family, however, soon called his attention, and required his exertions to secure them from being captured by the enemy, who were then triumphantly marching through New Jersey. His family residence lay in the supposed rout of their march; and the American army was so reduced, and in such a suffering condition, that it could afford no protection to the inhabitants. The families of those who had signed the instrument which severed the colonies from the parent state, were peculiarly obnoxious to the British forces; and Mr. Stockton was constrained to retire from congress to convey his own to a place of safety. After having conducted them into the county of Monmouth, about thirty miles from his residence, he resided with Mr. Covenhoven, a patriotic friend of his; and he, together with Mr. Covenhoven, was surprised, and made a prisoner, by a party of refugees, who had been informed of the place of his temporary residence, by a treacherous wretch. They were dragged from their beds at a late hour of the night; stripped and plundered of their property, and conducted to New York. They first conveyed him to Amboy, shut him in the common gaol, exposed him, thus destitute, to severe suffering by the cold weather; and in New York, he was subjected to a similar confinement, and extreme suffering. The severities he endured, during his imprisonment in Amboy and New York, laid the foundation for the disease which closed his life not long after. While in the latter place, the enemy withheld from him, not only the comforts, but even the necessaries of life; and this, notwithstanding his respectability of character and standing in life, and a very delicate state of health. At one time he was left absolutely without food more than twenty-four hours; and afterwards supplied with that which was coarse in quality, and scanty in amount. This treatment of Mr. Stockton, by the British, engaged the attention of congress, and General Howe was informed, if Mr. Stockton was not treated in a manner becoming his condition, and in conformity to the dictates of humanity, which had been observed by the Americans towards their prisoners, and which the established rules of modern warfare demanded, he might expect a practical retaliation on those of the British who might fall into the power of the Americans.

The complicated sufferings he endured while in captivity, the burning of his papers and fine library, the plundering of his property, particularly of his stock of horses and cattle; the general depredations committed on his estate, real and personal, wherever it was exposed to the ravages of an incensed foe, and the losses he sustained by reason of the ruinous depreciation of the continental paper currency, left him only the remnants of a large fortune, exhausted so entirely that it seemed to him only a mass of ruins; and finding himself so destitute of the means for providing comfortably for his family, he was compelled to resort to friends for a temporary accommodation, to procure the absolute necessaries of life. This caused a depression of spirits, out of which he never fully rose; and aggravated a lingering disease which terminated his life. He languished for a time under this calamity which, in the latter part of his life, was much increased by a cancer in his neck, whose insidious and fatal approaches are always clearly perceived, without the least hope of remedy. He died on the twenty-eighth day of February, 1781, in the fifty-first year of his age.

A minute delineation of character, does not comport with the design or limits of this work; only a brief summary can be given. The character of Mr. Stockton as a patriot, inflexibly devoted to the liberty, rights, and independence of his country, may be easily understood by what has been already stated. He not only pledged "his life, his fortune, and his sacred honor," for the attainment of his country's independence; but he fully redeemed the pledge by becoming a martyr to her cause. His life was a sacrifice; his fortune was nearly so; and his sacred honor attended him to his grave; and remains behind him an untarnished legacy to his posterity and his country.

—From Nathaniel Dwight, *The Lives of the Signers,* 1876

❧

Abigail Adams to John Adams, June 18, 1775, and John to Abigail, July 7, 1775

DURING THEIR courtship, Abigail Adams asked John: "Don't you think me a courageous being? Courage is laudable, a glorious virtue in your sex, why not in mine?"

Abigail's courage was to be later tested many times and in many different ways during the revolutionary war years. The following exchange between John and Abigail Adams takes place shortly after the

Battle of Bunker Hill (which actually took place on Breed's Hill). John
was in Philadelphia serving in the Second Continental Congress; Abigail
was alone, taking care of the farm and their four children in Braintree,
Massachusetts. On a hill near her farm with her young son Johnny,
Abigail watched the smoke rising above Charlestown from the battle of
Bunker Hill. A week later, John's "heroine" would reassure him that
although she and others "live in continual Expectation of Hostilities"
that "like good Nehemiah[,] having made our prayer with God, and set
the people with their Swords, their Spears[,] and their bows[,] we will
say unto them, Be not affraid of them."* And she was not afraid.

A B I G A I L   A D A M S   T O   J O H N   A D A M S

Dearest Friend

The Day; perhaps the decisive Day is come on which the fate of
America depends. My bursting Heart must find vent at my pen. I have
just heard that our dear Friend Dr. Warren is no more but fell gloriously
fighting for his Country—saying better to die honourably in the field
than ignominiously hang upon the Gallows. Great is our Loss. He has
distinguished himself in every engagement, by his courage and fortitude,
by animating the Soldiers and leading them on by his own example. A
particular account of these dreadful, but I hope Glorious Days will be
transmitted you, no doubt in the exactest manner.

The race is not to the swift, nor the battle to the strong, but the God
of Israel is he that giveth strength and power unto his people. Trust in
him at all times, ye people pour out your hearts before him. God is a
refuge for us.—Charlstown is laid in ashes. The Battle began upon our
intrenchments upon Bunkers Hill, a Saturday morning about 3 o'clock
and has not ceased yet and tis now 3 o'clock Sabbeth afternoon.

Tis expected they will come out over the Neck to night, and a dreadful
Battle must ensue. Almighty God cover the heads of our Country men,
and be a shield to our Dear Friends. How [many ha]ve fallen we know
not—the constant roar of the cannon is so [distre]ssing that we can not
Eat, Drink or Sleep. May we be supported and sustaind in the dreadful
conflict. I shall tarry here till tis thought unsafe by my Friends, and then
I have secured myself a retreat at your Brothers who has kindly offerd
me part of his house. I cannot compose myself to write any further at
present. I will add more as I hear further.

* Abigail to John, June 25, 1775. I've adjusted the punctuation slightly.

JOHN ADAMS TO ABIGAIL ADAMS

It gives me more Pleasure than I can express to learn that you sustain with so much Fortitude, the Shocks and Terrors of the Times. You are really brave, my dear, you are an Heroine. And you have Reason to be. For the worst that can happen, can do you no Harm. A soul, as pure, as benevolent, as virtuous and pious as yours has nothing to fear, but every Thing to hope and expect from the last of human Evils.

Am glad you have secured an Assylum, tho I hope you will not have occasion for it.

∞

"Give Me Liberty Or Give Me Death" Patrick Henry, Speech at St. Johns Church, March 23, 1775

THIS IS one of the most famous speeches of the revolutionary era and helped to infuse the citizens of Virginia with a sense of national spirit. With the growing presence of British forces in the colonies, Patrick Henry introduced a set of resolutions for organizing and arming a state militia and putting the colony of Virginia on defensive footing.

The church in which Henry gave the speech was packed, and the windows were thrown open to allow more people to hear. When Henry finished, his fellow delegates, who included Jefferson and Washington, sat in awed silence.

[NOTE: The accuracy of the speech cannot be attested to—some attribute the famous last lines to an early biographer, William Wirt, but it has been passed down from generation to generation as Henry's speech ever since.]

"*We* have petitioned—we have remonstrated—we have supplicated —we have prostrated ourselves before the throne, and have implored its interposition to arrest the tyrannical hands of the ministry and parliament. Our petitions have been slighted; our remonstrances have produced additional violence and insult; our supplications have been disregarded; and we have been spurned, with contempt, from the foot of the throne. In vain, after these things, may we indulge the fond hope of peace and reconciliation. *There is no longer any room for hope.* If we wish to be free—if we mean to preserve inviolate those inestimable privileges for which we have been so long contending—if we mean not basely to abandon the noble struggle in which we have been so long engaged, and which we have pledged ourselves never to abandon, until the glorious object of our contest shall be obtained—we must fight!—I repeat it, sir, we must fight!! An appeal to arms and to the God of hosts, is all that is left us!

"They tell us, sir," continued Mr. Henry, "that we are weak—unable to cope with so formidable an adversary. But when shall we be stronger. Will it be the next week or the next year? Will it be when we are totally disarmed, and when a British guard shall be stationed in every house? Shall we gather strength by irresolution and inaction? Shall we acquire the means of effectual resistance by lying supinely on our backs, and hugging the delusive phantom of hope, until our enemies shall have bound us hand and foot? Sir, we are not weak, if we make a proper use of those means which the God of nature hath placed in our power. Three millions of people armed in the holy cause of liberty, and in such a country as that which we possess, are invincible by any force which our enemy can send against us. Besides, sir, we shall not fight our battles alone. There is a just God who presides over the destinies of nations, and who will raise up friends to fight our battles for us. The battle, sir, is not to the strong alone; it is to the vigilant, the active, the brave. Besides, sir, we have no election. If we were base enough to desire it, it is now too late to retire from the contest. There is no retreat but in submission and slavery! Our chains are forged. Their clanking may be heard on the plains of Boston! The war is inevitable—and let it come!! I repeat it, sir, let it come!!!

"It is vain, sir, to extenuate the matter. Gentlemen may cry, peace, peace—but there is no peace. The war is actually begun! The next gale that sweeps from the north will bring to our ears the clash of resounding arms! Our brethren are already in the field! Why stand we here idle? What is it that gentlemen wish? What would they have? Is life so dear, or peace so sweet, as to be purchased at the price of chains and slavery? Forbid it, Almighty God!—I know not what course others may take; but as for me," cried he, with both his arms extended aloft, his brows knit, every feature marked with the resolute purpose of his soul, and his voice swelled to its boldest note of exclamation—"give me liberty, or give me death!"

—From William Wirt, *Sketches of the Life and Character of Patrick Henry*

∽

Thomas Paine, The American Crisis, December 19, 1776

THE AMERICAN Revolution was fought with both the sword and the pen. Thomas Paine, the Englishman who adopted the American cause as his own, delivered words as if they were bullets and effectively defined and sustained the American colonists throughout the Revolutionary War. For those colonists who didn't know why American independence was so important and worth fighting for, Paine's famous pamphlet *Common Sense*, released in January 1776, told them. The following excerpt is taken from a later work, *The American Crisis*, written at a critical juncture of the Revolution. George Washington was leading the Continental Army on a retreat through New Jersey after a disastrous defeat in New York. Paine accompanied Washington and his troops and saw firsthand the growing despondency among the rebels. The army had dwindled down to around 4,000 men (to the 20,000 British troops). Many were ready to give up and reconcile with Great Britain. It looked as if the rebellion was coming to an abrupt end.

Paine wrote *The American Crisis*—reportedly using a battle drum for a desk—by the light of campfire to boost morale. He left the camp for Philadelphia to have copies printed, which George Washington ordered to be read aloud to his men on Christmas Eve 1776. After it was read, the American troops crossed the Delaware and launched a surprise attack on the Hessian soldiers at Trenton. The American victory at Trenton infused new life into the patriots' cause and showed the British that the American army was not ready to bow out just yet.

NUMBER I.

These are the times that try men's souls. The summer soldier and the sunshine patriot will, in this crisis, shrink from the service of his country; but he that stands it NOW, deserves the love and thanks of man and woman. Tyranny, like hell, is not easily conquered; yet we have this consolation with us, that the harder the conflict, the more glorious the triumph. What we obtain too cheap, we esteem too lightly: 'tis dearness only that gives every thing its value. Heaven knows how to put a proper price upon its goods; and it would be strange indeed, if so celestial an article as FREEDOM should not be highly rated. Britain, with an army to enforce her tyranny, has declared that she has a right (*not only to* TAX) but "to BIND *us in* ALL CASES WHATSOEVER," and if being *bound in that manner,* is not slavery, then is there not such a thing as slavery upon earth. Even the expression is impious, for so unlimited a power can belong only to God. . . .

Quitting this class of men, I turn with the warm ardor of a friend to those who have nobly stood, and are yet determined to stand the matter out: I call not upon a few, but upon all: not on *this* state or *that* state, but on *every* state; up and help us; lay your shoulders to the wheel; better have too much force than too little, when so great an object is at stake. Let it be told to the future world, that in the depth of winter, when nothing but hope and virtue could survive, the city and the country, alarmed at one common danger, came forth to meet and to repulse it. Say not that thousands are gone, turn out your tens of thousands; throw not the burden of the day upon Providence, but *"show your faith by your works,"* that God may bless you. It matters not where you live, or what rank of life you hold, the evil or the blessing will reach you all. The far and the near, the home counties and the back, the rich and the poor, will suffer or rejoice alike. The heart that feels not now, is dead: the blood of his children will curse his cowardice, who shrinks back at a time when a little might have saved the whole, and made *them* happy. I love the man that can smile in trouble, that can gather strength from

distress, and grow brave by reflection. 'Tis the business of little minds to shrink; but he whose heart is firm, and whose conscience approves his conduct, will pursue his principles unto death. My own line of reasoning is to myself as straight and clear as a ray of light. Not all the treasures of the world, so far as I believe, could have induced me to support an offensive war, for I think it murder; but if a thief breaks into my house, burns and destroys my property, and kills or threatens to kill me, or those that are in it, and to *"bind me in all cases whatsoever,"* to his absolute will, am I to suffer it? What signifies it to me, whether he who does it is a king or a common man; my countryman or not my countryman: whether it be done by an individual villain, or an army of them? If we reason to the root of things we shall find no difference; neither can any just cause be assigned why we should punish in the one case and pardon in the other. Let them call me rebel, and welcome, I feel no concern from it; but I should suffer the misery of devils, were I to make a whore of my soul by swearing allegiance to one whose character is that of a sottish, stupid, stubborn, worthless, brutish man.

I thank God that I fear not. I see no real cause for fear. I know our situation well, and can see the way out of it.

By perseverance and fortitude we have the prospect of a glorious issue; by cowardice and submission, the sad choice of a variety of evils —a ravaged country—a depopulated city—habitations without safety, and slavery without hope—our homes turned into barracks and bawdy-houses for Hessians, and a future race to provide for, whose fathers we shall doubt of. Look on this picture and weep over it! and if there yet remains one thoughtless wretch who believes it not, let him suffer it unlamented.

∞

Marquis de Lafayette, "The Knight of Liberty"

WHEN GENERAL John J. "Black Jack" Pershing arrived in France in World War I with allied American troops, he reportedly said: "Lafayette, we are here."

Marie Gilbert Roch Yves du Moitier Marquis de Lafayette was certainly here for us during the critical years of the Revolutionary War. Born an aristocrat, he defied his family and his king by buying his own ship, *Victory,* that he might come to our shores and aid our cause. To explain such defiance, he famously added the words *"Cur non?"* ("Why not?") to his family motto. Other European aristocrats came to aid America's cause. Baron Friedrich Wilhelm von Steuben was a lieutenant general in the Prussian army, who came to Valley Forge and offered his services, without pay, to help train the American soldiers. He spoke little if any English, but by using a translator managed to instill discipline and order, without which the inexperienced and untrained American soldiers probably would have lost the war.

While Lafayette might have come to America initially for his own glory, he soon became a firm believer in the principles of America and sought to establish them once he returned to France.

The park facing the White House is called Lafayette Park. How fitting that this Frenchman who captured America's heart is honored in the heart of its capital.

As soon as La Fayette arrived in Philadelphia, he presented himself before Congress, then in session. The moment was inauspicious. Mr. Deane had given so many foreigners the same promises, that Congress found itself in a very embarrassing situation. Many of these foreigners were brave men, and true, who had come to America with philanthropic motives, but others were mere adventurers, and Congress therefore received the young Marquis de La Fayette with coldness and indifference, which he illy deserved, and which in the light of after events proved a mortifying mistake. La Fayette laid his stipulations with Mr. Deane before Congress, but, with surprise and chagrin, he was informed by the chairman of the Committee on Foreign Affairs that there was little hope that his request would be granted.

Imagine the feelings of the noble young marquis of nineteen. He had sacrificed home, family, friends, and fortune, to give his aid to this struggling nation, and his immense personal sacrifices were thus insultingly thrown into his face. What blindness in Congress! What heroic magnanimity in La Fayette! Pride and patriotism battled in his sensitive soul. But unselfish patriotism conquered, and never does he appear more truly great than at this moment. Seizing a pen, he writes to Congress this brief but immortal note:—

"After the sacrifices I have made, I have a right to exact two favors: one is, to serve at my *own expense;* the other is, to serve as a *volunteer.*"

Astonished at such unprecedented generosity, and conscious of their mistake in classing the young marquis with other foreigners, who were actuated by selfish avarice and love of adventure, Congress accordingly passed the following preamble and resolution on the 31st of July, 1777:—

"*Whereas,* the Marquis de La Fayette, out of his great zeal in the cause of liberty in which the United States are engaged, has left his family and connections, and, at his own expense, come over to offer his service to the United States, without pension or particular allowance, and is anxious to risk his life in our cause;

"*Resolved,* That his services be accepted, and that in consideration of his zeal, illustrious family and connections, he have the rank and commission of a Major-General in the army of the United States."

—From *The Life of Lafayette, The Knight of Liberty* by Lydia Farmer, 1898

∽

Abigail Adams to John Adams, June 17, 1782

JOHN ADAMS recalled to Benjamin Rush something he once said to Abigail when he was elected as a Boston delegate to the General Court in 1770. He told Abigail, "I have accepted a seat in the House of Representatives, and thereby have consented to my own ruin, to your ruin, and the ruin of our children. I give you this warning, that you may prepare your mind for your fate." Abigail burst into tears and, according to Adams, "cried out in a transport of magnanimity, 'Well, I am willing in this cause to run all risks with you, and be ruined with you, if you are ruined.' " Adams told Rush: "These were the times, my friend, in Boston, which tried women's souls as well as men's."

John Adams's service to his country took him away from Abigail for a total of ten years during their marriage. Below, as John served a diplomatic mission in France, Abigail gives voice to the form of patriotism that she and so many other women displayed. We should all agree with her that the sacrifices women then made, and still make, for our country are "equal to the most heroic" of men. Her "argument" in this letter for women's patriotic virtue deriving from profound sacrifice is extremely powerful.

Ardently as I long for the return of my dearest Friend, I cannot feel the least inclination to a peace but upon the most liberal foundation. Patriotism in the female Sex is the most disinterested of all virtues. Excluded from honours and from offices, we cannot attach ourselves to the

State or Government from having held a place of Eminence. Even in the freeest countrys our property is subject to the controul and disposal of our partners, to whom the Laws have given a soverign Authority. Deprived of a voice in Legislation, obliged to submit to those Laws which are imposed upon us, is it not sufficient to make us indifferent to the publick Welfare? Yet all History and every age exhibit Instances of patriotick virtue in the female Sex; which considering our situation equals the most Heroick of yours. "A late writer observes that as Citizens we are calld upon to exhibit our fortitude, for when you offer your Blood to the State, it is ours. In giving it our Sons and Husbands we give more than ourselves. You can only die on the field of Battle, but we have the misfortune to survive those whom we Love most."

I will take praise to myself. I feel that it is my due, for having sacrificed so large a portion of my peace and happiness to promote the welfare of my country which I hope for many years to come will reap the benifit, tho it is more than probable unmindfull of the hand that blessed them.

∞

"On Patriotism," October 20, 1773

BENJAMIN RUSH shares here some of his thoughts on what patriotism means—how it incorporates both a moral and religious duty.

To His Fellow Countrymen

Patriotism is as much a virtue as justice, and is as necessary for the support of societies as natural affection is for the support of families. The Amor Patriae is both a moral and a religious duty. It comprehends not only the love of our neighbors but of millions of our fellow creatures, not only of the present but of future generations. This virtue we find constitutes a part of the first characters in history. The holy men of old, in proportion as they possessed a religious were endowed with a public spirit. What did not Moses forsake and suffer for his countrymen! What shining examples of Patriotism do we behold in Joshua, Samuel, Maccabeus, and all the illustrious princes, captains, and prophets amongst the Jews! St. Paul almost wishes himself accursed for his countrymen and kinsmen after the flesh. Even our Saviour himself gives a sanction to this virtue. He confined his miracles and gospel at first to his own country.

∽

John Adams, Dissertation on the Canon and Feudal Law, 1765

IN 1765, the British Parliament passed the Stamp Act, which levied a direct tax on nearly all forms of paper, including pamphlets, newspapers, legal documents, even playing cards. The reach of the Stamp Act affected the lives of almost all the colonists, who believed it to be a violation of their cherished rights as Englishmen and a threat to their liberties in the colonies. Riots ensued in Boston and an effigy of the stamp distributor was burned.

John Adams disapproved of the riots but sensed that something had permanently changed in the colonies. In his *Diary*, Adams observed that the Act "raised and spread, thro the whole Continent, a Spirit that will be recorded to our Honour, with all future Generations" and had made the colonists "more attentive to their liberties, more inquisitive about them, and more determined to defend them."

In the same year that the Stamp Act was passed, Adams had earlier begun to publish in installments his *Dissertation on the Canon and Feudal Law*. The work was an attempt to make the colonists "more attentive" not only to their rights and liberties but also to the accomplishments of the first settlers of the colonies. It is a good set of reminders for our age in which there is evidence of a dearth of "civil affection." Here is a portrait of an energetic people in love with their freedom.

This spirit, however, without knowledge, would be little better than a brutal rage. Let us tenderly and kindly cherish, therefore, the means of knowledge. Let us dare to read, think, speak, and write. Let every order and degree among the people rouse their attention and animate their resolution. Let them all become attentive to the grounds and principles of government, ecclesiastical and civil. Let us study the law of nature; search into the spirit of the British constitution; read the histories of ancient ages; contemplate the great examples of Greece and Rome; set before us the conduct of our own British ancestors, who have defended for us the inherent rights of mankind against foreign and domestic tyrants and usurpers, against arbitrary kings and cruel priests, in short, against the gates of earth and hell. Let us read and recollect and impress upon our souls the views and ends of our own more immediate forefathers, in exchanging their native country for a dreary, inhospitable wilderness. Let us examine into the nature of that power, and the cruelty of that oppression, which drove them from their homes. Recollect their amazing fortitude, their bitter sufferings—the hunger, the nakedness, the cold, which they patiently endured—the severe labors of clearing their grounds, building their houses, raising their provisions, amidst dangers from wild beasts and savage men, before they had time or money or materials for commerce. Recollect the civil and religious principles and hopes and expectations which constantly supported and carried them through all hardships with patience and resignation. Let us recollect it was liberty, the hope of liberty for themselves and us and ours, which conquered all discouragements, dangers, and trials. In such researches as these, let us all in our several departments cheerfully engage—but especially the proper patrons and supporters of law, learning, and religion!

Let the pulpit resound with the doctrines and sentiments of religious liberty. Let us hear the danger of thraldom to our consciences from ignorance, extreme poverty, and dependence, in short, from civil and political slavery. Let us see delineated before us the true map of man. Let us hear the dignity of his nature, and the noble rank he holds among the works of God—that consenting to slavery is a sacrilegious breach of trust, as offensive in the sight of God as it is derogatory from our own honor or interest or happiness—and that God Almighty has promulgated from heaven liberty, peace, and good-will to man!

∞

"Yankee Doodle"

THE ORIGINS of this famous tune are unclear. According to the Oxford English Dictionary, the tune was written by a British surgeon in 1755 out of "derision of the provincial troops." "Yankee" was a derogatory term for a New Englander; "doodle" meant a "silly or foolish fellow"; and "macaroni" meant a "fop or dandy."

The American colonists, however, soon appropriated "Yankee Doodle" as their own song, and sang it with pride.

> Yankee Doodle went to town,
> A-ridin' on a pony,

Stuck a feather in his cap
And called it Macaroni.

Father and I went down to camp,
Along with Captain Gooding,
And there we saw the men and boys
As thick as hasty pudding.

And there we saw a thousand men,
As rich as Squire David;
And what they wasted every day,
I wish it could be saved.

And there was Captain Washington
Upon a slapping stallion,
A-giving orders to his men;
I guess there was a million.

And there I saw a little keg,
Its head was made of leather;
They knocked upon it with two sticks
To call the men together.

And there I saw a swamping gun,
As big as a log of maple,
Upon a mighty little cart,
A load for father's cattle.

And every time they fired it off
It took a horn of powder,
And made a noise like father's gun.
Only a nation louder.

I can't tell you half I saw,
They kept up such a smother,
So I took my hat off, made a bow
And scampered home to mother.

Yankee Doodle is the tune
Americans delight in,
'Twill do to whistle, sing or play
And just the thing for fightin'.

CHORUS:
Yankee Doodle, keep it up,
Yankee Doodle Dandy,
Mind the music and the step
And with the girls be handy.

George Washington Refuses Pay as Commander-in-Chief and a Presidential Salary

WASHINGTON UNDERSTOOD what it meant to be a true patriot. A true patriot would serve his country selflessly, without pay. So in order to set an example, Washington refused payment for his services to his country, first in his role as commander-in-chief and later as president, which is recounted below.

Even when we cannot meet the standard Washington set, its selfless spirit should be our guide and inspiration.

RETOLD BY JAMES BALDWIN

On the following day Washington was officially notified that he had been unanimously chosen to be commander in chief of all the forces of the American colonies.

In that dignified manner which was his, Washington arose and thanked the Congress for the great honor which it had conferred upon him. The duties that would be required of him were many and great, and he was not at all sure that he would be able to perform them wisely; yet he declared himself ready to give all his time, all his energies, his life if need be, to the defense of his country.

"As to the pay," he said, "I beg leave to say that no amount of money could tempt me to undertake this difficult work. I have no wish to make any profit from it. But I will keep an exact amount of my expenses, and if these are paid I shall want nothing more."

Thus, the united American colonies entered upon a long and uncertain war in defense of their liberties. They had as yet no efficient army; they had no money: but their delegates in the Continental Congress felt an unwavering faith in the righteousness of their cause.

To the preceeding observations I have one to add, which will be most properly addressed to the House of Representatives. It concerns myself, and will therefore be as brief as possible. When I was first honoured with a call into the Service of my Country, then on the eve of an arduous struggle for its liberties, the light in which I contemplated my duty required that I should renounce every pecuniary compensation. From this resolution I have in no instance departed. And being still under the impressions which produced it, I must decline as inapplicable to myself, any share in the personal emoluments, which may be indispensably included in a permanent provision for the Executive Department; and must accordingly pray that the pecuniary estimates for the Station in which I am placed, may, during my continuance in it, be limited to such actual expenditures as the public good may be thought to require.

∾

Nathan Hale, Captain in the American Army

NATHAN HALE'S inspiring example of patriotism is here retold. The young can learn what is meant by "a sense of duty" and how sacred honor has a claim on us.

After the unfortunate engagement on Long Island, General Washington called a council of war, who determined on an immediate retreat to New York. The intention was prudently concealed from the army, who knew not whither they were going, but imagined it was to attack the enemy. The field artillery, tents, baggage, and about nine thousand men, were conveyed to the city of New York, over the East River, more than a mile wide, in less than thirteen hours, and without the knowledge of the British, though not six hundred yards distant. Providence in a remarkable manner favoured the retreating army. The wind, which seemed to prevent the troops getting over at the appointed hour, afterward shifted to their wishes.

Perhaps the fate of America was never suspended by a more brittle thread than previously to this memorable retreat. A spectacle is here presented of an army destined for the defence of a great continent, driven to the narrow borders of an island, with a victorious army double its number in front, with navigable waters in its rear; constantly liable to

have its communication cut off by the enemy's navy, and every moment exposed to an attack. The presence of mind which animated the commander-in-chief in this critical situation, the prudence with which all the necessary measures were executed, redounded as much or more to his honour than the most brilliant victories. An army, to which America looked for safety, preserved; a general who was considered as an host himself, saved for the future necessities of his country. Had not, however, the circumstances of the night, of the wind and weather, been favourable, the plan, however well concerted, must have been defeated. To a good Providence, therefore, are the people of America indebted for the complete success of an enterprise so important in its consequences.

This retreat left the British in complete possession of Long Island. What would be their future operations remained uncertain. To obtain information of their situation, their strength, and future movements, was of high importance. For this purpose, General Washington applied to Colonel Knowlton, who commanded a regiment of light infantry, which formed the rear of the American army, and desired him to adopt some mode of gaining the necessary information. Colonel Knowlton communicated this request to Captain NATHAN HALE, of Connecticut, who was a captain in his regiment.

This young officer, animated by a sense of duty, and considering that an opportunity presented itself by which he might be useful to his country, at once offered himself a volunteer for this hazardous service. He passed in disguise to Long Island, and examined every part of the British army, and obtained the best possible information respecting their situation and future operations.

In his attempt to return, he was apprehended, carried before Sir William Howe, and the proof of his object was so clear, that he frankly acknowledged who he was, and what were his views. Sir William Howe at once gave an order to have him executed the next morning.

The order was accordingly executed in the most unfeeling manner, and by as great a savage as ever disgraced humanity. A clergyman, whose attendance he desired, was refused him; a Bible, for a few moments' devotion, was not procured, although he wished it. Letters which, on the morning of his execution, he wrote to his mother and other friends, were destroyed; and this very extraordinary reason given by the provost-martial, *"That the rebels should not know they had a man in their army who could die with so much firmness."*

Unknown to all around him, without a single friend to offer him the least consolation, thus fell as amiable and as worthy a young man as America could boast, with this as his dying observation, that *"he only lamented that he had but one life to lose for his country."*

Although the manner of this execution will ever be abhorred by every friend to humanity and religion, yet there cannot be a question but that the sentence was conformable to the rules of war, and the practice of nations in similar cases.

It is, however, but justice to the character of Captain Hale to observe, that his motives for engaging in this service were entirely different from those which generally influence others in similar circumstances. Neither expectation of promotion, nor pecuniary reward, induced him to this attempt. A sense of duty, a hope that he might in this way be useful to his country, and an opinion which he had adopted, that every kind of service necessary to the general good became honourable by being necessary, were the great motives which induced him to engage in an enterprise by which his connexions lost a most amiable friend, and his country one of its most promising supporters.

—From *Lives of the Heroes of the American Revolution*
by John Frost, 1848

❧

"The Atlas of Independence,"
John Adams to Timothy Pickering, August 6, 1822

JOHN ADAMS performed many patriotic deeds. He served in the First
and Second Continental Congress, was the leading advocate for independence at the Second Continental Congress, served abroad in Europe
to help secure loans to finance the revolutionary war and establish
peace alliances, served as vice-president under George Washington, and
was our second president, and the father of our sixth president.

However, there were in addition two decisions of his that were to
have a most monumental impact on this country: one was his nomina-
tion of George Washington as commander-in-chief of the Continental
Army; the second was his selection of Thomas Jefferson to write the
Declaration of Independence. Two decisions without which this nation
would not have been born were both made by this astounding and
underappreciated man.

Adams and Jefferson served on the subcommittee to draft the Declaration of Independence, along with Roger Sherman, Benjamin Franklin,
and Robert R. Livingston. Below, Adams records the thoughts that led
to his endorsement of Jefferson to write the Declaration. Adams had
the dream of American independence long before most Americans.
Richard Stockton, delegate from New Jersey, called Adams "the Atlas of
Independence." It has been written that later on in life, Adams smarted
a little every Fourth of July when all credit was given to Jefferson. It
was no small sacrifice to give the pen to his friend, but Adams, always
a patriot, put the cause ahead of his own fame. In recent surveys Jefferson has been regarded by many as the most influential man of the last
millennium. The case can be made that he is such for no small part
because Adams handed him the pen in Philadelphia.

These were men of enormous self-knowledge. Adams here candidly
admits to his own shortcomings and trades on them to make Jefferson
take the lead in the drafting and in history.

August 6, 1822

Mr. Jefferson came into Congress in June, 1775, and brought with
him a reputation for literature, science, and a happy talent of composi-

tion. Writings of his were handed about, remarkable for the peculiar felicity of expression. Though a silent member in Congress, he was so prompt, frank, explicit and decisive upon committees and in conversation—not even Samuel Adams was more so—that he soon seized upon my heart; and upon this occasion I gave him my vote, and did all in my power to procure the votes of others. I think he had one more vote than any other, and that placed him at the head of the committee. I had the next highest number, and that placed me the second. The committee met, discussed the subject, and then appointed Mr. Jefferson and me to make the draught, I suppose because we were the two first on the list.

The sub-committee met. Jefferson proposed to me to make the draught.

I said, "I will not."

"You should do it."

"Oh! no."

"Why will you not? You ought to do it."

"I will not."

"Why?"

"Reason enough."

"What can be your reasons?"

"Reason first—You are a Virginian, and a Virginian ought to appear at the head of this business. Reason second—I am obnoxious, suspected and unpopular. You are very much otherwise. Reason third—You can write ten times better than I can."

"Well," said Jefferson, "if you are decided, I will do as well as I can."

"Very well. When you have drawn it up, we will have a meeting."

A meeting we accordingly had, and conned the paper over. I was delighted with its high tone and the flights of oratory with which it abounded, especially that concerning Negro slavery, which, though I knew his Southern brethren would never suffer to pass in Congress, I certainly never would oppose. There were other expressions which I would not have inserted, if I had drawn it up, particularly that which called the King tyrant. I thought this too personal; for I never believed George to be a tyrant in disposition and in nature; I always believed him to be deceived by his courtiers on both sides of the Atlantic, and, in his official capacity only, cruel. I thought the expression too passionate, and too much like scolding, for so grave and solemn a document; but as Franklin and Sherman were to inspect it afterwards, I thought it would not become me to strike it out. I consented to report it, and do not now remember that I made or suggested a single alteration.

We reported it to the committee of five. It was read, and I do not remember that Franklin or Sherman criticized any thing. We were all in haste. Congress was impatient, and the instrument was reported, as I believe, in Jefferson's handwriting, as he first drew it. Congress cut off about a quarter of it, as I expected they would; but they obliterated some of the best of it, and left all that was exceptionable, if any thing in it was. I have long wondered that the original draught has not been published. I suppose the reason is the vehement philippic against Negro slavery.

∝

Longfellow, "Paul Revere's Ride," April 1775

DURING THE spring of 1775, tensions had been heating up between the British troops and the American colonists in Massachusetts. The growing presence and quartering of British troops in Massachusetts caused anger and alarm among the colonists, who began storing up ammunition in Concord, Massachusetts. On April 18, 1775, British troops began marching down to the Boston Commons, where there were boats waiting for them. It looked as if the British were going to sail across the river toward Lexington to seize the rebel leaders—John Hancock and Samuel Adams—and then move on to Concord to confiscate the colonists' supply of arms. Someone had to warn Adams and Hancock and to prepare the Minute Men to defend Concord. The "shot heard 'round the world" was soon to follow.

Paul Revere, a gifted and accomplished silversmith, veteran of the Boston Tea Party of 1773, and principal rider for Boston's Committee of Safety was chosen for the mission to warn the colonists of the British invasion. His task was not easy—the roads were heavily guarded by British patrols, who eventually captured Revere on his famous ride and threatened to kill him.

It has been said that Revere, an ardent patriot, wore one of his military uniforms every day until his death in 1818. Below is Longfellow's famous poem on the midnight ride of Paul Revere. The poem is not accurate in its details—it doesn't mention that Revere was apprehended by the British. But it is true to the spirit of the time, and grants Revere his much deserved immortality.

> Listen, my children, and you shall hear
> Of the midnight ride of Paul Revere,
> On the eighteenth of April, in Seventy-five;
> Hardly a man is now alive
> Who remembers that famous day and year.

He said to his friend, "If the British march
By land or sea from the town tonight,
Hang a lantern aloft in the belfry arch
Of the North Church tower as a signal light—
One, if by land, and two, if by sea;
And I on the opposite shore will be,
Ready to ride and spread the alarm
Through every Middlesex village and farm,
For the country folk to be up and to arm."

Then he said, "Good-night!" and with muffled oar
Silently rowed to the Charlestown shore,
Just as the moon rose over the bay,
Where swinging wide at her moorings lay
The Somerset, British man-of-war;
A phantom ship, with each mast and spar
Across the moon like a prison bar,
And a huge black hulk, that was magnified
By its own reflection in the tide.

Meanwhile, his friend, through alley and street,
Wanders and watches with eager ears,

Till in the silence around him he hears
The muster of men at the barrack door,
The sound of arms, and the tramp of feet,
And the measured tread of the grenadiers,
Marching down to their boats on the shore.

Then he climbed the tower of the Old North Church
By the wooden stairs, with stealthy tread,
To the belfry-chamber overhead,
And startled the pigeons from their perch
On the sombre rafters, that round him made
Masses and moving shapes of shade—
By the trembling ladder, steep and tall,
To the highest window in the wall,
Where he paused to listen and look down
A moment on the roofs of the town,
And the moonlight flowing over all.

Beneath, in the churchyard, lay the dead,
In their night-encampment on the hill,
Wrapped in silence so deep and still
That he could hear, like a sentinel's tread,
The watchful night wind, as it went
Creeping along from tent to tent,
And seeming to whisper, "All is well!"
A moment only he feels the spell
Of the place and the hour, and the secret dread
Of the lonely belfry and the dead;
For suddenly all his thoughts are bent
On a shadowy something far away,
Where the river widens to meet the bay—
A line of black that bends and floats
On the rising tide, like a bridge of boats.

Meanwhile, impatient to mount and ride,
Booted and spurred, with a heavy stride
On the opposite shore walked Paul Revere.
Now he patted his horse's side,
Now gazed at the landscape far and near,
Then, impetuous, stamped the earth,
And turned and tightened his saddle-girth;

But mostly he watched with eager search
The belfry-tower of the Old North Church,
As it rose above the graves on the hill,
Lonely and spectral and sombre and still.
And lo! as he looks, on the belfry's height
A glimmer, and then a gleam of light!
He springs to the saddle, the bridle he turns,
But lingers and gazes, till full on his sight
A second lamp in the belfry burns!

A hurry of hoofs in a village street,
A shape in the moonlight, a bulk in the dark,
And beneath, from the pebbles, in passing, a spark
Struck out by a steed flying fearless and fleet;
That was all! And yet, through the gloom and the light,
The fate of a nation was riding that night;
And the spark struck out by that steed, in his flight,
Kindled the land into flame with its heat.

He has left the village and mounted the steep,
And beneath him, tranquil and broad and deep,
Is the Mystic, meeting the ocean tides;
And under the alders that skirt its edge,
Now soft on the sand, now loud on the ledge,
Is heard the tramp of his steed as he rides.

It was twelve by the village clock
When he crossed the bridge into Medford town.
He heard the crowing of the cock
And the barking of the farmer's dog,
And felt the damp of the river fog
That rises after the sun goes down.

It was one by the village clock
When he galloped into Lexington.
He saw the gilded weathercock
Swim in the moonlight as he passed,
And the meeting-house windows, blank and bare,
Gaze at him with a spectral glare,
As if they already stood aghast
At the bloody work they would look upon.

It was two by the village clock
When he came to the bridge in Concord town.
He heard the bleating of the flock
And the twitter of birds among the trees,
And felt the breath of the morning breeze
Blowing over the meadows brown.
And one was safe and asleep in his bed
Who at the bridge would be first to fall,
Who that day would be lying dead,
Pierced by a British musket-ball.

You know the rest. In the books you have read,
How the British Regulars fired and fled—
How the farmers gave them ball for ball
From behind each fence and farm yard wall,
Chasing the red-coats down the lane,
Then crossing the fields to emerge again
Under the trees at the turn of the road,
And only pausing to fire and load.

So through the night rode Paul Revere;
And so through the night went his cry of alarm
To every Middlesex village and farm—
A cry of defiance and not of fear,
A voice in the darkness, a knock at the door,
And a word that shall echo forevermore.
For, borne on the night-wind of the Past,
Through all our history, to the last,
In the hour of darkness and peril and need,
The people will waken and listen to hear
The hurrying hoof-beats of that steed,
And the midnight message of Paul Revere.

∞

"An Eminent Patriot,"
Samuel Adams to Mrs. Betsy Adams,
November 29, 1776

BENJAMIN RUSH described Samuel Adams as "one of the most active instruments of the American Revolution." Adams, a second cousin of John Adams, was the chief agitator for rebellion years before the Revolutionary War actually commenced. He actively campaigned against the presence of British troops in Boston, formed the revolutionary group "Sons of Liberty," and was a leader in the Stamp Act riots and the Boston Tea Party. He was such a troublemaker that British General Thomas Gage sent an agent to deliver the message that if the impoverished Adams would cease agitating the colonists against Great Britain, he would be repaid "with great gifts and advancement." According to Adams's daughter, "Adams listened with apparent interest to this recital, until the messenger had concluded. Then, rising, Adams replied, glowing with indignation: 'Sir, I trust I have long since made my peace with the King of kings. No personal consideration shall induce me to abandon the righteous cause of my country. Tell Governor Gage it is the advice of Samuel Adams to him no longer to insult the feelings of an exasperated people.' **'

Although Adams may not have been an astute businessman, he was a great patriot whose allegiance to the colonies was unshakable. Shortly before the Battle of Bunker Hill, the British General Gage attempted to end all hostilities with the colonists by issuing pardons to all rebels who laid down their arms, with the *exception* of "only . . . Samuel Adams and John Hancock, whose offenses are of too flagitious a nature to admit of any other consideration than that of condign punishment."

In the passage below, Adams displays his unwavering devotion to the cause of independence when he is singled out again by the British.

.———I am told that Lord Howe has lately issued a Proclamation offering a general Pardon with the Exception of only four Persons viz Dr Franklin Coll Richard Henry Lee Mr John Adams and my self. I am not

---

* James K. Hosmer, *Samuel Adams*, 1885, pp. 271–72.

certain of the Truth of this Report. If it be a Fact I am greatly obligd to his Lordship for the flattering opinion he has given me of my self as being a Person obnoxious to those who are desolating a once happy Country for the sake of extinguishing the remaining Lamp of Liberty, and for the singular Honor he does me in ranking me with Men so eminently patriotick.

∞

"The Shot Heard Round the World"
Ralph Waldo Emerson, "Concord Hymn"

THE BRITISH troops marched to Concord in order to seize the stores of ammunition collected by the colonists. They were met by a small group of Massachusetts farmers—the "Minutemen," who, having been forewarned by Paul Revere, turned the British back. These "embattled farmers stood" and fought and began America's great journey to become a nation. Emerson wrote this poem commemorating the "spirit that made those heroes dare" at the Battle of Concord. May their spirit never die in us.

> By the rude bridge that arched the flood,
> Their flag to April's breeze unfurled,
> Here once the embattled farmers stood,
> And fired the shot heard round the world.
>
> The foe long since in silence slept,
> Alike the conqueror silent sleeps.
> And Time the ruined bridge has swept
> Down the dark stream which seaward creeps.
>
> On this green bank, by this soft stream,
> We set to-day a votive stone;
> That memory may their deed redeem,
> When, like our sires, our sons are gone.
>
> Spirit that made those heroes dare
> To die, and leave their children free,
> Bid Time and Nature gently spare
> The shaft we raise to them and thee.

∞

Israel Putnam at Bunker Hill

SHORTLY BEFORE the Battle of Bunker Hill on June 17, 1775, Abigail Adams made the following observation about the valor of her fellow patriots: "Courage I know we have in abundance, conduct I hope shall not want, but powder—where shall we get a sufficient supply?"

American troops fought valiantly at Bunker Hill and miraculously held off two charges by the British. They could have fought the redcoats off even longer had they had enough ammunition, but they ran out. Still, it was a great victory for the colonists to have stood up to the British Army. The Minute Men who fought on that day were led by Israel Putnam, who later became a major general in the Continental Army.

Legend has it that Putnam once faced down an angry wolf in a cave. Redcoats (with more ammunition) did not frighten him either.

At the close of the war, in 1764, Putnam went home, hung up his sword, swung over his door a signboard with General Wolfe's picture on it, and for ten years was a quiet farmer and innkeeper. On the 20th of April, in 1775, he had eaten his dinner and gone out to the field with his oxen. Suddenly he heard the sound of a drum. A man was galloping furiously along the road, beating his drum and calling, "To arms! To arms! The British have fired upon us! The country is ablaze!" Then Putnam forgot his beloved farm. He forgot to say good-by to his family. He forgot that he was an officer, and was going to war without his uniform. He forgot everything except which of his horses was the swiftest. He leaped upon its back, and while the oxen stood in the field waiting patiently for him to return, he was galloping along the road to make his second visit to Boston, one hundred miles away.

The Continental Army had gathered from all directions. The British were in possession of Boston. "We must seize those hills," declared the British General Gage, "if we are to stay in the city."

"We must seize those hills," declared the Americans, "if we are to drive the British out of the city." Colonel Prescott and General Putnam marched out by night and began to fortify Breed's Hill and Bunker Hill.

At daybreak the British discovered what was going on. "We might take Charlestown Neck," said one officer, "and starve them out."

"That's too slow," objected another. "I believe the best way will be to charge upon them."

"Not so easy to charge up that hill."

"Why not? They're only farmers. They don't know anything about fighting. The chances are that they will run long before we are at the foot of the hill."

So the British talked, and at length they decided to make a charge. The march began. The scarlet lines came nearer and nearer. Prescott and Putnam were going back and forth among their men at the top of the hill. "Remember there isn't much powder," they said. And Putnam added, "Men, you know how to aim. Don't fire till you can see the whites of their eyes."

Up the hill marched the British, stopping only to fire; but the Americans stood motionless. It seemed to them hours before the word rang out, "Fire!" That fire was like a cannonade, and the British, brave old soldiers as they were, ran pell-mell down the hill. "Hurrah! hurrah!" shouted the Americans. The British formed and rushed up the hill again; again the lines broke, and they retreated. They came a third time, but now no volleys met them; the powder had given out. The Americans had no bayonets, but they fought furiously with stones and the butt ends of their muskets, with clubs, knives, even with their fists; but no such weapons could withstand British veterans, and the Americans had to retreat.

News of the battle went through the colonies like wildfire. All their lives the Americans had looked up to the British regulars as the greatest of soldiers: and they, the untrained colonists who had never seen two regiments in battle, had twice driven them back! The hill was lost, but to repulse the British regulars was a mighty victory. Couriers galloped from one colony to another to carry the news. Everywhere there was rejoicing; but Putnam could not bear to think that after such a fight the hill had at last been given up, and he growled indignantly, "We ought to have stood. Powder or no powder, we ought to have stood."

—From Eva March Tappan, *American Hero Stories*

"*The Colossus of the Debate*"
John Adams, Autobiography, *July 1, 1776*

"HAD MR. ADAMS been so restrained, Congress would have lost the benefit of his bold and impressive avocations of the rights of Revolution.

For no man's confident and fervid addresses, more than Mr. Adams's, encouraged and supported us through the difficulties surrounding us, which, like the ceaseless action of gravity weighed on us by night and by day."

So wrote Thomas Jefferson to his friend James Madison, nearly fifty years after the great speech Adams made to convince his fellow delegates to adopt the resolution for American independence. Jefferson viewed Adams as the "colossus of the debate."

On June 7, 1776, Richard Henry Lee of Virginia had proposed a resolution for independence before the Continental Congress. Not all of the colonies were ready for this, and the vote was postponed until July 1. The case had to be made for independence, and the vote had to be unanimous.

On July 1, John Dickinson of Pennsylvania, Adams's chief antagonist, gave a speech "with great Ingenuity and Eloquence" arguing against independence. When he finished speaking, a great silence filled the hall. All eyes turned to Adams.

Though John Adams himself acknowledges that he was often found to be off-putting by his fellow delegates, he rose to give a stirring rebuttal. There is no copy of the actual speech he gave, but below is John Adams's account of the day. It is only appropriate that in arguing and winning the day for this most fundamental of American documents, Adams by his own account relies not on "ancient oratory" but on "plain understanding and common sense."

I am not able to recollect whether it was on this or some preceding day that the greatest and most solemn debate was had on the question of independence. The subject had been in contemplation for more than a year, and frequent discussions had been had concerning it. At one time and another all the arguments for it and against it had been exhausted and were become familiar. I expected no more would be said in public, but that the question would be put and decided. Mr. Dickinson, however, was determined to bear his testimony against it with more formality. He had prepared himself apparently with great labor and ardent zeal, and in a speech of great length, and with all his eloquence, he combined together all that had before been written in pamphlets and newspapers, and all that had from time to time been said in Congress by himself and others. He conducted the debate not only with great ingenuity and eloquence, but with equal politeness and candor, and was answered in the same spirit.

No member rose to answer him, and after waiting some time in hopes that some one less obnoxious than myself, who had been all along for a year before, and still was, represented and believed to be the author of all the mischief, would move, I determined to speak.

It has been said by some of our historians that I began by an invocation to the god of eloquence. This is a misrepresentation. Nothing so puerile as this fell from me. I began by saying that this was the first time of my life that I had ever wished for the talents and eloquence of the ancient orators of Greece and Rome, for I was very sure that none of them ever had before him a question of more importance to his country and to the world. They would probably, upon less occasions than this, have begun by solemn invocations to their divinities for assistance; but the question before me appeared so simple that I had confidence enough in the plain understanding and common sense that had been given me to believe that I could answer, to the satisfaction of the House, all the arguments which had been produced, notwithstanding the abilities which had been displayed, and the eloquence with which they had been enforced.

❧

"Liberty Bell," Anonymous

THE PROCEEDINGS of the Second Continental Congress had been highly confidential and secret. The Declaration of Independence was published on July 8, 1776, four days after it had been approved by the delegates. On July 8 the Pennsylvania State House's Liberty Bell, bearing the inscription, "Proclaim liberty throughout the land unto all the inhabitants thereof" (Leviticus 25:10) pealed forth to Philadelphians the final outcome of Congress's deliberations: American independence!

> There was tumult in the city,
> In the quaint old Quaker town,
> And the streets were rife with people,
> Pacing restless up and down,
> People gathering at corners,
> Where they whispered, each to each,
> And the sweat stood on their temples,
> With the earnestness of speech.

As the bleak Atlantic currents
Lash the wild Newfoundland shore,
So they beat against the State House,
So they surged against the door;

And the mingling of their voices
Made a harmony profound,
Till the quiet street of Chestnut
Was all turbulent with sound.

"Will they do it?"—"Dare they do it?"
"Who is speaking?"—"What's the news?"—
"What of Adams?"—"What of Sherman?"—
"Oh, God grant they won't refuse!"—

Aloft in that high steeple
Sat the bellman, old and gray;
He was weary of the tyrant
And his iron-sceptered sway;
So he sat with one hand ready
On the clapper of the bell,
When his eye should catch the signal,
Very happy news to tell.

See! see! the dense crowd quivers
Through all its lengthy line,
As the boy beside the portal
Looks forth to give the sign.
With his small hands upward lifted,
Breezes dallying with his hair,
Hark! with deep, clear intonation,
Breaks his young voice on the air.

Hushed the people's swelling murmur,
List the boy's strong, joyous cry—
"Ring!" he shouts aloud, *"Ring, Grandpa!*
Ring! Oh, ring for Liberty!"
And, straightway, at the signal,
The old bellman lifts his hand,
And sends the good news, making
Iron music through the land.

How they shouted! What rejoicing!
How the old bell shook the air,
Till the clang of Freedom ruffled
The calm, gliding Delaware!
How the bonfires and the torches
Illumed the night's repose!
And from the flames, like Phoenix,
Fair Liberty arose!

That old bell now is silent,
And hushed its iron tongue,
But the spirit it awakened
Still lives—forever young.
And, while we greet the sunlight,
On the fourth of each July,
We'll ne'er forget the bellman
Who, 'twixt the earth and sky,
Rung out OUR INDEPENDENCE;
Which, please God, *shall never die!*

∞

John Adams to Abigail Adams, July 3, 1776

ON JUNE 7, 1776, Richard Henry Lee of Virginia proposed a resolution in the Second Continental Congress: "That these United Colonies are and of right ought to be free and independent states." On July 2, 1776, the delegates of twelve colonies (New York abstained) voted unanimously to adopt Lee's resolution for independence, thanks to Adams's leadership. The next day in a letter to his wife, Adams shares his thoughts on how American independence would be celebrated by future generations—with pomp and parade, games and sports.

Of course, we celebrate American Independence on July 4, the date that the Declaration of Independence was approved, rather than on July 2, the date that the resolution for independence was adopted. Adams may have predicted the wrong date for future celebrations, but his thoughts are indeed prophetic. In the midst of our barbecues and fireworks, I hope Americans will take a minute or two to remember this brave warrior who made the birth of our nation possible and remember as well his words about toil, blood, treasure and trust in God.

But the Day is past. The Second Day of July 1776, will be the most memorable Epocha, in the History of America.—I am apt to believe that it will be celebrated, by succeeding Generations, as the great anniversary Festival. It ought to be commemorated, as the Day of Deliverance by solemn Acts of Devotion to God Almighty. It ought to be solemnized with Pomp and Parade, with Shews, Games, Sports, Guns, Bells, Bonfires and Illuminations from one End of this Continent to the other from this Time forward forever more.

You will think me transported with Enthusiasm but I am not.—I am well aware of the Toil and Blood and Treasure, that it will cost Us to maintain this Declaration, and support and defend these States.—Yet through all the Gloom I can see the Rays of ravishing Light and Glory. I can see that the End is more than worth all the Means. And that Posterity will tryumph in that Days Transaction, even altho We should rue it, which I trust in God We shall not.

∽

"Betty Zane," by Thomas Dunn English

IN SEPTEMBER of 1777, Fort Henry in West Virginia was attacked by British and Indian soldiers. The Americans were low on powder, and Betty Zane volunteered to leave the fort to get more. She returned with the needed ammunition and thus played a decisive role in the defense of Fort Henry. Here's a wonderful poem celebrating a woman who showed "a front of iron" and did "bold things in a quiet way."

> Women are timid, cower and shrink
> At show of danger, some folk think;
> But men there are who for their lives
> Dare not so far asperse their wives.
> We let that pass—so much is clear,
> Though little perils they may fear,
> When greater perils men environ,
> Then women show a front of iron;
> And, gentle in their manner, they

Do bold things in a quiet way,
And so our wondering praise obtain,
As on a time did Betty Zane.

A century since, out in the West,
A block-house was by Girty pressed—
Girty, the renegade, the dread
Of all that border, fiercely led
Five hundred Wyandots, to gain
Plunder and scalp-locks from the slain;
And in this hold—Fort Henry then,
But Wheeling now—twelve boys and men
Guarded with watchful ward and care
Women and prattling children there,
Against their rude and savage foes,
And Betty Zane was one of those. . . .

Now Betty's brothers and her sire
Were with her in this ring of fire,

And she was ready, in her way,
To aid their labor day by day,
In all a quiet maiden might.
To mould the bullets for the fight,
And, quick to note and so report,
Watch every act outside the fort;
Or, peering through the loopholes, see
Each phase of savage strategy—
These were her tasks, and thus the maid
The toil-worn garrison could aid.

Still, drearily the fight went on
Until a week had nearly gone,
When it was told—a whisper first,
And then in loud alarm it burst—
Their powder scarce was growing; they
Knew where a keg unopened lay
Outside the fort at Zane's—what now?
Their leader stood with anxious brow.
It must be had at any cost,
Or toil and fort and lives were lost.
Some one must do that work of fear;
What man of men would volunteer?

Two offered, and so earnest they,
Neither his purpose would give way;
And Shepherd, who commanded, dare
Not pick or choose between the pair.
But ere they settled on the one
By whom the errand should be done,
Young Betty interposed, and said,
"Let me essay the task instead.
Small matter 'twere if Betty Zane,
A useless woman, should be slain;
But death, if dealt on one of those,
Gives too much vantage to our foes."

Her father smiled with pleasure grim—
Her pluck gave painful pride to him;
And while her brothers clamored "No!"
He uttered, "Boys, let Betty go!

She'll do it at less risk than you;
But keep her steady in your view,
And be your rifles shields for her.
If yonder foe make step or stir,
Pick off each wretch who draws a bead,
And so you'll serve her in her need.
Now I recover from surprise,
I think our Betty's purpose wise."

The gate was opened, on she sped;
The foe, astonished gazed, 'tis said,
And wondered at her purpose, till
She gained that log-hut by the hill.
But when, in apron wrapped, the cask
She backward bore, to close her task,
The foemen saw her aim at last,
And poured their fire upon her fast.
Bullet on bullet near her fell,
While rang the Indians' angry yell;
But safely through that whirring rain,
Powder in arms, came Betty Zane.

They filled their horns, both boys and men
And so began the fight again.
Girty, who there so long had stayed,
By this new feat of feats dismayed,
Fired houses round and cattle slew,
And moved away—the fray was through.
But when the story round was told
How they maintained the leaguered hold,
It was agreed, though fame was due
To all who in that fight were true,
The highest meed of praise, 'twas plain,
Fell to the share of Betty Zane.

A hundred years have passed since then;
The savage never came again.
Girty is dust; alike are dead
Those who assailed and those bestead.
Upon those half-cleared, rolling lands,
A crowded city proudly stands;

But of the many who reside
By green Ohio's rushing tide,
Not one has lineage prouder than
(Be he or poor or rich) the man
Who boasts that in his spotless strain
Mingles the blood of Betty Zane.

∞

"Banish Unmanly Fear"
John Jay: To the General Committee
of Tryon County,
July 22, 1777

THE BRITISH expected an early victory as Washington and his men retreated across New Jersey after being soundly defeated and out-gunned in the Battle of Long Island. Taking advantage of the sinking morale of the American troops, the British commander offered a pardon and protection for any American who would return his allegiance to Great Britain.

John Jay wrote the following address to deter any such defections. It is a rousing call to courage and conviction.

In Council of Safety *

Gentlemen:

We have received your letter, and several others from different parts of your county, and are no less affected by the dangers than the fears of the people of Tryon. It is with the utmost concern that we hear of the universal panic, despair, and despondency which prevail throughout your county. We flattered ourselves that the approach of the enemy would have animated, and not depressed their spirits. What reason is there to expect that Heaven will help those who refuse to help them-selves; or that Providence will grant liberty to those who want courage

---

* The above letter is credited by his biographer to Mr. Jay, vol. i., p. 71. Jay seems to have conducted a large part of the correspondence for the Council of Safety; its proceedings contain or refer to drafts of letters by him to Washington, Clinton, Schuyler, Trumbull, and others.

to defend it. Are the great duties they owe to themselves, their country, and posterity, so soon forgotten? Let not the history of the present glorious contest declare to future generations that the people of your county, after making the highest professions of zeal for the American cause, fled at the first appearance of danger, and behaved like women. This unmanly conduct gives us great concern. We feel too much for your honour and reputation not to be uneasy. Instead of supplicating the protection of your enemies, meet them with arms in your hands—make good your professions, and let not your attachment to freedom be manifested only in your words.

We could scarcely have believed that a man among you would have thought of *protections* (as they are falsely called) from the enemy. Of what advantage have they been to the deluded wretches who accepted them in Jersey, New York, Westchester, and Long Island? After being seduced from their duty to their county, they were plundered, robbed, cast into prison, treated as slaves, and abused in a manner almost too savage and cruel to be related. We ought to profit by the woful experience of others, and not with our eyes open run to destruction. Nor imagine you will remain unsupported in the hour of trial. We consider you as part of the State, and as equally entitled with other counties to the aid of the whole. . . .

Let all differences among you cease. Let the only contest be, who shall be foremost in defending his country. Banish unmanly fear, acquit yourselves like men, and with firm confidence trust the event with that Almighty and benevolent Being who hath commanded you to hold fast the liberty with which he has made you free; and who is able as well as willing to support you in performing his orders. If you can prevail on your people to exert their own strength, all will be well. Let us again beseech and entreat you, for the honour and reputation, as well as the safety of the State, to behave like men.

∞

Gouverneur Morris

GOUVERNEUR MORRIS, diplomat and one of the drafters of the United States Constitution, may not have fought on the battlefield of the American Revolution, but he fought his own private battles and did so with courage. In 1778, at the age of twenty-five, Morris was elected a member of the Continental Congress in Philadelphia. He failed to win reelection in 1779, but stayed in Philadelphia and published a series of essays seeking ways to reform the near-crisis state of American currency and finances. During this time, he sustained injuries in a carriage accident. The doctors—perhaps wrongly—believed that these injuries required the amputation of one leg, from the knee down. In the following selection, we see how gallantly a twenty-eight-year-old Morris faced such a devastating blow.

In Philadelphia in May, 1780, while trying to control a pair of runaway horses, Morris was thrown from his phaëton, dislocated his ankle, and fractured the bones of his left leg. The two physicians who were called to him recommended an immediate amputation as the only means of saving his life, and, although this must have been a painful alternative for so young a man to contemplate, he submitted to the decree of the doctors with philosophy and even cheerfulness, and to the operation with extreme fortitude. The leg was taken off below the knee, and the operation has been cited by physicians knowing the particulars as most unskillful and hasty. The day after it took place a friend called upon him, full of sympathy and prepared to offer all the possible consolation on an event so melancholy. He painted in vivid words the good effect that such a trial should produce on his character and moral temperament, enlarging on the many temptations and pleasures of life into which young men are apt to be led, and of the diminished inducement Morris would now have to indulge in the enjoyment of such pleasures. "My good sir," replied Mr. Morris, "you argue the matter so handsomely and point out so clearly the advantages of being without legs, that I am almost tempted to part with the other." Morris seems to have felt the force of his friend's arguments in regard to the balancing effect on his character of the loss of a portion of his person, for to another friend, also deeply sympathetic and full of regret that he should have met with so grave a misfortune, he remarked: "Sir, the loss is much less than you imagine; I shall doubtless be a *steadier* man with one leg than with two." For the remainder of his life he wore a wooden leg, of primitive simplicity, not much more than a rough oak stick with a wooden knob on the end of it.

∞

"A Fine Fox Chase, My Boys!"
George Washington at Princeton, January 1777

THERE WAS not much time for Washington to celebrate his victory at Trenton, where his men, after making a perilous crossing over the frozen Delaware River, attacked mercenary Hessian troops. The victory at Trenton proved to be the major turning point of the war and was a much needed boost to morale. But Washington soon faced another problem: The British, after their defeat at Trenton, had fortified their troops and were closing in on the American army, while the enlistments for the bulk of Washington's troops were soon to expire. Washington could not once again retreat across the impassable Delaware River. He implored his weary men, who often marched barefoot, to remain with him for a little longer and offered a bonus for each man who stayed. As for the British, they were already beginning the celebrations. According to Washington biographer Washington Irving, British General Charles Cornwallis declared that they had finally trapped General Washington, and "would bag the fox in the morning" and finally end the war.

Under these conditions, the American troops marched to Princeton with muffled wheels to launch a surprise attack on the British. Washington sent General Hugh Mercer and some troops in advance to take out a strategic bridge. Mercer encountered bayonet-wielding soldiers, who attacked the American troops with great ferocity. Mercer fell, and his frightened men began to retreat.

Washington, riding upon a white horse directly in front of enemy fire, came to the rescue. With a torrent of bullets swirling about him, Washington stopped his horse, exposing himself, it seemed, to certain death. His aides begged Washington to take cover—one aide, John Fitzgerald, could not bear to see Washington cut down, so he used his hat to cover his eyes. When Fitzgerald looked up, however, Washington was still very much alive, rousing the troops to fight on. At the end of the battle, it was not Cornwallis but Washington, atop his horse, who shouted to his men, "A fine fox chase, my boys!"* as British soldiers hastily retreated.

* Cited in A. J. Langguth, *Patriots*, p. 428.

The poem that follows captures the glorious deeds of Washington and his soldiers at the Battle of Princeton.

BALLAD OF PRINCETON BATTLE
BY HENRY VAN DYKE

Along Assunpink's woody bank we left our
campfires bright,
While like a fox with padded feet we stole
away by night;
Cornwallis watched his Trenton trap,
And drained his glass, and took his nap;
But the ragged troops of Washington out-
flanked him in the night—
Up and away for Princeton,
By a secret road to Princeton—
We dragged our guns with muffled wheels to
win another fight.

The icy trail was hard as iron, our footprints
marked it red;
Our frosty breath went up like smoke to the
winking stars o'erhead;
By Bear Swamp and by Miry Run,
Our muskets weighed at least a ton;
We shivered, till o'er Stony Brook we saw
that sun rise red;
Weary we tramped to Princeton;
But all of us at Princeton
Would follow our chief through thick and thin
till the last of us was dead.

We looked beyond the upper bridge, across
the swollen stream,
And there along the king's highway we saw
the Redcoats gleam;
'Twas Mawhood's regiment marching down
To finish us off at Trenton Town!
"Go cut the bridge"—and Mercer's men
crept up along the stream.
But the British turned towards Princeton,

Came bravely back for Princeton;
And all the rest of that dim hour was wilder
than a dream.

They rushed thro' Will Clark's orchard,
among the naked trees;
With horse and foot they hammered hard;
their bullets sang like bees;
And Mercer fell, and Haslet fell;
The bayonets cut us up like hell;
The chain shot mowed a bloody path beneath
the twisted trees.
It looked all black for Princeton,
We lost our hopes of Princeton;
We wavered, and we broke and fled as leaves
before the breeze.

Then down the hill from Tom Clark's house
rode Washington aflame
With holy ire; through smoke and fire, like
mighty Mars he came.
"Come on, my men, parade with me,
We'll make the braggart Redcoats flee"—
And up the hill, against the guns, rode
Washington aflame.
He turned the tide at Princeton;
The land was saved at Princeton;
And they who fought, and they who fell, won
liberty and fame.

Men praise our chief for weighty words, for
counsel calm and high,
For prudence and enduring will, for cool,
farseeing eye;
One thing he had all else above—
Courage that caught the soldier's love,
And made the soldier's loyal heart in danger's
hour beat high.
We saw it clear at Princeton;
'Twas written here at Princeton:
THE MEN WHO MAKE A NATION GREAT ARE
MEN WHO DARE TO DIE.

∞

"I Have Not Yet Begun to Fight"
John Paul Jones's Victory, September 23, 1779

IN AUGUST 1779, John Paul Jones, a native of Scotland and volunteer in the new Continental Navy, was given command of a ship which he renamed the *Bonhomme Richard* in honor of Benjamin Franklin for his *Poor Richard's Almanacks*. Jones was small in stature—barely over five feet tall—but had a big and courageous heart. Captain Jones engaged the *Bonhomme Richard* in a fierce naval battle with the British ship *Serapis*. The *Serapis* had more guns and more men, but Jones and his men on the *Bonhomme Richard* were undaunted. They won one of the greatest naval battles ever in American history simply by sheer guts and will, stubbornly refusing to surrender. The ships were pounding away at each other at close range. When the British called for Jones's surrender, legend has it that he replied: "I have not yet begun to fight."

Here is a poem that celebrates his courage.

> An American frigate, a frigate of fame,
> With guns mounting forty, the *Richard* by name,
> Sail'd to cruise in the channels of old England,
>
> With valiant commander, Paul Jones was the man,
> Hurrah! Hurrah! Our country for ever, Hurrah!
> We had not cruised long, before he espies
> A large forty-four, and a twenty likewise;
> Well-manned with bold seamen, well laid in with stores,
> In consort to drive us from old England's shores.
> Hurrah! Hurrah! Our country for ever, Hurrah!
>
> About twelve at noon Pearson came alongside,
> With a loud speaking trumpet, "Whence came you?" he cried,
> "Return me an answer, I hail'd you before,
> Or if you do not, a broadside I'll pour."
> Hurrah! Hurrah! Our country for ever, Hurrah!
>
> Paul Jones then said to his men, every one,
> "Let every true seaman stand firm to his gun!
> We'll receive a broadside from this bold Englishman,
> And like true Yankee sailors return it again."
> Hurrah! Hurrah! Our country for ever, Hurrah!
>
> The contest was bloody, both decks ran with gore,
> And the sea seemed to blaze, while the cannon did roar;
> "Fight on, my brave boys," then Paul Jones he cried:
> "And soon we will humble this bold Englishman's pride."
> Hurrah! Hurrah! Our country for ever, Hurrah!
>
> "Stand firm to your quarters—your duty don't shun,
> The first one that shrinks, through the body I'll run;
> Though their force is superior, yet they shall know,
> What true, brave American seamen can do."
> Hurrah! Hurrah! Our country for ever, Hurrah!

The battle rolled on, till bold Pearson cried:
"Have you yet struck your colors? then come alongside!"
But so far from thinking that the battle was won,
Brave Paul Jones replied, "I've not yet begun!"
Hurrah! Hurrah! Our country for ever, Hurrah!

We fought them eight glasses, eight glasses so hot,
Till seventy bold seamen lay dead on the spot.
And ninety brave seamen lay stretched in their gore,
While the pieces of cannon most fiercely did roar.
Hurrah! Hurrah! Our country for ever, Hurrah!

Our gunner, in great fright to Captain Jones came,
"We gain water quite fast and our side's in a flame;"
Then Paul Jones said in the height of his pride,
"If we cannot do better, boys, sink along-side!"
Hurrah! Hurrah! Our country for ever, Hurrah!

The *Alliance* bore down, and the *Richard* did rake,
Which caused the bold hearts of our seamen to ache;
Our shot flew so hot that they could not stand us long,
And the undaunted Union of Britain came down.
Hurrah! Hurrah! Our country for ever, Hurrah!

To us they did strike and their colors hauled down;
The fame of Paul Jones to the world shall be known;
His name shall rank with the gallant and brave,
Who fought like a hero our freedom to save.
Hurrah! Hurrah! Our country for ever, Hurrah!

Now all valiant seamen where'er you may be,
Who hear of this combat that's fought on the sea,
May you all do like them, when called for the same,
And your names be enrolled on the pages of fame.
Hurrah! Hurrah! Our country for ever, Hurrah!

Your country will boast of her sons that are brave,
And to you she will look from all dangers to save;
She'll call you dear sons, in her annals you'll shine,
And the brows of the brave with green laurels entwine.
Hurrah! Hurrah! Our country for ever, Hurrah!

So now, my brave boys, have we taken a prize—
A large 44, and a 20 like-wise!
Then God bless the mother whose doom is to weep
The loss of her sons in the ocean so deep.
Hurrah! Hurrah! Our country for ever, Hurrah!

∞

Washington's Glasses

HERE'S A story of the inimitable example of George Washington. In 1783, unpaid officers from the Continental Army threatened a military coup to overthrow Congress. Washington could have been America's first dictator. Instead, he persuaded his fellow officers to live under the rule of law. On and off the field of battle, this man was a leader of the highest principles.

At the end of the Revolutionary War, the new United States came close to disaster. The government owed back pay to many officers in the army, men who had fought long and hard for the nation's freedom. But Congress had no money, and rumors abounded that it intended to disband the armed forces and send them home without pay.

As the weeks passed, the army's cry for pay grew louder. The soldiers insisted that they had performed their duty faithfully, and now the government should do the same. They sent appeals to Congress, with no effect. Patience began to wear thin. Tempers smoldered. At last some of the officers, encamped at Newburgh, New York, issued what amounted to a threat. The army would not disband until paid; if necessary, it would march on Congress. Mutiny was close at hand.

There was no doubt in anyone's mind that one man alone could persuade the army to give the government more time.

On March 15, 1783, George Washington strode into the Temple of Virtue, a large wooden hall built by the soldiers as a chapel and dance hall. A hush fell over the gathered officers as the tall figure took to the lectern at the front of the room. These men had come to love their commander-in-chief during the lean, hard years of fighting; now, for the first time, they glared at him with restless and resentful eyes. A deathlike stillness filled the room.

Washington began to speak. He talked of his own dedicated service, and reminded the group that he himself had served without pay. He spoke of his love for his soldiers. He urged them to have patience, and pointed out that Congress in the past had acted slowly, but in the end would act justly. He promised he would do everything in his power to see that the men received what they deserved.

He asked them to consider the safety and security of their new country, begging them not to "open the flood gates of civil discord, and deluge our rising empire in blood." He appealed to their honor. "Let me entreat you, gentlemen, on your part," he said, "not to take any measures which, viewed in the calm light of reason, will lessen the dignity and sully the glory you have hitherto maintained."

He paused. A restlessness pervaded the air. His audience did not seem moved. The men stared at him tensely.

Washington produced a letter from a congressman explaining the difficulties the government now faced. He would read it to them. It would help them comprehend the new government's difficulties. He unfolded the paper. He started to read, slowly. He stumbled over some of the words, then stopped. Something was wrong. The general seemed lost, slightly confused. The officers leaned forward.

Then Washington pulled from his pocket something the men had never seen their commander-in-chief use before—spectacles.

"Gentlemen, you must pardon me," he said quietly. "I have grown gray in your service, and now find myself growing blind."

It was not merely what the beloved general said, but the way he spoke the few, simple words. The humble act of this majestic man touched the soldiers in a way his arguments had failed to do. There were lumps in many throats, tears in every eye. The general quietly left the hall, and the officers voted to give the Congress more time.

George Washington had saved his new country from armed rebellion. As Thomas Jefferson later said, "The moderation and virtue of a single character probably prevented this Revolution from being closed, as most others have been, by a subversion of that liberty it was intended to establish."

Benjamin Franklin Defends the Constitution, 1787

FRANKLIN, THEN aged eighty-one, was the oldest delegate to the Constitutional Convention. Jared Sparks observed in his journal that, "at the

Convention, Dr. Franklin seldom spoke. As he was too feeble to stand long at a time, his speeches were generally written. He would arise and ask the favor of one of his colleagues to read what he had written." * Franklin, who suffered from gout, was carried each day to the convention in a sedan chair, propped up on poles carried by prisoners from the local jail.

On September 17, 1787, Franklin rose and handed the following written speech to James Wilson to read aloud. Franklin was not without his own reservations about the Constitution — for example, he believed in a one house legislature instead of two and opposed giving the president a salary. Nonetheless, Franklin showed intellectual and moral courage; he sacrificed his own ideas and endorsed the Constitution and gave a motion for a unanimous vote from the delegates from the eleven states who were present. Not all the delegates to the Constitutional Convention were in agreement — of the fifty-five delegates, only thirty-nine actually signed the Constitution.

This speech was, perhaps, Franklin's last political contribution to a nation he had been so instrumental in building. Toward the end of the signing, Franklin approached the President's chair on which there was painted a rising sun, and commented: "I have often and often in the course of the Session, and the vicissitudes of my hopes and fears as to its issue, looked at that behind the President without being able to tell whether it was rising or setting: But now at length I have the happiness to know that it is a rising and not a setting Sun."

What follows is James Madison's account of the speech.

Monday Sep. 17, 1787: In Convention
The engrossed Constitution being read,
Doc.ᴿ Franklin rose with a speech in his hand, which he had reduced to writing for his own conveniency, and which Mr. Wilson read in the words following.

Mr. President
I confess that there are several parts of this constitution which I do not at present approve, but I am not sure I shall never approve them: For having lived long, I have experienced many instances of being obliged by better information, or fuller consideration, to change opinions even on important subjects, which I once thought right, but found to be otherwise. It is therefore that the older I grow, the more apt I am to doubt my own judgment, and to pay more respect to the judgment of

* Max Farrand, ed., *The Records of the Federal Convention*, vol. 3, p. 481.

others. Most men indeed as well as most sects in Religion, think themselves in possession of all truth, and that wherever others differ from them it is so far error. Steele a Protestant in a Dedication tells the Pope, that the only difference between our Churches in their opinions of the certainty of their doctrines is, the Church of Rome is infallible and the Church of England is never in the wrong. But though many private persons think almost as highly of their own infallibility as of that of their sect, few express it so naturally as a certain french lady, who in a dispute with her sister, said "I don't know how it happens, Sister but I meet with no body but myself, that's always in the right—*Il n'y a que moi qui a toujours raison.*"

In these sentiments, Sir, I agree to this Constitution with all its faults, if they are such; because I think a general Government necessary for us, and there is no form of Government but what may be a blessing to the people if well administered, and believe farther that this is likely to be well administered for a course of years, and can only end in Despotism, as other forms have done before it, when the people shall become so corrupted as to need despotic Government, being incapable of any other. I doubt too whether any other Convention we can obtain, may be able to make a better Constitution. For when you assemble a number of men to have the advantage of their joint wisdom, you inevitably assemble with those men, all their prejudices, their passions, their errors of opinion, their local interests, and their selfish views. From such an assembly can a perfect production be expected? It therefore astonishes me, Sir, to find this system approaching so near to perfection as it does; and I think it will astonish our enemies, who are waiting with confidence to hear that our councils are confounded like those of the Builders of Babel; and that our States are on the point of separation, only to meet hereafter for the purpose of cutting one another's throats. Thus I consent Sir, to this Constitution because I expect no better, and because I am not sure, that it is not the best. The opinions I have had of its errors, I sacrifice to the public good. I have never whispered a syllable of them abroad. Within these walls they were born and here they shall die. If every one of us in returning to our Constituents were to report the objections he has had to it, and endeavor to gain partizans in support of them, we might prevent its being generally received, and thereby lose all the salutary effects & great advantages resulting naturally in our favor among foreign Nations as well as among ourselves, from our real or apparent unanimity. Much of the strength & efficiency of any Government in procuring and securing happiness to the people, depends, on opinion, on the general opinion of the goodness of the Government, as well as of the wisdom and integrity of its Governors. I hope therefore that for our own sakes as a part of the people, and for the sake of posterity, we shall act heartily and unanimously in recommending this Constitution (if approved by Congress & confirmed by the Conventions) wherever our influence may extend, and turn our future thoughts & endeavors to the means of having it well administred.

On the whole, Sir, I can not help expressing a wish that every member of the Convention who may still have objections to it, would with me, on this occasion doubt a little of his own infallibility, and to make manifest our unanimity, put his name to this instrument.—

He then moved that the Constitution be signed by the members and offered the following as a convenient form viz. "Done in Convention by the unanimous consent of *the States* present the 17th of Sept &c—In Witness whereof we have hereunto subscribed our names."

∞

Alexander Hamilton, Federalist No. 1, *October 27, 1787*

AFTER MONTHS of arduous work, the delegates to the Constitutional Convention submitted the Constitution before the people of each state for ratification. Adoption of the Constitution was not a foregone conclusion—there were many opponents to it, known as the "Anti-Federalists," who worried that the Constitution consolidated national power at the expense of the state governments.

Adopting the pen name "Publius," Alexander Hamilton, James Madison, and John Jay wrote a series of essays urging passage of the Constitution. These eighty-five essays appeared in newspapers mainly in New York and were later compiled in book form as *The Federalist.* They are a genuine work of political theory and still do a better job of explaining the principles of American government than any other book I know. I would encourage every American to read and reread them.

In this, one of the most famous passages from *The Federalist,* Alexander Hamilton explains why love of America means so much more. The fate of *our* republic is tied up with the fate of the universal principles upon which it is founded. As Hamilton points out, the spirit of patriotism *and* philanthropy support America's founding.

To the People of the State of New York

After an unequivocal experience of the inefficacy of the subsisting Federal Government, you are called upon to deliberate on a new Constitution for the United States of America. The subject speaks its own importance; comprehending in its consequences, nothing less than the existence of the Union, the safety and welfare of the parts of which it is composed, the fate of an empire, in many respects, the most interesting in the world. It has been frequently remarked, that it seems to have been reserved to the people of this country, by their conduct and example, to decide the important question, whether societies of men are really capable or not, of establishing good government from reflection and choice, or whether they are forever destined to depend, for their political constitutions, on accident and force. If there be any truth in the remark, the crisis, at which we are arrived, may with propriety be regarded as the æra in which that decision is to be made; and a wrong election of the part we shall act, may, in this view, deserve to be considered as the general misfortune of mankind.

This idea will add the inducements of philanthropy to those of patriotism to heighten the solicitude, which all considerate and good men must feel for the event.

∽

"One Great Respectable and Flourishing Empire"
James Madison, Federalist No. 14, *November 30, 1787*

MADISON HAS rightfully been called the "father of the Constitution." But Madison himself would not take sole credit and wrote that the Constitution "was not, like the fabled Goddess of Wisdom, the offspring of a single brain. It ought to be regarded as the work of many heads and many hands"*

Madison could protest as much as he wanted—as the scholar T. V. Smith once wrote, Madison had a "passion for anonymity," but he was the principal mind and force behind the Constitution. He passed up an enticing invitation from his friend Thomas Jefferson to go to Europe, even withdrawing his name for consideration for a diplomatic post

---

* James Madison to William Cogswell, March 10, 1834.

abroad, so that he could spend two years studying how America's political institutions might be restructured. From his extensive readings, Madison learned important lessons about the causes of decline and dissolution of ancient and modern confederacies. He brought these lessons to bear at the Convention. The result, of course, is the world's longest surviving written Constitution.

Madison arrived eleven days early in Philadelphia for the Constitutional Convention so that he could get a running start on the proceedings. A fellow delegate noted that his "spirit of industry and application" made Madison the "best informed Man of any point in debate" and that he was a "Gentleman of great modesty—with a remarkable sweet temper."* Madison took copious notes during the four months that the delegates met, and his notes serve as the most accurate and most elaborate account of the secret proceedings. Madison wrote that "I was not absent a single day, nor more than a casual fraction of an hour in any day, so that I could not have lost a single speech, unless a very short one."

In *Federalist No. 14,* Madison explains why the "experiment of an extended republic" is not something to dismiss simply because it has never been tried before. Hitherto, most republics had been small and homogeneous states, rocked by factions and convulsions and decline. It was Madison's vision that America could become "one great respectable and flourishing empire."

Is it not the glory of the people of America, that whilst they have paid a decent regard to the opinions of former times and other nations, they have not suffered a blind veneration for antiquity, for custom, or for names, to overrule the suggestions of their own good sense, the knowledge of their own situation, and the lessons of their own experience? To this manly spirit, posterity will be indebted for the possession, and the world for the example of the numerous innovations displayed on the American theatre, in favor of private rights and public happiness. Had no important step been taken by the leaders of the revolution for which a precedent could not be discovered, no government established of which an exact model did not present itself, the people of the United States might, at this moment, have been numbered among the melancholy victims of misguided councils, must at best have been labouring under the weight of some of those forms which have crushed the liberties

---

* Farrand, *The Records of the Federal Convention,* vol. 3, pp. 94–95.

of the rest of mankind. Happily for America, happily we trust for the whole human race, they pursued a new and more noble course. They accomplished a revolution which has no parallel in the annals of human society: They reared the fabrics of governments which have no model on the face of the globe. They formed the design of a great confederacy, which it is incumbent on their successors to improve and perpetuate. If their works betray imperfections, we wonder at the fewness of them. If they erred most in the structure of the union; this was the work most difficult to be executed; this is the work which has been new modelled by the act of your Convention, and it is that act on which you are now to deliberate and to decide.

—Publius

∞

"To Vindicate the Honor of the Human Race"
Alexander Hamilton, Federalist No. 11

CORNELIUS DE PAUW was a Dutch scientist who wrote a treatise arguing that living creatures degenerate in America; that America was a diseased continent. He even argued that European dogs, transported to the New World, ceased to bark. De Pauw was not alone in these beliefs —other Europeans, such as the Count de Buffon, made similar arguments about the degeneracy of American soil. There is still among some foreigners a sense of superiority toward America and Americans. In 1787, Hamilton sets the record straight in this *Federalist* paper and attempts to teach the Europeans—"that assuming brother" some "moderation."

I shall briefly observe, that our situation invites, and our interests prompt us, to aim at an ascendant in the system of American affairs. The world may politically, as well as geographically, be divided into four parts, each having a distinct set of interests. Unhappily for the other three, Europe by her arms and by her negociations, by force and by fraud, has, in different degrees, extended her dominion over them all. Africa, Asia, and America have successively felt her domination. The superiority, she has long maintained, has tempted her to plume herself as the Mistress of the World, and to consider the rest of mankind as created for her benefit. Men admired as profound philosophers have, in direct terms, attributed to her inhabitants a physical superiority; and have gravely asserted that all animals, and with them the human species, degenerate in America—that even dogs cease to bark after having breathed a while in our atmosphere. Facts have too long supported these arrogant pretensions of the European. It belongs to us to vindicate the honor of the human race, and to teach that assuming brother moderation. Union will enable us to do it. Disunion will add another victim to his triumphs. Let Americans disdain to be the instruments of European greatness! Let the thirteen States, bound together in a strict and indissoluble union, concur in erecting one great American system, superior to the controul of all trans-atlantic force or influence, and able to dictate the terms of the connection between the old and the new world!

—Publius

∞

"I Am an American"
Gouverneur Morris, Speech, 1800

G OUVERNEUR M ORRIS of New York spoke more at the Constitutional Convention than any other delegate, including Madison. A fellow delegate, William Pierce, described him as "one of those Genius's in whom every species of talents combine to render him conspicuous and flourishing in public debate: He winds through all mazes of rhetoric and throws around him such a glare that he charms, captivates, and leads away the senses of all who hear him."*

At the Constitutional Convention, Morris was firmly committed to erecting a strong national government and instilling in the disparate states a strong spirit of nationhood. For those who resisted the idea of a strong United States, Morris reportedly said, "This generation will die away and give place to a race of Americans." †

Full of "youthful Hope" for the new nation, Morris gave this rousing speech predicting that America's "high, haughty, generous, and noble" national spirit will give rise to one of the greatest countries of all time.

---

* Farrand, *The Records of the Federal Convention*, vol. 3, p. 92.
† Catherine Drinker Bowen, *Miracle at Philadelphia*, p. 42.

NATIONAL GREATNESS

Thus then We have seen that a People may be numerous powerful wealthy free brave and inured to War without being Great, and by reflecting on the Reason why a Combination of those Qualities and Circumstances will not alone suffice. We are close to the true Source and Principle of national Greatness. It is in the national Spirit. It is in that high, haughty, generous and noble Spirit which prizes Glory more than wealth and holds Honor dearer than Life. It is that Spirit, the inspiring Soul of Heroes which raises Men above the Level of Humanity. It is present with us when we read the Story of antient Rome. It [s]wells our Bosoms at the View of her gigantic Deeds and makes us feel that we must ever be irresistible while human Nature shall remain unchanged. I have called it a high haughty generous and noble Spirit. It is high—Elevated above all low and vulgar Considerations. It is haughty—Despising whatever is little and mean whether in Character Council or Conduct. It is generous—granting freely to the weak and to the Indigent Protection and Support. It is noble—Dreading Shame and Dishonor as the greatest Evil, esteeming Fame and Glory beyond all Things human.

When this Spirit prevails the Government, whatever it's Form, will be wise and energetic because such Government alone will be borne by such Men. And such a Government seeking the true Interest of those over whom they preside will find it in the Establishment of a national Character becoming the Spirit by which the Nation is inspired. Foreign Powers will then know that to withhold a due Respect and Deference is dangerous. That Wrongs may be forgiven but that Insults will be avenged. As a necessary Result every Member of the Society bears with him every where full Protection & when he appears his firm and manly Port mark him of a superior Order in the Race of Man. The Dignity of Sentiment which he has inhaled with his native Air gives to his Manner an Ease superior to the Politeness of Courts and a Grace unrivalled by the Majesty of Kings.

These are Blessings which march in the train of national Greatness and come on the Pinions of youthful Hope. I anticipate the Day when to command Respect in the remotest Regions it will be sufficient to say I am an American. Our Flag shall then wave in Glory over the Ocean and our Commerce feel no Restraint but what our own Government may impose. Happy thrice happy Day. Thank God, to reach this envied State we need only to Will. Yes my countrymen. Our Destiny depends on our Will. But if we would stand high on the Record of Time that Will must be inflexible.

∞

James Madison, National Gazette, November 19, 1791

W E   H A V E   always been and will always be a nation of immigrants, and this is reflected in our idea of patriotism. Any individual, from any country, can become an American by going through a process by which he or she learns about and accepts the principles of the American creed. Thomas Jefferson noted that "every species of government has its specific principles [and] ours perhaps are more peculiar than those of any other in the universe." Madison wrote that the immigrant to America must "incorporate himself into our society." It was the hope of the Founders that immigrants would continue to "incorporate" themselves fully in the "peculiar" principles of equality and liberty which have made this nation a great one.

Emigrations may augment the population of the country permitting them. The commercial nations of Europe, parting with emigrants, to America, are examples. The articles of consumption demanded from the former, have created employment for an additional number of manufactures. The produce remitted from the latter, in the form of raw materials, has had the same effect—whilst imports and exports of every kind, have multiplied European merchants and mariners. Where the settlers have doubled every twenty or twenty-five years, as in the United States, the increase of products and consumption in the new country, and consequently of employment and people in the old, has had a corresponding rapidity. . . .

Freedom of emigration is due to the general interests of humanity. The course of emigrations being always, from places where living is more difficult, to places where it is less difficult, the happiness of the emigrant is promoted by the change: and as a more numerous progeny is another effect of the same cause, human life is at once made a greater blessing, and more individuals are created to partake of it.

❧

John Adams Scolds Benjamin Rush: Benjamin Rush to John Adams, June 13, 1808, and Adams to Rush, June 20, 1808

NEARLY THIRTY-TWO years after signing the Declaration of Independence, Benjamin Rush grimly assessed the American scene. He saw a nation split by growing political factions and, of most concern to him, evidence of the decline of republican simplicity and the rise of money worshiping. He thought America was becoming a "bedollared nation" —that is, a nation obsessed with money. He even told his good friend John Adams, now in retirement as well, that he sometimes regretted ever signing the Declaration of Independence.

Even though Adams believed that his own contributions to his country were often overlooked, unappreciated, or misinterpreted, he rose to defend America, and in a wonderful letter, scolded his "friend of '74" for such unpatriotic thoughts.

RUSH TO ADAMS

𝓘 feel pain when I am reminded of my exertions in the cause of what we called liberty, and sometimes wish I could erase my name from the Declaration of Independence. In case of a rupture with Britain or France, which shall we fight for? For our Constitution? I cannot meet with a man who loves it. It is considered as too weak by one half of our citizens and too strong by the other half. Shall we rally round the standard of a popular chief? Since the death of Washington there has been no such center of Union. Shall we contend for our paternal acres and dwelling houses? Alas! how few of these are owned by the men who will in case of war be called to the helm of our government. Their property consists chiefly in bank stock, and that to such an extent that among some of them it is considered as a mark of bad calculation for a man to live in a house of his own. I lately attended an old man who died under my care in the 81st year of his age. Of course he knew America in her youthful and innocent days. In speaking of the change in the principles and morals of our people which has taken place since the Revolution, he said: "They had all become idolaters; they worshipped but one god it is true, but that god was GOD DOLLARS." Were I permitted to coin a word suggested by my patient's remark, I would say we were a "bedollared nation." In walking our streets I have often been struck with the principal subjects of conversation of our citizens. Seldom have I heard a dozen words of which *"Dollar, discount,* and a *good Spec"* did not compose a part. "O! Civitas mox peritura si emptorem invenias."* St. Paul places covetousness and uncleanness together as improper subjects of conversation. But not only our streets but our parlors are constantly vocal with the language of a broker's office, and even at our convivial dinners "Dollars" are a standing dish upon which all feed with rapacity and gluttony.

ADAMS TO RUSH

My dear Physical and Medical Philosopher,
I give you this title for the present only. I shall scarcely allow you to be a political, moral, or Christian philosopher till you retract some of the complaints, lamentations, regrets, and penitences in your letter of the 13th. . . .
You and I, in the Revolution, acted from principle. We did our duty, as we then believed, according to our best information, judgment, and consciences. Shall we now repent of this? God forbid! No! If a banishment to Cayenne or to Botany Bay,† or even the guillotine, were to be the necessary consequences of it to us, we ought not to repent. Repent? This is impossible. How can a man repent of his virtues?

∞

George Washington, Farewell Address, September 19, 1796

HERE IS a man whose dedication to his country was as consistent as it was deep. For his leadership on the battlefield and for his willingness to serve as our first President, despite his well-known preference for private life, Washington is remembered, in the words of Henry Lee, as "first in war, first in peace, and first in the hearts of his countrymen."

Washington, the greatest American, was very clear about the "just claim" that government has on us. We have lost sight of that in the anti-government climate that so dominates public discourse.

---

* "O City soon to perish if you find a buyer."
† Cayenne and Botany Bay were French and British penal colonies.

Devoting more than half his life to the service of his country, Washington here gives a moving farewell address as he repairs to private life.

. . . *The* impressions, with which I first undertook the arduous trust, were explained on the proper occasion. In the discharge of this trust, I will only say, that I have, with good intentions, contributed towards the Organization and Administration of the government, the best exertions of which a very fallible judgment was capable. Not unconscious, in the outset, of the inferiority of my qualifications, experience in my own eyes, perhaps still more in the eyes of others, has strengthened the motives to diffidence of myself; and every day the encreasing weight of years admonishes me more and more, that the shade of retirement is as necessary to me as it will be welcome. Satisfied that if any circumstances have given peculiar value to my services, they were temporary, I have the consolation to believe, that while choice and prudence invite me to quit the political scene, patriotism does not forbid it.

In looking forward to the moment, which is intended to terminate the career of my public life, my feelings do not permit me to suspend the deep acknowledgment of that debt of gratitude wch. I owe to my beloved country, for the many honors it has conferred upon me; still more for the stedfast confidence with which it has supported me; and for the opportunities I have thence enjoyed of manifesting my inviolable attachment, by services faithful and persevering, though in usefulness unequal to my zeal. If benefits have resulted to our country from these services, let it always be remembered to your praise, and as an instructive example in our annals, that, under circumstances in which the Passions agitated in every direction were liable to mislead, amidst appearances sometimes dubious, viscissitudes of fortune often discouraging, in situations in which not unfrequently want of Success has countenanced the spirit of criticism, the constancy of your support was the essential prop of the efforts, and a guarantee of the plans by which they were effected. Profoundly penetrated with this idea, I shall carry it with me to my grave, as a strong incitement to unceasing vows that Heaven may continue to you the choicest tokens of its beneficence; that your Union and brotherly affection may be perpetual; that the free constitution, which is the work of your hands, may be sacredly maintained; that its Administration in every department may be stamped with wisdom and Virtue; that, in fine, the happiness of the people of these States, under the auspices of liberty, may be made complete, by so careful a preservation and so prudent a use of this blessing as will acquire to them the glory of recommending it to the applause, the affection, and adoption of every nation which is yet a stranger to it. . . .

This government, the offspring of our own choice uninfluenced and unawed, adopted upon full investigation and mature deliberation, completely free in its principles, in the distribution of its powers, uniting security with energy, and containing within itself a provision for its own amendment, has a just claim to your confidence and your support. Respect for its authority, compliance with its Laws, acquiescence in its measures, are duties enjoined by the fundamental maxims of true Liberty. The basis of our political systems is the right of the people to make and to alter their Constitutions of Government. But the Constitution which at any time exists, 'till changed by an explicit and authentic act of the whole People, is sacredly obligatory upon all.

∞

James Madison, "Advice to My Country," Fall 1834

MADISON LIVED to the age of eighty-five and was the last surviving member of the Philadelphia Constitutional Convention. He died on June 28, 1836—six days before the sixtieth anniversary of America's independence. It has been reported that someone suggested to Madison that he take some medicine to delay his death until July 4, so that he could die a patriotic death on that date just as former presidents Thomas Jefferson, John Adams, and James Monroe had done. Madison thought the suggestion was ridiculous and that a man should die when he was meant to.*

Though in a state of physical debilitation, his mind remained sharp to the end, and he continued dictating letters and signing them with a trembling hand. One visitor during his last days remarked that "never have I seen so much mind in so little matter!"

His death, like his life, was full of serene dignity. Here's one account: "That morning Sukey brought him breakfast, as usual. He could not swallow. His niece, Mrs. Wilis, said: 'What is the matter, Uncle James?'

" 'Nothing more than a change of *mind,* my dear.' His head instantly dropped. and he ceased breathing as quietly as the snuff of a candle goes out." †

Madison continued to give advice from the grave. Madison's "Advice

---

* Cited in Rutland, *James Madison.*

† Paul Jennings, *A Colored Man's Reminiscences of James Madison,* 1865, cited in Andrienne Koch, *Madison's "Advice to My Country,"* pp. 156–57.

to My Country" was his final contribution to a nation that he had been so instrumental in building. As John Quincy Adams said of Madison: "Is it not in a pre-eminent degree by emanations from *his* mind, that we are assembled here as the representatives of the people and the states of this union? Is it not transcendentally by his exertions that we address each other here by the endearing appellations of country-men and fellow citizens?"*

As the last, and perhaps the greatest, of the Founding Fathers, no one was more entitled to give advice.

As this advice, if it ever see the light will not do it till I am no more, it may be considered as issuing from the tomb, where truth alone can be respected, and the happiness of man alone consulted. It will be entitled therefore to whatever weight can be derived from good intentions, and from the experience of one who has served his country in various stations through a period of forty years, who espoused in his youth and adhered through his life to the cause of its liberty, and who has borne a part in most of the great transactions which will constitute epochs of its destiny.

The advice nearest to my heart and deepest in my convictions is that the Union of the States be cherished and perpetuated. Let the open enemy to it be regarded as a Pandora with her box opened; and the disguised one, as the Serpent creeping with his deadly wiles into Paradise.

∞

George Washington, Last Will and Testament, July 1799, and George Mason, Last Will and Testament

WASHINGTON AND Mason's love of country knew no bounds. At the Constitutional Convention, Mason said: "If I had a vein which did not beat with the love of my country, I myself would open it." † Washington, in his First Inaugural speech, said that "I was summoned by my Country, whose voice I can never hear but with veneration and love."

Here, even in death, their patriotism is passed on to their descendants.

---

* Cited in Koch, *Madison's "Advice to My Country,"* p.158.
† Bowen, *Miracle at Philadelphia*, p. 76.

To each of my Nephews, William Augustine Washington, George Lewis, George Steptoe Washington, Bushrod Washington and Samuel Washington, I give one of the Swords or Cutteaux of which I may die possessed; and they are to chuse in the order they are named. These Swords are accompanied with an injunction not to unsheath them for the purpose of shedding blood, except it be for self defence, or in defence of their Country and its rights; and in the latter case, to keep them unsheathed, and prefer falling with them in their hands, to the relinquishment thereof.

> —From the last will and testament
> of George Washington

I recommend it to my sons, from my own experience in life, to prefer the happiness of independence and a private station to the troubles and vexations of public business; but if either their own inclinations or the necessity of the times should engage them in public affairs, I charge them, on a father's blessing, never to let the motives of private interest or ambition to induce them to betray, nor the terrors of poverty and disgrace, or the fear of danger or of death deter them from asserting the liberty of their country, and endeavoring to transmit to their posterity those sacred rights to which themselves were born.

> —From the last will and testament
> of George Mason

∞

"Independence Forever!"
Deaths of John Adams and Thomas Jefferson,
July 4, 1826

Thomas Jefferson and John Adams were blessed with longevity—Jefferson lived to the age of eighty-three; Adams to ninety-one. They had more time than most men of their era (who were lucky to live beyond thirty-four years of age)* to think about the meaning of death. When Jefferson asked Adams if he feared death, he responded that death "is not an evil. It is a blessing to the individual, and to the world. Yet we

---

* This is according to Jefferson's citation of contemporary mortality charts that showed that for all men reaching the age of twenty-one, the average life span was thirty-four years.

ought not to wish for it till life becomes insupportable; we must wait the pleasure and convenience of this great teacher." Jefferson seemed to agree, as he wrote to Adams: "There is a ripeness of time for death, regarding others as well as ourselves, when it is reasonable we should drop off, and make room for another growth. When we have lived our generation out, we should not wish to encroach on another."

On July 4, 1826—the fiftieth anniversary of the adoption of the Declaration of Independence—Jefferson, the author of that document, and Adams, its leading advocate, died. It was surely one of the great coincidences of history—one might say, providential. Perhaps the two Founders sensed they could finally rest, their work now complete, and turn the American experiment over to a new generation of Americans. In life and in death, these men were patriots.

It was as if Adams and Jefferson willed themselves to live to see July 4, 1826. There was much anticipation regarding the Fiftieth Anniversary of America's Independence in Adams's hometown of Quincy, Massachusetts. Adams was too weak to attend any of the planned festivities, so a local committee approached him in late June to ask him for a toast. Adams replied, "Independence forever!" and refused to add another word. Though bedridden, when the great anniversary arrived, Adams asked to be seated in his chair in front of the window, so that he could take in the festivities. Soon after he slipped into a state of unconsciousness, and his doctor predicted he would not live to see another day. Adams's last thought—at least the last one he uttered out loud—was of his friend and fellow laborer for independence, Thomas Jefferson. Adams woke from his coma and said, "Jefferson still survives." Those were his last words. He died that evening.*

But Adams was mistaken—Jefferson did not survive him. Jefferson's health had been on the decline. He told his grandson in the spring of 1826 that he did not expect to live to see midsummer. In mid-June, he sent for his physician to stay with him at Monticello. In the weeks that followed, Jefferson prepared for his death. He met with all his grandchildren and told them "to pursue virtue, be true and truthful."† His thoughts during his last days kept returning to the revolutionary years—as he began his final decline he said something about warning the Committee of Safety. On the morning of July 3, Jefferson's doctor reported that his "stupor" or coma was "almost permanent." However, Jefferson woke up at seven o'clock in the evening and asked the doctor, "Is it the Fourth?" The doctor assured him it soon would be. According to the testimony of

---

* Charles Francis Adams, *Life and Works of John Adams*, vol. 1, pp. 634–44.
† Testimony of Thomas Jefferson Randolph, *Domestic Life of Jefferson*.

his doctor, those were Jefferson's last words. He clung to life long enough to die peacefully at around one o'clock in the afternoon on July 4, 1826.

"Adams and Jefferson are no more," said Daniel Webster in his famous eulogy of both men:

"On our fiftieth anniversary, the great day of national jubilee, in the very hour of public rejoicing, in the midst of echoing and reechoing voices of thanksgiving, while their own names were on all tongues, they took their flight together to the world of spirits. . . . Poetry itself has hardly terminated illustrious lives, and finished the career of earthly renown, by such a consummation. . . . It has closed; our patriots have fallen; but so fallen, at such age, with such coincidence, on such a day, that we cannot rationally lament that that end has come, which we knew could not be long deferred. . . . Their work doth not perish with them."

Independence forever!

JEFFERSON'S EPITAPH:

Here was buried
Thomas Jefferson

Author of the Declaration of American Independence,
of the Statute of Virginia for religious freedom
& Father of the University of Virginia

Jefferson explained his selection of these achievements by the following: "because by these, as testimonials that I have lived, I wish most to be remembered."

John Quincy Adams composed the following epitaph for his parents. It is located at a church which John Quincy Adams attended, in Quincy, Massachusetts.

LIBERTATEM, AMICITIAM, FIDEM RETINEBIS
"Freedom, Friendship, Faith Thy Soul Engage"

D. O. M.
"God the best, the greatest"

Beneath these walls
Are deposited the mortal remains of

JOHN ADAMS.

Son of John and Susanna (Boylston) Adams,
Second President of the United States;
Born $\frac{19}{30}$ October, 1735.
On the Fourth of July, 1776,
He pledged his Life, Fortune, and sacred Honor
To the INDEPENDENCE OF HIS COUNTRY.
On the third of September, 1783,
He affixed his seal to the definitive treaty with Great Britain,
Which acknowledged that independence,
And consummated the redemption of his pledge.
On the Fourth of July, 1826,
He was summoned
To the Independence of Immortality,
And to the JUDGMENT OF HIS GOD.
This House will bear witness to his piety;
This Town, his birthplace, to his munificence;
History to his patriotism;
Posterity to the depth and compass of his mind.

At his side
Sleeps, till the trump shall sound,

ABIGAIL,

His beloved and only wife,
Daughter of William and Elizabeth (Quincy) Smith;
In every relation of life a pattern
Of filial, conjugal, maternal, and social virtue.
Born November $\frac{11}{22}$, 1744,
Deceased 28 October, 1818,
Aged 74.

————

Married 25 October, 1764.
During an union of more than half a century
They survived, in harmony of sentiment, principle, and affection,
The tempests of civil commotion;
Meeting undaunted and surmounting

The terrors and trials of that Revolution,
Which secured the Freedom of their Country;
Improved the condition of their times;
And brightened the prospects of Futurity
To the race of man upon Earth.

PILGRIM.

From lives thus spent thy earthly duties learn;
From fancy's dreams to active virtue turn;
Let Freedom, Friendship, Faith, thy soul engage,
And serve, like them, thy country and thy age.

II

*L*OVE
AND
COURTSHIP

❦

"It has ever been a maxim with me through life, neither to promote nor to prevent a matrimonial connection, unless there should be something indispensably requiring interference in the latter. I have always considered marriage as the most interesting event of one's life, the foundation of happiness or misery."

GEORGE WASHINGTON TO BURWELL BASSETT, MAY 23, 1785

We know the Founders best as *public* men and women, as statesmen. We admire and attempt to emulate their good sense, their patriotism, their profound learning; but they, like us, were also *private* men and women who wrestled with the most tempestuous passions of the human heart. Like all human beings, they longed for and gave and received love —and moreover valued, perhaps above all else in this world a happy marriage and tranquil domestic life. George Washington wrote of how he, with "heartfelt satisfaction," gave up the glories of public life for the pleasure of sitting "under my own Vine and Fig tree."

But if love and the charms of domestic life are private matters, they are not without public effects. Alexis de Tocqueville, one of the most astute observers of the American scene, wrote that "the American derives from his home that love of order which he carries over into affairs of state." And so the philosopher Jean Jacques Rousseau noted that it is the attachments we feel in family life that enable us to form attachments to our fellow citizens; and Aristotle began his study of politics with a discussion of the family or the "household." In other words, the bringing together of a man and a woman to form a little platoon, as it were, has great significance for the larger platoon, or country.

It is for this reason that I included in this book a chapter on love and courtship. For one cannot begin to talk about good citizens without consideration of the basic building block of citizenship—the family. The state is made up of many households where the love of a man and a woman is directed toward the raising of decent and honorable children —and good citizens.

The attraction between the opposite sexes constitutes an early spark of our natural sociability. If the relations between the sexes are gentle and well governed, then chances are, relations among our fellow citizens will be too. The Founders understood this better than we do today. Public felicity depends upon domestic tranquility. And thus, our political life will improve only if we halt the disintegration of the American family and restore the lost trust between the sexes. How we go about courtship (a word sadly underused today) and marriage, then, is full of political significance.

The most famous courtship and marriage among the founding generation was that between John and Abigail Adams. It occupies a large part of this chapter. To describe Abigail ("Diana" or "Portia" or "Miss Adorable," as John affectionately called her) as a remarkable woman "for her times," is to damn her with faint praise; she would be remarkable in any age. Some of Abigail Adams's contemporaries—Thomas Jefferson being the most notable—favorably compared her to Venus, the Roman goddess of courtship. She wrote to John Adams that their hearts were "cast in the same mould" with perhaps an "eaqual quantity of Steel." In his autobiography, John Adams described their marriage as "a connection which has been the source of all my felicity." And so too, the correspondence between Benjamin Rush and his soon-to-be bride shows an ideal of love and marriage, with piety at its center, from which we can learn today.

Not all of the Founders left behind their love letters for our perusal. Martha Washington, having shared so much of her husband with the public for most of her life, decided that their most intimate exchanges would remain a private matter between the two of them. She burned their love letters at his death. Similarly, Jefferson, so stricken with grief when his wife died that he fell into a state of unconsciousness, also destroyed most of the written evidence of their love, and even wrote the epitaph on her gravestone in Greek to limit the audience that would be privileged to know his feelings for his wife. And James Madison was probably so happy finally to have married at the age of forty-three that it was rare that he was apart from Dolley for more than a few days. So we are lucky to have the treasury of letters between Abigail and John.

Of course, some of the Founders were more successful in love than others, and some of their marriages were happier. And there were clearly lapses among them when it came to their love lives—Franklin candidly admits that he had difficulties controlling "that hard-to-be-governed passion of youth" and often fell into "intrigues with low women." He also reports that marriage saved him from getting into any further "intrigues." Hamilton, a man of many passions, did not remain faithful to his wife and paid a heavy price for it. Yet it is precisely their faults as much as their virtues—and especially their candid discussions of how they governed and failed to govern their passions, of how they approached love and marriage—that recommends the Founders to us, the children of the sexual revolution. They were at once romantics and realists in matters of the heart.

The correspondence I have gathered for this section shows the human side of the Founders, one that is frequently overlooked. Washington, in his letter to his granddaughter Eleanor Parke Custis, asks that she assess carefully the character of the "invader" of her heart. Thomas Jefferson tells his daughter that marriage is a series of compromises, and that a husband and wife should always attempt to be of one will. Samuel Adams advises his future son-in-law that husbands and wives should overlook "trifling disputes," which are the source of so much ill-will in marriage. And Benjamin Franklin, always serious in his playfulness, offers this advice to young people: "Keep your eyes wide open before marriage, half shut afterwards."

⚮

Thomas Jefferson to John Page, October 7, 1763

THOMAS JEFFERSON was a student at William and Mary College in Virginia when he fell in love with Rebecca Burwell. Jefferson called her "Belinda" and often wrote to his good friend John Page about romantic developments. Looking back, it might be surprising to see just how shy and awkward Thomas Jefferson—the future author of the Declaration of Independence and President of the United States—was around his first love. His Belinda, perhaps from impatience at his diffidence, married somebody else.

I think most of us can relate to a time in our lives when we were just as tongue-tied as the twenty-one-year-old Jefferson at the dance he describes in the following letter. The man whose words, perhaps more than any other, have shaped the modern political world couldn't find any to say to a young girl at a dance.

In the most melancholy fit that ever any poor soul was, I sit down to write to you. Last night, as merry as agreeable company and dancing with Belinda in the Apollo could make me, I never could have thought the succeeding sun would have seen me so wretched as I now am! I was prepared to say a great deal: I had dressed up in my own mind, such thoughts as occurred to me, in as moving language as I knew how, and expected to have performed in a tolerably creditable manner. But, good God! When I had an opportunity of venting them, a few broken sentences, uttered in great disorder, and interrupted with pauses of uncommon length, were the too visible marks of my strange confusion! The whole confab I will tell you, word for word, if I can, when I see you, which God send may be soon. . . . The court is now at hand, which I must attend constantly, so that unless you come to town, there is little probability of my meeting with you any where else. For God's sake come.

∞

Alexander Hamilton to Catherine Livingston, April 11, 1777

SOME HISTORIANS record that Alexander Hamilton was the most handsome of the Founding Fathers, and this letter showcases his considerable charm. Hamilton had grown up in the West Indies—his father had never married his mother and abandoned the family. Thus, Hamilton came to America without the family background that would offer entree to the highest families or social circles in America. Still, with sheer brilliance, superior talents (and his charm, no doubt), Hamilton, as we all know, rose to become one of the greatest of all Americans.

This letter was written to Kitty Livingston, who was the daughter of the royal governor of New Jersey. It is not a serious attempt at courtship —Hamilton knew Kitty would not take someone with his family background seriously. But it still shows, I think, how men then went about the business of courting the woman of their dreams.

After knowing exactly your taste, and whether you are of a romantic, or discreet temper, as to love affairs, I will endeavour to regulate myself by it. If you would choose to be a goddess, and to be worshipped as such, I will torture my imagination for the best arguments, the nature of the case will admit, to prove you so. You shall be one of the graces, or Diana, or Venus, or something surpassing them all. And after your deification, I will cull out of every poet of my acquaintance, the choicest delicacies, they possess, as offerings at your Goddesships' shrine. But if, conformable to your usual discernment, you are content with being a mere mortal, and require no other incense, than is justly due to you, I will talk to you like one [in] his sober senses; and, though it may be straining the point a little, I will even stipulate to pay you all the rational tribute properly applicable to a fine girl.

∞

John Adams to Abigail Smith, October 4, 1762; 1762–1763; February 14, 1763

I N H I S *Autobiography,* Adams described himself as possessing "an amorous disposition" and confessed that "very early, from ten or eleven years of age, he was very fond of the society of females." Instead of studying, Adams also confessed that he often wasted the day "gallanting the girls" of his neighborhood. Adams was soon to court and marry one of the most exceptional women in American history, Abigail Adams. However, it was not love at first sight.

Adams met Abigail Smith, daughter of a minister, when she was but fifteen years old. Of that first encounter, Adams wrote that Abigail and her sister, Mary Smith, are "wits" but also that they are not "fond, not frank, not candid" and do not display much "tenderness."

But two years later, upon seeing Abigail again, Adams wrote in his diary, without explicity naming her, that she is "a constant feast. Tender, feeling, sensible, friendly. A friend. Not an imprudent, not an indelicate, not a disagreeable word or action. Prudent, modest, delicate, soft, sensible, obliging, active." Soon, Adams was riding his horse the four miles to Weymouth, Massachusetts, to do legal business by day and to court Abigail by night.

As was the common practice of the day, Abigail and John adopted names from literary and classical figures in their correspondence. Abigail took the name "Diana"—the Roman goddess of purity and love, and John was "Lysander" the great Spartan admiral.

Whoever thought of the Puritans as repressed beings will be surprised by the passionate nature of young John and Abigail's courtship. Full of ardor and longing, these letters provide a wonderful example of what love can be. In the following three selections, we get a delightful perspective on John Adams as the impatient and amorous pursuer—in one case, delivering a letter to "Miss Adorable" that calls for kisses upon receipt.

In reading their love letters, I am reminded of Washington's dictum that, until there is a new order of things, men and women will experience passionate yearnings for each other.

JOHN ADAMS TO ABIGAIL SMITH

Miss Adorable

By the same Token that the Bearer hereof *satt up* with you last night I hereby order you to give him, as many Kisses, and as many Hours of your Company after 9 O'Clock as he shall please to Demand and charge them to my Account: This Order, or Requisition call it which you will is in Consideration of a similar order Upon Aurelia for the like favour, and

I presume I have good Right to draw upon you for the Kisses as I have given two or three Millions at least, when one has been received, and of Consequence the Account between us is immensely in favour of yours,

John Adams

JOHN ADAMS TO ABIGAIL SMITH

Dr. Miss Jemima   *Braintree*
I have taken the best Advice, on the subject of your Billet, and I find you cannot compell me *to pay* unless I refuse Marriage; which I never did, and never will, but on the Contrary am ready to *have you* at any Time.
Yours,   Jonathan

JOHN ADAMS TO ABIGAIL SMITH

Dear Madam   *Braintree*
Accidents are often more Friendly to us, than our own Prudence.—I intended to have been at Weymouth Yesterday, but a storm prevented. —Cruel, Yet perhaps blessed storm!—Cruel for detaining me from so much friendly, social Company, and perhaps blessed to you, or me or both, for keeping me at *my Distance.* For every experimental Phylosopher knows, that the steel and the Magnet or the Glass and feather will not fly together with more Celerity, than somebody And somebody, when brought within the striking Distance—and, Itches, Aches, Agues, and Repentance might be the Consequences of a Contact in present Circumstances. Even the Divines pronounce casuistically, I hear, "unfit to be touched these three Weeks."
I mount this moment for that noisy, dirty Town of Boston, where Parade, Pomp, Nonsense, Frippery, Folly, Foppery, Luxury, Polliticks, and the soul-Confounding Wrangles of the Law will give me the Higher Relish for Spirit, Taste and Sense, at Weymouth, next Sunday.

∞

Alexander Hamilton to John Laurens, April 1779

JOHN LAURENS of South Carolina was Alexander Hamilton's best friend. They were both members of Washington's military "family," serving as fellow aides to the great general. This letter is obviously meant in some jest—Hamilton ended it by asking "what could have put it into my head to hazard this *jeu de folie?*" But I think we can all say we're glad he wrote it. I, for one, think the advice to look in Carolina for a wife is very sound (I've been blessed with a Carolina wife for fifteen years), though I don't agree with some of the rest.

And Now my Dear as we are upon the subject of wife, I empower and command you to get me one in Carolina. Such a wife as I want will, I know, be difficult to be found, but if you succeed, it will be the stronger proof of your zeal and dexterity. Take her description—She must be young, handsome (I lay most stress upon a good shape) sensible (a little learning will do), well bred (but she must have an aversion to the word *ton*) chaste and tender (I am an enthusiast in my notions of fidelity and fondness) of some good nature, a great deal of generosity (she must neither love money nor scolding, for I dislike equally a termagent and an œconomist). In politics, I am indifferent what side she may be of; I think I have arguments that will easily convert her to mine. As to religion a moderate stock will satisfy me. She must believe in god and hate a saint. But as to fortune, the larger stock of that the better. You know my temper and circumstances and will therefore pay special attention to this article in the treaty. Though I run no risk of going to Purgatory for my avarice; yet as money is an essential ingredient to happiness in this world —as I have not much of my own and as I am very little calculated to get more either by my address or industry; it must needs be, that my wife, if I get one, bring at least a sufficiency to administer to her own extravagancies. NB You will be pleased to recollect in your negotiations that I have no invincible antipathy to the *maidenly beauties* & that I am willing to take the *trouble* of them upon myself.

If you should not readily meet with a lady that you think answers my description you can only advertise in the public papers and doubtless you will hear of many competitors for most of the qualifications required, who will be glad to become candidates for such a prize as I am. To excite their emulation, it will be necessary for you to give an account of the lover—his *size,* make, quality of mind and *body,* achievements, expectations, fortune, &c. In drawing my picture, you will no doubt be civil to your friend; mind you do justice to the length of my nose.

Abigail Smith to John Adams,
August 11, 1763

I N TH IS letter, Abigail shows solicitude for John's illness. She also dis-
cusses, beautifully, the growing and indissoluble bond she is feeling for
her suitor. Men and women who are lucky enough to feel such an
attachment to another are truly blessed.

My Friend

If I was sure your absence to day was occasioned, by what it generally
is, either to wait upon Company, or promote some good work, I freely
confess my Mind would be much more at ease than at present it is. Yet
this uneasiness does not arise from any apprehension of Slight or neglect,
but a fear least you are indisposed, for that you said should be your only
hindrance.

Humanity obliges us to be affected with the distresses and Miserys of
our fellow creatures. Friendship is a band yet stronger, which causes us
to [fee]l with greater tenderness the afflictions of our Friends.

And there is a tye more binding than Humanity, and stronger than
Friendship, which makes us anxious for the happiness and welfare of
those to whom it binds us. It makes their Misfortunes, Sorrows and
afflictions, our own. Unite these, and there is a threefold cord—by this
cord I am not ashamed to own myself bound, nor do I [believe] that you
are wholly free from it. Judg[e you then] for your Diana has she not this
day [had sufficien]t cause for pain and anxiety of mind?

She bids me [tell] you that Seneca, for the sake of his Paulina was
careful and tender of his health. The health and happiness of Seneca she
says was not dearer to his Paulina, than that of Lysander to his Diana.

The Fabrick often wants repairing and if we neglect it the Deity will
not long inhabit it, yet after all our care and solisitude to preserve it, it is
a tottering Building, and often reminds us that it will finally fall.

Adieu may this find you in better health than I fear it will, and happy
as your Diana wishes you.

Accept this hasty Scrawl warm from the Heart of Your Sincere

Diana

∞

John Adams to Abigail Smith, August 1763, and Abigail to John, September 12, 1763

IN THESE two charming letters, John and Abigail flirtatiously discuss "apparitions" of each other that appeared in their homes, no doubt a reflection of the powerful longing they felt for each other. In today's casual style of courtship, where obstacles to immediate gratification are like May snowfalls—rare, brief, and easily melted—the imagination is often left flat. We no longer believe in, or have a need for, "apparitions." I'm not sure that love lives are the better for it.

JOHN ADAMS TO ABIGAIL SMITH

My dear Diana   *Saturday morning*
Germantown is at a great Distance from Weymouth Meeting-House, you know; The No. of Yards indeed is not so prodigious, but the Rowing and Walking that lyes between is a great Discouragement to a weary Traveller. Could my Horse have helped me to Weymouth, Braintree would not have held me, last Night.—I lay, in the well known Chamber, and dreamed, I saw a Lady, tripping it over the Hills, on Weymouth shore, and Spreading Light and Beauty and Glory, all around her. At first I thought it was Aurora, with her fair Complexion, her Crimson Blushes and her million Charms and Graces. But I soon found it was Diana, a Lady infinitely dearer to me and more charming.—Should Diana make her Appearance every morning instead of Aurora, I should not sleep as I do, but should be all awake and admiring by four, at latest.—You may be sure I was mortifyed when I found, I had only been dreaming. The Impression however of this dream awaked me thoroughly, and since I had lost my Diana, I enjoy'd the Opportunity of viewing and admiring Miss Aurora. She's a sweet Girl, upon my Word. Her breath is wholesome as the sweetly blowing Spices of Arabia, and therefore next to her fairer sister Diana, the Properest Physician, for your drooping

J. Adams

ABIGAIL SMITH TO JOHN ADAMS

Weymouth
You was pleas'd to say that the receipt of a letter from your Diana always gave you pleasure. Whether this was designed for a complement,

(a commodity I acknowledg that you very seldom deal in) or as a real truth, you best know. Yet if I was to judge of a certain persons Heart, by what upon the like occasion passess through a cabinet of my own, I should be apt to suspect it as a truth. And why may I not? when I have often been tempted to believe; that they were both cast in the same mould, only with this difference, that yours was made, with a harder mettle, and therefore is less liable to an impression. Whether they have both an eaquil quantity of Steel, I have not yet been able to discover, but do not imagine they are either of them deficient. Supposing only this difference, I do not see, why the same cause may not produce the same Effect in both, tho perhaps not eaquil in degree.

Have you heard the News? that two Apparitions were seen one evening this week hovering about this house, which very much resembled you and a Cousin of yours. How it should ever enter into the head of an Apparition to assume a form like yours, I cannot devise. When I was told of it I could scarcly believe it, yet I could not declare the contrary, for I did not see it, and therefore had not that demonstration which generally convinces me, that you are not a Ghost.

The original design of this letter was to tell you, that I would next week be your fellow traveler provided I shall not be any encumberance to you, for I have too much pride to be a clog to any body. You are to determine that point. For your—

A. Smith

∞

Alexander Hamilton to Elizabeth Schuyler,
October 27, 1780

HAMILTON COURTED and wooed Elizabeth Schuyler, daughter of General Philip and Catherine Van Rensselaer Schuyler. They were a very prominent New York family who did not look down on Hamilton's low birth. In fact, General Schuyler became extremely fond of his future son-in-law.

In the following letter, Hamilton turns on the charm for his future wife. Unfortunately, the charm of a suitor does not always make him a good husband. Hamilton would later have an extramarital affair.

I had a charming dream two or three night ago. I thought I had just arrived at Albany and found you asleep on a green near the house, and beside you in an inclined posture stood a Gentleman whom I did not know. He had one of your hands in his, and seemed fixed in silent admiration. As you may imagine, I reproached him with his presumption and asserted my claim. He insisted on a prior right; and the dispute grew (heated). This I fancied (awoke) you, when yielding to a sudden impulse of joy, you flew into my arms and decided the contention with a kiss. I was so delighted that I immediately waked, and lay the rest of the night exulting in my good fortune. Tell me I pray you who is this rival of mine. Dreams you know are the messengers of Jove.

∞

John Adams to Abigail Smith, May 7, 1764, Abigail to John, May 9, 1764, and John to Abigail, September 30, 1764

ABIGAIL ADAMS was clearly a woman of courage. How many of us would have the confidence to ask our lover to provide a catalogue of our faults? But that's just what Abigail did. In April of 1764, she asked John to be her "second conscience" and to provide her with a list of her faults. She acknowledged that "although it is vastly disagreeable to be accused of faults yet no person ought to be offended when such accusations are delivered in the spirit of friendship."

It took several weeks for John Adams to answer her request, as he told Abigail that he had tried for three weeks to add more to his initial list, but found nothing more, everything else about her being "bright and luminous." John Adams finally sent the following affectionately frank assessment of his future wife.

This exchange indicates several things. It brings to light the deep bonds of trust that had developed between these young lovers. It also showcases the gallant spirit of Abigail Adams. You'll note her feisty reply to his catalogue, welcoming his criticism as most people would embrace praise. For, as she wrote, to "appear agreeable in the eyes of Lysander" is her highest ambition.

But in the end, it seemed that Adams was the one who had the most serious faults in need of reform—and he freely admitted so. In the third letter of this series, Adams writes a letter to his fiancée one month before their wedding date, telling her that she, and only she, will form him into the man he has always wanted but struggled to be. And isn't this a large part of what marriage is all about—bringing out our beloved's finer qualities and completing each other?

JOHN ADAMS TO ABIGAIL SMITH

Boston

I promised you, Sometime agone, a Catalogue of your Faults, Imperfections, Defects, or whatever you please to call them. I feel at present, pretty much at Leisure, and in a very suitable Frame of Mind to perform my Promise. But I must caution you, before I proceed to recollect yourself, and instead of being vexed or fretted or thrown into a Passion, to resolve upon a Reformation—for this is my sincere Aim, in laying before you, this Picture of yourself.

In the first Place, then, give me leave to say, you have been extreamly negligent, in attending so little to Cards. You have very litle Inclination, to that noble and elegant Diversion, and whenever you have taken an Hand you have held it but aukwardly and played it, with a very uncourtly, and indifferent, Air. Now I have Confidence enough in your good sense, to rely upon it, you will for the future endeavour to make a better Figure in this elegant and necessary Accomplishment.

Another Thing, which ought to be mentioned, and by all means amended, is, the Effect of a Country Life and Education, I mean, a certain Modesty, sensibility, Bashfulness, call it by which of these Names you will, that enkindles Blushes forsooth at every Violation of Decency, in Company, and lays a most insupportable Constraint on the freedom of Behaviour. Thanks to the late Refinements of modern manners, Hypocrisy, superstition, and Formality have lost all Reputation in the World and the utmost sublimation of Politeness and Gentility lies, in Ease, and Freedom, or in other Words in a natural Air and Behaviour, and in expressing a satisfaction at whatever is suggested and prompted by Nature, which the aforesaid Violations of Decency, most certainly are.

In the Third Place, you could never yet be prevail'd on to learn to sing. This I take very soberly to be an Imperfection of the most moment of any. An Ear for Musick would be a source of much Pleasure, and a Voice and skill, would be a private solitary Amusement, of great Value when no other could be had. You must have remarked an Example of this in Mrs. Cranch, who must in all probability have been deafened to Death with the Cries of her Betcy, if she had not drowned them in Musick of her own.

In the Fourth Place you very often hang your Head like a Bulrush.

You do not sit, erected as you ought, by which Means, it happens that you appear too short for a Beauty, and the Company looses the sweet smiles of that Countenance and the bright sparkles of those Eyes.—This Fault is the Effect and Consequence of another, still more inexcusable In a Lady. I mean an Habit of Reading, Writing and Thinking. But both the Cause and the Effect ought to be repented and amended as soon as possible.

Another Fault, which seems to have been obstinately persisted in, after frequent Remonstrances, Advices and Admonitions of your Frends, is that of sitting with the Leggs across. This ruins the figure and the Air, this injures the Health. And springs I fear from the former source vizt. too much Thinking.—These Things ought not to be!

A sixth Imperfection is that of Walking, with the Toes bending inward. This imperfection is commonly called Parrot-toed, I think, I know not for what Reason. But it gives an Idea, the reverse of a bold and noble Air, the Reverse of the stately strutt, and the sublime Deportment.

Thus have I given a faithful Portraiture of all the Spotts, I have hitherto discerned in this Luminary. Have not regarded Order, but have painted them as they arose in my Memory. Near Three Weeks have I conned and studied for more, but more are not to be discovered. All the rest is bright and luminous.

Having finished the Picture I finish my Letter, lest while I am re-counting Faults, I should commit the greatest in a Letter, that of tedious and excessive Length. There's a prettily turned Conclusion for You! from yr.

Lysander

ABIGAIL SMITH TO JOHN ADAMS

Weymouth

Welcome, Welcome thrice welcome is Lysander to Braintree, but ten times more so would he be at Weymouth, whither you are affraid to come.—Once it was not so. May not I come and see you, at least look thro a window at you? Should you not be glad to see your Diana? I flatter myself you would.

Your Brother brought your Letter, tho he did not let me see him, deliverd it the Doctor from whom received it safe. I thank you for your Catalogue, but must confess I was so hardned as to read over most of my Faults with as much pleasure, as an other person would have read their perfections. And Lysander must excuse me if I still persist in some of them, at least till I am convinced that an alteration would contribute to his happiness. Especially may I avoid that Freedom of Behaviour which according to the plan given, consists in Voilations of Decency, and which would render me unfit to Herd even with the Brutes. And permit me to tell you Sir, nor disdain to be a learner, that there is such a thing as Modesty without either Hypocricy or Formality.

As to a neglect of Singing, that I acknowledg to be a Fault which if posible shall not be complaind of a second time, nor should you have had occasion for it now, if I had not a voice harsh as the screech of a peacock.

The Capotal fault shall be rectified, tho not with any hopes of being lookd upon as a Beauty, to appear agreeable in the Eyes of Lysander, has been for Years past, and still is the height of my ambition.

The 5th fault, will endeavour to amend of it, but you know I think that a gentleman has no business to concern himself about the Leggs of a Lady, for my part I do not apprehend any bad effects from the practise, yet since you desire it, and that you may not for the future trouble Yourself so much about it, will reform.

The sixth and last can be cured only by a Dancing School.

But I must not write more. I borrow a hint from you, therefore will not add to my faults that of a tedious Letter—a fault I never yet had reason to complain of in you, for however long, they never were otherways than agreeable to your own

A Smith

JOHN ADAMS TO ABIGAIL SMITH

Oh my dear Girl, I thank Heaven that another Fortnight will restore you to me—after so long a separation. My soul and Body have both been thrown into Disorder, by your Absence, and a Month or two more would make me the most insufferable Cynick, in the World. I see nothing but Faults, Follies, Frailties and Defects in any Body, lately. People have lost all their good Properties or I my Justice, or Discernment.

But you who have always softened and warmed my Heart, shall restore my Benevolence as well as my Health and Tranquility of mind. You shall polish and refine my sentiments of Life and Manners, banish all the unsocial and ill natured Particles in my Composition, and form me to that happy Temper, that can reconcile a quick discernment with a perfect Candour.

Believe me, now & ever yr. faithful

Lysander

James Madison to Dolley Payne Todd,
August 18, 1794

For most of his young adult life, James Madison seemed to have been more interested in books than in women. Perhaps for us it's a good thing that he poured all his energies into writing the world's most imitated political document—the Constitution. Still, at the age of thirty-two, he was ready to settle down, and he became engaged to marry Kitty Floyd, who was then sixteen. Madison's friend Thomas Jefferson played a matchmaker of sorts by encouraging their union, hinting in secret code to Madison that marriage to Floyd "will render you happier than you can possibly be in a single state." Unfortunately for Madison, Floyd fell in love with someone else and broke off the engagement. Madison was devastated; Jefferson sought to comfort his friend for this "misadventure," advising him to keep busy and consoling him that "of all machines ours is the most complicated and inexplicable."

Eleven years were to pass since his failed engagement to Kitty Floyd before Madison met his future wife, the young and vivacious widow, Dorothea "Dolley" Payne Todd of Philadelphia. Madison was living in Philadelphia, serving in the Congress. This time, Aaron Burr provided matchmaking services. Dolley wrote a breathless letter to a friend: "Aaron Burr says that the great little Madison asked to be brought to see me this evening." Their meeting went well; Madison soon proposed marriage. But Dolley took some time to think it over before she finally accepted. Below, a relieved Madison responds to her acceptance:

> I recd some days ago your precious favor from Fredg. I cannot express, but hope you will conceive the joy it gave me. The delay in hearing of your leaving Hanover which I regarded as the only satisfactory proof of your recovery, had filled me with extreme . . . inquietude, and the consummation of that welcome event was endeared to me by the *stile* in which it was conveyed. I hope you will never have another *deliberation* on that subject. If the sentiments of my heart can guarantee those of yours, they assure me there can never be cause for it.

The great French novelist Colette distinguished between marrying "at once" and marrying "at last." Though Madison married later than most, it is no exaggeration to say that he is remembered not only for writing the Constitution but also for his extraordinary wife. William Rives, one of Madison's biographers, described Dolley as "the faithful and tender companion of his bosom, the partner of his joys and sorrows . . ." James and Dolley were married for over forty years.

∞

Benjamin Rush to Julia Stockton Rush, November 15, 1775

DR. BENJAMIN Rush, a brilliant doctor with a philosophic bent, was fourteen years older than his wife, Julia Stockton Rush. She was only sixteen years old when they married. He wrote a series of beautiful love letters to her during their courtship.

It might seem that Rush carried his thoughts on marriage and the different stages of love to an excess. But before the emergence in our century of a "divorce culture," Americans understood that marriage was to be taken very seriously and, indeed, not to be entered into lightly. Thus there was much soul-searching and introspection when it came to making the most important decision of their lives, choosing a marriage partner.

My dearest Julia,

It is a received opinion among many people that there is no medium in matrimony between extreme happiness & misery. I beg leave to controvert this opinion, and for this purpose I shall divide conjugal happiness by a scale. You may call it if you chuse a matrimonial thermometer.

The 1ˢᵗ or lowest degree of conjugal happiness consists in a sympathy in <u>animal love</u>. The Indians in this country enjoy no other happiness in matrimony than what is derived from this source. It is but a small degree above the happiness of brutes.—

The 2ⁿᵈ degree of conjugal happiness consists in a sympathy of <u>manners</u>. I mean no more here than mutual politeness between married people. Although it confers no real happiness, yet it is the best vehicle for it. If it does not prevent disputes, it tends much to soften them, and thus leaves the door of reconcilliation always open.

The 3rd degree consists in a sympathy of <u>opinions</u>. The more married people think alike upon all subjects the less danger there is of their disputing. This is of great consequence when the parties are not happy in their dispositions.—

The 4th degree consists in a sympathy of <u>tastes</u>. By taste you know is meant a perception of what is proper—beautiful—& sublime in nature or art. When we consider how many objects of taste in building—furniture—gardening—& books of entertainment engage the minds of married people, it will appear to be of great importance that there should be a strict uniformity in them.—

The 5th degree consists in a sympathy of <u>sentiments</u>. By sentiment you know is meant a perception of what is just, or unjust, right or wrong in actions. It is a moral principle, & therefore requires the most perfect union between married people, especially if they have children. A diversity of opinions in matters which relate to morals will always be supported by a sense of duty, and therefore will be maintained with more obstinacy than disputes about other subjects. How many married people have been made unhappy by thinking differently upon the lawfulness, or unlawfulness of teaching children to dance!

The 6th degree consists in a sympathy of <u>understandings</u>. This includes an equality of capacity to perceive & relish truth in morals—politicks—philosophy—& religion, and forms an exalted source of happiness in matrimony.—

The 7th degree consists in a sympathy of <u>tempers</u>. This degree excludes anger—resentment—& pevishness in every shape. It supposes the most perfect uniformity in the wills of married people, leading them to just, benevolent—& charitable actions. This is so sweet a source of happiness in matrimony that it can only be exceeded by

The 8th & highest degree of conjugal happiness which consists in a sympathy in <u>religion</u>. This includes a sameness of ideas of the attributes & perfections of god with wills—affections, & actions mutually tending towards the honor of the deity, & the advancement of the soul in a resemblance to him.—The happiness of this degree is heightned by a sameness in a mode of worship.

The happiness of matrimony my dear Julia seems to be proportioned to the number of degrees which are included in this scale.—I beleive there is a progression in them among some people, & a retrogression among others.—I have known married people happy for a few months, or years 'till some new situation or connection in life produced a want of sympathy in some of the degrees of conjugal happiness. I have likewise known people who have been unhappy for a few years after matrimony 'till force, or a conviction of superiority in temper—taste—or understanding has produced the necessary sympathies between them. There is scarcely any one sympathy—perhaps the whole of them put together cannot supply the want of a sympathy of tempers.—If any sufferings in this world could entitle a man or woman to the happiness of heaven it would be to pass thro' life tied to a companion with a weak head & a bad disposition.

It gives me pleasure to reflect upon the very great uniformity which subsists my dear Julia, between our tastes—opinions—sentiments &c. I dare not ascend to the two last degrees in the scale of matrimonial happiness. But you may be asured that it shall be the study of my life to cultivate in them both, a conformity to you.

—I have communicated these thoughts to paper with some diffidence, having never mentioned them before to anybody. If <u>you</u> approve of them, I shall think them just.—But is it now time to descend from Pisgah's mount. Although I have been viewing matrimony with a telescope yet I find no obstacles from you in the way to my happiness in it. On the contrary, I am now more anxious than ever to take possession of the promised land.—

I am afraid to tell you how much I suffered from my last excursion to Morven. My patients declare they will excuse but one more visit, before that which shall bring matters to a conclusion. I wish my amiable Julia you would think once more of completing my happiness in december. I am afraid the public will accuse you of————————if it is delayed much longer. Have compassion my dearest girl upon a heart that loves you above all things. I can relish no pleasure without you. And heaven can witness that I never wish to enjoy a pleasure in this world in which you will not be a sharer.

Please to let me know when you think it probable your Papa will return from Burlington, for as I already begin to count the hours before our jaunt to Eliz^th town, I want to know exactly how many I must endure before we set out together. I shall [have] a thousand things to say to you on our journey, but the scope of them all will be only to convince you how superlatively you are esteemed, & how ardently you are beloved by your <u>own</u>.

Benjamin Franklin, Autobiography

FRANKLIN DID not make a good first impression on his future wife, Deborah Read. As he recounts in his *Autobiography* he first arrived in Philadelphia a poor man: As is mentioned elsewhere in this volume, his pockets were stuffed with shirts and stockings (his only possessions) and he was carrying two huge loaves of bread under each arm, while eating another. His wife-to-be watched from not too far a distance, probably laughing at him, Franklin imagines, as he made a "most awkward, ridiculous appearance."

Not too long after, in the summer of 1724, Franklin began courting Deborah Read. Though they wanted to marry, Deborah's mother thought they were too young. Franklin exchanged "some promises with Miss Read" to marry and set sail for London with his good friend James Ralph (whom he described as a man "lax" in "principles of religion").

Franklin found work at a printing house in London, while Ralph idled his time away. They were soon spending all of Franklin's hard-earned money on "plays and other places of amusements." As a result, Ralph and Franklin were leading a "hand to mouth" existence. Though Ralph was married and had a child in America, he soon made it clear to Franklin that he had decided to abandon them. Perhaps due to the bad influence of his friend, Franklin decided to abandon his fiancée. As he recalls, Ralph "seemed quite to forget his wife and child, and I by degrees my engagement with Miss Read, to whom I never wrote more than one letter, and that was to let her know that I was not likely soon to return. This was another of the great errata of my life, which I should wish to correct if I were to live it over again."

Spurned by Franklin, Deborah Read married another man who, it was later rumored, was already married to someone else. Bigamist or not, he was impossible to live with, and Deborah returned home to live with her family (he left for the West Indies, where he died).

As this letter recounts, Franklin woefully regretted this great "erratum." And he atoned for it by finally marrying Deborah Read, and they, in his words, "throve together."

But this affair having turned my thoughts to marriage, I look'd round me and made overtures of acquaintance in other places; but soon found that, the business of a printer being generally thought a poor one, I was not to expect money with a wife, unless with such a one as I should not otherwise think agreeable. In the mean time, that hard-to-be-governed passion of youth hurried me frequently into intrigues with low women that fell in my way, which were attended with some expense and great inconvenience, besides a continual risque to my health by a distemper which of all things I dreaded, though by great good luck I escaped it. A friendly correspondence as neighbours and old acquaintances had continued between me and Mrs. Read's family, who all had a regard for me from the time of my first lodging in their house. I was often invited there and consulted in their affairs, wherein I sometimes was of service. I piti'd poor Miss Read's unfortunate situation, who was generally dejected, seldom cheerful, and avoided company. I considered my giddiness and inconstancy when in London as in a great degree the cause of her unhappiness, tho' the mother was good enough to think the fault more her own than mine, as she had prevented our marrying before I went thither, and persuaded the other match in my absence. Our mutual affection was revived, but there were now great objections to our union. The match was indeed looked upon as invalid, a preceding wife being said to be living in England; but this could not easily be prov'd, because of the distance; and, tho' there was a report of his death, it was not certain. Then, tho' it should be true, he had left many debts, which his successor might be call'd upon to pay. We ventured, however, over all these difficulties, and I took her to wife, September 1st, 1730. None of the inconveniences happened that we had apprehended; she proved a good and faithful helpmate, assisted me much by attending the shop; we throve together, and have ever mutually endeavour'd to make each other happy. Thus I corrected that great *erratum* as well as I could.

∞

Gouverneur Morris Weds, December 25, 1809

GOUVERNEUR MORRIS was fifty-six years old when he finally married. Morris cut a very striking figure; he was handsome and extremely popular with women, both in America and in France, despite the wooden leg that was his bequest from a carriage accident. Yet at fifty-six years old, he decided to marry, having fallen in love with a woman nearly half his age, Anne Cary Randolph. Though Randolph came from a prominent

Virginia family—she was related to Thomas Jefferson—she was penniless and haunted by a scandal when Morris decided to marry her against
his family wishes. When Gouverneur was sixty-four years old, he wrote
of his domestic bliss, telling a friend that he "descends with tottering
steps the bottom of life's hill, supported by a kind companion, a tender
female friend and cheered by a little prattler [his son], who bids fair, if
God shall spare his life, to fill in due time the space his father leaves."

In matters of the heart, Gouverneur makes plain that wise men and
women are their best judges. He also demonstrates that one is never
too old to settle down.

On Christmas-day there was a family dinner party at Morrisania. Morris
enumerates his guests, but says he had expected many more members of

his family, "who are detained by the bad weather. I marry this day Anne Cary Randolph, no small surprise to my guests," is the only mention he made of this event at the moment. There was, indeed, no small surprise occasioned by the step he had taken, and no little indignation, as may be gathered from the following letter to his niece Mrs. Meredith, of Philadelphia, who undertook to call him to account for the audacity he had shown in taking to himself a wife at his time of life. "I received your letter, my dear child, yesterday, and perceive in it two charges; viz., that I have committed a folly in marrying, and have acted undutifully in not consulting you. I can only say to the first that I have not yet found cause to repent, and to the second that I hope you will pardon me for violating an obligation of which I was not apprised. The decision of that great question, whether the liberty of a bachelor be more virtuous than the bondage of a married man, must be left to you and your friend Cato; it is beyond my competence. If I had married a rich woman of seventy the world might think it wiser than to take one of half that age without a farthing, and, if the world were to live with my wife, I should certainly have consulted its taste; but as that happens not to be the case, I thought I might, without offending others, endeavor to suit myself, and look rather into the head and heart than into the pocket. Perhaps it would gratify a laudable curiosity to say what I discovered; but that must be omitted, to avoid the charge of partiality—and the rather as the step I have taken gives sufficient evidence of my opinion.

∞

Noah Webster, "Advice to the Young," 1834

THERE IS much confusion about how men are supposed to treat women—there was then, there still is now. But things have changed for women (and much of it for the better) since Noah Webster wrote. Yet one thing has not changed: Men should still treat women with "kindness, delicacy and respect." Now, while some of Webster's advice might rub modern sensibilities the wrong way, Webster's aim to turn young males into gentlemen is still a worthy one today. Many young men today view women with purely predatory intentions and do not meet the responsibilities they owe to the women and children in their lives. By encouraging all young men to respect women, we could go a long way in reversing these troubling trends.

50. To young men I would recommend that their treatment of females should be always characterized by kindness, delicacy and respect. The tender sex look to men for protection and support. Females when properly educated and devoted to their appropriate duties, are qualified to add greatly to the happiness of society, and of domestic life. Endowed with finer sensibilities than men, they are quick to learn and to practice the civilities and courtesies of life; their reputation requires the nice observance of the rules of decorum; and their presence and example impose most salutary restraints on the ruder passions and less polished manners of the other sex. In the circle of domestic duties, they are cheerful companions of their husbands; they give grace and joy to prosperity; consolation and support to adversity. When we see an affectionate wife devoted to her domestic duties, cheering her husband with smiles, and as a mother, carefully tending and anxiously guarding her children and forming their minds to virtue and to piety; or watching with conjugal or maternal tenderness over the bed of sickness; we cannot fail to number among the chief temporal advantages of Christianity; the elevation of the female character. Let justice then be done to their merits; guard their purity; defend their honor; treat them with tenderness and respect.

—From Noah Webster, *Value of the Bible and Excellence of the Christian Religion*

∞

Benjamin Franklin: Reply to a Piece of Advice, Pennsylvania Gazette, *1734*

BENJAMIN FRANKLIN here responds to a published poem warning men against the cares and bondage of marriage. Franklin defended the institution of marriage against such naysayers and here shows the advantages of the marital state. While Franklin chose to emphasize the practical side of married life, he also believed that husbands and wives could be "like a faithful Pair of Doves" relieving "one another by turns."

Nor is it true that *as soon as a Man weds, his expected Bliss dissolves into slavish Cares and Bondage.* Every Man that is really a Man is Master of his own Family; and it cannot be *Bondage* to have another submit to one's Government. If there be any Bondage in the Case, 'tis the Woman enters into it, and not the Man. And as to the *Cares,* they are chiefly what attend the bringing up of Children; and I would ask any Man who has experienced it, if they are not the most delightful Cares in the World; and if from that Particular alone, he does not find the *Bliss* of a double State much greater, instead of being less than he expected. In short this *Bondage* and these *Cares* are like the Bondage of having a beautiful and fertile Garden, which a Man takes great Delight in; and the Cares are the Pleasure he finds in cultivating it, and raising as many beautiful and useful Plants from it as he can. And if common Planting and Gardening be an Honourable Employment, (as 'tis generally allow'd, since the greatest Heroes have practic'd it without any Diminution to their Glory) I think *Human Planting* must be more Honourable, as the Plants to be raised are more excellent in their Nature, and to bring them to Perfection requires the greater Skill and Wisdom.

In the next Place he insinuates, that *a Man by marrying, acts contrary to his Interest, loses his Liberty and his Friends, and soon finds himself undone.* In which he is as much mistaken as in any of the rest. A Man does not act contrary to his Interest by Marrying; for I and Thousands more know very well that we could never thrive till we were married; and have done well ever since; What we get, the Women save; a Man being fixt in Life minds his Business better and more steadily; and he that cannot thrive married, could never have throve better single; for the Idleness and Negligence of Men is more frequently fatal to Families, than the Extravagance of Women. Nor does a Man *lose his Liberty* but encrease it; for when he has no Wife to take Care of his Affairs at Home, if he carries on any Business there, he cannot go Abroad without a Detriment to that; but having a Wife, that he can confide in, he may with much more Freedom be abroad, and for a longer Time; thus the Business goes on comfortably, and the good Couple relieve one another by turns, like a faithful Pair of Doves. Nor does he *lose Friends* but gain them, by prudently marrying; for there are all the Woman's Relations added to his own, ready to assist and encourage the new-married Couple; and a Man that has a Wife and Children, is sooner trusted in Business, and can have Credit longer and for larger Sums than if he was single, inasmuch as he is look'd upon to be more firmly settled, and under greater Obligations to behave honestly, for his Family's Sake.

∞

Samuel Adams to Thomas Wells, November 22, 1780

SAMUEL ADAMS, though always at the center of the revolutionary cause, was not so distracted that he couldn't offer some good advice to Thomas Wells, who was soon to marry Adams's daughter, Hannah. As Adams aptly notes, so many of the blowups between husband and wife arise from the most trifling matters, such as whether a turkey is served boiled or roasted. 'Twas so then and still is. And it's still good advice to overlook such things.

The Marriage State was designd to complete the Sum of human Happiness in this Life. It some times proves otherwise; but this is owing to the Parties themselves, who either rush into it without due Consideration, or fail in point of Discretion in their Conduct towards each other afterwards. It requires Judgment on both Sides, to conduct with exact Propriety; for though it is acknowledgd, that the Superiority is & ought to be in the Man, yet as the Mannagement of a Family in many Instances necessarily devolves on the Woman, it is difficult always to determine the Line between the Authority of the one & the Subordination of the other. Perhaps the Advice of the good Bishop of St Asaph on another Occasion, might be adopted on this, and that is, not to govern too much. When the married Couple strictly observe the great Rules of Honor & Justice towards each other, Differences, if any happen, between them, must proceed from small & trifling Circumstances. Of what Consequence is it, whether a Turkey is brought on the Table boild or roasted? And yet, how often are the Passions sufferd to interfere in such mighty Disputes, till the Tempers of both become so sowerd, that they can scarcely look upon each other with any tolerable Degree of good Humor. I am not led to this particular Mode of treating the Subject from an Apprehension of more than common Danger, that such Kind of Fricas will frequently take Place in that Connection, upon which, much of my future Comfort in Life will depend. I am too well acquainted with the Liberality of your Way of thinking, to harbour such a Jealousy; and I think I can trust to my Daughters Discretion if she will only promise to exercise it. I feel myself at this Moment so domestically disposd that I could say a thousand things to you, if I had Leisure. I could dwell on the Importance of Piety &

Religion, of Industry & Frugality, of Prudence, Œconomy, Regularity & an even Government, all which are essential to the Well being of a Family. But I have not Time. I cannot however help repeating Piety, because I think it indispensible. Religion in a Family is at once its brightest Ornament & its best Security. The first Point of Justice, says a Writer I have met with, consists in *Piety;* Nothing certainly being so great a Debt upon us, as to render to the Creator & Preserver those Acknowledgments which are due to Him for our Being, and the hourly Protection he affords us.

∞

George Washington to Eleanor (Nelly) Parke Custis, January 16, 1795

GEORGE AND Martha Washington adopted two of Martha's grandchildren and raised them as their own children. One of these grandchildren was Eleanor (Nelly) Custis, a favorite of both George and Martha. Several years after writing the following letter, Washington invited his nephew, Lawrence Lewis, to live at Mount Vernon and serve as his secretary. On Washington's birthday in 1799, Nelly married Lawrence. On her wedding day, according to Woodrow Wilson, who wrote a biography of Washington, she reportedly begged Washington to wear the brand new "grand embroidered uniform" made recently for the undeclared war with the French. Instead, Washington wore his old and worn buff and blue uniform that had served him in the American Revolutionary War. Woodrow Wilson records that "the delighted girl told him, with her arm around his neck, that she loved him better in that" anyway.

This letter, which is full of both levity and seriousness, gives good advice about the "inclinations" and "passions" men and women have felt toward each other since time immemorial. Nobody, President Washington tells his spirited daughter, is immune to the stirrings of the heart, but we can still direct these feelings toward people worthy of our affections.

Let me touch a little now on your Georgetown ball, and happy, thrice happy, for the fair who were assembled on the occasion, that there was a man to spare; for had there been 79 ladies and only 78 gentlemen, there might, in the course of the evening, have been some disorder among the caps; notwithstanding the apathy which *one* of the company entertains for the *"youth"* of the present day, and her determination "never to give herself a moment's uneasiness on account of any of them." A hint here; men and women feel the same inclinations to each other *now* that they always have done, and which they will continue to do until there is a new order of things, and *you*, as others have done, may find, perhaps, that the passions of your sex are easier raised than allayed. Do not therefore boast too soon or too strongly of your insensibility to, or resistance of, its powers. In the composition of the human frame there is a good deal of inflammable matter, however dormant it may lie for a time, and like an intimate acquaintance of yours, when the torch is put to it, *that* which is *within you* may burst into a blaze; for which reason and especially to, as I have entered upon the chapter of advices, I will read you a lecture drawn from this text.

Love is said to be an involuntary passion, and it is, therefore, contended that it cannot be resisted. This is true in part only, for like all things else, when nourished and supplied plentifully with aliment, it is rapid in its progress; but let these be withdrawn and it may be stifled in its birth or much stinted in its growth. For example, a woman (the same may be said of the other sex) all beautiful and accomplished, will, while her hand and heart are undisposed of, turn the heads and set the circle in which she moves on fire. Let her marry, and what is the consequence? The madness *ceases* and all is quiet again. Why? not because there is any diminution in the charms of the lady, but because there is an end of hope. Hence it follows, that love may and therefore ought to be under the guidance of reason, for although we cannot avoid first impressions, we may assuredly place them under guard; and my motives for treating on this subject are to show you, while you remain Eleanor Parke Custis, spinster, and retain the resolution to love with moderation, the propriety of adhering to the latter resolution, at least until you have secured your game, and the way by which it may be accomplished.

When the fire is beginning to kindle, and your heart growing warm, propound these questions to it. Who is this invader? Have I a competent knowledge of him? Is he a man of good character; a man of sense? For, be assured, a sensible woman can never be happy with a fool? What has been his walk in life? Is he a gambler, a spendthrift, or drunkard? Is his fortune sufficient to maintain me in the manner I have been accustomed to live, and my sisters do live, and is he one to whom my friends can have no reasonable objection? If these interrogatories can be satisfactorily answered, there will remain but one more to be asked, that, however, is an important one. Have I sufficient ground to conclude that his affections are engaged by me? Without this the heart of sensibility will struggle against a passion that is not reciprocated; delicacy, custom, or call it by what epithet you will, having precluded all advances on your part. The declaration, without the *most indirect* invitation of yours, must proceed from the man, to render it permanent and valuable, and nothing short of good sense and an easy unaffected conduct can draw the line between prudery and coquetry. It would be no great departure from truth to say, that it rarely happens otherwise than that a thorough-paced coquette dies in celibacy, as a punishment for her attempts to mislead others, by encouraging looks, words, or actions, given for no other purpose than to draw men on to make overtures that they may be rejected.

∽

Benjamin Franklin, "Rules and Maxims for Promoting Matrimonial Happiness," Pennsylvania Gazette, *October 8, 1730*

FRANKLIN FAMOUSLY said that a man without a wife is like "Half of a Pair of Scissars"—incomplete and dysfunctional. He didn't say the same about women. Instead, Franklin praised women, observing: "Good wives usually make good husbands." Perhaps from this, one can infer that Franklin believed men were imperfect without women, whereas women were full moral beings, even without the presence of men. In this essay, for example, he reminds women that they will marry a man, not an angel. Thus, Franklin addresses this advice column to women because they are less intractable than men—perhaps even superior—though he says that most of these rules can be applied to men, too. (In fact, Franklin himself lived by most of these rules.)

> *Ver novum, ver jam canorum, vere natus Orirs est:*
> *Vere concordant amores, vere nubent alites—Carul.*

> "The new spring, now harmonious spring,
> in spring the world is born: In spring
> loves are in harmony, in spring
> they marry one another."

I am now about to lay down such Rules and Maxims as I think most practicable and conducive toward the End and Happiness of Matrimony. And these I address to all Females that would be married, or are already so; not that I suppose their Sex more faulty than the other, and most to want Advice, for I assure them, upon my Honour, I believe the quite contrary; but the Reason is, because I esteem them better disposed to receive and practice it, and therefore am willing to begin, where I may promise myself the best Success. Besides, if there is any Truth in Proverbs, *Good Wives* usually make *Good Husbands*.

RULES and MAXIMS for promoting Matrimonial
Happiness. *Address'd to all* Widows, Wives, *and* Spinsters.

The likeliest Way, either to obtain a *good Husband,* or to keep one *so,* is to be *Good* yourself.

Be not over sanguine before Marriage, nor promise your self Felicity without Alloy, for that's impossible to be attain'd in this present State of Things. Consider beforehand, that the Person you are going to spend your Days with is a Man, and not an Angel; and if, when you come together you discover any Thing in his Humour or Behaviour that is not altogether so agreeable as you expected, *pass it over as a humane Frailty:* smooth your Brow; compose your Temper; and try to amend it by *Cheerfulness* and Good-nature. . . .

In your Prayers be sure to add a Clause for Grace to make you a good Wife; and at the same Time, resolve to do your utmost endeavour towards it.

Always wear your Wedding Ring, for therein lies more Virtue than usually is imagined. If you are ruffled unawares, assaulted with improper Thoughts, or tempted in any kind against your Duty, cast your Eyes upon it, and call to Mind who gave it you, where it was received, and what passed that solemn Time.

Let the Tenderness of your conjugal Love be expressed with such Decency, Delicacy and Prudence, as that it may appear plainly and thorowly distinct from the designing Fondness of an Harlot.

Have you any Concern for your own Ease, or for your Husband's Esteem? then, have a due Regard to his Income and Circumstances in all your Expenses and Desires: For if Necessity should follow, you run the greatest Hazard of being deprived of both.

Let not many Days pass together without a serious Examination how you have behaved as a Wife, and if upon Reflection you find your self guilty of any Foibles or Omissions, the best Attonement is, to be exactly careful of your future Conduct.

I am fully persuaded, that a strict Adherence to the foregoing Rules would equally advance the Honour of Matrimony, and the *Glory* of the *Fair Sex:* And since the greatest Part of them, with a very little Alteration, are as proper for Husbands as for Wives to practice, I recommend them accordingly to their Consideration, and hope, in a short time to receive Acknowledgments from *married Persons* of *both Sexes* for the Benefit they receive thereby.

And now, in behalf of my *unlearned Readers,* I beg Leave of my *learned Ones,* to conclude this Discourse with M *Creech*'s Translation of that Part of *Horace* which I have taken for the *Motto* of this Paper.

> *Thrice happy* They, *that free from* Strife,
> *Maintain a* Love *as long as Life:*
> *Whose fixt and binding Vows,*
> *No intervening* Jealousy,
> *No* Fears *and no* Debates *untye;*
> *And* Death *alone can loose.*

∞

Thomas Jefferson to Mary Eppes, January 7, 1798

T HOMAS J EFFERSON had two daughters who survived into adulthood. The younger one was Mary "Polly" Jefferson Eppes. She married her cousin John Wayles Eppes, whom she had grown up with while Jefferson was away in France, a match of which Jefferson approved. Jefferson reputedly would not give toasts to brides and grooms at weddings, believing it best to wait a year—when they would then need it. Anyhow, here he offers some good advice to the young newlyweds. Mainly he reminds his daughter that a husband and wife are no longer separate individuals; they are one. As such, they must support each other and try to avoid being at "cross-purposes."

When we see ourselves in a situation which must be endured and gone through, it is best to make up our minds to it. Meet it with firmness and accomodate every thing to it in the best way practicable. This lessens the evil, while fretting and fuming only serves to increase our own torment. The errors and misfortunes of others should be a school for our own instruction. Harmony in the marriage state is the very first object to be aimed at. Nothing can preserve affections uninterrupted but a firm resolution never to differ in will and a determination in each to consider the love of the other as of more value than any object whatever on which a wish has been fixed. How light in fact is the sacrifice of any other wish, when weighed against the affections of one with whom we are to pass our whole life and though opposition in a single instance will hardly of itself produce alienation; yet every one has their pouch into which all these little oppositions are put. While that is filling, the alienation is insensibly going on, and when filled, it is complete. It would puzzle either to say why; because no one difference of opinion has been marked enough to produce a serious effect by itself. But he finds his affections wearied out by a constant string of little checks and obstacles. Other sources of discontent, very common indeed, are the little cross purposes of husband and wife in common conversation, a disposition either to criticise and question whatever the other says, a desire always to demonstrate and make him feel himself in the wrong, and especially in company. Nothing is so goading. Much better therefore, if our companion views a thing in a light different from what we do to leave him in quiet possession of his view. What is the use of rectifying him if the thing be unimportant; and if important let it pass for the present, and wait a softer moment and more conciliatory occasion of revising the subject together. It is wonderful how many persons are rendered unhappy by inattention to these little rules of prudence. I have been insensibly led, by the particular case you mention, to sermonize to you on the subject generally. However if it is the means of saving you from a single heart-ache, it will have contributed a great deal to my happiness.

∞

George Washington to Martha Washington, June 18, 1775

THIS IS one of the few surviving letters between Martha and George Washington. Martha destroyed most of their letters to each other upon her husband's death. Their love for each other was not meant, in her eyes, for public display.

In Philadelphia, on June 15, 1775, the Second Continental Congress unanimously voted George Washington to be the commander in chief of the military. Though Washington seeks to reassure Martha in the letter that he will return safely to her, he includes a copy of his will. The separation between them would not go uninterrupted. Martha stayed at Mount Vernon in the spring and summer, but joined Washington at his winter quarters—at Cambridge, Morristown, Philadelphia, Valley Forge, and, finally, Newburgh. Reportedly, the other officers' wives were surprised by her plain and simple dress. Her presence among the suffering troops greatly boosted morale. Not only did she enliven the social scene and play the good hostess, but she also tended the sick, prayed for the dying, and was beloved not only by Washington but by all his troops as well.

My Dearest:

I am now set down to write to you on a subject which fills me with inexpressible concern, and this concern is greatly aggravated and increased, when I reflect upon the uneasiness I know it will give you. It has been determined in Congress, that the whole army raised for the defence of the American cause shall be put under my care, and that it is necessary for me to proceed immediately to Boston to take upon me the command of it.

You may believe me, my dear Patsy, when I assure you, in the most solemn manner that, so far from seeking this appointment, I have used every endeavor in my power to avoid it, not only from my unwillingness to part with you and the family, but from a consciousness of its being a trust too great for my capacity, and that I should enjoy more real happiness in one month with you at home, than I have the most distant prospect of finding abroad, if my stay were to be seven times seven years. But as it has been a kind of destiny, that has thrown me upon this service, I shall hope that my undertaking it is designed to answer some good purpose. You might, and I suppose did perceive, from the tenor of my letters, that I was apprehensive I could not avoid this appointment, as I did not pretend to intimate when I should return. That was the case. It was utterly out of my power to refuse this appointment, without exposing my character to such censures, as would have reflected dishonor upon myself, and given pain to my friends. This, I am sure, could not, and ought not, to be pleasing to you, and must have lessened me considerably in my own esteem. I shall rely, therefore, confidently on that Providence, which has heretofore preserved and been bountiful to me, not doubting but that I shall return safe to you in the fall. I shall feel no pain from the toil or the danger of the campaign; my unhappiness will flow from the uneasiness I know you will feel from being left alone. I therefore beg, that you will summon your whole fortitude, and pass your time as agreeably as possible. Nothing will give me so much sincere satisfaction as to hear this, and to hear it from your own pen. My earnest and ardent desire is, that you would pursue any plan that is most likely to produce content, and a tolerable degree of tranquillity; as it must add greatly to my uneasy feelings to hear, that you are dissatisfied or complaining at what I really could not avoid.

As life is always uncertain, and common prudence dictates to every man the necessity of settling his temporal concerns, while it is in his power, and while the mind is calm and undisturbed, I have, since I came to this place (for I had not time to do it before I left home) got Colonel Pendleton to draft a will for me, by the directions I gave him, which will I now enclose. The provision made for you in case of my death will, I hope, be agreeable.

I shall add nothing more, as I have several letters to write, but to desire that you will remember me to your friends, and to assure you that I am with the most unfeigned regard, my dear Patsy, your affectionate, &c.

∽

Abigail Adams to John Adams, March 31, 1776, and John to Abigail, April 14, 1776

THIS IS one of the more famous exchanges between Abigail and John. A few months before America had declared independence from Great Britain, Abigail was urging her husband, then serving in the Continental Congress, to promote independence for women. "Remember the Ladies," she declared. She never pressed the matter too much, and even here, one can detect a tone of playfulness in her request (and certainly in John's reply). Certainly, Abigail did not count her husband as one of the tyrants. In another letter shortly after this one, she wrote "all my desires and all my ambition is to be esteemed and loved by my partner, to join with him in the education and instruction of our little ones, to set under our own vines in peace, liberty and safety."

But one also detects a seed of justified discontent, one that would grow in the decades to come. In 1929, Virginia Woolf famously called for "A Room of One's Own." Once while visiting a relative, Abigail described with joy a little alcove in the house to which she could escape, and think, and write. She confided to John that she at times wished for a similar room in her own house—"a closet with a window which I could more peculiarly call my own."

ABIGAIL ADAMS TO JOHN ADAMS

I have sometimes been ready to think that the passion for Liberty cannot be Eaquelly Strong in the Breasts of those who have been accustomed to deprive their fellow Creatures of theirs. Of this I am certain that it is not founded upon that generous and christian principal of doing unto others as we would that others should do unto us.

—I long to hear that you have declared an independancy—and by the way in the new Code of Laws which I suppose it will be necessary for you to make I desire you would Remember the Ladies, and be more generous and favourable to them than your ancestors. Do not put such unlimited power into the hands of the Husbands. Remember all Men would be tyrants if they could. If perticuliar care and attention is not paid to the Laidies we are determined to foment a Rebelion, and will not hold ourselves bound by any Laws in which we have no voice, or Representation.

That your Sex are Naturally Tyrannical is a Truth so thoroughly established as to admit of no dispute, but such of you as wish to be happy willingly give up the harsh title of Master for the more tender and endearing one of Friend. Why then, not put it out of the power of the vicious and the Lawless to use us with cruelty and indignity with impunity. Men of Sense in all Ages abhor those customs which treat us only as the vassals of your Sex. Regard us then as Beings placed by providence under your protection and in immitation of the Supreem Being make use of that power only for our happiness.

JOHN ADAMS TO ABIGAIL ADAMS

As to your extraordinary Code of Laws, I cannot but laugh. We have been told that our Struggle has loosened the bands of Government every where. That Children and Apprentices were disobedient—that schools and Colledges were grown turbulent—that Indians slighted their Guardians and Negroes grew insolent to their Masters. But your Letter was the first Intimation that another Tribe more numerous and powerfull than all the rest were grown discontented.—This is rather too coarse a Compliment but you are so saucy, I won't blot it out.

Depend upon it, We know better than to repeal our Masculine systems. Altho they are in full Force, you know they are little more than Theory. We dare not exert our Power in its full Latitude. We are obliged to go fair, and softly, and in Practice you know We are the subjects. We have only the Name of Masters, and rather than give up this, which would compleatly subject Us to the Despotism of the Peticoat, I hope General Washington, and all our brave Heroes would fight. I am sure every good Politician would plot, as long as he would against Despotism, Empire, Monarchy, Aristocracy, Oligarchy, or Ochlocracy.—A fine Story indeed. I begin to think the Ministry as deep as they are wicked. After stirring up Tories, Landjobbers, Trimmers, Bigots, Canadians, Indians, Negroes, Hanoverians, Hessians, Russians, Irish Roman Catholicks, Scotch Renegadoes, at last they have stimulated the [women] to demand new Priviledges and threaten to rebell.

∞

Abigail Adams to John Adams, October 25, 1782, and Abigail to John, December 23, 1782

ABIGAIL SPENT ten of their fifty-four years of marriage apart from John. John left Abigail in 1774 for Philadelphia, where he spent more than three years as a delegate to the First and Second Continental Congresses, visiting Abigail between sessions. Next, in 1777, Adams sailed for France with their son John Quincy to serve as an American commissioner, joining Benjamin Franklin and Arthur Lee. He returned to America briefly in 1779 and then sailed back to France. Abigail was finally able to join him in 1784.

Abigail and John endured these painful separations by writing to each other. It wasn't easy being separated—Abigail and John felt the strain, and naturally had some slight misunderstandings and disagreements. Sometimes, Abigail would go for months without hearing from John, whose letters were often lost in the mail. Often, John's letters were filled with reports of official and public business rather than the sentiments of his heart. After once scolding him for his dearth of correspondence, Abigail apologized and quoted the poet who wrote: "The falling out of lovers is the renewal of love."

Abigail had not seen John for three years when these two letters were written; the first notes the passage of their eighteenth wedding anniversary, the other might well have been Abigail's anticipating yet another Christmas without John and two of her oldest sons. Abigail's devotion to John was so complete that she once told a friend that "when he is wounded, I bleed."

A B I G A I L   T O   J O H N   A D A M S

My Dearest Friend   *October 25, 1782*
The family are all retired to rest, the Busy scenes of the day are over, a day which I wished to have devoted in a particular manner to my dearest Friend, but company falling in prevented nor could I claim a moment untill this silent watch of the Night.

Look—(is there a dearer Name than Friend; think of it for me;) Look to the date of this Letter—and tell me, what are the thoughts which arise in your mind? Do you not recollect that Eighteen years have run their annual Circuit, since we pledged our mutual Faith to each other, and the Hymeneal torch was Lighted at the Alter of Love. Yet, yet it Burns with unabating fervour, old ocean has not Quenched it, nor old Time smooth-erd it, in the Bosom of Portia. It cheers her in the Lonely Hour, it comforts her even in the gloom which sometimes possesses her mind.

It is my Friend from the Remembrance of the joys I have lost that the arrow of affliction is pointed. I recollect the untitled Man to whom I gave my Heart, and in the agony of recollection when time and distance present themse[l]ves together, wish he had never been any other. Who shall give me back Time? Who shall compensate to me those *years* I cannot recall? How dearly have I paid for a titled Husband; should I wish you less wise, that I might enjoy more happiness? I cannot find that in my Heart. Yet providence has wisely placed the real Blessings of Life within the reach of moderate abilities, and he who is wiser than his Neighbour sees so much more to pitty and Lament, that I doubt whether the balance of happiness is in his Scale.

I feel a disposition to Quarrel with a race of Beings who have cut me of, in the midst of my days from the only Society I delighted in. Yet No Man liveth for himself, says an authority I will not dispute. Let me draw satisfaction from this Source and instead of murmuring and repineing at my Lot consider it in a more pleasing view. Let me suppose that the same Gracious Being who first smiled upon our union and Blessed us in each other, endowed *(him)* my Friend with powers and talents for the Benifit of Mankind and gave him a willing mind, to improve them for the service of his Country.

You have obtaind honour and Reputation at Home and abroad. O may not an inglorious Peace wither the Laurels you have won.

ABIGAIL TO JOHN ADAMS

December 23, 1782
Weymouth

There are few occurences in this Northen climate at this Season of the year to divert or entertain you—and in the domestick way, should I draw you the picture of my Heart, it would be what I hope you still would Love; tho it containd nothing New; the early possession you obtained there, and the absolute power you have ever maintained over it, leaves not the smallest space unoccupied. I look back to the early days of our acquaintance, and Friendship, as to the days of Love and Innocence, and with an undiscribable pleasure I have seen near a score of years roll over our Heads, with an affection heightned and improved by time—nor have the dreary years of absence in the smallest degree effaced from my mind the Image of the dear untittled Man to whom I gave my Heart. I cannot sometimes refrain considering the Honours with which he is invested as badges of my unhappiness. The unbounded confidence I have in your attachment to me, and the dear pledges of our affection, has soothed the solitary hour, and renderd your absence more supportable; for had I [not] loved you with the same affection it must have been misiry to have doubted. Yet a cruel world too often injures my feelings, by wondering how a person possesst of domestick attachments can sacrifice them by absenting himself *for years*.

If you had known said a person to me the other day, that Mr. A[dam]s would have remained so long abroad, would you have consented that he should have gone? I recollected myself a moment, and then spoke the real dictates of my Heart. If I had known Sir that Mr. A. could have affected what he has done, I would not only have submitted to the absence I have endured, painfull as it has been; but would not have opposed it, even tho 3 years more should be added to the Number, which Heaven avert! I feel a pleasure in being able to sacrifice my selfish passions to the general good, and in imitating the example, which has taught me to consider myself and family but as the small dust of the balance when compaired with the great community.

Benjamin Rush to Mrs. Julia Rush, June 11, 1812: Poem

B E N J A M I N R U S H , the physician, wrote this lovely tribute to his wife.

> To Mrs Julia Rush
> from her husband
> Benjamin Rush
> 36 years after their marriage.

1

When tossed upon the bed of pain,
And every healing art was vain,
Whose prayers brought back my life again?
                              my Julia's.

2

When shafts of scandal round me flew,
And ancient friends no longer knew,
My humble name, whose heart was true?
                              my Julia's.

3

When falsehood aimed its poisoned dart,
And treachery peirced by bleeding heart,
Whose friendship did a cure impart?
                              my Julia's

4

When hope was weak, and faith was dead,
And every earthly joy was fled,
Whose hand sustained my drooping head?
                              my Julia's

5

When worn by age, and sunk in years,
My shadow at full length appears,
Who shall participate my cares?
                    my Julia.

6

When life's low wick shall feebly blaze,
And weeping children on me gaze,
Who shall assist my prayers & praise,
                    my Julia.

7

And when my mortal part shall lay,
Waiting in hope, the final day,
Who shall mourn o're my sleeping clay,
my Julia.

8

And when the stream of time shall end,
And the last trump, my grave shall rend,
Who shall with me to Heaven ascend?
my Julia.

Death of Martha Jefferson, September 6, 1792,

We began this chapter with an example of Jefferson's awkwardness around women; we end it with an example of the inexpressible love he shared with his wife.

Jefferson enjoyed ten years of married life before his wife, Martha, died. For much of their marriage, Martha was in frail health. According to their daughter, while his wife was dying Jefferson "was never out of calling" and nursed her tenderly. On Martha's deathbed, Jefferson supposedly made a promise to her that he would never remarry; and he never did.

Below is a copy of a poem by Laurence Sterne that Martha and Thomas Jefferson had read together.* Martha began writing the first part; Jefferson finished the rest. After his death, a worn envelope containing the poem, which had been frequently opened and closed over the years, was found in his private drawer.

The first part of the poem is in Martha's handwriting:

Time wastes too fast: every letter
I trace tells me with what rapidity

---

* Cited in Andrew Burstein, *The Inner Jefferson: Portrait of a Grieving Optimist*, pp. 61–62.

life follows my pen. The days and hours
are flying over our heads like
clouds of windy day never to return—
more.
Everything presses on—

Jefferson here finishes the rest:

and every time I kiss thy hand to bid adieu, every absence
which follows it, are preludes to that eternal separation
which we are shortly to make!

On her gravestone, Jefferson had the following epitaph engraved, in Greek to preserve some privacy, on his wife's grave. It is taken from Homer's *Iliad*:

If in the melancholy shades below,
The flames of friends and lovers cease to glow,
Yet mine shall sacred last; mine undecayed
Burn on through death and animate my shade.

III

CIVILITY
AND
FRIENDSHIP

I find friendship to be like wine, raw when new, ripened with age, the true old man's milk and restorative cordial.

THOMAS JEFFERSON TO BENJAMIN RUSH, AUGUST 17, 1811

Humans are not merely *social*, like bees or wolves, but *political* . . . political in the original meaning of the word. It is no coincidence that our words for politics and politeness derive from the same Greek root which assumed that the only proper choice for man was life in a *polis*, or a democratic city-state, with all of the social and civic connections that such a life entails. We interact with strangers, coworkers, business associates, and friends and know intuitively that there are different modes of conduct appropriate for these different relationships. With our closest friends, we should be loyal and true; with strangers or associates, we should always attempt to be civil; with the suffering and the poor, we should be generous and solicitous. As Franklin summed it up: "Be civil to *all;* serviceable to *many;* familiar with *few;* Friend to *one;* Enemy to *none.*" This chapter explores the Founders' views on civility, charity, and friendship—virtues we cannot do without if we are to have a healthy political community and fulfilled lives.

Much has been said and written about how in America today, a general coarsening of relations among citizens has taken hold—a good deal of anger, rudeness, and impatience. Sometimes it seems as if the old ethic of self-restraint has been replaced with a new one of self-aggrandizement.

It was not always so. For a long time, Americans observed certain rules of behavior, known generally as "civility." As we have lost the original meaning of "politics," we retain an awareness of civility. The word "civility" comes from the Latin root "civitas," meaning city and "civis," meaning citizen. Civility, then, is behavior worthy of citizens living in a city or in common with others.

The Founders' understanding of civility was meant to fit the needs of a large commercial republic. This understanding had many sources, the English philosopher John Locke being one of the most important of them. Here's how he defined civility: ". . . that general good will and regard for all people, which makes any one have a care not to show, in his carriage, any contempt, disrespect, or neglect of them." The Founders certainly did not expect that all Americans would become friends, but they could at least be polite or civil to each other. John Adams wrote his son John Quincy: "Treat the world with modesty, decency, and respect."

While guides to polite behavior might today seem stuffy or prudish, there was much at stake in cultivating civility. In the ancient republics there was no private sphere per se; the laws of the regime reached to most spheres (even those we today would call "private") of human existence. The Founders, in contrast, carved out, for the first time really, a private sphere—of conscience, of religious belief, and of thought— which the government could not, and should not, infringe upon. But the private sphere was not simply private, in the sense of isolation; rather, it involved considerable interaction with one's fellows, whether in the marketplace, or in one's place of worship, or in the classroom, or even in conversation. The interaction among citizens in this private sphere would have to be regulated somehow, not by the government, however, but by rules of etiquette, propriety, and, it was hoped, generosity. How citizens carried on with each other in their private transactions would determine, perhaps more than anything else, the degree to which Americans truly enjoyed "domestic tranquillity." The requirements of civility, at least compared to the older notions of citizenship, are not very exacting. Civility asks simply that we respect the rights and dignity of our fellow citizens.

Civility uplifts our common life, and makes it more pleasant, but it also acts as an important, though indirect, moral teacher of character. "Politeness," Jefferson noted to his grandson, "is artificial good humor, it covers the natural want of it, and ends by rendering habitual a substitute nearly equivalent to the real virtue." Jefferson means the following: By observing the formalities of civility in daily life—even against our more self-regarding inclinations—we learn to control our passions, and we become mindful of how our actions and words affect others. At some point, the learned formalities become second nature. Perhaps with enough practice and repetition, we will be able to fulfill Franklin's advice: "What you seem to be, be really."

The art of civility is precisely that, an art that requires constant application. George Washington, as a young boy, entered into his copybook

110 "Rules of Civility and Decent Behavior in Company and Conversation," some of which are included in this chapter. By studying and practicing these "Rules of Civility," Washington eventually learned to master his infamous bad temper. Thus, said Gouverneur Morris, Washington's "first victory was over himself."[*]

Practiced at its best, civility involves restraining the self and acting with due regard to others. Washington's example of civility appears very formal, dignified, even stern; while Franklin and Jefferson's call to be good-humored seems more informal and inviting. But all three men were attempting to do the same thing—to control selfish inclinations and show respect for those around them. While Franklin doubted that he ever overcame his own pride in "reality," he noted that he made "quite an appearance of it." He must have fooled even Jefferson, who called Franklin "the most amiable of men in society."

The Founders knew that like national friendship, universal friendship among citizens would be impossible—as impossible as regarding the world as a universal family. That's why civility is so important. But if friendship on a wide scale is impossible, friendship on a small scale certainly is not. President George Washington began all eight of his annual messages by addressing Congress as his "fellow citizens." But for his final message, the Farewell Address, he spoke to "*friends* and fellow citizens." Perhaps Washington added "friends" because he was addressing the world—those who aren't fellow citizens. But by adding "friends," Washington also indicated that the ideal political life is to be conducted among citizens animated not just by laws or rights but also by a spirit of friendship or comity. As Aristotle wrote, friendship among citizens of an ideal state would make justice unnecessary, as friends do not injure but only do what is good for each other. Such an ideal world is just that, an ideal. So we cannot do without justice (see chapter 6). But neither can we do without friendship.

Friendships come in all different shapes and sizes. One kind of friendship is based on pleasure and utility and is characterized mainly by civility rather than by deep affection. These friendships may not last forever; they end when the pleasure or the usefulness of the association ends. For example, Franklin formed a club for the mutual improvement of its members, which he called the "Junto," and which lasted for many years. The club existed to further the business interests of each member, but it also performed many community services, such as establishing a volunteer fire department and the first subscription library. Such associa-

[*] *Eulogies and Orations on the Life and Death of General Washington*, pp. 44–45.

tion, the mark of a successful civil society because it makes everyday life more pleasing and communal, is something we could use more of today.

The Founders exemplified, however, a nobler form of friendship as well, providing a model for us all. Though not always in agreement—a few of them became bitter antagonists—they offered each other mutual assistance, hospitality, and good will during "the times that try men's souls." Aristotle observed that during the prime of life, friends "prompt us to noble actions." The Founders could not have acted with such great nobility had they not been surrounded by so many great friends. "Laboring always at the same oar," Jefferson recalled to Adams of their revolutionary days, "we rode through the storm with heart and hand and made a happy port."

Jefferson's capacity for friendship is well known—his daughter once remarked that her father never gave up an opinion, or a friend. Jefferson's friendship with James Madison went uninterrupted for nearly fifty years, while his reconciliation with John Adams (engineered by a mutual friend, Benjamin Rush, which I've documented in this chapter) proves how much more dear friendship is than political differences. Jefferson once wrote to Adams that theirs was "a friendship co-eval with our government;" Adams that Jefferson "soon seized upon my heart" at the Continental Congress. It was only appropriate that these two statesmen died on the same day, July 4, 1826, the fiftieth anniversary celebrating the product of their friendship, American independence. The last words on Adams's lips were: "Jefferson still survives," though Jefferson had actually died a few hours before. From Proverbs 27:17, we learn that "Iron sharpeneth iron; so a man sharpeneth the countenance of his friend." These great men shaped each other's minds and hearts and, in turn, shaped our country.

Of course, not all of the Founders were friends, and as I noted earlier, some of them became bitter political rivals (though some of them transcended rivalries, such as Adams and Jefferson). Aaron Burr's refusal to overlook political differences with Alexander Hamilton led to a duel, in which Hamilton was killed.

True friendship does not come easy. Unlike all other types of human relationships, friendship alone is necessarily reciprocal. Let me illustrate: One can be "in love" without having that love returned. Not so friendship, where the bonds and ties must be mutually felt if one is to count as a friend. The feelings of friendship are almost by definition shared equally. Another difficulty of friendship is that unlike other familial connections which we do not choose, we must choose our friends. We choose to unite with them at a spiritual level and must work at keeping them. As Jefferson once remarked: "Of those connected by blood, the number does not depend on us. But friends we have if we have merited them." A man who is a friend in the fullest sense, Aristotle said, is a virtuous man, for the highest friendship is that between two individuals who share a love of the good and who seek in others the good. It is in the company of such friends that we ourselves become virtuous. No wonder, then, that Washington warned his grandson to be careful in choosing his friends, to "weigh their dispositions and character *well*." Or Franklin, who cautioned: "Be slow in chusing a friend, slower in changing."

For those of us who think we are too busy to make friends, we might learn something from the Founders. They lived in extraordinary times and shared in some of the most exciting political ferments ever. For their friends, however, they found the time and made the effort. They gave comfort to each other in their private lives, grieving over the deaths of their friends' spouses and children and supporting each other through personal and public trials. In matters of friendship, as in much else, we have much to learn from the Founding of America.

⚭

Benjamin Franklin, "Rules for Making Oneself a Disagreeable Companion," Pennsylvania Gazette, *November 15, 1750*

BENJAMIN FRANKLIN freely admitted that there was a time in his life when he himself followed these rules for making himself disagreeable in company. In his *Autobiography,* Franklin confessed that he was often "disputatious" in his manners. Franklin noted that a friend once told him that he could be quite rude and argumentative when he was trying to make a point. This friend made an impression, and Franklin changed. Here Franklin, with his usual sharp wit, offers some advice to those who still don't get it. "Self-esteem," as Franklin describes it, is certainly not a virtue, for it ends up esteeming itself.

Rules, by the Observation of which, a Man of Wit and Learning may nevertheless make himself a disagreeable *Companion.*

Your Business is to *shine;* therefore you must by all means prevent the shining of others, for their Brightness may make yours the less distinguish'd. To this End,

1. If possible engross the whole Discourse; and when other Matter fails, talk much of your-self, your Education, your Knowledge, your Circumstances, your Successes in Business, your Victories in Disputes, your own wise Sayings and Observations on particular Occasions, &c. &c. &c.

2. If when you are out of Breath, one of the Company should seize the Opportunity of saying something; watch his Words, and, if possible, find somewhat either in his Sentiment or Expression, immediately to contradict and raise a Dispute upon. Rather than fail, criticise even his Grammar.

3. If another should be saying an indisputably good Thing; either give no Attention to it; or interrupt him; or draw away the Attention of others; or, if you can guess what he would be at, be quick and say it before him; or, if he gets it said, and you perceive the Company pleas'd with it, own it to be a good Thing, and withal remark that it had been said by *Bacon, Locke, Bayle,* or some other eminent Writer; thus you deprive him of the Reputation he might have gain'd by it, and gain some yourself, as you hereby show your great Reading and Memory.

4. When modest Men have been thus treated by you a few times, they will chuse ever after to be silent in your Company; then you may shine on without Fear of a Rival; rallying them at the same time for their Dullness, which will be to you a new Fund of Wit.

Thus you will be sure to please *yourself.* The polite Man aims at pleasing *others,* but you shall go beyond him even in that. A Man can be present only in one Company, but may at the same time be absent in twenty. He can please only where he *is,* you where-ever you are *not.*

∽

Thomas Jefferson to Benjamin Rush, January 3, 1808, and Thomas Jefferson to Thomas Jefferson Randolph, November 24, 1808

JEFFERSON RANKED "good humor" as the most important quality of the mind. It can't be undervalued: A sharp mind does not compensate for a disagreeable disposition.

In the second letter, Jefferson explains to his grandson and namesake why "good humor" is so essential. Most important, it elevates social and political interactions that might otherwise be unbearable or too coarse. It also can't hurt one's reputation to have a conciliatory disposition. According to Jefferson, it's the secret that will get you ahead in life. By being good-humored and polite, people are apt to take you more seriously. Good humor and civility certainly helped the quiet and agreeable young Jefferson, who spoke no more than three words in the Continental Congress in 1776. Fellow delegates, almost all of them older, chose him to write the Declaration of Independence. And yes, the world listened and is still listening to this gentleman from Virginia.

To Doctor Benjamin Rush

In the ensuing autumn, I shall be sending on to Philadelphia a grandson of about fifteen years of age, to whom I shall ask your friendly attentions. Without that bright fancy which captivates, I am in hopes he possesses sound judgment and much observation; and, what I value more than all things, good humor. For thus I estimate the qualities of the mind: 1, good humor; 2, integrity; 3, industry; 4, science. The preference of the first to the second quality may not at first be acquiesced in; but certainly we had all rather associate with a good-humored, light-principled man, than with an ill-tempered rigorist in morality.

To Thomas Jefferson Randolph

I have mentioned good humor as one of the preservatives of our peace and tranquillity. It is among the most effectual, and it's effect is so well imitated and aided artificially by politeness, that this also becomes an acquisition of first rate value. In truth, politeness is artificial good humor, it covers the natural want of it, and ends by rendering habitual a substitute nearly equivalent to the real virtue. It is the practice of sacrificing to those whom we meet in society all the little conveniences and preferences which will gratify them, and deprive us of nothing worth a moment's consideration; it is the giving a pleasing and flattering turn to our expressions which will conciliate others, and make them pleased with us as well as themselves. How cheap a price for the good will of another! When this is in return for a rude thing said by another, it brings him to his senses, it mortifies and corrects him in the most salutary way, and places him at the feet of your good nature in the eyes of the company.

∞

George Washington's "Rules of Civility"

GEORGE WASHINGTON was not born good—only practice and habit made him so. He was, for instance, known to have had a bad temper. Gouverneur Morris said that Washington had those "tumultuous passions that accompany greatness" and that his "wrath" could be "terrible." But Morris also noted that these strong passions were "controlled by his stronger mind." A famous anecdote records that Henry Lee told Martha and George Washington that the portrait artist Gilbert Stuart had remarked that George had a bad temper. While George Washington thought this over, Martha Washington, being the good wife, immediately objected. Lee responded that Stuart had also said that Washington had his temper under "wonderful control." George Washington replied with a smile: "Mr. Stuart is right." *

In large measure, Washington began the process of controlling his temper and other passions by copying, at a very young age, a translated version of a French book of etiquette, dating back to the sixteenth century. This book contained 110 rules of civility. By regularly reminding himself of these rules and practicing them when the occasion presented itself, Washington learned to master his worst inclinations.

Here's an excerpt of some of the rules. I believe that the general spirit of the rules still applies. We tend to think that liberation means breaking the rules. But it is only by respecting time-honored rules of decency, as Washington himself did, that we truly become masters of ourselves and worthy members of civil society.

1. Every action in company ought to be with some sign of respect to those present.
2. In the presence of others sing not to yourself with a humming voice, nor drum with your fingers or feet.
3. Speak not when others speak, sit not when others stand, and walk not when others stop.
4. Turn not your back to others, especially in speaking; jog not the table or desk on which another reads or writes; lean not on anyone.

---

* Richard Norton Smith, *Patriarch*, p. 263.

5. Be no flatterer, neither play with anyone that delights not to be played with.

6. Read no letters, books, or papers in company; but when there is a necessity for doing it, you must ask leave. Come not near the books or writings of anyone so as to read them unasked; also look not nigh when another is writing a letter.

7. Let your countenance be pleasant, but in serious matters somewhat grave.

8. Show not yourself glad at the misfortune of another, though he were your enemy.

9. They that are in dignity or office have in all places precedency, but whilst they are young, they ought to respect those that are their equals in birth or other qualities, though they have no public charge.

10. It is good manners to prefer them to whom we speak before ourselves, especially if they be above us, with whom in no sort we ought to begin.

11. Let your discourse with men of business be short and comprehensive.

12. In visiting the sick do not presently play the physician if you be not knowing therein.

13. In writing or speaking give to every person his due title according to his degree and the custom of the place.

14. Strive not with your superiors in argument, but always submit your judgment to others with modesty.

15. Undertake not to teach your equal in the art he himself professes; it savors of arrogancy.

16. When a man does all he can, though it succeeds not well, blame not him that did it.

17. Being to advise or reprehend anyone, consider whether it ought to be in public or in private, presently or at some other time, also in what terms to do it; and in reproving show no signs of choler, but do it with sweetness and mildness.

18. Mock not nor jest at anything of importance; break no jests that are sharp or biting; and if you deliver anything witty or pleasant, abstain from laughing thereat yourself.

19. Wherein you reprove another be unblamable yourself, for example is more prevalent than precept.

20. Use no reproachful language against anyone, neither curses nor revilings.

21. Be not hasty to believe flying reports to the disparagement of anyone.

22. In your apparel be modest, and endeavor to accommodate nature rather than procure admiration. Keep to the fashion of your equals, such as are civil and orderly with respect to time and place.

23. Play not the peacock, looking everywhere about you to see if you be well decked, if your shoes fit well, if your stockings set neatly and clothes handsomely.

24. Associate yourself with men of good quality if you esteem your own reputation, for it is better to be alone than in bad company.

25. Let your conversation be without malice or envy, for it is a sign of tractable and commendable nature; and in all causes of passion admit reason to govern.

26. Be not immodest in urging your friend to discover a secret.

27. Utter not base and frivolous things amongst grown and learned men, nor very difficult questions or subjects amongst the ignorant, nor things hard to be believed.

28. Speak not of doleful things in time of mirth nor at the table; speak not of melancholy things, as death and wounds; and if others mention them, change, if you can, the discourse. Tell not your dreams but to your intimate friends.

29. Break not a jest when none take pleasure in mirth. Laugh not aloud, nor at all without occasion. Deride no man's misfortunes, though there seem to be some cause.

30. Speak not injurious words, neither in jest or earnest. Scoff at none, although they give occasion.

31. Be not forward, but friendly and courteous, the first to salute, hear and answer, and be not pensive when it is time to converse.

32. Detract not from others, but neither be excessive in commending.

33. Go not thither where you know not whether you shall be welcome or not. Give not advice without being asked; and when desired, do it briefly.

34. If two contend together, take not the part of either unconstrained, and be not obstinate in your opinion; in things indifferent be of the major side.

35. Reprehend not the imperfection of others, for that belongs to parents, masters, and superiors.

36. Gaze not on the marks or blemishes of others, and ask not how they came. What you may speak in secret to your friend deliver not before others.

37. Speak not in an unknown tongue in company, but in your own language; and that as those of quality do, and not as the vulgar. Sublime matters treat seriously.

38. Think before you speak; pronounce not imperfectly, nor bring out your words too hastily, but orderly and distinctly.

39. When another speaks, be attentive yourself, and disturb not the audience. If any hesitate in his words, help him not, nor prompt him without being desired; interrupt him not, nor answer him till his speech be ended.

40. Treat with men at fit times about business, and whisper not in the company of others.

41. Make no comparisons; and if any of the company be commended for any brave act of virtue, commend not another for the same.

42. Be not apt to relate news if you know not the truth thereof. In discoursing of things you have heard, name not your author always. A secret discover not.

43. Be not curious to know the affairs of others, neither approach to those that speak in private.

44. Undertake not what you cannot perform; but be careful to keep your promise.

45. When you deliver a matter, do it without passion and indiscretion, however mean the person may be you do it to.

46. When your superiors talk to anybody, hear them; neither speak nor laugh.

47. In disputes be not so desirous to overcome as not to give liberty to each one to deliver his opinion, and submit to the judgment of the major part, especially if they are judges of the dispute.

48. Be not tedious in discourse, make not many digressions, nor repeat often the same matter of discourse.

49. Speak no evil of the absent, for it is injust.

50. Be not angry at table, whatever happens; and if you have reason to be so show it not; put on a cheerful countenance, especially if there be strangers, for good humor makes one dish a feast.

51. Set not yourself at the upper end of the table; but if it be your due, or the master of the house will have it so, contend not, lest you should trouble the company.

52. When you speak of God or his attributes, let it be seriously, in reverence and honor, and obey your natural parents.

53. Let your recreations be manful, not sinful.

54. Labor to keep alive in your breast that little spark of celestial fire called conscience.

Benjamin Franklin, Autobiography, *On His Newspapers*

THE FIRST patron saint of printers was St. Augustine of Hippo. But in America, the title goes to Benjamin Franklin. The oldest of America's Founders began his career in insurgency and in printing simultaneously when, at the age of twelve, he rebelled against his father's desire that he become a tallow candle maker and instead became a printer's apprentice for his brother in Boston. Franklin later fled his apprenticeship, found work for a printer in Philadelphia, mastered his craft in England, and returned home, where he produced some of the most famous editorial broadsides in American history and published both the *Pennsylvania Gazette* and *Poor Richard's Almanack.*

At the end of a long life accumulating honors as a scientist, diplomat, businessman, philosopher, and statesman, he chose to begin his Last Will and Testament with the words, "I, Benjamin Franklin, printer . . ." His self-composed epitaph reads:

> The body of
> B. Franklin, Printer
> (Like the Cover of an Old book
> Its Contents torn Out
> And Stript of its Lettering and Gilding)
> Lies Here, Food for Worms.
> But the Work shall not be Lost;
> For it will (as he Believ'd) Appear Once More
> In a New and More Elegant Edition
> Revised and Corrected
> By the Author.

Please note that his actual tombstone reads, rather more modestly:

Benjamin and Deborah Franklin: 1790

In this age of tabloid journalism, Franklin's standards for what is fit to print and his worry about a polluted press are highly instructive.

In the Conduct of my Newspaper I carefully excluded all Libelling and Personal Abuse, which is of late Years become so disgraceful to our Country. Whenever I was solicited to insert any thing of that kind, and the Writers pleaded as they generally did, the Liberty of the Press, and that a Newspaper was like a Stage Coach in which any one who would pay had a Right to a Place, my Answer was, that I would print the Piece separately if desired, and the Author might have as many Copies as he pleased to distribute himself, but that I would not take upon me to spread his Detraction, and that having contracted with my Subscribers to furnish them with what might be either useful or entertaining, I could not fill their Papers with private Altercation in which they had no Concern without doing them manifest Injustice. Now many of our Printers make no scruple of gratifying the Malice of Individuals by false Accusations of the fairest Characters among ourselves, augmenting Animosity even to the producing of Duels, and are moreover so indiscreet as to print scurrilous Reflections on the Government of neighbouring States, and even on the Conduct of our best national Allies, which may be attended with the most pernicious Consequences.—These Things I mention as a Caution to young Printers, & that they may be encouraged not to pollute their Presses and disgrace their Profession by such infamous Practices, but refuse steadily; as they may see by my Example; that such a Course of Conduct will not on the whole be injurious to their Interests.—

∽

George Washington and Gouverneur Morris at the Constitutional Convention

WASHINGTON'S FIRST rule of civility was that "every action in company ought to be done with some sign of respect to those present." This anecdote recounts Gouverneur Morris's violation of that rule. Morris was a good friend of Washington—Washington often dined with him in Philadelphia during the Constitutional Convention. But for Washington, even good friends must observe rules of decorum, especially when they are involved in important public events. At the very least such rules of mutual respect make society pleasant; more important, they remind us of the dignity of the public realm. (The rules of the convention were strictly formal. The delegates were even told that when the president of the convention rises to speak, "None shall pass between them or hold discourse with another, or read a book, pamphlet or paper, printed or manuscript. . . .")

As the following story shows, Morris came to regret his imprudent behavior—he reportedly told a friend in another version of this story that as soon as he slapped Washington on the shoulder: "How I wish the floor would open and I could descend to the cellar!"

When the Convention to form a Constitution was sitting in Philadelphia in 1787, of which General Washington was president, he had stated evenings to receive the calls of his friends. At an interview between Hamilton, the Morrises, and others, the former remarked that Washington was reserved and aristocratic even to his intimate friends, and allowed no one to be familiar with him. Gouverneur Morris said that was a mere fancy, and he could be as familiar with Washington as with any of his other friends. Hamilton replied, "If you will, at the next reception evenings, gently slap him on the shoulder and say, 'My dear General, how happy I am to see you look so well!' a supper and wine shall be provided for you and a dozen of your friends." The challenge was accepted. On the evening appointed, a large number attended; and at an early hour Gouverneur Morris entered, bowed, shook hands, laid his left hand on Washington's shoulder, and said, "My dear General, I am very happy to see you look so well!" Washington withdrew his hand, stepped suddenly back, fixed his eye on Morris for several minutes with an angry frown, until the latter retreated abashed, and sought refuge in the crowd. The company looked on in silence. At the supper, which was provided by Hamilton, Morris said, "I have won the bet, but paid dearly for it, and nothing could induce me to repeat it."
—From James Parton, *Life of Thomas Jefferson* (1874), p. 369.

∞

George Washington to Bushrod Washington, November 10, 1787

WASHINGTON'S NEPHEW, Bushrod Washington, had been elected to the Virginia State Assembly. Here Washington gives Bushrod some advice about how to be an effective legislator. Civility figures large.

You have I find broke the Ice; the only advice I will offer to you on the occasion (if you have a mind to command the attention of the House) is to speak seldom, but to important Subjects, except such as particularly relate to your Constituents, and, in the former case make yourself *perfectly* master of the Subject. Never exceed a *decent* warmth, and submit your sentiments with diffidence. A dictatorial Stile, though it may carry conviction, is always accompanied with disgust. I am, &c.

∞

Abigail Adams to Mary Cranch, January 5, 1790

JOHN ADAMS served as America's first vice-president under George Washington. This meant for Abigail Adams many official duties and parties to attend. During these official receptions, the wife of the vice-president was to stand to the right of Mrs. Washington. Abigail Adams, who had never been particularly comfortable with the formalities of court life when she served as a diplomat's wife in Europe, was sometimes confused as to what she should do and where she should stand. Sometimes, other women would step in her place next to Mrs. Washington. But Washington was always mindful of making others comfortable and often came to Abigail's rescue by restoring her to her rightful place. The following description of Washington, by a grateful Abigail, captures the gentility and gracious bearing of Washington that won him the respect not only of Abigail but of a whole nation as well.

Here is the wife of the second president of the United States expressing her hope that the tenure of the first president will last "for many, many years."

In the Evening I attended the drawing Room, it being Mrs. W[ashington']s publick day. It was as much crowded as a Birth Night at St. James, and with company as Briliantly drest, diamonds & great hoops excepted. My station is always at the right hand of Mrs. W.; through want of knowing what is right I find it sometimes occupied, but on such an occasion the President never fails of seeing that it is relinquished for me, and having removed Ladies several times, they have now learnt to rise & give it me, but this between our selves, as *all distinction* you know is unpopu-

lar. Yet this same P[resident] has so happy a faculty of appearing to
accommodate & yet carrying his point, that if he was not really one of
the best intentiond men in the world he might be a very dangerous
one. He is polite with dignity, affable without familiarity, distant without
Haughtyness, Grave without Austerity, Modest, wise & Good. These are
traits in his Character which peculiarly fit him for the exalted station he
holds, and God Grant that he may Hold it with the same applause &
universal satisfaction for many many years, as it is my firm opinion that
no other man could rule over this great people & consolidate them into
one mighty Empire but He who is set over us.

Benjamin Franklin, Autobiography

BENJAMIN FRANKLIN called pride the strongest of all our natural
passions. Franklin tried to conquer his ample portion of pride, but like
most of us, he admits he never overcame it. That didn't seem to bother
him, however, for he notes, with wit and some jocularity, that if he
conquered his pride he would probably be proud of his humility. Franklin settled for *appearing* to be humble. He marveled at how "soon" he
"found the advantage of this change in his manners." Franklin's point is
not that we be hypocrites but that where moral purity is impossible the
practice of good manners is not. And who knows, the more we practice,
the better we may actually become.

My list of virtues contain'd at first but twelve; but a Quaker friend
having kindly informed me that I was generally thought proud; that my
pride show'd itself frequently in conversation; that I was not content with
being in the right when discussing any point, but was overbearing, and
rather insolent, of which he convinc'd me by mentioning several instances; I determined endeavouring to cure myself, if I could, of this vice
or folly among the rest, and I added *Humility* to my list, giving an
extensive meaning to the word.

I cannot boast of much success in acquiring the *reality* of this virtue,
but I had a good deal with regard to the *appearance* of it. I made it a
rule to forbear all direct contradiction to the sentiments of others, and all
positive assertion of my own. I even forbid myself, agreeably to the old
laws of our Junto, the use of every word or expression in the language
that imported a fix'd opinion, such as *certainly, undoubtedly,* etc., and I

adopted, instead of them, *I conceive, I apprehend,* or *I imagine* a thing to be so or so; or it *so appears to me at present.* When another asserted something that I thought an error, I deny'd myself the pleasure of contradicting him abruptly, and of showing immediately some absurdity in his proposition; and in answering I began by observing that in certain cases or circumstances his opinion would be right, but in the present case there *appear'd* or *seem'd* to me some difference, etc. I soon found the advantage of this change in my manner; the conversations I engag'd in went on more pleasantly. The modest way in which I propos'd my opinions procur'd them a readier reception and less contradiction; I had less mortification when I was found to be in the wrong, and I more easily prevail'd with others to give up their mistakes and join with me when I happened to be in the right.

And this mode, which I at first put on with some violence to natural inclination, became at length so easy, and so habitual to me, that perhaps for these fifty years past no one has ever heard a dogmatical expression escape me. And to this habit (after my character of integrity) I think it principally owing that I had early so much weight with my fellow-citizens when I proposed new institutions, or alterations in the old, and so much influence in public councils when I became a member; for I was but a bad speaker, never eloquent, subject to much hesitation in my choice of words, hardly correct in language, and yet I generally carried my points.

In reality, there is, perhaps, no one of our natural passions so hard to subdue as *pride.* Disguise it, struggle with it, beat it down, stifle it, mortify it as much as one pleases, it is still alive, and will every now and then peep out and show itself; you will see it, perhaps, often in this history; for, even if I could conceive that I had compleatly overcome it, I should probably be proud of my humility.

∞

George Washington to Bushrod Washington, January 15, 1783, and George Washington to Lund Washington, November 26, 1775

THESE TWO letters showcase Washington's charity to the needy. He was generous to friends and strangers in need, but was careful to make a distinction between the "deserving" and "undeserving" poor. He made this distinction not out of mean-spiritedness or ignorance that fortune can make waste to even the most hard-working men. Rather, it was his sense that not to make such distinctions, to lump the deserving and undeserving into one category, such as we do today by such terms as the "underclass," insults and degrades the working and virtuous poor.

In the middle of commanding the battles of the Revolutionary War, George Washington found the time to write to his cousin, Lund, who was in charge of running Mount Vernon, that he remember and be generous to the poor who came to the estate.

To Bushrod Washington

Let your *heart* feel for the affliction, and distresses of every one, and let your *hand* give in proportion to your purse; remembering always, the estimation of the Widows mite. But, that it is not every one who asketh, that deserveth charity; all however are worthy of the enquiry, or the deserving may suffer.

To Lund Washington

"*It* is the greatest, indeed it is the only comfortable reflexion I enjoy on this score, to think that my business is in the hands of a person in whose integrity I have not a doubt, and on whose care I can rely. Was it not for this, I should feel very unhappy on Account of the situation of my affairs; but I am persuaded you will do for me as you would for yourself, and more than this I cannot expect."

"Let the Hospitality of the House, with respect to the poor, be kept up; Let no one go hungry away. If any of these kind of People should be in want of Corn, supply their necessities, provided it does not encourage them in idleness; and I have no objection to your giving my Money in Charity, to the Amount of forty or fifty Pounds a Year, when you think it well bestowed. What I mean, by having no objection, is, that it is my desire that it should be done. You are to consider that neither myself or Wife are now in the way to do these good Offices. In all other respects, I recommend it to you, and have no doubts, of your observing the greatest Œconomy and frugality; as I suppose you know that I do not get a farthing for my services here more than my Expenses; It becomes necessary, therefore, for me to be saving at home."

The above is copied, not only to remind myself of my promises, and requests; but others also, if any mischance happens to G. Washington.

∞

Thomas Jefferson to Marquis de Lafayette, April 11, 1787

WHILE IN France, Thomas Jefferson studied the hard life of peasants and wrote to Lafayette of ways of improving their life prospects, and doing it "absolutely incognito."

From the first olive fields of Pierrelate, to the orangeries of Hieres, has been continued rapture to me. I have often wished for you. I think you have not made this journey. It is a pleasure you have to come, and an improvement to be added to the many you have already made. It will be a great comfort to you to know, from your own inspection, the condition of all the provinces of your own country, and it will be interesting to them at some future day to be known to you. This is perhaps the

only moment of your life in which you can acquire that knolege. And to do it most effectually you must be absolutely incognito, you must ferret the people out of their hovels as I have done, look into their kettles, eat their bread, loll on their beds under pretence of resting yourself, but In fact to find if they are soft. You will feel a sublime pleasure in the course of this investigation, and a sublimer one hereafter when you shall be able to apply your knolege to the softening of their beds, or the throwing a morsel of meat into the kettle of vegetables. You will not wonder at the subjects of my letter: they are the only ones which have been present to my mind for some time past, and the waters must always be what are the fountain from which they flow. According to this indeed I should have intermixed from beginning to end warm expressions of friendship to you: but according to the ideas of our country we do not permit ourselves to speak even truths when they may have the air of flattery. I content myself therefore with saying once for all that I love you, your wife and children. Tell them so and Adieu. Your's affectionately,

TH: JEFFERSON

∞

George Washington to William Ramsay, January 29, 1769

THE SPIRIT of generosity in Washington's support of his friend's promising son is unparalleled. Washington takes it upon himself to support this child simply upon hearing that he would like to go to the College of New Jersey (now Princeton University). Washington gives with the hope that this young man will receive an education that will promote the general welfare of others. Washington also does not wish to get recognition for his generosity, assuring his friend that his gift will "never be known" to others.

Having once or twice of late hear you Speak highly in praise of the Jersey College, as if you had a desire of sending your Son William there (who I am told is a youth fond of study and instruction, and disposed to a sedentary studious life; in following of which he may not only promote his own happiness, but the future welfare of others) I shou'd be glad, if you have no other objection to it than what may arise from the expence, if you wou'd send him there as soon as it is convenient and depend on me for Twenty five pounds this Currency a year for his support so long as it may be necessary for the completion of his Education. If I live to see the accomplishment of this term, the sum here stipulated shall be annually paid, and if I die in the mean while, this letter shall be obligatory upon my Heirs or Executors to do it according to the true intent and meaning hereof. No other return is expected, or wished for this offer, than that you will accept it with the same freedom and good will with which it is made, and that you may not even consider it in the light of an obligation, or mention it as such; for be assur'd that from me it will never be known. I am, &c.

∾

John Adams, Autobiography, *September 1776*

IN SEPTEMBER of 1776, the Continental Army suffered a disastrous defeat at the Battle of Long Island. The British military commanders — the brothers Sir William Howe and Admiral Lord Howe — offered to negotiate with the colonists. The Continental Congress selected John Adams, Benjamin Franklin, and Edward Rutledge to meet with the British in a diplomatic mission. According to John Adams, Lord Howe told the delegation that he "could not confer with us as members of Congress, or public characters, but only as private persons and British subjects." To which John Adams "answered somewhat quickly, '[y]our Lordship may consider me, in what light you please; and indeed I should be willing to consider myself, for a few moments, in any character which would be agreeable to your Lordship, *except that of a British subject.'* Howe turned to the other two delegates and said, 'Mr. Adams is a decided character.' "

Following is a humorous story that shows the camaraderie of Adams and Franklin on their way to this ill-fated meeting. Adams and Franklin were to have a falling-out a few years later when they were both in France. But at this critical juncture of the revolution, these two patriots seem to have gotten along quite fine, as the story indicates.

The Taverns were so full We could with difficulty obtain Entertainment. At Brunswick, but one bed could be procured for Dr. Franklin and me, in a Chamber little larger than the bed, without a Chimney and with only one small Window. The Window was open, and I, who was an invalid and afraid of the Air in the night *(blowing upon me)*, shut it close. Oh! says Franklin dont shut the Window. We shall be suffocated. I answered I was afraid of the Evening Air. Dr. Franklin replied, the Air within this Chamber will soon be, and indeed is now worse than that without Doors: come! open the Window and come to bed, and I will convince you: I believe you are not acquainted with my Theory of Colds. Opening the Window and leaping into Bed, I said I had read his Letters to Dr. Cooper in which he had advanced, that Nobody ever got cold by going into a cold Church, or any other cold Air: but the Theory was so little consistent with my experience, that I thought it a Paradox: However I had so much curiosity to hear his reasons, that I would run the risque of a cold. The Doctor then began an harrangue, upon Air and cold and Respiration and Perspiration, with which I was so much amused that I soon fell asleep, and left him and his Philosophy together: but I believe they were equally sound and insensible, within a few minutes after me, for the last Words I heard were pronounced as if he was more than half asleep. . . . I remember little of the Lecture, except, that the human Body, by Respiration and Perspiration, destroys a gallon of Air in a minute: that two such Persons, as were now in that Chamber, would consume all the Air in it, in an hour or two: that by breathing over again the matter thrown off, by the Lungs and the Skin, We should imbibe the real Cause of Colds, not from abroad but from within. I am not inclined to introduce here a dissertation on this Subject. There is much Truth I believe, in some things he advanced: but they warrant not the assertion that a Cold is never taken from cold air. I have often conversed with him since on the same subject: and I believe with him that Colds are often taken in foul Air, in close Rooms: but they are often taken from cold Air, abroad too. I have often asked him, whether a Person heated with Exercise, going suddenly into cold Air, or standing still in a current of it, might not have his Pores suddenly contracted, his Perspiration stopped, and that matter thrown into the Circulations or cast upon the Lungs which he acknowledged was the cause of Colds. To this he never could give me a satisfactory Answer. And I have heard that in the Opinion of his own able Physician Dr. Jones he fell a Sacrifice at last, not to the Stone but to his own Theory; having caught the violent Cold, which finally choaked him, by sitting for some hours at a Window, with the cool Air blowing upon him.

∾

Thomas Jefferson and Benjamin Franklin
at the Second Continental Congress

PART OF being a true friend is knowing just the right words to give comfort to and cheer up a friend. Here's a great example.

After this had been adopted Congress went into Committee of the Whole to consider Jefferson's statement of the reasons which had led to this act; but the hour being late, it was agreed to postpone discussion to another day. On the 3d of July further reasons for delay presented themselves, but on the 4th the way was clear, and the Declaration as Jefferson wrote it had to stand the criticism of one surveyor, one planter, one clergyman, one shoemaker, one sailor, one general, one printer, one soldier, eight merchants, two statesmen, six farmers, six doctors and twenty-four lawyers, who made up the Continental Congress. Some suggested verbal changes. Others wanted to strike out whole paragraphs. Objection was made to calling King George a tyrant. Somebody took exception to Jefferson's observations on the wickedness of slavery. Between them all they discarded about a quarter of what he had written— "as I expected," said John Adams, who felt that some of the best passages had been sacrificed. Timothy Pickering, on the other hand, thought the document distinctly improved. To Jefferson the well-meant changes seemed little short of butchery. He sat quiet, however, leaving the task of defense to Mr. Adams, and glad that Mr. Adams was a good fighter. . . .

On the day when his work was running the gauntlet of discussion, Benjamin Franklin, seated near Jefferson, noted with sympathy, not untinged by amusement, that his young friend "writhed a little," and to divert him told under his breath an incident of his own youth, which had taught him, he said, never to write anything to be offered for public criticism. An acquaintance of his, a hatter's apprentice, about to set up in business for himself, devised a fine new sign and exhibited it with pride to his friends. It read: "John Thompson Hatter makes and sells hats for ready money," this information being followed by an impressive picture of a hat. Asked what they thought of it, one man said the word "hatter" might be dispensed with, since it was followed by "makes hats." Another thought "makes" quite superfluous, the public not caring who made the hats; and so it went on until nothing was left except John Thompson's name and the portrait of a hat. If Jefferson failed to see any humor in this while his masterpiece was being hacked to pieces, he savored it to the full later on, and the story, with Franklin's kindly intent in telling it, strongly emphasized, became one of his favorite anecdotes.

—From Helen Nicolay, *Boys Life of Thomas Jefferson*

∞

George Washington to Bushrod Washington, January 15, 1783

BUSHROD WASHINGTON was George Washington's favorite nephew. Bushrod was studying law in Philadelphia when Washington, "as a friend," gave him some moral guidance. Washington couldn't resist giving out a little advice every now and then to his extended family members. To give more incentive to Bushrod to behave properly, he told him, at the end of this letter, that it makes him happy "to find those, to whom I am so nearly connected, pursuing the right walk of life." Bushrod grew up to become an associate justice of the U.S. Supreme Court.

That the Company in which you will improve most, will be least expensive to you; and yet I am not such a Stoic as to suppose you will, or to think it right that you ought, always to be in Company with Senators and Philosophers; but, of the young and juvenile kind let me advise you to be choice. It is easy to make acquaintances, but very difficult to shake them off, however irksome and unprofitable they are found after we have once committed ourselves to them; the indiscretions, and scrapes which very often they involuntarily lead one into, proves equally distressing and disgraceful.

Be courteous to all, but intimate with few, and let those few be well tried before you give them your confidence; true friendship is a plant of slow growth, and must undergo and withstand the shocks of adversity before it is entitled to the appellation.

George Washington to George Washington Custis, November 28, 1796

GEORGE WASHINGTON CUSTIS was Washington's adopted grandson, whom he raised, along with Custis's sister, Eleanor, at Mount Vernon. George Washington Custis was a student at Princeton University when George wrote the letter of advice. Custis needed a lot of guidance. He was a handful—not very disciplined and prone to idleness. He dropped out of Princeton University and returned to Mount Vernon.

'*Tis* well to be on good terms with all your fellow students, and I am pleased to hear you are so, but while a courteous behavior is due to all, select the most deserving only for your friendships, and before this becomes intimate, weigh their dispositions and character *well*. True friendship is a plant of slow growth; to be sincere, there must be a congeniality of temper and pursuits. Virtue and vice can not be allied; nor can idleness and industry; of course, if you resolve to adhere to the two former of these extremes, an intimacy with those who incline to the latter of them, would be extremely embarrassing to you; it would be a stumbling-block in your way, and act like a millstone hung to your neck, for it is the nature of idleness and vice to obtain as many votaries as they can.

Thomas Jefferson to Martha Jefferson Randolph, July 17, 1790

MARTHA'S FATHER-IN-LAW was about to remarry a woman half his age. This had agitated Martha and her husband. Jefferson wrote the following note stressing the importance of comity between those we must live with.

If the lady has any thing difficult in her dispositions, avoid what is rough, and attach her good qualities to you. Consider what are otherwise

as a bad stop in your harpsichord. Do not touch on it, but make yourself
happy with the good ones. Every human being, my dear, must thus be
viewed according to what it is good for, for none of us, no not one, is perfect; and were we to love none who had imperfections, this world would
be a desart for our love. All we can do is to make the best of our friends:
love and cherish what is good in them, and keep out of the way of what is
bad: but no more think of rejecting them for it than of throwing away a
piece of music for a flat passage or two. Your situation will require peculiar
attentions and respects to both parties. Let no proof be too much for either
your patience or acquiescence. Be you my dear, the link of love, union,
and peace for the whole family. The world will give you the more credit
for it, in proportion to the difficulty of the task. And your own happiness
will be the greater as you percieve that you promote that of others.

∞

Benjamin Franklin, Autobiography, *and "Rules for a Club Formerly Established in Philadelphia"*

A s a young man, poor and struggling to establish his business in Philadelphia, Franklin began the formation of a club for "mutual improvement." He called the club the Junto. It consisted of poor men, mainly
tradesmen and artisans who were trying to get ahead. Franklin limited
the membership to twelve, after the twelve apostles. The group existed
mainly to help advance the careers and business interests of each member. For example, they were asked to share information on any local
businesses that seemed to be thriving, or any that have failed. But the
club also took an interest in the community, asking at every meeting,
for example, if members had heard of any "deserving stranger in town"
for whom they could be of service. The Junto took on many projects to
help the community, such as establishing the first subscription library
in North America. The club lasted for thirty years and spawned many
other similar clubs. This is what a robust civil society is all about.

I should have mentioned before, that, in the autumn of the preceding
year, I had form'd most of my ingenious acquaintance into a club of
mutual improvement, which we called the JUNTO; we met on Friday
evenings. The rules that I drew up required that every member, in his

turn, should produce one or more queries on any point of Morals, Politics, or Natural Philosophy, to be discuss'd by the company; and once in three months produce and read an essay of his own writing, on any subject he pleased. Our debates were to be under the direction of a president, and to be conducted in the sincere spirit of inquiry after truth, without fondness for dispute, or desire of victory; and, to prevent warmth, all expressions of positiveness in opinions, or direct contradiction, were after some time made contraband, and prohibited under small pecuniary penalties.

RULES FOR A CLUB ESTABLISHED FOR MUTUAL IMPROVEMENT
PREVIOUS QUESTION, TO BE ANSWERED AT EVERY MEETING

Have you read over these queries this morning, in order to consider what you might have to offer the Junto touching any one of them? viz.

1. Have you met with any thing in the author you last read, remarkable, or suitable to be communicated to the Junto? particularly in history, morality, poetry, physic, travels, mechanic arts, or other parts of knowledge.

2. What new story have you lately heard agreeable for telling in conversation?

3. Hath any citizen in your knowledge failed in his business lately, and what have you heard of the cause?

4. Have you lately heard of any citizen's thriving well, and by what means?

5. Have you lately heard how any present rich man, here or elsewhere, got his estate?

6. Do you know of a fellow citizen, who has lately done a worthy action, deserving praise and imitation; or who has lately committed an error, proper for us to be warned against and avoid?

7. What unhappy effects of intemperance have you lately observed or heard; of imprudence, of passion, or of any other vice or folly?

8. What happy effects of temperance, of prudence, of moderation, or of any other virtue?

9. Have you or any of your acquaintance been lately sick or wounded? If so, what remedies were used, and what were their effects?

10. Whom do you know that are shortly going voyages or journeys, if one should have occasion to send by them?

11. Do you think of any thing at present, in which the Junto may be serviceable to *mankind*, to their country, to their friends, or to themselves?

12. Hath any deserving stranger arrived in town since last meeting,

that you have heard of? And what have you heard or observed of his character or merits? And whether, think you, it lies in the power of the Junto to oblige him, or encourage him as he deserves?

13. Do you know of any deserving young beginner lately set up, whom it lies in the power of the Junto any way to encourage?

14. Have you lately observed any defect in the laws of your *country,* of which it would be proper to move the legislature for an amendment? Or do you know of any beneficial law that is wanting?

15. Have you lately observed any encroachment on the just liberties of the people?

16. Hath any body attacked your reputation lately? And what can the Junto do towards securing it?

17. Is there any man whose friendship you want, and which the Junto, or any of them, can procure for you?

18. Have you lately heard any member's character attacked, and how have you defended it?

19. Hath any man injured you, from whom it is in the power of the Junto to procure redress?

20. In what manner can the Junto, or any of them, assist you in any of your honourable designs?

21. Have you any weighty affair on hand, in which you think the advice of the Junto may be of service?

22. What benefits have you lately received from any man not present?

23. Is there any difficulty in matters of opinion, of justice, and injustice, which you would gladly have discussed at this time?

24. Do you see any thing amiss in the present customs or proceedings of the Junto, which might be amended?

Any person to be qualified [as a member of the JUNTO], to stand up, and lay his hand upon his breast, and be asked these questions, viz.

1. Have you any particular disrespect to any present members? *Answer.* I have not.

2. Do you sincerely declare, that you love mankind in general, of what profession or religion soever? *Answer.* I do.

3. Do you think any person ought to be harmed in his body, name, or goods, for mere speculative opinions, or his external way of worship? *Answer.* No.

4. Do you love truth for truth's sake, and will you endeavour impartially to find and receive it yourself, and communicate it to others. *Answer.* Yes.

∞

Thomas Jefferson to Maria Cosway,
"Dialogue Between the Head and the Heart,"
October 12, 1786

JEFFERSON MET Maria Cosway when he was serving as the American minister to France. He was a lonely widower; she a charming and beautiful artist who happened to be married. So taken was Jefferson with Maria that when she and her husband left Paris, he wrote his famous letter, the "dialogue between the head and the heart." In the dialogue, Jefferson considered what friendship means.

Head. Everything in this world is a matter of calculation. Advance then with caution, the balance in your hand. Put into one scale the pleasures which any object may offer; but put fairly into the other the pains which are to follow, and see which preponderates. The making an acquaintance is not a matter of indifference. When a new one is proposed to you, view it all round. Consider what advantages it presents, and to what inconveniences it may expose you. Do not bite at the bait of pleasure till you know there is no hook beneath it. The art of life is the art of avoiding pain: and he is the best pilot who steers clearest of the rocks and shoals with which it is beset. Pleasure is always before us; but misfortune is at our side: while running after that, this arrests us. The most effectual means of being secure against pain is to retire within ourselves, and to suffice for our own happiness. Those, which depend on ourselves, are the only pleasures a wise man will count on: for nothing is ours which another may deprive us of. Hence the inestimable value of intellectual pleasures. Ever in our power, always leading us to something new, never cloying, we ride, serene and sublime, above the concerns of this mortal world, contemplating truth and nature, matter and motion, the laws which bind up their existence, and that eternal being who made and bound them up by these laws. Let this be our employ. Leave the bustle and tumult of society to those who have not talents to occupy themselves without them. Friendship is but another name for an alliance with the follies and the misfortunes of others. Our own share of miseries is sufficient: why enter then as volunteers into those of another? Is there so little gall poured into our own cup that we must needs help to drink that of our neighbor? A friend dies or leaves us:

we feel as if a limb was cut off. He is sick: we must watch over him, and participate of his pains. His fortune is shipwrecked: ours must be laid under contribution. He loses a child, a parent or a partner: we must mourn the loss as if it was our own.

Heart. And what more sublime delight than to mingle tears with one whom the hand of heaven hath smitten! To watch over the bed of sickness, and to beguile it's tedious and it's painful moments! To share our bread with one to whom misfortune has left none! This world abounds indeed with misery: to lighten it's burthen we must divide it with one another. But let us now try the virtues of your mathematical balance, and as you have put into one scale the burthens of friendship, let me put it's comforts into the other. When languishing then under disease, how grateful is the solace of our friends! How are we penetrated with their assiduities and attentions! How much are we supported by their encouragements and kind offices! When Heaven has taken from us some object of our love, how sweet is it to have a bosom whereon to recline our heads, and into which we may pour the torrent of our tears! Grief, with such a comfort, is almost a luxury! In a life where we are perpetually exposed to want and accident, yours is a wonderful proposition, to insulate ourselves, to retire from all aid, and to wrap ourselves in the mantle of self-sufficiency! For assuredly nobody will care for him who cares for nobody. But friendship is precious not only in the shade but in the sunshine of life: and thanks to a benevolent arrangement of things, the greater part of life is sunshine.

Believe me then, my friend, that that is a miserable arithmetic which would estimate friendship at nothing, or at less than nothing.

∞

John Jay to Egbert Benson, March 1781

WE'VE ALL heard the expression "make new friends, but keep the old. One is silver and the other is gold." Jay writes a sweet letter about the value of old friends, but it's also important, as the song goes, to replenish the capital of friendships along the way of life.

The vulgar proverb, *out of sight, out of mind,* always appeared to me in the light of a vulgar error, when applied to old *friends and companions.* I hope I have not been mistaken, especially as the contrary of that proposition is true with respect to myself. I never loved or admired America so much as since I left it, and my attachment to my friends in it seems to have increased, in proportion as distance of time and place separated me from them. The remark that we seldom estimate blessings justly till we are about to lose them for a time, or altogether, is, I believe, frequently true, and perhaps that circumstance has tightened the cords which bind me to my friends and country. I could carry your recollection back to days that are past, and entertain you with the shades of many departed pleasures, in which we had been partakers. These shades speak a language that I hope your heart understands as well as mine, and I flatter myself that their voice, though not loud, will be sufficient to awaken a remembrance of the sincere attachment and regard, with which I have long been, and still am,

Your affectionate friend and servant,

JOHN JAY.

∞

Alexander Hamilton, Private Papers, 1804

SHAKESPEARE WROTE of Henry V: "If it be a sin to covet honor, he was the most offending soul alive." The same may be said of Alexander Hamilton. Hamilton entered a gun duel with Aaron Burr to defend his honor. In it, he lost his life.

The animosity between Burr and Hamilton escalated during the presidential election of 1800. The vote in the electoral college ended in a tie between the two Republican candidates Jefferson and Burr. As provided in article 2, section 2 of the still-new Constitution, the election was thrown to the House of Representatives, where the results were far from certain. Though Hamilton had strong and long-established political differences with Jefferson, he threw his support (reluctantly) behind Jefferson for the good of the country. Hamilton wrote to a friend that Burr was "the most unfit man in the U.S. for the office of President," a man "without probity" or for that matter, any "principle[,] public or private." Believing that Burr's ambitions would not be satisfied with the office of the presidency and that he would be a serious threat to the stability of the young republic, Hamilton urged fellow Federalists to "save our country from so great a calamity." With the help of Hamilton, Jefferson won.

Their paths crossed again a few years later when Burr was nominated for governor in New York. Hamilton again spoke out against him and played a prominent role in Burr's defeat. Burr heard of some derogatory remarks Hamilton had made about him. He demanded an apology. Hamilton and Burr exchanged several letters; Burr, however, was not satisfied with Hamilton's responses and thus challenged him to a duel.

Hamilton, who had lost a son to a duel, did not believe in the practice of dueling and worried that his example might encourage others. Many wonder why he couldn't have resolved his differences with Burr peaceably. But Hamilton had an aristocratic idea of honor and believed that, given his out-of-wedlock birth, he had much to prove, as his honor was often held in question. Thus he acquiesced.

Some reports indicate that Hamilton never intended to shoot at Burr and fired his gun into the air. Burr had no such qualms and with his first shot delivered a fatal wound to Hamilton's chest. After much suffering, Hamilton died the next day. As for Burr, he was indicted but fled. He later engaged in secessionist plans to break up the Union for which he was tried but not convicted for lack of evidence.

Gouverneur Morris said that Hamilton "was ambitious of glory only" and told mourners at his funeral to "protect his fame. It is all that he has left. . . ." There is no denying that this out-of-wedlock son of a Scotsman certainly achieved that.

On my expected interview with Col. Burr, I think it proper to make some remarks explanatory of my conduct, motives, and views. I was certainly desirous of avoiding this interview for the most cogent reasons:

(1) My religious and moral principles are strongly opposed to the practice of dueling, and it would ever give me pain to be obliged to shed the blood of a fellow-creature in a private combat forbidden by the laws.

(2) My wife and children are extremely dear to me, and my life is of the utmost importance to them in various views.

(3) I feel a sense of obligation towards my creditors; who, in case of accident to me by the forced sale of my property, may be in some degree sufferers. I did not think myself at liberty as a man of probity lightly to expose them to this hazard.

(4) I am conscious of no ill-will to Col. Burr, distinct from political opposition, which, as I trust, has proceeded from pure and upright motives.

Lastly, I shall hazard much and can possibly gain nothing by the issue of the interview.

But it was, as I conceive, impossible for me to avoid it. There were intrinsic difficulties in the thing and artificial embarrassments, from the manner of proceeding on the part of Col. Burr.

Intrinsic, because it is not to be denied that my animadversions on the political principles, character, and views of Col. Burr have been extremely severe; and on different occasions I, in common with many others, have made very unfavorable criticisms on particular instances of the private conduct of this gentleman. In proportion as these impressions were entertained with sincerity and uttered with motives and for purposes which might appear to me commendable, would be the difficulty (until they could be removed by evidence of their being erroneous) of explanation or apology.

The disavowal required of me by Col. Burr in a general and indefinite form was out of my power, if it had really been proper for me to submit to be questioned, but I was sincerely of opinion that this could not be, and in this opinion I was confirmed by that of a very moderate and judicious friend whom I consulted. Besides that, Col. Burr appeared to me to assume, in the first instance, a tone unnecessarily peremptory and menacing, and, in the second, positively offensive.

Yet I wished, as far as might be practicable, to leave a door open to accommodation. This, I think, will be inferred from the written communication made by me and by my directions, and would be confirmed by the conversations between Mr. Van Ness and myself which arose out of the subject. I am not sure whether, under all the circumstances, I did not go further in the attempt to accommodate than a punctilious delicacy will justify. If so, I hope the motives I have stated will excuse me.

It is not my design, by what I have said, to affix any odium on the conduct of Col. Burr in this case. He doubtless has heard of animadversions of mine which bore very hard upon him, and it is probable that as usual they were accompanied with some falsehoods. He may have supposed himself under a necessity of acting as he has done. I hope the grounds of his proceeding have been such as ought to satisfy his own conscience.

I trust, at the same time, that the world will do me the justice to believe that I have not censured him on light grounds nor from unworthy inducements. I certainly have had strong reasons for what I have said, though it is possible that in some particulars I may have been influenced by misconstruction or misinformation. It is also my ardent wish that I may have been more mistaken than I think I have been; and that he, by his future conduct, may show himself worthy of all confidence and esteem and prove an ornament and a blessing to the country. As well, because it is possible that I may have injured Col. Burr, however convinced myself that my opinions and declarations have been well-founded, as from my general principles and temper in relation to similar affairs, I have resolved, if our interview is conducted in the usual manner and if pleases God to give me the opportunity to reserve and throw away my first fire, and I have thoughts even of reserving my second fire, and thus giving a double opportunity to Col. Burr to pause and reflect.

It is not, however, my intention to enter into any explanations on the ground. Apology from principle, I hope, rather than pride, is out of the question. To those who, with me, abhorring the practice of duelling, may think that I ought on no account to have added to the number of bad examples, I answer that my relative situation, as well in public as private, enforcing all the considerations which constitute what men of the world denominate honor, imposed on me (as I thought) a peculiar necessity not to decline the call. The ability to be in future useful, whether in resisting mischief or in effecting good, in those crises of our public affairs which seem likely to happen, would probably be inseparable from a conformity with public prejudice in this particular.

∞

Comity at Valley Forge

GEORGE WASHINGTON described the plight of the continental army at Valley Forge in the following: "To see Men without Cloathes to cover their nakedness, without Blankets to lay on, without Shoes, by which their Marches might be traced by the blood from their feet, and almost as often without Provisions as with; Marching through frost and Snow, and at Christmas taking up their Winter Quarters within a day's March of the enemy, without a House or Hutt to cover them till they could be built and submitting to it without a murmur, is a mark of patience and obedience which in my opinion can scarce be parallel'd."

Despite the suffering and death, the brutal conditions of Valley Forge could not suppress a spirit of comity that arose among the officers and their men. Below is a narrative describing the fellow feeling that characterized the relationships among Washington's men.

Howe's troops lay through the cold weather in comfort in the city, while the privations in Washington's gloomy camp were the most severe that the Americans were called upon to endure. But during the terrible winter at Valley Forge, Washington's ragged host was welded into an army of which any general might be proud. He was proud of them. "Naked and starving as they are," he wrote, "we cannot sufficiently admire the incomparable patience and fidelity of the soldiers." The weather was intensely cold. There was not enough food or shelter or clothing. The barefooted soldiers left bloody footprints in the snow, and men actually died of starvation. Conspiracy tried to undermine faith in Washington, even to bribe to its side the gallant young Lafayette who had come to America in time to receive his wound at Brandywine. Lafayette was as loyal as his heart was big, and his presence was not the least among the small bits of comfort that Washington was able to extract from the situation.

Before he knew Lafayette, Washington's personal dealings with

Frenchmen had been limited to those he met in the French and Indian War, and his experience of officers who had served abroad to such unfortunate examples as Charles Lee and General Horatio Gates, a little man with a plausible tongue and a cuckoo's gift for slipping into places to which he had no right. Washington had been distinctly uncordial in thought toward the foreign officers who came over during the summer of 1777 to join his army and, fearing that Lafayette would put on airs, was annoyed at having to welcome him. But their meeting proved a case of friendship at first sight, which speedily deepened into real affection. Far from putting on airs the young Frenchman was willing and eager to bear his share of hardship. One of his small acts of kindness that only came to light half a century after it happened was done during this cold winter at Valley Forge. The last time Lafayette was in America an aged man came up to shake his hand. He was dressed in a faded Continental uniform, and across his shoulders he wore a piece of old and dingy blanket. He asked the general if he remembered a stormy night when he took the musket from the hands of a shivering sentry and sent him to his own tent with orders to bring back stockings and a blanket, promising to do duty for him till he returned. The soldier found that even a general at Valley Forge owned only one covering for his bed, but when he brought the desired articles, Lafayette bade him put on the stockings and, taking out his sword, fraternally divided the blanket in half.

The story not only portrays the want in that winter camp, but the spirit in which it was borne. John Marshall, who was in after years to become America's great chief justice, joked about his discomforts. Young Alexander Hamilton, whom Washington loved like a son, was there to ease his chief's burden where he could, giving long and laborious days to clerical duty, using that wonderful brain of his on a thousand perplexing problems, and seasoning the fare at the frugal mess-table with his brilliant talk. Scores of officers proved their mettle that winter; thousands of soldiers, their heroism. In December, Baron von Steuben brought his great knowledge and skill to the camp and gave officers and men alike what would now be called "intensive training." They came out from the trial welded in a spirit of comradeship and devotion that was destined to be the seed of the spirit of a great nation.

—From Helen Nicolay, *The Book of American Wars*

∞

Washington's Farewell to Military Officers

WASHINGTON, AS a leader, worked to preserve some distance from those he led. Thus, his conduct was often marked by formality. Yet, underneath this exterior was a warm heart that formed the firmest and deepest attachments to his fellow military officers. Below is a moving testament to Washington's capacity for friendship and love.

In the course of a few days Washington prepared to depart for Annapolis, where Congress was assembling, with the intention of asking leave to resign his command. A barge was in waiting about noon on the 4th of December [1783] at Whitehall Ferry to convey him across the Hudson to Paulus Hook. The principal officers of the army assembled at Fraunces's Tavern in the neighborhood of the ferry to take a final leave of him.

On entering the room and finding himself surrounded by his old companions in arms, who had shared with him so many scenes of hardship, difficulty and danger, his agitated feelings overcame his usual self-command. Filling a glass of wine and turning upon them his benignant but saddened countenance, "With a heart full of love and gratitude," said he, "I now take leave of you, most devoutly wishing that your latter days may be as prosperous and happy as your former ones have been glorious and honorable."

Having drunk this farewell benediction, he added with emotion, "I cannot come to each of you to take my leave, but shall be obliged if each of you will come and take me by the hand."

General Knox, who was nearest, was the first to advance. Washington, affected even to tears, grasped his hand and gave him a brother's embrace. In the same affectionate manner he took leave severally of the rest. Not a word was spoken. The deep feeling and manly tenderness of these veterans in the parting moment could find no utterance in words. Silent and solemn they followed their loved commander as he left the room, passed through a corps of light infantry and proceeded on foot to Whitehall Ferry. Having entered the barge, he turned to them, took off his hat and waved a silent adieu. They replied in the same manner, and having watched the barge until the intervening point of the battery shut it from sight, returned, still solemn and silent, to the place where they had assembled.

—From Washington Irving's *Life of Washington*

✺

Falling Out Between George Washington
and Alexander Hamilton

AS COMMANDER-IN-CHIEF of the American army, Washington had to maintain a strict discipline and some distance between himself and his men. Hamilton was one of his favorite aides-de-camp—he treated him almost as if he were his own son. Here Hamilton, a passionate and proud young man, reports the incident that led to their falling out.

In matters of official business Washington was a hard taskmaster, expecting his aides to give their time day in and day out, with the same unwearied persistence that he displayed himself. But he had imagination enough most of the time to realize that it might be harder for them than for himself. Sometimes the strain was too great, even for his strong self-control. His parting with his beloved aide-de-camp, Alexander Hamilton, was due, according to Hamilton, to a sudden flare-up of impatience on the part of Washington and an answering bit of temper on his own. He wrote his father-in-law:

> I am no longer a member of the General's family. Two days ago the General and I passed each other on the stairs; he told me he wanted to speak to me—I answered that I would wait upon him immediately. I went below and delivered Mr. Tilghman a letter to be sent to the commissary. . . . Returning to the General I was stopped on the way by the Marquis de Lafayette, and we conversed together about a minute on a matter of business. He can testify how impatient I was to get back; and that I left him in a manner which, but for our intimacy, would have been more than abrupt. Instead of finding the General, as is usual, in his room, I met him at the head of the stairs, accosting me in an angry tone, "Colonel Hamilton," he said, "you have kept me waiting at the head of the stairs these ten minutes; —I must tell you, sir, you treat me with disrespect." I replied without petulancy, but with decision, "I am not conscious of it, sir, but since you have thought it necessary to tell me so, we part." "Very well, sir," he said, "if it be your choice," or something to that effect, and we separated. I sincerely believe my absence which gave so much umbrage, did not last two minutes. In less than an hour after Tilghman came to me in the General's name, assuring me of his great confidence in my abilities, integrity,

usefulness, &c.; and of his desire, in a candid conversation to heal the difference which could not have happened but for a moment of passion.

A handsome apology certainly, considering their relative ages and rank; but the younger man, very much on his dignity, refused the proffered interview, though intimating his willingness to continue his duties until a successor could be found, adding with boyish hauteur that "in the meantime it depended upon him to let our behavior to each other be the same as if nothing had happened." It was an answer that, in the circumstances, must have called for some self-control on the part of the general. Very likely both Washington and Hamilton were sorry when the actual time of parting came; but the elder could scarcely be expected to make further advances, or the young ask to be retained.

—From Helen Nicolay, *The Book of American Wars*

∞

Marquis de Lafayette and George Washington Correspondence, 1779–1784

LAFAYETTE CAME to America from France at the age of nineteen to volunteer in the struggling continental army. Without ever seeing any pictures of Washington, Lafayette was able to identify him right away at their first encounter at a dinner in Philadelphia. Lafayette wrote: "The majesty of his countenance and his figure made it impossible not to recognize him." Lafayette, like many others, recognized Washington's greatness. But Washington also admired Lafayette. He had heard about Lafayette's zeal to leave the luxuries of his aristocratic France, against the wishes of his family, for the American cause.

Washington invited Lafayette to become a member of his military "family." Lafayette had lost his father in battle when he was just two years old. Washington became like a father to Lafayette; Lafayette a loyal son to the childless Washington.

Lafayette endured the hardships of Valley Forge and stood loyally by Washington. During this time, a cabal of army officers and some congressmen plotted to replace Washington as commander-in-chief. Unbeknownst to Lafayette, they were attempting to pull the young and ambitious Frenchman into their schemes by offering him command of a northern expedition into Canada. During a dinner with this group of conspirators, toast after toast was given to everyone except Washington. Lafayette grew increasingly outraged, and finally rose to his feet and proposed a toast to George Washington, their noble commander-in-chief. By his actions, he made it clear to everyone that he wanted no part in their schemes.

Lafayette was also there to comfort Washington when he first learned of Benedict Arnold's betrayal. Lafayette named one of his sons George Washington (and a daughter Virginia). Lafayette, as it turns out, was not only one of Washington's best friends but America's as well.

Below is some of their correspondence. It is readily apparent that Lafayette brings out the most affectionate side of George Washington.

G EORGE W ASHINGTON TO L AFAYETTE , S EPTEMBER 30, 1779

Your forward zeal in the cause of liberty; Your singular attachment to this infant World; Your ardent and persevering efforts, not only in America but since your return to France to serve the United States; Your polite attention to Americans, and your strict and uniform friendship for *me,* has ripened the first impressions of esteem and attachment which I imbibed for you into such perfect love and gratitude that neither time nor absence can impair which will warrant my assuring you, that whether in the character of an Officer at the head of a Corps of gallant French (if circumstances should require this) whether as a Major Genl. commanding a division of the American Army; Or whether, after our Swords and Spears have given place to the plough share and pruning hook, I see you as a private Gentleman, a friend and Companion, I shall welcome you in all the warmth of friendship to Columbia's shore; and in the latter case, to my rural Cottage, where homely fare and a cordial reception shall be substituted for delicacies and costly living. this from past experience I know *you* can submit to; and if the lovely partner of your happiness will consent to participate with *us* in such rural entertainment and amusemts. I can undertake in behalf of Mrs. Washington that she will do everything in her power to make Virginia agreeable to the Marchioness. My inclination and endeavours to do this cannot be doubted when I assure you that I love everybody that is dear to you.

LAFAYETTE TO WASHINGTON, JUNE 29, 1782

Adieu, my dear General, I hope you will approuve my conduct and in every thing I do I first consider what your opinion would be had I an opportunity to consult it. I anticipate the happiness to be again with you, my dear General, and I hope I need not assuring you that nothing can exceed the sentiments of respect and tenderness I have the honor to be with

Your most h^{ble} serv and for
ever your most devoted affectionate
friend
Lafayette

WASHINGTON TO LAFAYETTE,
DECEMBER 8, 1784

In the moment of our separation upon the road as I travelled, and every hour since, I felt all that love, respect and attachment for you, with which length of years, close connexion and your merits have inspired me. I often asked myself, as our carriages distended, whether that was the last sight, I ever should have of you? And tho' I wished to say no, my fears answered yes. I called to mind the days of my youth, and found they had long since fled to return no more; that I was now descending the hill, I had been 52 years climbing, and that tho' I was blessed with a good constitution, I was of a short lived family, and might soon expect to be entombed in the dreary mansions of my father's. These things darkened the shades and gave a gloom to the picture, consequently to my prospects of seeing you again: but I will not repine, I have had my day.

It is unnecessary, I persuade myself to repeat to you my Dr. Marqs. the sincerity of my regards and friendship, nor have I words which could express my affection for you, were I to attempt it.

LAFAYETTE TO WASHINGTON

On board the Nimph Newyork Harbour
December the 21st 1784

My dear General
I have received your affectionate letter of the 8th inst, and from the known sentiments of my heart to you, you will easely guess what my feelings have been in perusing the tender expressions of your friendship

—No, my beloved General, our late parting was not by any means a last interwiew. My whole soul revolts at the idea—and could I harbour it an instant, indeed my dear General, it would make miserable. I well see you never will go to France—The unexpressible pleasure of embracing you in my own house, of well coming you in a family where your name is adored, I do not much expect to experience—But to you, I shall return, and in the walls of Mount Vernon we shall yet often speack of old times. My firm plan is to visit now and then my friends on this side of the Atlantick, and the most beloved of all friends I ever had, or ever will have any where, is too strong an inducement for me to return to him, not to think that, when ever it is possible, I will renew my so pleasing visits to Mount Vernon. . . .

Adieu, adieu, my dear General, it is with unexpressible pain that I feel I am going to be severed from you by the Atlantick—every thing that admiration, respect, gratitude, friendship, and filial love can inspire, is combined in my affectionate heart to devote me most tenderly to you— In your friendship I find a delight which words cannot express—Adieu, my dear General, it is not without emotion that I write this word—Altho' I know I shall soon visit you again—Be attentive to your health—Let me hear from you every month—Adieu, adieu.

L.f.

∞

Thomas Jefferson to Governor John Page, June 25, 1804

JEFFERSON MET John Page when they were both students at William and Mary College. They shared similar academic interests, though Page admitted that he didn't study as hard as Jefferson (who was said to have studied fifteen hours a day). It was to Page that Jefferson freely confided his early romantic woes. They stayed in close touch until Page's death in 1808.

In the following letter, Jefferson responds to a letter Page had written consoling Jefferson on the recent loss of his daughter, Mary. Jefferson tells Page that he looks forward to the day when he will be reunited with all his lost friends. But in the meantime, Jefferson intended to enjoy all the friends he had left, especially those from his earliest years.

JEFFERSON TO GOVERNOR JOHN PAGE, JUNE 25, 1804

When you and I look back on the country over which we have passed, what a field of slaughter does it exhibit! Where are all the friends who entered it with us, under all the inspiring energies of health and hope? As if pursued by the havoc of war, they are strewed by the way, some earlier, some later, and scarce a few stragglers remain to count the numbers fallen, and to mark yet, by their own fall, the last footsteps of their party. Is it a desirable thing to bear up through the heat of the action, to witness the death of all our companions, and merely be the last victim? I doubt it. We have, however, the traveller's consolation. Every step shortens the distance we have to go; the end of our journey is in sight, the bed wherein we are to rest, and to rise in the midst of the friends we have lost. "We sorrow not then as others who have no hope;" but look forward to the day which "joins us to the great majority." But whatever is to be our destiny, wisdom, as well as duty, dictates that we should acquiesce in the will of Him whose it is to give and take away, and be contented in the enjoyment of those who are still permitted to be with us. Of those connected by blood, the number does not depend on us. But friends we have, if we have merited them. Those of our earliest years stand nearest in our affections. But in this too, you and I have been unlucky. Of our college friends (and they are the dearest) how few have stood with us in the great political questions which have agitated our country; and these were of a nature to justify agitation. I did not believe the Lilliputian fetters of that day strong enough to have bound so many. Will not Mrs. Page, yourself and family, think it prudent to seek a healthier region for the months of August and September? And may we not flatter ourselves that you will cast your eye on Monticello? We have not many summers to live. While fortune places us then within striking distance, let us avail ourselves of it, to meet and talk over the tales of other times.

Marquis de Lafayette and Thomas Jefferson in 1824

AT THE invitation of Congress, Lafayette returned to America for a tour in 1824. The reception for America's adopted son—the "knight of liberty"—was overwhelming. Jefferson told Lafayette that he was afraid

Lafayette would "be killed with kindness." Throngs of Americans turned out in all towns and cities across the nation to welcome Lafayette. He spent some time alone at the tomb of Washington and tried to visit many surviving heroes of the Revolutionary War years. That included Jefferson, whom Lafayette had known both in America and in France (Jefferson had assisted Lafayette in writing France's "Declaration of the Rights of Man"). Of Lafayette's contribution to the American founding, Jefferson said: "In truth, I only held the nail; he drove it. Honor him then as your benefactor in peace as well as in war." They were reunited at Monticello: Jefferson was eighty-one years old and Lafayette was sixty-six. Thomas Jefferson Randolph, Jefferson's grandson, recounts the emotional reunion of these aging heroes of the Revolutionary War.

The lawn on the eastern side of the house at Monticello contains not quite an acre. On this spot was the meeting of Jefferson and Lafayette, on the latter's visit to the United States. The barouche containing Lafayette stopped at the edge of this lawn. His escort—one hundred and twenty mounted men—formed on one side in a semicircle extending from the carriage to the house. A crowd of about two hundred men, who were drawn together by curiosity to witness the meeting of these two venerable men, formed themselves in a semicircle on the opposite side. As Lafayette descended from the carriage, Jefferson descended the steps of the portico. The scene which followed was touching. Jefferson was feeble and tottering with age—Lafayette permanently lamed and broken in health by his long confinement in the dungeon of Olmutz. As they approached each other, their uncertain gait quickened itself into a shuffling run, and exclaiming, "Ah, Jefferson!" "Ah, Lafayette," they burst into tears as they fell into each other's arms. Among the four hundred men witnessing the scene there was not a dry eye—no sound save an occasional suppressed sob. The two old men entered the house as the crowd dispersed in profound silence.

∞

Thomas Jefferson to James Madison, February 20, 1784

JEFFERSON AND Madison met in 1776 as fellow delegates to the Virginia Assembly. Their friendship was to continue "uninterrupted" for fifty years.

It is impossible to understand either of them without understanding both of them. They often collaborated in political projects, and on the few occasions where disagreement made such cooperation impossible, it did not harm their friendship or their intellectual kinship. Their friendship was an education for both of them. It also fostered and secured some of the most important political developments and institutions of our nation, from the Virginia statute for religious liberty to the Bill of Rights.

When Jefferson went to France, he told Madison that "[i]n the purchase of books, pamphlets, etc. old and curious, or new and useful, I shall ever keep you in my eye." Madison asked Jefferson to send "whatever may throw light on the general constitution and *droit public* of the several confederacies which have existed." Jefferson sent hundreds of books on political philosophy, law, government, and history to Madison. These books helped Madison to become the most widely read and most capable member of the Constitutional Convention. Madison never set foot out of America, but he didn't have to—Jefferson gave him the best Europe had to offer through his generous gift boxes of books.

While Jefferson was out of the country, Madison kept him abreast of political developments, and sent him American-made goods—fruits, nuts, produce, and grafts of trees—so that Jefferson could proudly showcase to the Europeans the fecundity of American soil. Madison and Jefferson tested many profound political ideas and innovations on each other, such as ruminations about the possibility of an extended republic, the advisability of revolution, and the question of whether the Constitution should contain a Bill of Rights (Jefferson's enthusiasm for the latter no doubt swayed Madison to endorse and write them).

Jefferson also reached out to James Monroe and William Short. In this letter, Jefferson was attempting to lure these three young men to set up their homes near his Monticello. For as Jefferson put it in another letter, "Agreeable society is the first essential in constituting the happiness and of course the value of our existence."

There is something wondrous in Jefferson's ideal of friendship as a rational society in which the minds of each friend would be refined and sharpened by the others. No one can ascend intellectual or moral virtue alone—it must be done with the help of like-minded friends. One can imagine Albermarle County, Virginia, becoming the Athens of America under Jefferson's plan. Madison never relocated to Jefferson's neighborhood, but he always remained Jefferson's most constant intellectual partner and friend.

I hope you have found access to my library. I beg you to make free use of it. Key, the steward is living there now and of course will be always in the way. Monroe is buying land almost adjoining me. Short will do the same. What would I not give you could fall into the circle. With such a society I could once more venture home and lay myself up for the residue of life, quitting all it's contentions which grow daily more and more insupportable. Think of it. To render it practicable only requires you to think it so. Life is of no value but as it brings us gratifications. Among the most valuable of these is rational society. It informs the mind, sweetens the temper, chears our spirits, and promotes health. There is a little farm of 140 as. adjoining me, and within two miles, all of good land, tho' old, with a small indifferent house on it, the whole worth not more than £250. Such a one might be a farm of experiment and support a little table and houshold. It is on the road to Orange and so much nearer than I am. It is convenient enough for supplementary supplies from thence. Once more think of it, and Adieu.

∞

Thomas Jefferson to James Madison, February 17, 1826
James Madison to Thomas Jefferson, February 24, 1826
James Madison to N. P. Trist, July 6, 1826

JEFFERSON AND Madison once had a philosophic disagreement about the former's assertion that the "earth belongs to the living." Madison gently corrected his friend and argued to the contrary, that there was a "descent of obligations" transferred to each generation. Consistent with his view of obligations, Madison conscientiously labored to keep alive this nation's sense of debt to Jefferson once he died.

Nearing death, Jefferson worried about the future state of his beloved University of Virginia and asked Madison to take care of both it and him. Upon Jefferson's death, Madison became the rector of the University of Virginia. He donated money to the university, gave books to the library, and devoted himself to making Jefferson's dream of a "general diffusion of knowledge" a reality. Madison also responded to many requests from biographers and historians about Jefferson's political views and legacy. He even corrected one biographer's unflattering description of Jefferson's nose (Madison told him that Jefferson's nose was "rather under, certainly not above, common size.")

Following is a moving account of the end of a beautiful friendship. The third letter of this series is one Madison wrote lamenting the death of his friend.

JEFFERSON TO MADISON

But why afflict you with these details? Indeed, I cannot tell, unless pains are lessened by communication with a friend. The friendship which has subsisted between us, now half a century, and the harmony of our political principles and pursuits, have been sources of constant happiness to me through that long period. And if I remove beyond the reach of attentions to the University, or beyond the bourne of life itself, as I soon must, it is a comfort to leave that institution under your care, and an assurance that it will not be wanting. It has also been a great solace to me, to believe that you are engaged in vindicating to posterity the course we have pursued for preserving to them, in all their purity, the blessings of self-government, which we had assisted too in acquiring for them. If ever the earth has beheld a system of administration conducted with a single and steadfast eye to the general interest and happiness of those committed to it, one which, protected by truth, can never know reproach, it is that to which our lives have been devoted. To myself you have been a pillar of support through life. Take care of me when dead, and be assured that I shall leave with you my last affections.

MADISON TO JEFFERSON

You cannot look back to the long period of our private friendship and political harmony, with more affecting recollections than I do. If

they are a source of pleasure to you, what ought they not to be to me? We cannot be deprived of the happy consciousness of the pure devotion to the public good with which we discharged the trusts committed to us. And I indulge a confidence that sufficient evidence will find its way to another generation, to ensure, after we are gone, whatever of justice may be withheld whilst we are here. The political horizon is already yielding in your case at least, the surest auguries of it. Wishing and hoping that you may yet live to increase the debt which our Country owes you, and to witness the increasing gratitude, which alone can pay it, I offer you the fullest return of affectionate assurances.

MADISON TO N.P. TRIST ON THE DEATH OF JEFFERSON

Dear Sir,

I have just received yours of the 4th. A few lines from Dr. Dunglison had prepared me for such a communication; and I never doubted that the last scene of *our* illustrious friend would be worthy of the life which it closed. Long as this has been spared to his Country and to those who loved him, a few years more were to have been desired for the sake of both. But we are more than consoled for the loss by the gain to him; and by the assurance that he lives and will live in the memory and gratitude of the wise and good as a luminary of science, as a votary of liberty, as a model of patriotism, and as a benefactor of human kind. In these characters I have known him, and not less in the virtues and charms of social life, for a period of fifty years, during which there has not been an interruption or diminution of mutual confidence and cordial friendship for a single moment, in a single instance. What I feel, therefore, now, need not, I should say, cannot, be expressed. If there be any possible way in which I can *usefully* give evidence of it, do not fail to afford me an opportunity. I indulge a hope that the unforeseen event will not be permitted to impair *any* of the beneficial measures which were in progress or in project. It cannot be unknown that the anxieties of the deceased were for others, not for himself.

∞

Abigail Adams to Thomas Jefferson, June 6, 1785, and Thomas Jefferson to Abigail Adams, September 25, 1785

THE ORIGINAL friendship between Thomas Jefferson and John and Abigail Adams deepened when they were in Paris. Abigail described Jefferson as "one of the choice ones of the earth." When John and Abigail Adams left Paris for London, Jefferson told John that "[t]he departure of your family has left me in the dumps. My afternoons hang heavily on me."

The following letter of Abigail Adams to Jefferson marks the beginning of a rich correspondence between the two. They wrote often to each other, filling their letters with a wide range of topics that included plenty of social and political gossip. They often made shopping requests for each other—for example, at Jefferson's request, Abigail sent a tablecloth with twenty napkins to Jefferson; Jefferson sent the shoes and lace material to Abigail that she had requested. Most important, when Jefferson sent for his seven-year-old daughter, Mary, also known as Polly, to join him in Paris, he first sent her to Abigail in London, where Abigail and John became quite attached to the girl.

Below is just one example of the letters they wrote to each other. Abigail initiated their correspondence, which Jefferson had "so much desired." Jefferson's comparison of Abigail to Venus is highly flattering —Venus was the Roman goddess of courtship.

A BIGAIL A DAMS TO J EFFERSON

Dear Sir

Mr. Adams has already written you that we arrived in London upon the 27 of May. We journey'd slowly and sometimes silently. I think I have somewhere met with the observation that nobody ever leaves paris but with a degree of tristeness. I own I was loth to leave my garden because I did not expect to find its place supplied. I was still more loth on account of the increasing pleasure, and intimacy which a longer acquaintance with a respected Friend promised, to leave behind me the only person with whom my Companion could associate with perfect freedom, and unreserve: and whose place he had no reason to expect supplied in the Land to which he is destinied.

I have to apologize for thus freely scribling to you. I will not deny that there may be a little vanity in the hope of being honourd with a line from you. Having heard you upon some occasions express a desire to hear from your Friends, even the Minutia respecting their Situation, I have ventured to class myself in that number and to subscribe myself, Sir, your Friend and Humble Servant,

A. ADAMS

J EFFERSON TO A BIGAIL A DAMS

Dear Madam,

Mr. Short's return the night before last availed me of your favour of Aug. 12. I immediately ordered the shoes you desired which will be ready tomorrow. I am not certain whether this will be in time for the departure of Mr. Barclay or of Colo. Franks, for it is not yet decided which of them goes to London. I have also procured for you three plateaux de dessert with a silvered ballustrade round them, and four figures of Biscuit. The former cost 192^{ft}, the latter 12^{ft} each, making together 240 livres or 10. Louis. The merchant undertakes to send them by the way of Rouen through the hands of Mr. Garvey and to have them delivered in London. There will be some additional expences of packing, transportation and duties here. Those in England I imagine you can save. When I know the amount I will inform you of it, but there will be no occasion to remit it here. With respect to the figures I could only find three of those you named, matched in size. These were Minerva, Diana, and Apollo. I was obliged to add a fourth, unguided by your choice. They offered me a fine Venus; but I thought it out of taste to have two at table at the same time. Paris and Helen were presented. I conceived it would be cruel to remove them from their peculiar shrine. When they shall pass the Atlantic, it will be to sing a requiem over our freedom and happiness. At length a fine Mars was offered, calm, bold, his faulchion not drawn, but ready to be drawn. This will do, thinks I, for the table of the American Minister in London, where those whom it may concern may look and learn that though Wisdom is our guide, and the Song and Chase our supreme delight, yet we offer adoration to that tutelar god also who rocked the cradle of our birth, who has accepted our infant offerings, and has shewn himself the patron of our rights and avenger of our wrongs. The groupe then was closed, and your party formed. Envy and malice will never be quiet. I hear it already whispered to you that in admitting Minerva to your table I have departed from the principle which made me reject Venus: in plain English that I have paid a just respect to the daughter but failed to the mother. No Madam, my respect to both is sincere. Wisdom, I know, is social. She seeks her fellows. But Beauty is jealous, and illy bears the presence of a rival—but, Allons, let us turn over another leaf, and begin the next chapter. I receive by Mr. Short a budget of London papers. They teem with every horror of which human nature is capable. Assassinations, suicides, thefts, robberies, and, what is worse than assassination, theft, suicide or robbery, the blackest slanders! Indeed the man must be of rock, who can stand all this; to Mr. Adams it will be but one victory the more. It would have illy suited me. I do not love difficulties. I am fond of quiet, willing to do my duty, but irritable by slander and apt to be forced by it to abandon my post. These are weaknesses from which reason and your counsels will preserve Mr. Adams. I fancy it must be the quantity of animal food eaten by the English which renders their character insusceptible of civilisation. I suspect it is in their kitchens and not in their churches that their reformation must be worked, and that Missionaries of that description from hence would avail more than those who should endeavor to tame them by precepts of religion or philosophy. But what do the foolish printers of America mean by retailing all this stuff in our papers? As if it was not enough to be slandered by one's enemies without circulating the slanders among his friends also.

To shew you how willingly I shall ever receive and execute your commissions, I venture to impose one on you. From what I recollect of the diaper and damask we used to import from England I think they were better and cheaper than here. You are well acquainted with those of both countries. If you are of the same opinion I would trouble you to send me two sets of table cloths and napkins for 20 covers each, by Colo. Franks or Mr. Barclay who will bring them to me. But if you think they can be better got here I would rather avoid the trouble this commission will give. I inclose you a specimen of what is offered me at 100. livres for the table cloth and 12 napkins. I suppose that, of the same quality, a table cloth 2. aunes wide and 4. aunes long, and 20 napkins of 1. aune each, would cost 7. guineas.—I shall certainly charge the publick my house rent and court taxes. I shall do more. I shall charge my outfit. Without this I can never get out of debt. I think it will be allowed. Congress is too reasonable to expect, where no imprudent expences are incurred, none but those which are required by a decent respect to the mantle with which they cover the public servants, that such expenses should be left as a burthen on our private fortunes. But when writing to you, I fancy myself at Auteuil, and chatter on till the last page of my paper awakes me from my reverie, and tells me it is time to assure you of the sincere respect and esteem with which I have the honour to be Dear Madam your most obedient and most humble servt.,

TH: JEFFERSON

P.S. The cask of wine at Auteuil, I take chearfully. I suppose the seller will apply to me for the price. Otherwise, as I do not know who he is, I shll not be able to find him out.

Abigail Adams to Thomas Jefferson, May 20, 1804, and Thomas Jefferson to Abigail Adams, June 13, 1804

ABIGAIL ADAMS could never quite forgive Thomas Jefferson in the same way that her husband eventually did. She was angry with him for what he and his political allies had done to discredit the political integrity of her husband, and strongly disagreed with the direction in which Jefferson's Republican party was taking the country. She had also been offended that Jefferson removed her son, John Quincy, from a government position. (Jefferson explained that he had known nothing about this—and Abigail said she accepted him at his word.)

Still, Abigail could not resist sending a condolence note to the man she had formerly considered her friend on the death of his daughter, Polly, the same daughter that Abigail and John had taken care of many years ago in England. Abigail had loved her dearly. Thomas Jefferson took Abigail's gesture as an opportunity to renew their correspondence and their friendship. Several letters followed, but Abigail ended their correspondence without fully reconciling with Jefferson.

ABIGAIL ADAMS TO JEFFERSON

Sir

Had you been no other than the private inhabitant of Monticello, I should e'er this time have addrest you, with that sympathy, which a recent event has awakened in my Bosom. But reasons of various kinds withheld my pen, untill the powerfull feelings of my heart, have burst through the restraint, and called upon me to shed the tear of sorrow over the departed remains, of your beloved and deserving daughter, an event which I most sincerely mourn.

The attachment which I formed for her, when you committed her to my care: upon her arrival in a foreign Land: has remained with me to this hour, and the recent account of her death, which I read in a late paper, brought fresh to my remembrance the strong sensibility she discovered, tho but a child of nine years of age at having been seperated from her Friends, and country, and brought, as she expressed it, "to a strange land amongst strangers." The tender scene of her seperation from me, rose to my recollection, when she clung around my neck and wet my Bosom with her tears, saying, "O! now I have learnt to Love you, why will they tear me from you."

It has been some time since that I conceived of any event in this Life, which could call forth, feelings of mutual sympathy. But I know how closely entwined around a parents heart, are those chords which bind the filial to the parental Bosom, and when snaped assunder, how agonizing the pangs of seperation.

I have tasted the bitter cup, and bow with reverence, and humility before the great dispenser of it, without whose permission, and over ruling providence, not a sparrow falls to the ground. That you may derive comfort and consolation in this day of your sorrow and affliction, from that only source calculated to heal the wounded heart—a firm belief in the Being: perfections and attributes of God, is the sincere and ardent wish of her, who once took pleasure in subscribing Herself your Friend

Abigail Adams

JEFFERSON TO ABIGAIL ADAMS

Dear Madam

The affectionate sentiments which you have had the goodness to express in your letter of May 20. towards my dear departed daughter, have awakened in me sensibilities natural to the occasion, and recalled your kindnesses to her which I shall ever remember with gratitude and friendship. I can assure you with truth they had made an indelible impression on her mind, and that, to the last, on our meetings after long separations, whether I had heard lately of you, and how you did, were among the earliest of her enquiries. In giving you this assurance I perform a sacred duty for her, and at the same time am thankful for the occasion furnished me of expressing my regret that circumstances should have arisen which have seemed to draw a line of separation between us. The friendship with which you honoured me has ever been valued, and fully reciprocated; and altho' events have been passing which might be trying to some minds, I never believed yours to be of that kind, nor felt that my own was. Neither my estimate of your character, nor the esteem founded in that, have ever been lessened for a single moment, although doubts whether it would be acceptable may have forbidden manifestations of it. Mr. Adams's friendship and mine began at an earlier date. It accompanied us thro' long and important scenes. The different conclusions we had drawn from our political reading and reflections were not permitted to lessen mutual esteem, each party being conscious they were the result of an honest conviction in the other. Like differences of opinion existing among our fellow citizens attached them to the one or the other of us, and produced a rivalship in their minds which did not exist in ours. We never stood in one another's way: for if either had been withdrawn at any time, his favorers would not have gone over to the other, but would have sought for some one of homogeneous opinions. This consideration was sufficient to keep down all jealousy between us, and to guard our friendship from any disturbance by sentiments of rivalship: and I can say with truth that one act of Mr. Adams's life, and one only, ever gave me a moment's personal displeasure. I did consider his last appointments to office as personally unkind. They were from among my most ardent political enemies, from whom no faithful cooperation could ever be expected and laid me under the embarrasment of acting thro' men whose views were to defeat mine; or to encounter the odium of putting others in their places. It seemed but common justice to leave a successor free to act by instruments of his own choice. If my respect for him did not permit me to ascribe the whole blame to the influence of others, it left something for friendship to forgive, and after brooding over it for some little time, and not always resisting the expression of it, I forgave it cordially, and returned to the same state of esteem and respect for him which had so long subsisted. Having come into life a little later than Mr. Adams, his career has preceded mine, as mine is followed by some other, and it will probably be closed at the same distance after him which time originally placed between us. I maintain for him, and shall carry into private life an uniform and high measure of respect and good will, and for yourself a sincere attachment. I have thus, my dear Madam, opened myself to you without reserve, which I have long wished an opportunity of doing; and, without knowing how it will be recieved, I feel relief from being unbosomed. And I have now only to entreat your forgiveness for this transition from a subject of domestic affliction to one which seems of a different aspect. But tho connected with political events, it has been viewed by me most strongly in it's unfortunate bearings on my private friendships. The injury these have sustained has been a heavy price for what has never given me equal pleasure. That you may both be favored with health, tranquility and long life, is the prayer of one who tenders you the assurances of his highest consideration and esteem.

TH: JEFFERSON

∽

Thomas Jefferson to John Adams, November 13, 1818

T HOMAS J EFFERSON wrote this beautiful letter of condolence to John Adams upon Abigail Adams's death.

The public papers, my dear friend, announce the fatal event of which your letter of Oct. 20. had given me ominous foreboding. Tried myself, in the school of affliction, by the loss of every form of connection which can rive the human heart, I know well, and feel what you have lost, what you have suffered, are suffering, and have yet to endure. The same trials have taught me that, for ills so immeasurable, time and silence are the only medecines. I will not therefore, by useless condolances, open afresh the sluices of your grief nor, altho' mingling sincerely my tears with yours, will I say a word more, where words are vain, but that it is of some comfort to us both that the term is not very distant at which we are to deposit, in the same cerement, our sorrows and suffering bodies, and to ascend in essence to an ecstatic meeting with the friends we have loved and lost and whom we shall still love and never lose again. God bless you and support you under your heavy affliction.

TH: JEFFERSON

*John Adams–Thomas Jefferson Reconciliation 1809–1812 **

ADAMS and Jefferson became friends in 1775, when they were both serving in the Continental Congress. They made an unlikely pair. Adams was a short and paunchy Northerner; Jefferson was a tall and lean Southerner. Adams, as he himself put it, was "obnoxious, suspected, and unpopular"; Jefferson was "very much otherwise." But they owned in common a fierce devotion to the cause of independence. Their dedication to this cause cemented a deep friendship that was to last for over fifty years.

However, political differences almost destroyed that friendship. Jefferson thought that Adams was betraying the spirit of the revolution by embracing monarchical sentiments. Jefferson wrote a letter to the printer of the American edition of Thomas Paine's *The Rights of Man* in which he indirectly attacked John Adams by voicing concern over the "political heresies which had of late sprung up among us." Much to Jefferson's horror, the letter was published as a preface to the book and his dispute with his friend became a public event. Although Jefferson later apologized to Adams, Adams viewed the letter as an "open personal attack" and was furious. He thought that Jefferson's radical republicanism and unqualified support for the French Revolution would itself subvert the experiment in self-government. Thus, shortly before leaving office, President Adams made "midnight appointments" of judges before Jefferson's inauguration, putting on the bench Federalist judges who would oppose the new president's initiatives. This time it was Jefferson who was infuriated.

---

* Details of the Adams–Jefferson reconciliation taken from L.H. Butterfield, "The Dream of Benjamin Rush: The Reconciliation of John Adams and Thomas Jefferson," *Yale Review,* vol. 40, 1950–1951.

They didn't speak to each other or exchange any correspondence for eleven years. Benjamin Rush, a fellow signer of the Declaration of Independence and mutual friend of both, wanted these two men to reconcile with each other. He believed that posterity would be made better off from a renewed correspondence between these eminent founders. But how could Rush get these two proud old men, each feeling hurt by the other, back together? Who would make the first move?

The following letters provide an overview of how Rush brought these two old friends back together. It is a very human story. I'm sure this little drama is replayed many times over between friends who let disagreements fester until they think it is too late to save their friendship. But the reconciliation between Jefferson and Adams shows what a little magnanimity, what a little swallowing of pride (along with the help of a third party) can do to save a friendship.

∞

Benjamin Rush to John Adams, October 16, 1809

RUSH INITIATED the reunion by sharing with Adams a prophetic dream he claimed he had in which Adams and Jefferson were reunited. It is rather amazing that Rush's predictions came so close to being true: He predicted their reunion; he predicted that the world would be made better off by their observations in a renewed correspondence; and he predicted that these two men would fall into their graves at nearly the same time. That was true.

"What book is that in your hands?" said I to my son Richard a few nights ago in a DREAM. "It is the history of the United States," said he. "Shall I read a page of it to you?" "No, no," said I. "I believe in the truth of no history but in that which is contained in the Old and New Testaments." "But, sir," said my son, "this page relates to your friend Mr. Adams." "Let me see it then," said I. I read it with great pleasure and herewith send you a copy of it.

"1809"

Among the most extraordinary events of this year was the renewal of the friendship and intercourse between Mr. John Adams and Mr. Jefferson, the two ex-Presidents of the United States. They met for the first time in the Congress of 1775. Their principles of liberty, their ardent attachment to their country, and their views of the importance and probable issue of the struggle with Great Britain in which they were engaged being exactly the same, they were strongly attracted to each other and became personal as well as political friends. They met in England during the war while each of them held commissions of honor and trust at two of the first courts of Europe, and spent many happy hours together in reviewing the difficulties and success of their respective negotiations. A difference of opinion upon the objects and issue of the French Revolution separated them during the years in which that great event interested and divided the American people. The predominance of the party which favored the French cause threw Mr. Adams out of the Chair of the United States in the year 1800 and placed Mr. Jefferson there in his stead. The former retired with resignation and dignity to his seat at Quincy, where he spent the evening of his life in literary and philosophical pursuits surrounded by an amiable family and a few old and affectionate friends. The latter resigned the Chair of the United States in the year 1808, sick of the cares and disgusted with the intrigues of public life, and retired to his seat at Monticello in Virginia, where he spent the remainder of his days in the cultivation of a large farm agreeably to the new system of husbandry. In the month of November 1809, Mr. Adams addressed a short letter to his friend Mr. Jefferson in which he congratulated him upon his escape to the shades of retirement and domestic happiness, and concluded it with assurances of his regard and good wishes for his welfare. This letter did great honor to Mr. Adams. It discovered a magnanimity known only to great minds. Mr. Jefferson replied to this letter and reciprocated expressions of regard and esteem. These letters were followed by a correspondence of several years, in which they mutually reviewed the scenes of business in which they had been engaged, and candidly acknowledged to each other all the errors of opinion and conduct into which they had fallen during the time they filled the same station in the service of their country. Many precious aphorisms, the result of observation, experience, and profound reflection, it is said, are contained in these letters. It is to be hoped the world will be favored with a sight of them when they can neither injure nor displease any persons or families whose ancestors' follies or crimes were mentioned in them. These gentlemen sunk into the grave nearly at the same time, full of years and rich in the gratitude and praises of their country (for they outlived the heterogeneous parties that were opposed to them), and to their numerous merits and honors posterity has added that they were rival friends.

∽

John Adams to Benjamin Rush, October 25, 1809

ADAMS SCOFFED at Rush's dream, claiming that there was no ill-will between himself and Jefferson. But this is Adams's pride speaking, trying to convince himself that nothing is amiss with his old friend.

A dream again! I wish you would dream all day and all night, for one of your dreams puts me in spirits for a month. I have no other objection to your dream but that it is not history. It may be prophecy. There has never been the smallest interruption of the personal friendship between me and Mr. Jefferson that I know of. You should remember that Jefferson was but a boy to me. I was at least ten years older than him in age and more than twenty years older than him in politics. I am bold to say that I was his preceptor in politics and taught him everything that has been good and solid in his whole political conduct. I served with him on many committees in Congress, in which we established some of the most important regulations of the army &c., &c., &c.

∽

Benjamin Rush to Thomas Jefferson, January 2, 1811, and Rush to Jefferson, February 1, 1811

A FEW years passed before Rush began working on Jefferson. He sent the following letter to Jefferson and appealed to Jefferson's patriotism and fond memories of his old friend from 1776.

Jefferson thanked Rush for the solicitude he showed in wanting to reunite him with Adams, but expressed some doubts as to its possibility. Below (February 1, 1811) Rush attempts to persuade Jefferson that political differences should not keep them apart.

January 2, 1811

When I consider your early attachment to Mr. Adams, and his to you; when I consider how much the liberties and independence of the United States owe to the concert of your principles and labors; and when I reflect upon the sameness of your opinions at present upon most of the subjects of government and all the subjects of legislation, I have ardently wished a friendly and epistolary intercourse might be revived between you before you take a final leave of the common object of your affections. Such an intercourse will be honorable to your talents and patriotism and highly useful to the course of republicanism not only in the United States but all over the world. Posterity will revere the friendship of two ex-Presidents that were once opposed to each other. Human nature will be a gainer by it. I am sure an advance on your side will be a cordial to the heart of Mr. Adams. Tottering over the grave, he now leans wholly upon the shoulders of his old Revolutionary friends. The patriots generated by the funding system, &c., are all his enemies. Adieu! my dear friend, and believe me to be yours truly and affectionately,

February 1, 1811

I was induced to make the proposal to you of reviving a farewell intercourse with Mr. Adams before you meet in another world, in consequence of his having reverted back to the opinions and feelings of his early life upon several interesting subjects of government, and of his having in one of his letters expressed favorable sentiments towards you and a decided approbation of one of the unpopular acts of your administration.

Many are the evils of a political life, but none so great as the dissolution of friendships and the implacable hatreds which too often take their place. Mr. Adams' letters to me contain many affecting proofs of his sufferings from this quarter.

∞

Thomas Jefferson to Benjamin Rush, December 5, 1811

T wo o f Jefferson's neighbors went to visit John Adams in Massachusetts. Upon returning to Virginia, they told Jefferson that Adams had spoken very highly of his old friend, even saying that he had always loved Jefferson, and still did.

Jefferson shares this happy report with Rush. Moving closer to reconciliation, Jefferson is still worried about the "certain awkwardness" of reviving a friendship that has been long since dormant.

I recur, therefore, to the subject of your kind letters relating to Mr. Adams and myself, which a late occurrence has again presented to me.

Two of the Mr. _____, my neighbors and friends, took a tour to the northward during the last summer. In Boston they fell into company with Mr. Adams, and by his invitation passed a day with him at Braintree. He spoke out to them everything which came uppermost, and as it ocurred to his mind, without any reserve; and seemed most disposed to dwell on those things which happened during his own administration. He spoke of his *masters,* as he called his Heads of departments, as acting above his control, and often against his opinions. Among many other topics, he adverted to the unprincipled licentiousness of the press against myself, adding, "I always loved Jefferson, and still love him."

This is enough for me. I only needed this knowledge to revive towards him all the affections of the most cordial moments of our lives. Changing a single word only in Dr. Franklin's character of him, I knew him to be always an honest man, often a great one, but sometimes incorrect and precipitate in his judgments; and it is known to those who have ever heard me speak of Mr. Adams, that I have ever done him justice myself, and defended him when assailed by others with the single exception as to political opinions. But with a man possessing so many other estimable qualities, why should we be dissocialized by mere differences of opinions in politics, in religion, philosophy, or anything else? His opinions are as honestly formed as my own. Our different views of the same subject are the result of a difference in our organization and experience. I never withdrew from the society of any man on this account, although many have done it from me; much less should I do it from one with whom I had gone through, with hand and heart, so many trying scenes. I wish, therefore, but for an apposite occasion to express to Mr. Adams my unchanged affections for him. There is an awkwardness which hangs over the resuming a correspondence so long discontinued, unless something could arise which should call for a letter. Time and chance may perhaps generate such an occasion, of which I shall not be wanting in promptitude to avail myself. From this fusion of mutual affections, Mrs. Adams is of course separated. It will only be necessary that I never name her. In your letters to Mr. Adams, you can, perhaps, suggest my continued cordiality towards him, and knowing this, should an occasion of writing first present itself to him, he will perhaps avail himself of it, as I certainly will, should it first occur to me. No ground for jealousy now existing, he will certainly give fair play to the natural warmth of his heart. Perhaps I may open the way in some letter to my old friend Gerry, who I know is in habits of the greatest intimacy with him.

I have thus, my friend, laid open my heart to you, because you were so kind as to take an interest in healing again revolutionary affections, which have ceased in expression only, but not in their existence. God ever bless you, and preserve you in life and health.

∞

Benjamin Rush to John Adams, December 16, 1811

BUOYED BY Jefferson's expression of interest in reconciling with Adams, Rush attempts to persuade Adams to receive the "olive branch." Rush, in his enthusiasm, even sends a draft letter of reconciliation for Adams to send to Jefferson.

And now, my dear friend, permit me again to suggest to you to receive the olive branch which has thus been offered to you by the hand of a man who still loves you. Fellow laborers in erecting the great fabric of American independence!—fellow sufferers in the calumnies and falsehoods of party rage!—fellow heirs of the gratitude and affection of posterity!—and fellow passengers in a stage that must shortly convey you both into the presence of a Judge with whom the forgiveness and love of enemies is the condition of acceptance!—embrace—embrace each other! Bedew your letters of reconciliation with tears of affection and joy. Bury in silence all the causes of your separation. Recollect that explanations may be proper between lovers but are *never* so between divided friends. Were I near to you, I would put a pen into your hand and guide it while it composed the following short address to Mr. Jefferson:

"Friend and fellow laborer in the cause of the liberty and independence of our common country, I salute you with the most cordial good wishes for your health and happiness.

John Adams."

Excuse the liberty I have taken, and be assured of the respect, affection, and gratitude of yours truly,

John Adams to Benjamin Rush,
December 25, 1811

ADAMS STILL claims that there is nothing to mend with Jefferson and that he had forgiven him long ago, even though eleven years have passed since they last communicated. Nevertheless, Adams resists Rush's urge to do something, and even scolds Rush for meddling. He also tells Rush to stop reminding him that he is to die soon. He already knows that.

I perceive plainly enough, Rush, that you have been teasing Jefferson to write to me, as you did me some time ago to write to him. You gravely advised me "to receive the olive branch," as if there had been war; but there has never beeen any hostility on my part, nor that I know, on his. When there has been no war, there can be no room for negotiations of peace.

Mr. Jefferson speaks of my political opinions; but I know of no difference between him and myself relative to the Constitution, or to forms of government in general. In measures of administration, we have differed in opinion. . . .

In point of republicanism, all the differences I ever knew or could discover between you and me, or between Jefferson and me, consisted,

1. In the difference between speeches and messages. I was a monarchist because I thought a speech more manly, more respectful to Congress and the nation. Jefferson and Rush preferred messages.

2. I held levees once a week, that all my time might not be wasted by idle visits. Jefferson's whole eight years was a levee.

3. I dined a large company once or twice a week. Jefferson dined a dozen every day.

4. Jefferson and Rush were for liberty and straight hair. I thought curled hair was as republican as straight.

In these, and a few other points of equal importance, all miserable frivolities, that Jefferson and Rush ought to blush that they ever laid any stress upon them, I might differ; but I never knew any points of more consequence on which there was any variation between us.

You exhort me to "forgiveness and love of enemies," as if I considered, or had ever considered, Jefferson as my enemy. This is not so; I have always loved him as a friend. If I ever received or suspected any injury from him, I have forgiven it long and long ago, and have no nore resentment against him than against you.

You enforce your exhortations by the most solemn considerations that can enter the human mind. After mature reflection upon them, and laying them properly to heart, I could not help feeling that they were so unnecessary that you must excuse me if I had some inclination to be ludicrous.

You often put me in mind that I am soon to die; I know it, and shall not forget it. Stepping into my kitchen one day, I found two of my poor neighbors, as good sort of men as two drunkards could be. One had sotted himself into a consumption. His cough and his paleness and weakness showed him near the last stage. Tom, who was not so far gone as yet, though he soon followed, said to John, "You have not long for this world." John answered very quick: "I know it, Tom, as well as you do; but why do you tell me of it? I had rather you should strike me." This was one of those touches of nature which Shakspeare or Cervantes would have noted in his ivory book.

But why do you make so much ado about nothing? Of what use can it be for Jefferson and me to exchange letters? I have nothing to say to him, but to wish him an easy journey to heaven, when he goes, which I wish may be delayed as long as life shall be agreeable to him. And he can have nothing to say to me, but to bid me make haste and be ready. Time and chance, however, or possibly design, may produce ere long a letter between us.

∞

John Adams to Thomas Jefferson, January 1, 1812, and Jefferson to Adams, January 21, 1812

BELOW, ADAMS makes the first move and reaches out to his dear old friend. He uses the excuse of sending "two pieces of Homespun," which turned out to be his son John Quincy's treatise on rhetoric and oratory. Adams would later tell Jefferson that when they were in Paris, John Quincy "appeared to be as much your boy as mine."

Jefferson eagerly receives Adams's olive branch and begins a long series of reminiscences with his friend of '76.

ADAMS TO JEFFERSON

Dear Sir

As you are a Friend to American Manufactures under proper restrictions, especially Manufactures of the domestic kind, I take the Liberty of sending you by the Post a Packett containing two Pieces of Homespun lately produced in this quarter by One who was honoured in his youth with some of your Attention and much of your kindness.

All of my Family whom you formerly knew are well. My Daughter Smith is here and has successfully gone through a perilous and painful Operation, which detains her here this Winter, from her Husband and her Family at Chenango: where one of the most gallant and skilful Officers of our Revolution is probably destined to spend the rest of his days, not in the Field of Glory, but in the hard Labours of Husbandry.

I wish you Sir many happy New Years and that you may enter the next and many succeeding Years with as animating Prospects for the Public as those at present before Us. I am Sir with a long and sincere Esteem your Friend and Servant

JOHN ADAMS

JEFFERSON TO ADAMS

Dear Sir

. . . A letter from you calls up recollections very dear to my mind. It carries me back to the times when, beset with difficulties and dangers, we were fellow laborers in the same cause, struggling for what is most valuable to man, his right of self-government. Laboring always at the same oar, with some wave ever ahead threatening to overwhelm us and yet passing harmless under our bark, we knew not how, we rode through the storm with heart and hand, and made a happy port. Still we did not expect to be without rubs and difficulties; and we have had them. First the detention of the Western posts: then the coalition of Pilnitz, outlawing our commerce with France, and the British enforcement of the outlawry. In your day French depredations: in mine English, and the Berlin and Milan decrees: now the English orders of council, and the piracies they authorise: when these shall be over, it will be the impressment of our seamen, or something else: and so we have gone on, and so we shall go on, puzzled and prospering beyond example in the history of man. And I do believe we shall continue to growl, [i.e., grow] to multiply and prosper until we exhibit an association, powerful, wise and happy, beyond what has yet been seen by men. As for France and England, with all their pre-eminence in science, the one is a den of robbers, and the other pirates. And if science produces no better fruits than tyranny, murder, rapine and destitution of national morality, I would rather wish our country to be ignorant, honest and estimable as our neighboring savages are.

But whither is senile garrulity leading me? Into politics, of which I have taken final leave. I think little of them, and say less. I have given up newspapers in exchange for Tacitus and Thucydides, for Newton and Euclid; and I find myself much the happier. Sometimes indeed I look back to former occurrences, in remembrance of our old friends and fellow laborers, who have fallen before us. Of the signers of the Declaration of Independance I see now living not more than half a dozen on your side of the Potomak, and, on this side, myself alone. You and I have been wonderfully spared, and myself with remarkable health, and a considerable activity of body and mind. I am on horseback 3. or 4. hours of every day; visit 3. or 4. times a year a possession I have 90 miles distant, performing the winter journey on horseback. I walk little however; a single mile being too much for me; and I live in the midst of my grandchildren, one of whom has lately promoted me to be a great grandfather. I have heard with pleasure that you also retain good health, and a greater power of exercise in walking than I do. But I would rather have heard this from yourself, and that, writing a letter, like mine, full of egotisms, and of details of your health, your habits, occupations and enjoyments, I should have the pleasure of knowing that, in the race of life, you do not keep, in it's physical decline, the same distance ahead of me which you have done in political honors and atchievements. No circumstances have lessened the interest I feel in these particulars respecting yourself; none have suspended for one moment my sincere esteem for you; and I now salute you with unchanged affections and respect.

TH: JEFFERSON

∞

Benjamin Rush to John Adams, February 17, 1812

RUSH REJOICED in the reunion of these two friends and fellow patriots and wrote a wonderful tribute to them both.

ℐ rejoice in the correspondence which has taken place between you and your old friend Mr. Jefferson. I consider you and him as the North and South Poles of the American Revolution. Some talked, some wrote, and some fought to promote and establish it, but you and Mr. Jefferson *thought* for us all. I never take a retrospect of the years 1775 and 1776 without associating your opinions and speeches and conversations with all the great political, moral, and intellectual achievements of the Congresses of those memorable years.

∞

Thomas Jefferson to John Adams, October 12, 1823

THE REVIVED friendship between Adams and Jefferson was threatened by the publication of some disparaging remarks Adams had made about Jefferson many years before, at the height of their political rivalry. While Adams was early in his retirement, having been defeated by Jefferson in the presidential election of 1800, he criticized the character of his political rival. Jefferson magnanimously chose to ignore the publication, attributing the remarks to mere political differences. Adams was overjoyed when he received the following letter from Jefferson.

Putting aside these things however for the present, I write this letter as due to a friendship co-eval with our government, and now attempted to be poisoned, when too late in life to be replaced by new affections. I had for some time observed, in the public papers, dark hints and mysterious innuendoes of a correspondence of yours with a friend, to whom you had opened your bosom without reserve, and which was to be made public by that friend, or his representative. And now it is said to be actually published. It has not yet reached us, but extracts have been given, and such as seemed most likely to draw a curtain of separation between you and myself. Were there no other motive than that of indignation against the author of this outrage on private confidence, whose shaft seems to have been aimed at yourself more particularly, this would make it the duty of every honorable mind to disappoint that aim, by opposing to it's impression a seven-fold shield of apathy and insensibility. With me however no such armour is needed. The circumstances of the times, in which we have happened to live, and the partiality of our friends, at a particular period, placed us in a state of apparent opposition, which some might suppose to be personal also; and there might not be wanting those who wish'd to make it so, by filling our ears with malignant falsehoods, by dressing up hideous phantoms of their own creation, presenting them to you under my name, to me under your's, and endeavoring to instill into our minds things concerning each other the most destitute of truth. And if there had been, at any time, a moment when we were off our guard, and in a temper to let the whispers of these people make us forget what we had known of each other for so many years, and years of so much trial, yet all men who have attended to the workings of the human mind, who have seen the false colours under which passion sometimes dresses the actions and motives of others, have seen also these passions subsiding with time and reflection, dissipating, like mists before the rising sun, and restoring to us the sight of all things in their true shape and colours. It would be strange indeed if, at our years, we were to go an age back to hunt up imaginary, or forgotten facts, to disturb the repose of affections so sweetening to the evening of our lives. Be assured, my dear Sir, that I am incapable of receiving the slightest impression from the effort now made to plant thorns on the pillow of age, worth, and wisdom, and to sow tares between friends who have been such for near half a century. Beseeching you then not to suffer your mind to be disquieted by this wicked attempt to poison it's peace, and praying you to throw it by, among the things which have never happened, I add sincere assurances of my unabated, and constant attachment, friendship and respect.

∽

Thomas Jefferson to John Adams, March 25, 1826

THIS WAS to be the last letter Jefferson wrote to his friend. They both were soon to be reunited in death, "in an ecstatic meeting with the friends [they] have loved and lost," as Jefferson had once put it.

Dear Sir

My grandson Th: Jefferson Randolph, being on a visit to Boston, would think he had seen nothing were he to leave it without having seen you. Altho' I truly sympathise with you in the trouble these interruptions give, yet I must ask for him permission to pay to you his personal respects. Like other young people, he wishes to be able, in the winter nights of old age, to recount to those around him what he has heard and learnt of

the Heroic age preceding his birth, and which of the Argonauts particularly he was in time to have seen. It was the lot of our early years to
witness nothing but the dull monotony of colonial subservience, and of
our riper ones to breast the labors and perils of working out of it. Theirs
are the Halcyon calms succeeding the storm which our Argosy had so
stoutly weathered. Gratify his ambition then by recieving his best bow,
and my solicitude for your health by enabling him to bring me a favorable account of it. Mine is but indifferent, but not so my friendship and
respect for you.

IV

EDUCATION OF THE HEAD AND HEART

❦

"If Virtue & Knowledge are diffusd among the People, they will never be enslavd. This will be their great Security."

SAMUEL ADAMS TO JAMES WARREN, FEBRUARY 12, 1779

Without educated citizens, said James Madison, "popular government is but a Prologue to a Farce or a Tragedy; or, perhaps both." Popular government—that is government by consent—was not, in the view of the Founders, enough; *informed* consent was what the American republic would need. Our political institutions were designed, of course, to take into account human depravity and self-interest. But, as dynamic and as flexible as these institutions were, the Founders believed that more was needed. As I have said before, their hope was to raise up men —to improve not just the material condition of men but men themselves. The institutions of American democracy presuppose a virtuous and knowledgeable citizenry: "We, the people" should be enlightened and virtuous enough to govern ourselves, or at least select responsible and enlightened political officials to govern us. Schools and homes were the places in which we would learn of our civic responsibilities. Here we would be taught to temper our selfishness, respect the nation's laws, and become better human beings.

"What is the chief end of man?" Abigail Adams asked in a letter to her sister. A question that she thought all "rational creatures" should explore. This chapter shows how the Founders themselves wrestled with this question and expected their children, even at a very young age, to wrestle with it as well. We begin with the Founders' advice to young people, focusing on their attempts to shape the moral character of their children and other young charges. Their letters may seem rather austere and demanding by modern standards, but if so, so much the worse for modern standards. These men and women didn't wish to leave anything to chance when it came to raising decent human beings and good citizens.

John and Abigail Adams took the upbringing of their "lovely babes" most seriously, John once telling Abigail to "let our Anxiety be, to mould the minds and manners of our children." Their oldest son, John Quincy Adams, of course, grew up to become the sixth president of the United States. George Washington wrote many letters to his stepson and adopted grandson, urging them to cultivate the habits and virtues that would make them not only successful individuals but useful members of the commonwealth. Jefferson exhorted his children to be good and honest—to let their "internal monitors" (or consciences) be their guide.

Of course, the Founders were human; so were their children. And, just as the Founders made mistakes in raising their children, not all of their children or other relations grew up to be the kind of people they had hoped they would be. George and Martha Washington were often overly indulgent with their young charges, which was one of the reasons Washington had to write so many letters urging them to overcome their bad habits; James Madison exhausted a huge proportion of his savings covering the gambling debts of his wayward stepson, John Payne Todd; and one of Adams's sons died an alcoholic. But, despite some mistakes, their advice and thoughts are still, I think, quite sound and still highly relevant.

The remainder of the chapter explores the Founders' thoughts on the important role education would play in the new republic. A "general diffusion of knowledge," as Jefferson called it, would be necessary to turn Americans into informed, responsible citizens, or, in the words of Benjamin Rush, into "republican machines."

There were several reasons for promoting a general diffusion of knowledge. First was the creation of a "natural aristocracy," as Jefferson put it, of genius and virtue. This would be no aristocracy of wealth, caste, or privilege. Because genius and virtue are not limited to any particular class, but scattered randomly throughout the polity, Jefferson's reform of education would reach out to all Americans—the goal being to separate the "best geniuses . . . from the rubbish annually." Jefferson was not one to mince words, but his goal was an admirable one: All children, no matter what their background, were to be given an opportunity to rise to their potential. By separating the "wheat from the chaff," as Jefferson starkly put it, he hoped to elevate worthy persons to guard the sacred rights of liberty.

However, Jefferson and the other Founders were not content to rely simply on an *aristoi* or "elite"—no matter how natural—to safeguard the republic from tyranny. This was a democracy after all. As students of the histories of republics, the Founders knew all too well the tendency of republics to devolve into oligarchies or tyrannies. Ultimately, the people would have to rely on themselves to fend off tyranny. Schools provided the "best security against crafty and dangerous encroachments on the public liberty," observed Madison.

However, more was at stake than checking would-be tyrants. Character formation was also the business of educators. This meant that not only should teachers educate the "abilities" of children but also, and more important, according to Noah Webster, their "hearts" as well. Samuel Adams described the mission of educators as keeping alive the "moral sense" of children. "Great Learning and superior abilities, should you ever possess them," Abigail Adams told John Quincy, "will be of little value and small Estimation, unless Virtue, Honour, Truth and integrety are added to them."

But still more was to be asked of education. In addition to planting virtues in the heart, and cultivating Jefferson's "natural aristocracy," an education should harvest patriots. It must encourage children to love their country and to be useful citizens. The Founders believed that what was needed was a civic education, one that shaped both minds and hearts to prepare Americans for the requirements of self-government. This civic mission of education was regarded as fundamental to the future prosperity of America. Children would learn to revere their laws and to become acquainted with the heroes and ideas of their collective past. This education begins in the home and is carried on in the schools. As Noah Webster put it, as soon as a child "opens his lips . . . he should lisp the praise of liberty and of those illustrious heroes" of our founding; Washington wrote that children should learn reverence for the laws.

In the twentieth century, many confuse civic education with propaganda or reeducation camps found in totalitarian regimes. But this was certainly not the Founders' view. They thought that education was about more than acquiring skills; children should also learn to love their country and to take pride in and contribute to the American national character.

Let me close with Abraham Lincoln's defense of civic education:

> Let reverence for the laws . . . be taught in schools, in seminaries, and in colleges;—let it be written in Primmers, spelling books, and in Almanacs. . . . And in short, let it become the political religion of the nation; and let the old and the young, the rich and the poor, the grave and the gay, of all sexes and tongues, and colors and conditions, sacrifice increasingly upon its altars.

∽

"I Can't Tell a Lie"
Mason Weems, The Life of George Washington

"I CAN'T tell a lie" is perhaps the most famous quotation ever attributed to George Washington. As it happens, we don't know that he ever said it, but his biographer Parson Weems, who inserted it into the fifth edition of *The Life and Memorable Actions of George Washington,* has made it part of the Washington story.

While Weems took considerable artistic license in depicting the life of George Washington—which doubtless made for enjoyable reading—the integrity of his subject did not require any such embellishment. Washington himself said, "I hope I shall always possess firmness and virtue enough to maintain what I consider the most enviable of all titles, the character of an 'Honest Man.' " And Washington, by all accounts, always acted with that title more than anything else in mind, maintaining it throughout his life. However, it is in part thanks to Weems that we do remember Washington as an honest man, and for that reason, I have included Weems's famous account of Washington and the cherry tree in this chapter. But I do so not on my judgment alone. I can think of no higher recommendation for including it here than the fact that another famous president avidly read Weems's biography of Washington —Abraham Lincoln, whose moniker was "Honest Abe." Truth or fiction, myth or not, it certainly had an impact on this boy, who would later hail Washington as the "mightiest name" in "moral reformation."

"*When* George," said she, "was about six years old, he was made the wealthy master of a *hatchet!* of which, like most little boys, he was immoderately fond, and was constantly going about chopping every thing that came in his way. One day, in the garden, where he often amused himself hacking his mother's pea-sticks, he unluckily tried the edge of his hatchet on the body of a beautiful young English cherry-tree, which he barked so terribly, that I don't believe the tree ever got the better of it. The next morning the old gentleman finding out what had befallen his tree, which, by the by, was a great favourite, came into the house, and with much warmth asked for the mischievous author, declaring at the same time, that he would not have taken five guineas for his tree. Nobody could tell him any thing about it. Presently George and his hatchet made their appearance. *George, said his father, do you know who killed that beautiful little cherry-tree yonder in the garden?* This was a *tough question;* and George staggered under it for a moment; but quickly recovered himself: and looking at his father, with the sweet face of youth brightened with the inexpressible charm of all-conquering truth, he bravely cried out, *"I can't tell a lie, Pa; you know I can't tell a lie. I did cut it with my hatchet."—Run to my arms, you dearest boy,* cried his father in transports, *run to my arms; glad am I, George, that you killed my tree; for you have paid me for it a thousand fold. Such an act of heroism in my son, is more worth than a thousand trees, though blossomed with silver, and their fruits of purest gold.*

It was in this way, by interesting at once both his *heart* and *head,* that Mr. Washington conducted George with great ease and pleasure along the happy paths of virtue.

❀

Thomas Jefferson's Decalogue, February 25, 1825

A FRIEND asked Thomas Jefferson to pass on some advice to his young son, whom he had named after Jefferson. Jefferson wrote a letter of advice, attached a poem, and wrote a set of ten commandments for practical life.

Jefferson's wisdom is timeless—it's a good list of rules to remember.

The Portrait of a Good Man by the most sublime of Poets, for your Imitation.

Lord, who's the happy man that may to thy blest courts repair;
Not stranger-like to visit them, but to inhabit there?

'Tis he whose every thought and deed by rules of virtue moves;
Whose generous tongue disdains to speak the thing his heart disproves.

Who never did a slander forge, his neighbor's fame to wound;
Nor hearken to a false report by malice whispered round.

Who vice in all its pomp and power, can treat with just neglect;
And piety, though clothed in rags, religiously respect.

the want of truth, and at the same time so useless. Teach her never to be angry. Anger only serves to torment ourselves, to divert others, and alienate their esteem. And teach her industry and application to useful pursuits. I will venture to assure you that if you inculcate this in her mind you will make her a happy being in herself, a most inestimable friend to you, and precious to all the world. In teaching her these dispositions of mind, you will be more fixed in them yourself, and render yourself dear to all your acquaintance. Practice them then, my dear, without ceasing. If ever you find yourself in difficulty and doubt how to extricate yourself, do what is right, and you will find it the easiest way of getting out of the difficulty. Do it for the additional incitement of increasing the happiness of him who loves you infinitely, and who is my dear Patsy your's affectionately.

∞

George Washington to George Washington Custis

WASHINGTON WROTE the following letters to his adopted grandson, George Washington Custis, who was studying at Princeton. Custis was not a very serious student and often lacked self-discipline. Washington's advice to students about to enter upon "the grand theatre of life" (a.k.a. the real world) is as good today as it was then; Custis did not heed it and eventually dropped out of the College of New Jersey.

December 19, 1796

The same consequences would follow from inconstancy and want of steadiness—for 'tis to close application and constant perseverance, men of letters and science are indebted for their knowledge and usefulness; and you are now at that period of life (as I have observed to you in a former letter) when these are to be acquired, or lost for ever. But as you are well acquainted with my sentiments on this subject, and know how anxious all your friends are to see you enter upon the grand theatre of life, with the advantages of a finished education, a highly cultivated mind, and a proper sense of your duties to God and man, I shall only add one sentiment more before I close this letter (which, as I have others to write, will hardly be in time for the mail), and that is, to pay due respect and obedience to your tutors, and affectionate reverence to the president of the college, whose character merits your highest regards. Let no bad example, for such is to be met in all seminaries, have an improper influence upon your conduct. Let this be such, and let it be your pride, to demean yourself in such a manner as to obtain the good will of your superiors, and the love of your fellow-students.

Adieu—I sincerely wish you well, being your attached and affectionate friend,

January 11, 1797

Another thing I would recommend to you—not because *I* want to know how *you* spend your money—and that is, to keep an account-book, and enter therein every farthing of your receipts and expenditures. The doing of which would initiate you into a habit, from which considerable advantages would result. Where no account of this sort is kept, there can be no investigation; no correction of errors; no discovery from a recurrence thereto, wherein too much, or too little, has been appropriated to particular uses. From an early attention to these matters, important and lasting benefits may follow.

We are all well, and all unite in best wishes for you; and with sincere affection I am always yours,

∞

John Adams, "The Choice of Hercules"

"THE CHOICE of Hercules" was one of John Adams's favorite legends. Adams, who once wrote that he realized that the example of Hercules might not be an appropriate symbol for a modern nation like America, nevertheless proposed it for our official seal in 1776. He also hoped that his own children might follow in Hercules's example. The legend depicts Hercules stopping at a fork in the road where two women stood. One woman told him that her road was smooth and pleasant, with no toils or cares. The other woman pointed to her road and told him she could promise him nothing but what his own labor and strength would yield. He chose the latter road.

I have often told this story to audiences asking them which road they would choose. Some simply disbelieve that anyone would choose the second road, but it is surprising how many choose it, still. One young person has told me it sounded like the choice between television and homework.

It is noteworthy that Jefferson and Franklin proposed a biblical theme for our national seal. The Continental Congress eventually chose the eagle to be on the Great Seal of the United States of America. The eagle holds a ribbon in its beak which reads *"e pluribus unum"*—from many, one.

JOHN ADAMS TO ABIGAIL ADAMS, AUGUST 14, 1776

Dr. F. proposes a Device for a Seal. Moses lifting up his Wand, and dividing the Red Sea, and Pharaoh, in his Chariot overwhelmed with the Waters.—This Motto. Rebellion to Tyrants is Obedience to God.

Mr. Jefferson proposed. The Children of Israel in the Wilderness, led by a Cloud by day, and a Pillar of Fire by night, and on the other Side Hengist and Horsa, the Saxon Chiefs, from whom We claim the Honour of being descended, and whose Political Principles and Form of Government We have assumed.

I proposed the Choice of Hercules, as engraved by Gribeline in some Editions of Lord Shaftsburys Works. The Hero resting on his Clubb. Virtue pointing to her rugged Mountain, on one Hand, and perswading him to ascend. Sloth, glancing at her flowery Paths of Pleasure, wantonly reclining on the Ground, displaying the Charms both of her Eloquence and Person, to seduce him into Vice. But this is too complicated a Group for a Seal or Medal, and it is not original.

JOHN ADAMS TO ABIGAIL ADAMS, APRIL/MAY 1780

There is every Thing here that can inform the Understanding, or refine the Taste, and indeed one would think that could purify the Heart. Yet it must be remembered there is every thing here too, which can seduce, betray, deceive, deprave, corrupt and debauch it. Hercules marches here in full View of the Steeps of Virtue on one hand, and the flowery Paths of Pleasure on the other—and there are few who make the Choice of Hercules. That my Children may follow his Example, is my earnest Prayer: but I sometimes tremble, when I hear the syren songs of sloth, least they should be captivated with her bewitching Charms and her soft, insinuating Musick.

∞

Thomas Jefferson to Thomas Jefferson Randolph, November 24, 1808

W E H E A R a lot of talk today about the importance of "role models" and often debate about who is fit to be one. Some of the best ones, I believe, can be neighbors, teachers, people who truly take an interest in directing and shaping young minds and hearts. Writing in 1808 to his grandson, Thomas Jefferson recalled with great admiration the influence of three of his mentors. Wythe and Small were former teachers; Randolph was an uncle with whom he served in the Virginia House of Burgesses.

My dear Jefferson

I have just recieved the inclosed letter under cover from Mr. Bankhead which I presume is from Anne and will inform you she is well. Mr. Bankhead has consented to go and pursue his studies at Monticello, and live with us till his pursuits or circumstances may require a separate establishment. Your situation, thrown at such a distance from us and alone, cannot but give us all, great anxieties for you. As much has been secured for you, by your particular position and the acquaintance to which you have been recommended, as could be done towards shielding you from the dangers which surround you. But thrown on a wide world, among entire strangers without a friend or guardian to advise so young too and with so little experience of mankind, your dangers are great, and still your safety must rest on yourself. A determination never to do what is wrong, prudence, and good humor, will go far towards securing to you the estimation of the world. When I recollect that at 14. years of age, the whole care and direction of my self was thrown on my self entirely, without a relation or friend qualified to advise or guide me, and recollect the various sorts of bad company with which I associated from time to time, I am astonished I did not turn off with some of them, and become as worthless to society as they were. I had the good fortune to become acquainted very early with some characters of very high standing, and to feel the incessant wish that I could even become what they were. Under temptations and difficulties, I could ask myself what would Dr. Small, Mr. Wythe, Peyton Randolph do in this situation? What course in it will ensure me their approbation? I am certain that this mode of deciding on my conduct tended more to it's correctness than any reasoning powers I possessed. Knowing the even and dignified line they pursued, I could never doubt for a moment which of two courses would be in character for them. Whereas seeking the same object through a process of moral reasoning, and with the jaundiced eye of youth, I should often have erred. From the circumstances of my position I was often thrown into the society of horseracers, cardplayers, Foxhunters, scientific and professional men, and of dignified men; and many a time have I asked myself, in the enthusiastic moment of the death of a fox, the victory of a favorite horse, the issue of a question eloquently argued at the bar or in the great Council of the nation, well, which of these kinds of reputation should I prefer? That of a horse jockey? A foxhunter? An Orator? Or the honest advocate of my country's rights? Be assured my dear Jefferson, that these little returns into ourselves, this self-cathechising habit, is not trifling, nor useless, but leads to the prudent selection and steady pursuits of what is right?

∞

George Washington to George Steptoe Washington, December 5, 1790

GEORGE STEPTOE WASHINGTON was the son of George Washington's brother, Sam. When Sam died, Washington took on the responsibility of educating Sam's son. George Steptoe Washington was heading to college in Philadelphia when Washington wrote him the following letter. Knowledge without virtue would be incomplete, Washington tells his nephew. As John Locke put it: "Virtue is harder to be got than knowledge; and, if lost in a young man, is seldom recovered." We have lost sight of the fact that the proper end of any education is moral education. As Martin Buber wrote: "All education is the education of character."

Should you enter upon the course of studies here marked out you must consider it as the finishing of your education, and, therefore, as the time is limited, that every hour misspent is lost for ever, and that future *years* cannot compensate for lost *days* at this period of your life. This reflection must shew the necessity of an unremitting application to your studies. To point out the importance of circumspection in your conduct, it may be proper to observe that a good moral character is the first essential in a man, and that the habits contracted at your age are generally indelible, and your conduct here may stamp your character through life. It is therefore highly important that you should endeavor not only to be learned but virtuous. Much more might be said to shew the necessity of application and regularity, but when you must know that without them you can never be qualified to render service to your country, assistance to your friends, or consolation to your retired moments, nothing further need be said to prove their utility.

∞

James Madison to William Bradford, Jr., November 9, 1772

MADISON WROTE this letter when he was twenty-one years old. He had recently returned from Princeton where he had stayed an extra six months after graduation to study Hebrew and theology with his teacher John Witherspoon. Studying Hebrew and theology, not politics, Madison thought, would serve him well in the pursuit of public policy. He was right.

Back home, this young college graduate began educating his younger brothers and sisters. His health was never very good, and he had exhausted himself by his intellectual exertions at Princeton. But during this time, he suffered from what some historians say was a "nervous disorder" or depression. He was unsure of what he wanted to do in life —he didn't want to go into the ministry, but he found the study of law to be tedious. A good friend of his from Princeton, who had graduated early with him, had recently died. Madison thought that his life would be cut short as well, given his weak and frail constitution (some claim that he was barely five feet six inches and weighed ninety-eight pounds).

Like many young people today, he was having an "identity crisis" and thought very little of himself. Despite the low expectations expressed here, he was, of course, to become one of the greatest men in our history. Every soul has valleys of despair and self-doubt, even the souls of the greatest human beings.

This letter is to William Bradford, a good friend of his from the College of New Jersey (Princeton).

However nice and cautious we may be in detecting the follies of mankind, and framing our economy according to the precepts of Wisdom and Religion, I fancy there will commonly remain with us some latent expectation of obtaining more than ordinary happiness and prosperity till we feel the convincing argument of actual disappointment. Though I will not determine whether we shall be much the worse for it if we do not allow it to intercept our views towards a future state, because strong desires and great hopes instigate us to arduous enterprises, fortitude, and perseverance. Nevertheless, a watchful eye must be kept on ourselves, lest while we are building ideal monuments of renown and bliss here, we neglect to have our names enrolled in the annals of Heaven.

These thoughts come into my mind because I am writing to you, and thinking of you. As to myself, I am too dull and infirm now to look out for any extraordinary things in this world, for I think my sensations for many months past have intimated to me not to expect a long or healthy life; though it may be better with me after some time, [but] I hardly dare expect it, and therefore have little spirit and alacrity to set about anything that is difficult in acquiring and useless in possessing after one has exchanged time for eternity. But you have health, youth, fire, and genius, to bear you along through the high track of public life, and so may be more interested and delighted in improving on hints that respect the temporal though momentous concerns of man.

∞

John Quincy Adams to John Adams,
March 16, 1780,
and John Adams to John Quincy Adams,
March 17, 1780

TWELVE-YEAR-OLD John Quincy Adams was enrolled in school in Passy, a suburb of Paris. Here Adams carefully goes over his curriculum and even nags his son for his bad penmanship. It would be hard to have John Adams for a father. Then again the hard road can pay off. John Quincy Adams did become president of the United States, which John Adams lived to see. It is interesting that for Adams, one of the most brilliant and politically astute men of his time, it is Greek and Latin that he recommends above all to a future president. The same priorities are certainly not found in many schools or universities today.

JOHN QUINCY ADAMS TO JOHN ADAMS

My Work for a day.
  Make Latin,
  Explain Cicero
       Erasmus
        Appendix
  Peirce Phædrus
  Learn greek Racines
      greek Grammar
  Geography
  geometry
  fractions
  Writing
  Drawing

As a young boy can not apply himself to all those Things and keep a remembrance of them all I should desire that you would let me know what of those I must begin upon at first. I am your Dutiful Son,

John Quincy Adams

JOHN ADAMS TO JOHN QUINCY ADAMS

My dear Son
I have received your Letter giving an Account of your Studies for a day. You should have dated your Letter.

Making Latin, construing Cicero, Erasmus, the Appendix de Diis et Heroibus ethnicis, and Phædrus, are all Exercises proper for the Acquisition of the Latin Tongue; you are constantly employed in learning the Meaning of Latin Words, and the Grammar, the Rhetorick and Criticism of the Roman Authors: These Studies have therefore such a Relation to each other, that I think you would do well to pursue them all, under the Direction of your Master.

The Greek Grammar and the Racines I would not have you omit, upon any Consideration, and I hope your Master will soon put you into the Greek Testament, because the most perfect Models of fine Writing in history, Oratory and Poetry are to be found in the Greek Language.

Writing and Drawing are but Amusements and may serve as Relaxations from your studies.

As to Geography, Geometry and Fractions I hope your Master will not insist upon your spending much Time upon them at present; because altho they are Useful sciences, and altho all Branches of the Mathematicks, will I hope, sometime or other engage your Attention, as the most profitable and the most satisfactory of all human Knowledge, yet my Wish at present is that your principal Attention should be directed to the Latin and Greek Tongues, leaving the other studies to be hereafter attained, in your own Country.

I hope soon to hear that you are in Virgil and Tully's orations, or Ovid or Horace or all of them.

I am, my dear Child, your affectionate Father, John Adams
P.S. The next Time you write me, I hope you will take more care to write well. Cant you keep a steadier Hand?

∞

Thomas Jefferson to Martha Jefferson, December 11, 1783

PATSY JEFFERSON was only eleven years old when her father made her confront something that many adults avoid: that death "puts an end" to us all. To prepare for this is to find one's conscience—one's "internal monitor"—and to strive never to do wrong. Learning we are to die teaches us how to live right. It is a lesson that the young should learn—that in this coil life is not forever.

My Dear Patsy

. . . I hope you will have good sense enough to disregard those foolish predictions that the world is to be at an end soon. The almighty has never made known to any body at what time he created it, nor will he tell any body when he means to put an end to it, if ever he means to do it. As to preparations for that event, the best way is for you to be always prepared for it. The only way to be so is never to do or say a bad thing. If ever you are about to say any thing amiss or to do any thing wrong, consider before hand. You will feel something within you which will tell you it is wrong and ought not to be said or done: this is your conscience, and be sure to obey it. Our maker has given us all this faithful internal Monitor, and if you always obey it, you will always be prepared for the end of the world: or for a much more certain event which is death. This must happen to all: it puts an end to the world as to us, and the way to be ready for it is never to do a wrong act.

∞

Abigail Adams to Mercy Warren, July 6, 1773, and Mercy to Abigail, July 25, 1773

ABIGAIL ADAMS and Mercy Otis Warren were good friends who maintained a lifelong correspondence. As a young mother with four children under the age of five, Abigail was eager for advice on how to raise "the tender twigs alloted to my care." Warren recommends instilling in children, first and foremost, a "sacred regard for veracity." It makes everything else come easier.

ABIGAIL ADAMS TO MERCY WARREN

I am sensible I have an important trust committed to me; and tho I feel my-self very uneaquel to it, tis still incumbent upon me to discharge it in the best manner I am capable of. I was really so well pleased with your little offspring, that I must beg the favour of you to communicate to me the happy Art of "rearing the tender thought, teaching the young Idea how to shoot, and pouring fresh instruction o'er the Mind." May the Natural Benevolence of your Heart, prompt you to assist a young and almost inexperienced Mother in this Arduous Business, that the tender twigs alloted to my care, may be so cultivated as to do honour to their parents and prove blessing[s] to the riseing generation. When I saw the happy fruits of your attention in your well ordered family, I felt a Sort of Emulation glowing in my bosom, to imitate the

> "Parent who vast pleasure find's
> In forming of her childrens minds
> In midst of whom with vast delight
> She passes many a winters Night
> Mingles in every play to find
> What Bias Nature gave the mind

Resolving thence to take her aim
To guide them to the realms of fame
And wisely make those realms the way
To those of everlasting day.

Each Boisterous passion to controul
And early Humanize the Soul
In simple tales beside the fire,
The noblest Notions to inspire.
Her offspring conscious of her care
Transported hang around her chair."

MERCY WARREN TO ABIGAIL ADAMS

You ask if the sentiments of this Lady coincide with the Rules per-
scribed myself in the Regulation of my Little flock and to answer you
ingeneously I must acknowledge I fall so far short of the Methods I
heretofore Laid down as the Rule of my Conduct that I dispaire of Reaching those more perfect plans Exhibited by superior Hands. Much less
shall I presume to dictate to those who have had Equal advantages with
myself and who I think Likly to make a much better improvement
thereof. I shall Esteem it a happiness indeed if I can acquit myself of the
important Charge (by providence devovled on Every Mother), to the
approbation of the judicious Observer of Life, but a much more noble
pleasure is the conscious satisfaction of having Exerted our utmost Efforts
to rear the tender plant and Early impress the youthful mind, with such
sentiments that if properly Cultivated when they go out of our hands
they may become useful in their several departments on the present
theatre of action, and happy forever when the immortal mind shall be
introduced into more Enlarged and Glorious scenes.

But before I quit this subject I would ask if you do not think Generosity
of sentiment as it is mention'd in the ninth Letter of the above treatise
too Comprehensive a term to be given as the first principle to be impress'd on the infant mind. This temper doubtless includes many other
Virtues but does it argue an invariable Attachment to truth. I have ever
thought a careful Attention to fix a sacred regard to Veracity in the Bosom
of Youth the surest Gaurd to Virtue, and the most powerful Barrier
against the sallies of Vice through Every future period of Life. I cannot
but think it is of much the most importance of any single principle in the
Early Culture, for when it has taken deep root it usually produces not
only Generosity of mind but a train of other Exelent qualities. And when
I find a heart that will on no terms deviate from the Law of truth I

do not much fear its Course will Ever Run very Eccentrick from the path of Rectitude, provided we can obtain any degree of that Childs Confidence: A point at which I think Every mother should aim.

∞

George Washington to George Washington Custis, November 28, 1796

HERE WASHINGTON, serving as president in Philadelphia, encourages prudence and discretion in his adopted grandson and namesake, who was fifteen years old and in college.

𝒥 would guard you, too, against imbibing hasty and unfavorable impressions of any one. Let your judgment always balance well, before you decide; and even then, where there is no occasion for expressing an opinion, it is best to be silent, for there is nothing more certain than that it is at all times more easy to make enemies than friends. And besides, to speak evil of any one, unless there is unequivocal proofs of their deserving it, is an injury for which there is no adequate reparation.

For, as Shakespeare says, "He that robs me of my good name enriches not himself, but renders me poor indeed," or words to that effect. Keep in mind that scarcely any change would be agreeable to you at *first* from the sudden transition, and from never having been accustomed to shift or rough it. And, moreover, that if you meet with collegiate fare, it will be unmanly to complain. My paper reminds me it is time to conclude.

∞

Thomas Jefferson to Peter Carr, August 19, 1785

"HOW WOULD you act were all the world looking at you?" Jefferson asked his fifteen-year-old nephew, Peter Carr. "Act accordingly," he advised. Jefferson here offers some good advice that stands the test of time and scrutiny.

When your mind shall be well improved with science, nothing will be necessary to place you in the highest points of view but to pursue the interests of your country, the interests of your friends, and your own interests also with the purest integrity, the most chaste honour. The defect of these virtues can never be made up by all the other acquirements of body and mind. Make these then your first object. Give up money, give up fame, give up science, give [up] the earth itself and all it contains rather than do an immoral act. And never suppose that in any possible situation or under any circumstances that it is best for you to do a dishonourable thing however slightly so it may appear to you. Whenever you are to do a thing tho' it can never be known but to yourself, ask yourself how you would act were all the world looking at you, and act accordingly. Encourage all your virtuous dispositions, and exercise them whenever an opportunity arises, being assured that they will gain strength by exercise as a limb of the body does, and that exercise will make them habitual. From the practice of the purest virtue you may be assured you will derive the most sublime comforts in every moment of life and in the moment of death. If ever you find yourself environed with difficulties and perplexing circumstances, out of which you are at a loss how to extricate yourself, do what is right, and be assured that that will extricate you the best out of the worst situations. Tho' you cannot see when you fetch one step, what will be the next, yet follow truth, justice, and plain-dealing, and never fear their leading you out of the labyrinth in the easiest manner possible. The knot which you thought a Gordian one will untie itself before you. Nothing is so mistaken as the supposition that a person is to extricate himself from a difficulty, by intrigue, by chicanery, by dissimulation, by trimming, by an untruth, by an injustice. This increases the difficulties tenfold, and those who pursue these methods, get themselves so involved at length that they can turn no way but their infamy becomes more exposed. It is of great importance to set a resolution, not to be shaken, never to tell an untruth. There is no vice so mean, so pitiful, so contemptible and he who permits himself to tell a lie once, finds it much easier to do it a second and third time, till at length it becomes habitual, he tells lies without attending to it, and truths without the world's beleiving him. This falshood of the tongue leads to that of the heart, and in time depraves all it's good dispositions.

∞

Abigail Adams to John Quincy Adams, June 1778

ABIGAIL ADAMS shows what "tough love" is all about in this letter to her eleven-year-old son, John Quincy Adams, who was in Europe with his father. Her letter may seem overly stern, but she is well aware that "the welfare and prosperity of all countries, communities and I may add individuals depend upon their morals." Abigail Adams took to heart the fundamental task of the education of the young, knowing that self-government rests on the piety and moral seriousness of each new generation of citizens.

Her sentiment that she would prefer John Quincy dead to being immoral or "a Graceless child" may not be literally true, but it probably caught his attention. It would still catch a young ear.

My Dear Son
. . . The most amiable and most usefull disposition in a young mind is diffidence of itself, and this should lead you to seek advise and instruction from him who is your natural Guardian, and will always counsel and direct you in the best manner both for your present and future happiness. You are in possession of a natural good understanding and

of spirits unbroken by adversity, and untamed with care. Improve your understanding for acquiring usefull knowledge and virtue, such as will render you an ornament to society, an Honour to your Country, and a Blessing to your parents. Great Learning and superior abilities, should you ever possess them, will be of little value and small Estimation, unless Virtue, Honour, Truth and integrety are added to them. Adhere to those religious Sentiments and principals which were early instilled into your mind and remember that you are accountable to your Maker for all your words and actions. Let me injoin it upon you to attend constantly and steadfastly to the precepts and instructions of your Father as you value the happiness of your Mother and your own welfare. His care and attention to you render many things unnecessary for me to write which I might otherways do, but the inadvertency and Heedlessness of youth, requires line upon line and precept upon precept, and when inforced by the joint efforts of both parents will I hope have a due influence upon your Conduct, for dear as you are to me, I had much rather you should have found your Grave in the ocean you have crossd, or any untimely death crop you in your Infant years, rather than see you an immoral profligate or a Graceless child.

You have enterd early in life upon the great Theater of the world which is full of temptations and vice of every kind. You are not wholly unacquainted with History, in which you have read of crimes which your unexperienced mind could scarcly believe credible. You have been taught to think of them with Horrour and to view vice as

> a Monster of so frightfull Mein
> That to be hated, needs but to be seen.

Yet you must keep a strict guard upon yourself, or the odious monster will soon loose its terror, by becomeing familiar to you. The Modern History of our own times furnishes as Black a list of crimes as can be paralleld in ancient time, even if we go back to Nero, Caligula or Caesar Borgia. Young as you are, the cruel war into which we have been compelld by the Haughty Tyrant of Britain and the Bloody Emissarys of his vengance may stamp upon your mind this certain Truth, that the welfare and prosperity of all countries, communities and I may add individuals depend upon their Morals. That Nation to which we were once united as it has departed from justice, eluded and subverted the wise Laws which formerly governd it, sufferd the worst of crimes to go unpunished, has lost its valour, wisdom and Humanity, and from being the dread and terror of Europe, has sunk into derision and infamy.

◆◆◆

George Washington to Reverend Jonathan Boucher, December 16, 1770

WASHINGTON WROTE the following letter to the headmaster of the boarding school attended by his stepson, Jack Custis. Much of our education occurs outside the classroom—and so it is important that we not fall in with the wrong crowd.

The time of Life he is now advancing into requires the most friendly aid and Council (especially in such a place as Annapolis); otherwise, the warmth of his own Passions, assisted by the bad example of other Youth, may prompt him to actions derogatory of Virtue, & that Innocence of Manners which one coud wish to preserve him in: For wch reason I would beg leave to request, that he may not be suffered to sleep from under your own Roof, unless it be at such places as you are sure he can have no bad examples set him; nor allow him to be rambling about of Nights in Company with those who do not care how debauched and viceous his Conduct may be.

You will be so good I hope, as to excuse the liberty I have taken in offering my sentiments thus freely—I have his well-being much at Heart, & should be sorry to see him fall into any Vice, or evil course, which there is a possibility of restraining him from.

◆◆◆

John Adams to Abigail Adams, October 29, 1775

JOHN WAS in Philadelphia serving in the Second Continental Congress when he wrote the following letter to Abigail. They both took the task of parenting seriously. And they both knew about the virtues of fitness.

Human nature with all its infirmities and depravation is still capable of great things. It is capable of attaining to degrees of wisdom and of goodness, which, we have reason to believe, appear respectable in the

estimation of superior intelligences. Education makes a greater difference between man and man, than nature has made between man and
brute. The virtues and powers to which men may be trained, by early
education and constant discipline, are truly sublime and astonishing.

It should be your care, therefore, and mine, to elevate the minds of
our children and exalt their courage; to accelerate and animate their
industry and activity; to excite in them an habitual contempt of meanness, abhorrence of injustice and inhumanity, and an ambition to excel
in every capacity, faculty, and virtue. If we suffer their minds to grovel
and creep in infancy, they will grovel all their lives.

But their bodies must be hardened, as well as their souls exalted.
Without strength and activity and vigor of body, the brightest mental
excellencies will be eclipsed and obscured.

∞

James Madison, Federalist No. 55

HERE MADISON weighs the frailties of human nature against its potential. He is at once a realist and an idealist. There is enough virtue in
human nature to make republican government possible, but there is
also much depravity so that it is not certain.

The number of which the House of Representatives is to consist
forms another, and a very interesting point of view under which this
branch of the federal legislature may be contemplated. . . . The truth is,
that in all cases a certain number at least seems to be necessary to secure
the benefits of free consultaton and discussion, and to guard against too
easy a combination for improper purposes: As on the other hand, the
number ought at most to be kept within a certain limit, in order to avoid
the confusion and intemperance of a multitude. In all very numerous
assemblies, of whatever characters composed, passion never fails to
wrest the sceptre from reason. Had every Athenian citizen been a Socrates, every Athenian assembly would still have been a mob. . . .

As there is a degree of depravity in mankind which requires a certain
degree of circumspection and distrust: So there are other qualities in
human nature, which justify a certain portion of esteem and confidence.
Republican government presupposes the existence of these qualities in
a higher degree than any other form. Were the pictures which have been

drawn by the political jealousy of some among us, faithful likenesses of the human character, the inference would be that there is not sufficient virtue among men for self-government; and that nothing less than the chains of despotism can restrain them from destroying and devouring one another.

PUBLIUS.

∞

Abigail Adams to Mary Smith Cranch, February 20, 1785

IN THIS letter to her sister, Abigail Adams expresses what I have called "getting used to decadence." The setting and time are of course different, and today we might think Abigail's outrage at Parisian dancing girls quaint. But Abigail, as always, is onto something. As Dostoevsky's Raskolnikov put it: "Man gets used to everything—the beast!" Abigail Adams's observation that "there is no Sumit of virtue, and no Depth of vice, which Humane Nature is not capable of riseing to, on the one hand, or sinking into on the other" is on the mark. Few of us, though, are as self-aware and as candid as Abigail is in this letter.

This Day 3 Months I sailed for Europe since which many new and interesting Scenes have presented them selves before me. I have seen many of the Beauties and some of the Deformities of this old World. I have been more than ever convinced that there is no Sumit of virtue, and no Depth of vice which Humane Nature is not Capable of riseing to, on the one hand, or sinking into on the other. I have felt the force of an observation which I have read, that "daily example is the most subtle of prisons." I have found my taste reconciling itself to habits customs and fashions, which at first disgusted me. The first dance which I saw upon the Stage shoked me, the Dress'es and Beauty of the performers was enchanting, but no sooner did the Dance commence, than I felt my delicacy wounded, and I was ashamed to bee seen to look at them. Girls cloathd in the thinest Silk; and Gauze, with their peticoats short Springing two foot from the floor poising themselves in the air, with their feet flying, and as perfectly shewing their Garters and draws, as tho no peticoat had been worn, was a sight altogether new to me. Their motions are as light as air and as quick as lightning. They balance themselves to astonishment. No description can equal the reality. They are daily trained to it from early infancy at a Royal academy instituted for this purpose. You will very often see little creatures not more than 7 or 8 years old as undauntedly performing their parts as the eldest amongst them. Shall I speak a Truth and say that repeatedly seeing these Dances has worn of that disgust which I first felt, and that I see them now with pleasure. Yet when I consider the tendency of these things, the passions they must excite, and the known Character, even to a proverb, which is attached to an opera Girl, my abhorrence is not lessned, and neither my Reason or judgment have accompanied my Sensibility in acquiring any degree of callousness.

∞

"Is There No Virtue Among Us?" James Madison, Virginia Ratifying Convention, June 20, 1788

JAMES MADISON was the lead advocate for the Constitution at the Virginia Ratifying Convention. His chief antagonist was Patrick Henry. Henry was a dazzling speaker, much better than Madison, who had a weak voice and was often in frail health. But Madison persevered; James Barbour, a prominent Virginia statesman, described the Madison-Henry match-up by noting that Madison's voice, compared to Henry's, was "inconveniently feeble, so that when he rose to speak, the members, lest they should lose a word, were accustomed to gather around him. He used little or no gesture; his style of speaking was pure and simple, and without ornament. Yet, modestly confiding in his own vast resources, and strong in the conviction of the righteousness of his cause, day after day, for six weeks, he continued to wrestle successfully with his gigantic opponent . . . so that his words fell upon his audience like the response of an ancient oracle—adored for its truth and wisdom. In fine, the good genius of his country was in him personified." [*]

Here is one of Madison's speeches, delivered five days before Virginia ratified the Constitution. Though Madison devised America's institu-

---

[*] Cited in Koch, *Advice to My Country*, pp. 87–88.

tions with the understanding that human nature is fallen, here he explains that these institutions rely on the "virtue and wisdom" of the people for their success.

I have observed, that gentlemen suppose, that the general legislature will do every mischief they possibly can, and that they will omit to do every thing good which they are authorised to do. If this were a reasonable supposition, their objections would be good. I consider it reasonable to conclude, that they will as readily do their duty, as deviate from it: Nor do I go on the grounds mentioned by gentlemen on the other side—that we are to place unlimited confidence in them, and expect nothing but the most exalted integrity and sublime virtue. But I go on this great republican principle, that the people will have virtue and intelligence to select men of virtue and wisdom. Is there no virtue among us? If there be not, we are in a wretched situation. No theoretical checks— no form of government can render us secure. To suppose that any form of government will secure liberty or happiness without any virtue in the people, is a chimerical idea, if there be sufficient virtue and intelligence in the community, it will be exercised in the selection of these men. So that we do not depend on their virtue, or put confidence in our rulers, but in the people who are to choose them.

∞

Thomas Jefferson, To the Inhabitants of Albemarle County, Virginia, April 3, 1809

AFTER YEARS of public service in America and in the gilded halls of Europe, Thomas Jefferson retired to Albemarle County, Virginia, submitting his character to the judgment of his neighbors.

The part which I have acted on the theatre of public life, has been before them; and to their sentence I submit it; but the testimony of my native country, of the individuals who have known me in private life, to my conduct in its various duties and relations, is the more grateful, as proceeding from eye witnesses and observers, from triers of the vicinage. Of you, then, my neighbors, I may ask, in the face of the world, "whose ox have I taken, or whom have I defrauded? Whom have I oppressed, or of whose hand have I received a bribe to blind mine eyes therewith?"

On your verdict I rest with conscious security. Your wishes for my happiness are received with just sensibility, and I offer sincere prayers for your own welfare and prosperity.

James Madison Refuses to "Treat" Voters

MADISON WROTE in 1788 that under a republican form of government, there must be "sufficient virtue and intelligence in the community" in order for the people to elect officials with "virtue and wisdom." Madison acted on this belief early in his career when he ran for the Virginia General Assembly in 1777. The previous year, Madison had served as a delegate at the Virginia Convention and proposed an important revision to the Virginia Declaration of Rights that broadened the scope of religious liberties. At the age of twenty-six, he was a rising star.

He was defeated in this election, however, by a much less capable candidate because he refused to "treat" voters with alcoholic beverages. A long-held practice in England, Madison didn't think "treating" was a practice befitting a republican form of government. He didn't think men should win elections by getting the electorate drunk. As a result, he lost the election; but out of recognition for his talents and past contributions, the Virginia Assembly elected him to serve on the Council of State, which was the executive body of the new Virginia Constitution. He never lost another election, though we don't know if he continued his policy of not buying drinks.

On the day of their proceedings mentioned above, the General Assembly of Virginia adjourned, after a laborious and most important session of three months. At that time its meetings were semi-annual,—in May and in October. A new election of delegates took place annually in April. At the ensuing election of 1777, Mr. Madison was outvoted by candidates who brought to their aid a species of influence unfortunately not uncommon in that day, but against which he was firmly principled. The practice of *treating* at elections was one which, in England, had long and rankly flourished in spite of prohibitory enactments; and it had been transplanted, with the representative institutions which it tended to vitiate and corrupt, to the virgin soil of the new world. Mr. Madison, believing, to use his own language, that "the reputation and success of representative government depended on the purity of popular elections," resolved to give no countenance to a practice which he deemed so destructive of it; and he declined, therefore, to follow the example of his competitors in courting the suffrages of the electors by offering them treats. He fell a victim, as others have done before and since, to the inflexibility of his principles; but his self-respect raised him above the mortification of defeat. In a paper containing some reflections on the importance of maintaining the purity of popular elections, he has incidentally given an account of this early experience of his political life, which we cannot do better than to present in his own words to the reader.

"In Virginia, where the elections to the colonial legislature were septennial, and the original settlers of the prevailing sentiments and manners of the parent nation, the modes of canvassing for popular votes in that country were generally practised. The people not only tolerated, but expected and even required to be courted and treated. No candidate, who neglected those attentions, could be elected. His forbearance would have been ascribed to a mean parsimony, or to a proud disrespect for the voters.

"The spirit of the Revolution and the adoption of annual elections seeming to favor a more chaste mode of conducting elections in Virginia, my way of thinking on the subject determined me to attempt, by an example, to introduce it. It was found that the old habits were too deeply rooted to be suddenly reformed. Particular circumstances obtained for me success in the first election, at which I was a candidate. At the next, I was outvoted by two candidates, neither of them having superior pretensions, and one particularly deficient in them; but both of them availing themselves of all the means of influence familiar to the people. My reserve was imputed to want of respect for them, if to no other unpopular motive."

—William Rives, *Life and Times of James Madison*

∞

Abigail Adams to Mary Smith Cranch, January 20, 1787

THIS IS a typical letter of Abigail Adams—full of self-knowledge and "a train of moral reflections." The pursuit of happiness—running from one pleasure to another—she says, is not a fully human life. A fully human life rests on inward happiness—the cultivation of the mind and the soul.

To derive a proper improvement from company, it ought to be select, and to consist of persons respectable both for their morals and their understanding; but such is the prevailing taste, that provided you can be in a crowd, with here and there a glittering star, it is considered of little importance what the character of the person is who wears it. Few consider that the foundation stone, and the pillar on which they erect the fabric of their felicity, must be in their own hearts, otherwise the winds of dissipation will shake it, and the floods of pleasure overwhelm it in ruins. What is the chief end of man? is a subject well worth the investigation of every rational being. What, indeed, is life, or its enjoyments, without settled principle, laudable purposes, mental exertions, and internal comfort, that sunshine of the soul; and how are these to be acquired in the hurry and tumult of the world? My visit to Bath, and the scenes which I mixed in, instead of exciting a gayety of disposition, led me into a train of moral reflections, which I could not refrain from detailing to you in my account of it.

❧

Benjamin Franklin, "On Constancy," Pennsylvania Gazette, *April 4, 1734*

CONSTANCY—OR steadiness and perseverance—Franklin considered a great enabler to the other virtues. Indeed, he considered it a virtue in its own right. Having a high IQ or good intentions does not make one a good citizen or good friend or guarantee success in life. It is the virtue of perseverance that is a more likely ally.

When I have sometimes observ'd Men of Wit and Learning, in Spite of their excellent natural and acquir'd Qualifications, fail of obtaining that Regard and Esteem with Mankind, which their Inferiors in point of Understanding frequently arrive at, I have, upon a slight Reflection, been apt to think, that it was owing to the ill Judgment, Malice, or Envy of their Acquaintance: But of late two or three flagrant Instances of this kind have put me upon thinking and deliberating more maturely, and I find within the Compass of my Observation the greatest part of those fine

Men have been ruined for want of *CONSTANCY,* a Virtue never too highly priz'd, and whose true Worth is by few rightly understood.

A Man remarkably wavering and inconstant, who goes through with no Enterprize, adheres to no Purpose that he has resolv'd on, whose Courage is surmounted by the most trifling Obstacles, whose Judgment is at any time byass'd by his Fears, whose trembling and disturb'd Imagination will at every Turn suggest to him Difficulties and Dangers that actually have no Existence, and enlarge those that have; A Man, I say, of this Stamp, whatever natural and aquir'd Qualities he may have, can never be a truly useful Member of a Common-wealth, a sincere or amiable Friend, or a formidable Enemy; and when he is once incapable of bearing either of these Characters, 'tis no Wonder he is contemn'd and disregarded by Men of all Ranks and Conditions.

Without Steadiness or Perseverance no Virtue can long subsist; and however honest and well-meaning a Man's Principles may be, the Want of this is sufficient to render them ineffectual, and useless to himself or others. Nor can a Man pretend to enjoy or impart the lasting Sweets of a strict and glorious Friendship, who has not Solidity enough to despise the malicious Misrepresentations frequently made use of to disturb it, and which never fail of Success where a mutual Esteem is not founded upon the solid Basis of Constancy and Virtue. An Intimacy of this sort, contracted by chance, or the Caprice of an unstable Man, is liable to the most violent Shocks, and even an intire Ruin, from very trifling Causes. Such a Man's Incapacity for Friendship, makes all that know his Character absolutely indifferent to him: His known Fickleness of Temper renders him too inconsiderable to be fear'd as a Foe, or caress'd as a Friend.

I may venture to say there never was a Man eminently famous but what was distinguish'd by this very Qualification; and few if any can live comfortably even in a private Life without it; for a Man who has no End in View, no Design to pursue, is like an irresolute Master of a Ship at Sea, that can fix upon no one Port to steer her to, and consequently can call not one Wind favourable to his Wishes. . . .

∞

Thomas Jefferson to Dr. Walter Jones, *January 2, 1814*

HERE IS an apt description of George Washington's character by Thomas Jefferson, who chose to emphasize Washington's prudence. To

Aristotle and the ancient Greeks, prudence was one of the essential virtues of the good man and the good statesman. It was a type of intellectual quality that went beyond mere habituation and rote learning. In many ways the capstone of virtue, prudence is that character and habit of mind that enables the good and wise person to apply his erudition and experience to concrete events as they arise—to deliberate wisely.

Note the sobriety and balance of the description. Here is as subject one of the greatest Americans of all time. Jefferson doesn't exaggerate and notes the strengths and the weaknesses, both.

I think I knew General Washington intimately and thoroughly; and were I called on to delineate his character, it should be in terms like these.

His mind was great and powerful, without being of the very first order; his penetration strong, though not so acute as that of a Newton, Bacon, or Locke; and as far as he saw, no judgment was ever sounder. It was slow in operation, being little aided by invention or imagination, but sure in conclusion. Hence the common remark of his officers, of the advantage he derived from councils of war, where hearing all suggestions, he selected whatever was best; and certainly no General ever planned his battles more judiciously. But if deranged during the course of the action, if any member of his plan was dislocated by sudden circumstances, he was slow in re-adjustment. The consequence was, that he often failed in the field, and rarely against an enemy in station, as at Boston and York. He was incapable of fear, meeting personal dangers with the calmest unconcern. Perhaps the strongest feature in his character was prudence, never acting until every circumstance, every consideration, was maturely weighed; refraining if he saw a doubt, but, when once decided, going through with his purpose, whatever obstacles opposed. His integrity was most pure, his justice the most inflexible I have ever known, no motives of interest or consanguinity, of friendship or hatred, being able to bias his decision. He was, indeed, in every sense of the words, a wise, a good, and a great man. His temper was naturally high toned; but reflection and resolution had obtained a firm and habitual ascendancy over it. If ever, however, it broke its bonds, he was most tremendous in his wrath. In his expenses he was honorable, but exact; liberal in contributions to whatever promised utility; but frowning and unyielding on all visionary projects and all unworthy calls on his charity. His heart was not warm in its affections; but he exactly calculated every man's value, and gave him a solid esteem proportioned to it. His person, you know, was fine, his stature exactly what one would wish, his deportment easy, erect and noble; the best horseman of his age, and the most graceful figure that could be seen on horseback. Although in the circle of his friends, where he might be unreserved with safety, he took a free share in conversation, his colloquial talents were not above mediocrity, possessing neither copiousness of ideas, nor fluency of words. In public, when called on for a sudden opinion, he was unready, short and embarrassed. Yet he wrote readily, rather diffusely, in an easy and correct style. This he had acquired by conversation with the world, for his education was merely reading, writing and common arithmetic, to which he added surveying at a later day. His time was employed in action chiefly, reading little, and that only in agriculture and English history. His correspondence became necessarily extensive, and, with journalizing his agricultural proceedings, occupied most of his leisure hours within doors. On the whole, his character was, in its mass, perfect, in nothing bad, in few points indifferent; and it may truly be said, that never did nature and fortune combine more perfectly to make a man great, and to place him in the same constellation with whatever worthies have merited from man an everlasting remembrance. For his was the singular destiny and merit, of leading the armies of his country successfully through an arduous war, for the establishment of its independence; of conducting its councils through the birth of a government, new in its forms and principles, until it had settled down into a quiet and orderly train; and of scrupulously obeying the laws through the whole of his career, civil and military, of which the history of the world furnishes no other example.

∞

Benjamin Franklin to Joseph Priestley, September 19, 1772

JOSEPH PRIESTLEY was an English philosopher, scientist (the discoverer of oxygen), and clergyman, with whom Franklin often discussed his scientific experiments. Priestley asked Franklin for some advice on what we might today call a "career move." Franklin shares his method of moral or "prudential algebra" with his friend. We all face choices in our lives—here's a way of avoiding rash decisions. Many people use such a method today. I do.

Dear Sir,

In the Affair of so much Importance to you, wherein you ask my Advice, I cannot for want of sufficient Premises, advise you *what* to determine, but if you please I will tell you *how*. When these difficult Cases occur, they are difficult chiefly because while we have them under Consideration all the Reasons *pro* and *con* are not present to the Mind at the same time; but sometimes one Set present themselves, and at other times another, the first being out of Sight. Hence the various Purposes or Inclinations that alternately prevail, and the Uncertainty that perplexes us. To get over this, my Way is, to divide half a Sheet of Paper by a Line into two Columns, writing over the one *Pro,* and over the other *Con.* Then during three or four Days Consideration I put down under the different Heads short Hints of the different Motives that at different Times occur to me for or against the Measure. When I have thus got them all together in one View, I endeavour to estimate their respective Weights; and where I find two, one on each side, that seem equal, I strike them both out: If I find a Reason *pro* equal to some two Reasons *con,* I strike out the three. If I judge some two Reasons *con* equal to some three Reasons *pro,* I strike out the five; and thus proceeding I find at length where the Balance lies; and if after a Day or two of farther Consideration nothing new that is of Importance occurs on either side, I come to a Determination accordingly. And tho' the Weight of Reasons cannot be taken with the Precision of Algebraic Quantities, yet when each is thus considered separately and comparatively, and the whole lies before me, I think I can judge better, and am less likely to make a rash Step; and in fact I have found great Advantage from this kind of Equation, in what may be called *Moral* or *Prudential Algebra.* Wishing sincerely that you may determine for the best, I am ever, my dear Friend, Yours most affectionately

∞

George Washington: "A Vice Grown into Fashion"

FOR WASHINGTON, it was not enough to have an army of brave and courageous soldiers, they had to be pious as well. Here he warns them against the vice of "profane cursing." It is interesting that although Washington didn't make it a practice, he did swear—even famously at the Battle at the Monmouth Courthouse. There General Charles Lee, against the protests of Lafayette and Hamilton, began a retreat from British soldiers who he believed outnumbered his men. Washington was a few miles away on his horse when he learned of the retreat and rode furiously to the Courthouse. According to one report, Washington approached General Lee and swore "till the leaves shook on the trees. Charming! Delightful! Never have I enjoyed such swearing before or since. Sir, on that memorable day, he swore like an angel from heaven."[*] Lafayette was similarly impressed, and the Americans held the British to a draw on that day.

GENERAL ORDER

The General is sorry to be informed that the foolish and wicked practice of profane cursing and swearing, a vice heretofore little known in an American army, is growing into fashion. He hopes the officers will, by example as well as influence, endeavor to check it, and that both they and the men will reflect, that we can have little hope of the blessing of Heaven on our arms, if we insult it by our impiety and folly. Added to this, it is a vice so mean and low, without any temptation, that every man of sense and character detests and despises it.

∞

John Jay to Benjamin Rush, March 21, 1785

SOME SOUND thoughts from John Jay about the place of knowledge in a republic like America.

I consider knowledge to be the soul of a republic, and as the weak and the wicked are generally in alliance, as much care should be taken to diminish the number of the former as of the latter. Education is the way to do this, and nothing should be left undone to afford all ranks of people the means of obtaining a proper degree of it at a cheap and easy rate.

[*] Cited in Brookhiser, *Founding Father,* p. 32.

Benjamin Rush to Richard Price, May 25, 1786

WRITING A decade after American independence was first declared, Rush observes that the American Revolution is far from complete. A new form of government—republicanism—requires new kinds of "principles, opinions, and manners." A self-governing people must equip themselves with the knowledge and virtue to rule themselves. This is why Rush believed a system of popular education was so essential.

Most of the *distresses* of our country, and of the *mistakes* which Europeans have formed of us, have arisen from the mistaken belief that the American Revolution is *over*. This is so far from being the case that we have only finished the first act of the great drama. We have changed our forms of government, but it remains yet to effect a revolution in our principles, opinions, and manners so as to accommodate them to the forms of government we have adopted. This is the most difficult part of the business of the patriots and legislators of our country. It requires more wisdom and fortitude than to expel or to reduce armies into captivity. I wish to see this idea inculcated by your pen. Call upon the rulers of our country to lay the foundations of their empire in *knowledge* as well as virtue. Let our common people be compelled by law to give their children (what is commonly called) a good English education. Let schoolmasters of every description be supported in part by the public, and let their principles and morals be subjected to examination before we employ them. . . . This plan of general education alone will render the American Revolution a blessing to mankind.

∞

John Adams, "Dissertation on the Canon and Feudal Law," 1765

THIS EXCERPT from Adams's "Dissertation on the Canon and Feudal Law" was written in 1765, the same year that the Stamp Act was passed. Adams argues that Americans must be vigilant about protecting their rights — rights which the British were violating. The best way for Americans of all ranks, rich or poor, to guard the blessings of liberty is through education. Adams dares Americans to study and read and think about their principles of government, and their history, so that they will be able to safeguard its future.

Liberty cannot be preserved without a general knowledge among the people, who have a right, from the frame of their nature, to knowledge, as their great Creator, who does nothing in vain, has given them understandings, and a desire to know; but besides this, they have a right, an indisputable, unalienable, indefeasible, divine right to that most dreaded and envied kind of knowledge; I mean, of the characters and conduct of their rulers. Rulers are no more than attorneys, agents, and trustees, for the people; and if the cause, the interest and trust, is insidiously betrayed, or wantonly trifled away, the people have a right to revoke the authority that they themselves have deputed, and to constitute abler and better agents, attorneys, and trustees. And the preservation of the means of knowledge among the lowest ranks is of more importance to the public than all the property of all the rich men in the country. . . .

Let us dare to read, think, speak, and write. Let every order and degree among the people rouse their attention and animate their resolution.

Let the bar proclaim "the laws, the rights, the generous plan of power" delivered down from remote antiquity—inform the world of the mighty struggles and numberless sacrifices made by our ancestors in defense of freedom. Let it be known that original rights, conditions of original contracts, [are] coequal with prerogative and coeval with government; that many of our rights are inherent and essential, agreed on as maxims and established as preliminaries even before a parliament existed. Let them search for the foundations of British laws and government in the frame of human nature, in the constitution of the intellectual and moral world. There let us see that truth, liberty, justice, and benevolence are its everlasting basis, and if these could be removed, the superstructure is overthrown of course.

Let the colleges join their harmony in the same delightful concert. Let every declamation turn upon the beauty of liberty and virtue, and the deformity, turpitude, and malignity of slavery and vice. Let the public disputations become researches into the grounds and nature and ends of government, and the means of preserving the good and demolishing the evil. Let the dialogues, and all the exercises, become the instruments of impressing on the tender mind, and in spreading and distributing far and wide, the ideas of right and the sensations of freedom.

In a word, let every sluice of knowledge be opened and set a-flowing.

∞

Thomas Jefferson, Report of the Commissioners for the University of Virginia, Meeting in Rockfish Gap, Virginia, to the State Legislature

JEFFERSON WAS in France during the Constitutional Convention. When he learned of the results from friends, Jefferson was less than enthusiastic. In part, his lukewarm endorsement of the Constitution can be attributed to the absence of a Bill of Rights, which was later added. But also, Jefferson believed that institutional arrangements were of secondary importance—the main supports for freedom must come from the virtue of the people, and the best way to ensure that was through education. As Jefferson wrote to James Madison on December 20, 1787: "Above all things I hope the education of the common people will be attended to; convinced that on their good sense we may rely with the most security for the preservation of a due degree of liberty."

In his attempt to revise the laws of Virginia shortly after American independence was declared, Jefferson believed it important to restructure the system of education to support the new form of government. To this end, Jefferson proposed a public school system to reach all children. The aim of his plan was to make education widely available to the masses, to make the people "worthy" and "able to guard the sacred deposit of the rights and liberties of their fellow citizens." Jefferson believed that his bill for a more general diffusion of knowledge was "by far the most important bill in our whole code." The Virginia Legislature did not adopt Jefferson's bill, but passed a watered-down version of it that scarcely resembled his original and radical plan for public education.

Jefferson revisited the question of education reform about thirty years later in Rockfish Gap, Virginia, where he was meeting to prepare and plan for the opening of the University of Virginia. In the Rockfish Gap Report, Jefferson examined the purposes of education in the primary and secondary schools, before addressing the university. Early education, as well as higher education, Jefferson thought, should develop not only skills but, most especially, the morality and virtue of American students. This way they would not only be self-sufficient but good citizens and neighbors as well. Or as Jefferson put it, education would make Americans "examples of virtue to others, and of happiness within themselves."

The objects of this primary education determine its character and limits. These objects would be,

To give to every citizen the information he needs for the transaction of his own business;

To enable him to calculate for himself, and to express and preserve his ideas, his contracts and accounts, in writing;

To improve, by reading, his morals and faculties;

To understand his duties to his neighbors and country, and to discharge with competence the functions confided to him by either;

To know his rights; to exercise with order and justice those he retains; to choose with discretion the fiduciary of those he delegates; and to notice their conduct with diligence, with candor, and judgment;

And, in general, to observe with intelligence and faithfulness all the social relations under which he shall be placed.

To instruct the mass of our citizens in these, their rights, interests and duties, as men and citizens, being then the objects of education in the primary schools, whether private or public, in them should be taught reading, writing and numerical arithmetic, the elements of mensuration (useful in so many callings), and the outlines of geography and history. And this brings us to the point at which are to commence the higher branches of education, of which the Legislature require the development; those, for example, which are,

To form the statesmen, legislators and judges, on whom public prosperity and individual happiness are so much to depend;

To expound the principles and structure of government, the laws which regulate the intercourse of nations, those formed municipally for our own government, and a sound spirit of legislation, which, banishing all arbitrary and unnecessary restraint on individual action, shall leave us free to do whatever does not violate the equal rights of another;

To harmonize and promote the interests of agriculture, manufactures and commerce, and by well informed views of political economy to give a free scope to the public industry;

To develop the reasoning faculties of our youth, enlarge their minds, cultivate their morals, and instill into them the precepts of virtue and order;

To enlighten them with mathematical and physical sciences, which advance the arts, and administer to the health, the subsistence, and comforts of human life;

And, generally, to form them to habits of reflection and correct action, rendering them examples of virtue to others, and of happiness within themselves.

These are the objects of that higher grade of education, the benefits and blessings of which the Legislature now propose to provide for the good and ornament of their country, the gratification and happiness of their fellow citizens, of the parent especially, and his progeny, on which all his affections are concentrated.

They are sensible that the advantages of well-directed education, moral, political and economical, are truly above all estimate. Education generates habits of application, of order, and the love of virtue; and controls, by the force of habit, any innate obliquities in our moral organization. We should be far, too, from the discouraging persuasion that man is fixed, by the law of his nature, at a given point; that his improvement is a chimera, and the hope delusive of rendering ourselves wiser, happier or better than our forefathers were. As well might it be urged that the wild and uncultivated tree, hitherto yielding sour and bitter fruit only, can never be made to yield better; yet we know that the grafting art implants a new tree on the savage stock, producing what is more estimable both in kind and degree. Education, in like manner, engrafts a new man on the native stock, and improves what in his nature was vicious and perverse into qualities of virtue and social worth. And it cannot be but that each generation succeeding to the knowledge acquired by all those who preceded it, adding to it their own acquisitions and discoveries, and handing the mass down for successive and constant accumulation, must advance the knowledge and well-being of mankind, not *infinitely,* as some have said, but *indefinitely,* and to a term which no one can fix and foresee.

∞

George Washington, Eighth Annual Address, December 7, 1796

O NE OF George Washington's dreams was to establish a national university, where American youth would study the principles of their government. He hoped too that such a university would contribute to national unity—as our motto has it, "e pluribus unum." Washington urged Congress to set aside funds for the university, but it never happened.

The Assembly to which I address myself, is too enlightened not to be fully sensible how much a flourishing state of the Arts and Sciences, contributes to National prosperity and reputation. True it is, that our Country, much to its honor, contains many Seminaries of learning highly respectable and useful; but the funds upon which they rest, are too narrow, to command the ablest Professors, in the different departments of liberal knowledge, for the Institution contemplated, though they would be excellent auxiliaries.

Amongst the motives to such an Institution, the assimilation of the principles, opinions and manners of our Country men, but the common education of a portion of our Youth from every quarter, well deserves attention. The more homogeneous our Citizens can be made in these particulars, the greater will be our prospect of permanent Union; and a primary object of such a National Institution should be, the education of our Youth in the science of *Government*. In a Republic, what species of knowledge can be equally important? and what duty, more pressing on its Legislature, than to patronize a plan for communicating it to those, who are to be the future guardians of the liberties of the Country?

∞

"Liberty and Learning," James Madison to W.T. Barry, August 4, 1822

MADISON GIVES his reasons for the importance of a public system of education for all children, of all ranks. Other countries, such as Great Britain, limited education to the propertied classes out of fear that educating the masses would upset the class system. Some Americans resisted the idea of public education, believing that they should not have to pay for the education of someone whose family couldn't afford paying for it themselves. But Madison points out that, in America, the rich today will probably be the poor in a few generations. Thus the rich who support public education now will be supporting their own descendants. A popular education is too valuable and essential for Americans to limit it to the few.

The liberal appropriations made by the Legislature of Kentucky for a general system of Education cannot be too much applauded. A popular Government, without popular information, or the means of acquiring it, is but a Prologue to a Farce or a Tragedy; or, perhaps both. Knowledge will forever govern ignorance: And a people who mean to be their own Governors, must arm themselves with the power which knowledge gives. . . .

Without such Institutions, the more costly of which can scarcely be provided by individual means, none but the few whose wealth enables them to support their sons abroad can give them the fullest education; and in proportion as this is done, the influence is monopolized which superior information every where possesses. At cheaper & nearer seats of Learning parents with slender incomes may place their sons in a course of education putting them on a level with the sons of the Richest. Whilst those who are without property, or with but little, must be peculiarly interested in a System which unites with the more Learned Institutions, a provision for diffusing through the entire Society the education needed for the common purposes of life. A system comprizing the Learned Institutions may be still further recommended to the more indigent class of Citizens by such an arrangement as was reported to the General Assembly of Virginia, in the year 1779, by a Committee appointed to revise laws in order to adapt them to the genius of Republican Government. It made part of a "Bill for the more general diffusion of knowledge" that wherever a youth was ascertained to possess talents meriting an education which his parents could not afford, he should be carried forward at the public expence, from seminary to seminary, to the completion of his studies at the highest.

But why should it be necessary in this case, to distinguish the Society into classes according to their property? When it is considered that the establishment and endowment of Academies, Colleges, and Universities are a provision, not merely for the existing generation, but for succeeding ones also; that in Governments like ours a constant rotation of property results from the free scope to industry, and from the laws of inheritance, and when it is considered moreover, how much of the exertions and privations of all are meant not for themselves, but for their posterity, there can be little ground for objections from any class, to plans of which every class must have its turn of benefits. The rich man, when contributing to a permanent plan for the education of the poor, ought to reflect that he is providing for that of his own descendants; and the poor man who concurs in a provision for those who are not poor that at no distant day it may be enjoyed by descendants from himself. It does not require a long life to witness these vicissitudes of fortune.

. . . Throughout the Civilized World, nations are courting the praise of fostering Science and the useful Arts, and are opening their eyes to the principles and the blessngs of Representative Government. The American people owe it to themselves, and to the cause of free Government, to prove by their establishments for the advancement and diffusion of Knowledge, that their political Institutions which are attracting observation from evey quarter, and are respected as Models, by the new-born States in our own Hemisphere, are as favorable to the intellectual and moral improvement of Man as they are conformable to his individual & social Rights. What spectacle can be more edifying or more seasonable, than that of Liberty and Learning, each leaning on the other for their mutual & surest support?

∞

Thomas Jefferson to Benjamin Banneker, August 30, 1791

JEFFERSON, IN his *Notes on Virginia*, tentatively questioned the intellectual equality of blacks. In that work, he observed that blacks seemed inferior in their mental capacities. Later in life, however, he became more persuaded that the intellectual inferiority of blacks was due not to any intrinsic or natural difference but to their lack of education. They were, after all, slaves, who received no schooling whatsoever. He expresses this change of heart to Benjamin Banneker, who was a prominent black educator.

Sir,

I thank you sincerely for your letter of the 19th instant and for the Almanac it contained. No body wishes more than I do to see such proofs as you exhibit, that nature has given to our black brethren, talents equal to those of the other colors of men, and that the appearance of a want of them is owing merely to the degraded condition of their existence, both in Africa & America. I can add with truth, that no body wishes more ardently to see a good system commenced for raising the condition both of their body & mind to what it ought to be, as fast as the imbecility of their present existence, and other circumstances which cannot be neglected, will admit. I have taken the liberty of sending your Almanac to Monsieur de Condorcer, Secretary of the Academy of Sciences at Paris, and member of the Philanthropic society, because I considered it as a document to which your whole colour had a right for their justification against the doubts which have been entertained of them. I am with great esteem, Sir Your most obed⟨t⟩ humble serv⟨t⟩.

∞

Samuel Adams to Joseph Warren, November 4, 1775, and Samuel Adams to the Legislature, January 27, 1797

SAM ADAMS has been called the "last Puritan." Thomas Jefferson called him the "patriarch of liberty." Adams believed that morality and liberty go hand in hand. Here, the most rebellious of our patriots shares his thoughts on the central role of education in inculcating morality.

SAMUEL ADAMS TO JAMES WARREN

Let me talk with you a little about the Affairs of our own Colony. I perswade my self, my dear Friend, that the greatest Care and Circumspection will be used to conduct its internal Police with Wisdom and Integrity. The Eyes of Mankind will be upon you to see whether the Government, which is now more popular than it has been for many years past, will be productive of more Virtue moral and political. We may look up to Armies for our Defence, but Virtue is our best Security. It is not possible that any State shd long remain free, where Virtue is not supremely honord.

. . . Since private and publick Vices, are in Reality, though not always apparently, so nearly connected, of how much Importance, how necessary is it, that the utmost Pains be taken by the Publick, to have the Principles of Virtue early inculcated on the Minds even of children, and the moral Sense kept alive, and that the wise institutions of our Ancestors for these great Purposes be encouraged by the Government. For no people will tamely surrender their Liberties, nor can any be easily subdued, when knowledge is diffusd and Virtue is preservd. On the Contrary, when People are universally ignorant, and debauchd in their Manners, they will sink under their own weight without the Aid of foreign Invaders.

SAMUEL ADAMS TO THE LEGISLATURE OF MASSACHUSETTS

As Piety, Religion and Morality have a happy influence on the minds of men, in their public as well as private transactions, you will not think it unseasonable, although I have frequently done it, to bring to your remembrance the great importance of encouraging our University, town schools, and other seminaries of education, that our children and youth while they are engaged in the pursuit of useful science, may have their minds impressed with a strong sense of the duties they owe to their God, their instructors, and each other, so that when they arrive to a state of manhood, and take a part in any public transactions, their hearts having been deeply impressed in the course of their education with the moral feelings—such feelings may continue and have their due weight through the whole of their future lives.

∞

Thomas Jefferson, Aim and Curricula, University of Virginia, August 4, 1818

THIS WAS Thomas Jefferson's vision of an academic community. His University of Virginia was to be modeled after a family; professor and student were to take their cue from "the affectionate deportment between father and son." Unfortunately, this vision did not bear up to reality—a student riot involving one of Jefferson's great-nephews erupted a few years after the university was founded, and stricter disciplinary provisions were instituted. Still, it is a noble vision, one that Jefferson believed should be "woven into the American character."

The best mode of government for youth, in large collections, is certainly a desideratum not yet attained with us. It may be well questioned whether *fear* after a certain age, is a motive to which we should have ordinary recourse. The human character is susceptible of other incitements to correct conduct, more worthy of employ, and of better effect. Pride of character, laudable ambition, and moral dispositions are innate correctives of the indiscretions of that lively age; and when strengthened by habitual appeal and exercise, have a happier effect on future character than the degrading motive of fear. Hardening them to disgrace, to corporal punishments, and servile humiliations cannot be the best process for producing erect character. The affectionate deportment between father and son, offers in truth the best example for that of tutor and pupil; and the experience and practice of other* countries, in this respect, may be worthy of enquiry and consideration with us. It will then be for the wisdom and discretion of the Visitors to devise and perfect a proper system of government, which, if it be founded in reason and comity, will be more likely to nourish in the minds of our youth the combined spirit of order and self-respect, so congenial with our political institutions, and so important to be woven into the American character.

---

* A police exercised by the students themselves, under proper discretion, has been tried with success in some countries, and the father as forming them for initiation into the duties and practices of civil life.—T.J.

❧

John Adams, Massachusetts Constitution, 1780, and to Count Sarsfield

ADAMS'S HOPES for the new nation largely depend on the popular education and enlightenment of the people.

The Encouragement of Literature

Wisdom and knowledge, as well as virtue, diffused generally among the body of the people, being necessary for the preservation of their rights and liberties, and as these depend on spreading the opportunities and advantages of education in the various parts of the country, and among the different orders of the people, it shall be the duty of the legislatures and magistrates, in all future periods of this Commonwealth, to cherish the interests of literature and the sciences, and all seminaries of them; especially the university at Cambridge, public schools and grammar schools in the towns; to encourage private societies and public institutions, by rewards and immunities, for the promotion of agriculture, arts, sciences, commerce, trades, manufactures *and a natural history of the country;* to countenance and inculcate the principles of humanity and general benevolence, public and private charity, industry and frugality, honesty and punctuality in their dealings, sincerity, good humor and all social affections and generous sentiments among the people.

TO COUNT SARSFIELD, LONDON, FEBRUARY 3, 1786

. . . *It* has ever been my hobby-horse to see rising in America an empire of liberty, and a prospect of two or three hundred millions of freemen, without one noble or one king among them. You say it is impossible. If I should agree with you in this, I would still say, let us try the experiment, and preserve our equality as long as we can. A better system of education for the common people might preserve them long from such artificial inequalities as are prejudicial to society, by confounding the natural distinctions of right and wrong, virtue and vice.

∽

Benjamin Rush,
"Of the Mode of Education Proper in a Republic," 1798

TOCQUEVILLE ONCE observed that "everything which has a bearing on the status of women, their habits, and their thoughts is, in my view, of great political importance." Benjamin Rush believed that girls, like boys, "should be taught the principles of liberty and government" as they will have a decisive part in the perpetuation of America's institutions.

I beg pardon for having delayed so long to say any thing of the separate and peculiar mode of educaton proper for women in a republic. I am sensible that they must concur in all our plans of education for young men, or no laws will ever render them effectual. To qualify our women for this purpose, they should not only be instructed in the usual branches of female education, but they should be taught the principles of liberty and government; and the obligations of patriotism should be

inculcated upon them. The opinions and conduct of men are often regulated by the women in the most arduous enterprizes of life; and their
approbation is frequently the principal reward of the hero's dangers, and
the patriot's toils. Besides, the first impressions upon the minds of children are generally derived from the women. Of how much consequence,
therefore, is it in a republic, that they should think justly upon the great
subject of liberty and government!

The complaints that have been made against religion, liberty and
learning, have been, against each of them in a separate state. Perhaps
like certain liquors, they should only be used in a state of mixture. They
mutually assist in correcting the abuses, and in improving the good
effects of each other. From the combined and reciprocal influence of
religion, liberty and learning upon the morals, manners and knowledge
of individuals, of these, upon government, and of government, upon
individuals, it is impossible to measure the degrees of happiness and
perfection to which mankind may be raised. For my part, I can form no
ideas of the golden age, so much celebrated by the poets, more delightful, than the contemplation of that happiness which it is now in the
power of the legislature of Pennsylvania to confer upon her citizens, by
establishing proper modes and places of education in every part of the
state.

∞

Noah Webster,
"On the Education of Youth in America," 1788

NOAH WEBSTER, whose "blue back spellers" educated and unified
generations of Americans, was a constant advocate of what we today
would call civic education. During Webster's time, the case for a civic
education was made to promote unity and create a sense of national
spirit for a nation quite young. The case for it in the twentieth century
seems to me as strong as ever.

. . . *But* every child in America should be acquainted with his own
country. He should read books that furnish him with ideas that will be
useful to him in life and practice. As soon as he opens his lips, he should
rehearse the history of his own country; he should lisp the praise of

liberty, and of those illustrious heroes and statesmen who have wrought a revolution in her favor.

A selection of essays, respecting the settlement and geography of America; the history of the late revoluton and of the most remarkable characters and events that distinguished it, and a compendium of the principles of the federal and provincial governments, should be the principal school book in the United States. These are interesting objects to every man; they call home the minds of youth and fix them upon the interests of their own country, and they assist in forming attachments to it, as well as in enlarging the understanding.

"It is observed by the great Montesquieu, that the laws of education ought to be relative to the principles of the government."

In despotic governments, the people should have little or no education, except what tends to inspire them with a servile fear. Information is fatal to despotism.

In monarchies, education should be partial, and adapted to the rank of each class of citizens. But "in a republican government," says the same writer, "the whole power of education is required." Here every class of people should *know* and *love* the laws. This knowledge should be diffused by means of schools and newspapers; and an attachment to the laws may be formed by early impressions upon the mind.

Two regulations are essential to the continuance of republican governments: 1. Such a distribution of lands and such principles of descent and alienation, as shall give every citizen a power of acquiring what his industry merits. 2. Such a system of education as gives every citizen an opportunity of acquiring knowledge and fitting himself for places of trust. These are fundamental articles; the *sine qua non* of the existence of the American republics.

When I speak of a diffusion of knowledge, I do not mean merely a knowledge of spelling books, and the New Testament. An acquaintance with ethics, and with the general principles of law, commerce, money and government, is necessary for the yeomanry of a republican state. This acquaintance they might obtain by means of books calculated for schools, and read by the children, during the winter months, and by the circulation of public papers.

. . . Every small district should be furnished with a school, at least four months in a year, when boys are not otherwise employed. This school should be kept by the most reputable and well informed man in the district. Here children should be taught the usual branches of learning; submission to superiors and to laws; the moral or social duties; the history and transactions of their own country; the principles of liberty and government. Here the rough manners of the wilderness should be softened, and the principles of virtue and good behaviours inculcated. The *virtues* of men are of more consequence to society than their *abilities;* and for this reason, the *heart* should be cultivated with more assiduity than the *head.*

Such a general system of education is neither impracticable nor difficult; and excepting the formation of a federal government that shall be efficient and permanent, it demands the first attention of American patriots. Until such a system shall be adopted and pursued; until the Statesman and Divine shall unite their efforts in *forming* the human mind, rather than in loping its excrescences, after it has been neglected; until Legislators discover that the only way to make good citizens and subjects is to nourish them from infancy; and until parents shall be convinced that the *worst* of men are not the proper teachers to make the *best;* mankind cannot know to what a degree of perfection society and government may be carried. America affords the fairest opportunities for making the experiment, and opens the most encouraging prospect of success.

V

*I*NDUSTRY
AND
FRUGALITY

❦

"Let Frugality, and Industry, be our Virtues, if they are not of any others."

For generations, American children have been reminded by their parents of Benjamin Franklin's aphorism: "Early to bed, and early to rise, makes a man healthy, wealthy, and wise." The man behind the aphorism should know. As he himself tells us in his *Autobiography,* he "emerged from the poverty and obscurity" of his origins to "attain a degree of reputation in the world." The beginnings were as humble as the end was great. As a seventeen-year-old runaway he set sail from New York to Philadelphia. Landing at the Market Street wharf, "fatigued with traveling, rowing, and want of rest," his pockets "stuffed out with shirts and stockings," he had nothing to his name but a Dutch dollar and a copper shilling. Hungry, he went to a bakery and asked for three-penny's-worth of bread and, to his surprise, was given "three great puffy rolls," but "having no room in [his] pockets, [he] walked off with a roll under each arm, and eating the other." His future wife, Deborah Read, saw him as she stood outside her door on Market Street, and, as Franklin recounts, she "thought I made, as I certainly did, a most awkward, ridiculous appearance."

We can see in Franklin's humble beginnings and subsequent success as a scientist and statesman the story of the American Everyman. Ours is a country filled with men and women who began with little but a willingness to work and save and make good. And so this chapter focuses on industry and frugality—two qualities that ranked high in Franklin's catalogue of virtues and that have helped make our country what it is.

The philosopher John Locke, whose writings many of the Founders read, made the modern case for industry. Whereas in aristocratic ages there was a disdain for labor, Locke endorsed industry as a great virtue for a democratic people. Locke wrote: "God gave the world to men in common; but since he gave it them for their benefit and the greatest conveniences of life they were capable to draw from it, it cannot be supposed he meant it should always remain common and uncultivated. He gave it to the use of the industrious and rational (and *labour* was to be *his title* to it); not to the fancy or covetousness of the quarrelsome and contentious."

If our children are to grow up to be among the "industrious and rational" rather than the "quarrelsome and contentious," they must be raised with an appreciation of the importance of hard work. Work itself is the best way to learn about its own virtues and rewards; another good way is from understanding what is presented in this chapter.

As Locke observed, children generally hate to be idle, so it should come as no surprise that several of the entries here are letters from the Founders to their children. Industry comes naturally to children if only parents will see to it that they channel their "busy humour" into activities and pursuits that will be useful to them and to others.

As for adults, the Founders had a low opinion of idleness because they placed a high value on time. Here's Franklin: "Dost thou love Life? Then do not squander Time; for that's the stuff life is made of." (And he didn't know about television!) The Founders certainly set a very high standard when it comes to industriousness. It is well known that Jefferson took advantage of the minutes that made up his life, always rising before the sun and filling his day with worthwhile pursuits aimed at improving the mind and body. Or consider James Madison who graduated from Princeton in three years instead of four by, as he reports, bearing "five hours of sleep in twenty-four." It seems that he took to heart the admonition of his Princeton teacher and signer of the Declaration of Independence, John Witherspoon: "Do not live useless and die contemptible."

But why focus on work? Were the Founders what we could today pejoratively label "workaholics"? Certainly not. They were promoters of industriousness as a means of self-improvement. Industriousness begets leisure time in which we can pursue our other interests—for the Founders, this meant a variety of activities—horse riding, letter writing, conversation, etc. In Franklin's case, this meant life both as a world-renowned theoretical scientist and as an enormously gifted creator of useful inventions, such as the Franklin stove, which was widely used throughout the colonies because of the superior heating it provided. As Jefferson wrote to his daughter: "It is wonderful how much may be done if we are constantly doing."

Thus industriousness is more than a private or self-regarding virtue. It is about more than making a buck (Franklin never took out a patent on his ingenious stove). It is a public virtue, one that is of benefit to the general community. Communal projects cannot get done without a citizenry that is willing to contribute to the public weal—whether by voluntary efforts, such as Franklin's fire company, or more simply, by providing for one's family so that its members do not become a burden on the scarce resources of the community. "What maintains one vice," Franklin warned, "would bring up two children." Once again, I recur to Franklin on the public significance of this very American virtue: "Industry and constant Employment are great preservatives of the Morals and Virtue of a Nation."

It would be naive to dismiss entirely the plain fact that working hard can make life much more comfortable. By founding a commercial republic, where the pursuit of wealth would be open to all, the Founders provided a model of government that would increase the general welfare of all citizens. Thus the Founders embraced the idea that each citizen should do what he could to "better his condition" and make life more comfortable. Today, we call this pursuit the "American Dream." But the Founders were well aware that the unmitigated pursuit of wealth and affluence could lead to decadence. I'm thinking in particular of John and Samuel Adams who worried that the pursuit of riches would lead to a softening of morals and a relaxation of our first duty to God and country. John Adams famously asked Jefferson, "Will you tell me how to prevent luxury from producing effeminacy, intoxication, extravagance, vice and folly?"

John Adams understood the great danger of what is known today as the "cultural contradictions of capitalism." That is, though great wealth may lead to a more general prosperity, this prosperity can undermine itself by growing into decadence and hedonism. Franklin wrote that "prosperity discovers vice, adversity virtue." The injunctions to frugality, to simplicity, to plain dress may be difficult to heed in a nation grown accustomed to the great affluence of the last half-century. Yet we need to recover more of what the Founders believed. We have all heard the expression, "Clothes make the man." Not so according to George Washington, one of the wealthiest of the Founders. He wrote to his nephew Bushrod Washington: "Do not conceive that fine clothes make fine men. . . . A plain genteel dress is more admired and obtains more credit than lace and embroidery in the eyes of the judicious and sensible."

In our modern age of easy credit and consumer debt, of great affluence and great decadence, it is important to recall that industry and frugality are the sources not only of material success but of good and satisfactory living as well.

∞

Benjamin Franklin, Autobiography, *Plan for Moral Perfection*

WHILE STILL in his twenties, Benjamin Franklin embarked on a "bold and arduous project of arriving at moral perfection." In fact, he wrote his famous *Autobiography* largely to share with the world this project and to show how it might work for anybody willing to go through with it. At first glance, Franklin's plan may appear to be a stern attempt to take all the fun out of life. But this is not so—Franklin was not, as it turns out, a moral rigorist. If anything, Franklin's plan was to show how morality and virtue can work in one's self-interest. "Deny self for self's sake," Franklin suggested in *Poor Richard.* Virtue is an end in itself, but Franklin emphasizes how it can also be a means to making one happier and more successful in life. Morality and success, unlike today, were considered by Franklin to be inseparable.

Following is Franklin's list of the thirteen virtues. These are largely "bourgeois" virtues and have helped to make America an orderly and prosperous nation. And isn't there something especially American about Franklin's list? His list and his "method" in many ways represent the beginning of a long American tradition of self-improvement. The list, the virtues, and their corresponding vices are still familiar. Most of us have fallen short on most of them. But that is why we put them before us. For in this country, as Franklin observes, "one man of tolerable Abilities may work great Changes, and accomplish great Affairs among Mankind, if he first forms a good Plan, and . . . makes the Execution of that same Plan his sole Study and Business." There are so many self-help books these days, but Franklin's *Autobiography* is one of the best.

It was about this time I conceiv'd the bold and arduous project of arriving at moral perfection. I wish'd to live without committing any fault at any time; I would conquer all that either natural inclination, custom, or company might lead me into. As I knew, or thought I knew, what was right and wrong, I did not see why I might not always do the one and avoid the other. But I soon found I had undertaken a task of more difficulty than I had imagined. While my care was employ'd in guarding against one fault, I was often surprised by another; habit took the advantage of inattention; inclination was sometimes too strong for reason. I concluded, at length, that the mere speculative conviction that it was our interest to be completely virtuous, was not sufficient to prevent our slipping; and that the contrary habits must be broken, and good ones acquired and established, before we can have any dependence on a steady, uniform rectitude of conduct. For this purpose I therefore contrived the following method.

In the various enumerations of the moral virtues I had met with in my reading, I found the catalogue more or less numerous, as different writers included more or fewer ideas under the same name. Temperance, for example, was by some confined to eating and drinking, while by others it was extended to mean the moderating every other pleasure, appetite, inclination, or passion, bodily or mental, even to our avarice and ambition. I propos'd to myself, for the sake of clearness, to use rather more names, with fewer ideas annex'd to each, than a few names with more ideas; and I included under thirteen names of virtues all that at that time occurr'd to me as necessary or desirable, and annexed to each a short precept, which fully express'd the extent I gave to its meaning.

These names of virtues, with their precepts, were:

1. TEMPERANCE.

Eat not to dullness; drink not to elevation.

2. SILENCE.

Speak not but what may benefit others or yourself; avoid trifling conversation.

3. ORDER.

Let all your things have their places; let each part of your business have its time.

4. RESOLUTION.

Resolve to perform what you ought; perform without fail what you resolve.

5. FRUGALITY.

Make no expense but to do good to others or yourself; *i.e.,* waste nothing.

6. INDUSTRY.

Lose no time; be always employ'd in something useful; cut off all unnecessary actions.

7. SINCERITY.

Use no hurtful deceit; think innocently and justly, and, if you speak, speak accordingly.

8. JUSTICE.

Wrong none by doing injuries, or omitting the benefits that are your duty.

9. MODERATION.

Avoid extreams; forbear resenting injuries so much as you think they deserve.

10. CLEANLINESS.

Tolerate no uncleanliness in body, cloaths, or habitation.

11. TRANQUILLITY.

Be not disturbed at trifles, or at accidents common or unavoidable.

12. CHASTITY.

Rarely use venery but for health or offspring, never to dullness, weakness, or the injury of your own or another's peace or reputation.

13. HUMILITY.

Imitate Jesus and Socrates.

FRANKLIN DIDN'T leave anything to chance in his attempt to master the thirteen virtues. He devised a "method" to expunge each bad habit, one week at a time, and recorded his progress in a "little book." When public business and travels made him too busy to repeat the course, he still carried the little book with him always.

While this might seem extreme, even odd, the larger lesson here is, I think, that nobody is born good—it takes constant application to rid ourselves of bad habits. Today we see many analogues to Franklin's book—for cardiovascular health, nutritional health, even healthy relationships—then why not for moral health? The Founding Fathers, on good precedent, thought that kind of health more important. If it takes Franklin's method, then so be it.

My intention being to acquire the *habitude* of all these virtues, I judg'd it would be well not to distract my attention by attempting the whole at once, but to fix it on one of them at a time; and, when I should be master of that, then to proceed to another, and so on, till I should have gone thro' the thirteen; and, as the previous acquisition of some might facilitate the acquisition of certain others, I arrang'd them with that view, . . .

I made a little book, in which I allotted a page for each of the virtues. I rul'd each page with red ink, so as to have seven columns, one for each day of the week, marking each column with a letter for the day. I cross'd these columns with thirteen red lines, marking the beginning of each line with the first letter of one of the virtues, on which line, and in its proper column, I might mark, by a little black spot, every fault I found upon examination to have been committed respecting that virtue upon that day.

I determined to give a week's strict attention to each of the virtues successfully. Thus, in the first week, my great guard was to avoid every the least offence against *Temperance,* leaving the other virtues to their ordinary chance, only marking every evening the faults of the day. Thus, if in the first week I could keep my first line, marked T, clear of spots, I suppos'd the habit of that virtue so much strengthen'd, and its opposite weaken'd, that I might venture extending my attention to include the next, and for the following week keep both lines clear of spots. Proceeding thus to the last, I could go thro' a course compleat in thirteen weeks, and four courses in a year. And like him who, having a garden to weed, does not attempt to eradicate all the bad herbs at once, which would exceed his reach and strength, but works on one of the beds at a time, and, having accomplish'd the first, proceeds to a second, so I should have, I hoped, the encouraging pleasure of seeing on my pages the progress I made in virtue, by clearing successively my lines of their spots,

Form of the pages.

	S.	M.	T.	W.	T.	F.	S.
TEMPERANCE							
Eat not to dulness. Drink not to elevation.							
T.							
S.	*	*		*		*	
O.	**	*	*		*	*	*
R.			*			*	
F.		*			*		
I.			*				
S.							
J.							
M.							
C.							
T.							
C.							
H.							

till in the end, by a number of courses, I should be happy in viewing a clean book, after a thirteen weeks' daily examination.

WHILE FRANKLIN certainly worked hard at his "method" for attaining moral perfection, he admits he was not successful. He says here that he had the most trouble with the virtue of "order." But he didn't worry too much about it—he still affirms that the whole "endeavor" made him "a better and happier man." Below, he corrects those who aim for complete moral purity with his story of "speckled" versus "shiny" axes. Franklin is at his most charming here and shows that a little tolerance for human frailties and lapses is definitely in order.

My scheme of ORDER gave me the most trouble; and I found that, tho' it might be practicable where a man's business was such as to leave him the disposition of his time, that of a journeyman printer, for instance, it was not possible to be exactly observed by a master, who must mix with the world, and often receive people of business at their own hours. *Order,* too, with regard to places for things, papers, etc., I found extreamly difficult to acquire. I had not been early accustomed to it, and, having an exceeding good memory, I was not so sensible of the inconvenience attending want of method. This article, therefore, cost me so much painful attention, and my faults in it vexed me so much, and I made so little progress in amendment, and had such frequent relapses, that I was almost ready to give up the attempt, and content myself with a faulty character in that respect, like the man who, in buying an ax of a smith, my neighbour, desired to have the whole of its surface as bright as the edge. The smith consented to grind it bright for him if he would turn the wheel; he turn'd, while the smith press'd the broad face of the ax hard and heavily on the stone, which made the turning of it very fatiguing. The man came every now and then from the wheel to see how the work went on, and at length would take his ax as it was, without farther grinding. "No," said the smith, "turn on, turn on; we shall have it bright by-and-by; as yet, it is only speckled." "Yes," says the man, *"but I think I like a speckled ax best."* And I believe this may have been the case with many, who, having, for want of some such means as I employ'd, found the difficulty of obtaining good and breaking bad habits in other points of vice and virtue, have given up the struggle, and concluded that *"a speckled ax was best"*; for something, that pretended to be reason, was every now and then suggesting to me that such extream nicety as I exacted of myself might be a kind of foppery in morals, which, if it were known, would make me ridiculous; that a perfect character might be attended with the inconvenience of being envied and hated; and that a benevolent man should allow a few faults in himself, to keep his friends in countenance.

In truth, I found myself incorrigible with respect to Order; and now I am grown old, and my memory bad, I feel very sensibly the want of it. But, on the whole, tho' I never arrived at the perfection I had been so ambitious of obtaining, but fell far short of it, yet I was, by the endeavour, a better and a happier man than I otherwise should have been if I had not attempted it; as those who aim at perfect writing by imitating the engraved copies, tho' they never reach the wish'd for excellence of those copies, their hand is mended by the endeavour, and is tolerable while it continues fair and legible.

It may be well my posterity should be informed that to this little artifice, with the blessing of God, their ancestor ow'd the constant felicity of his life, down to his 79th year in which this is written.

∞

Thomas Jefferson to Martha Jefferson, November 28, 1783

TO GET a sense of what Thomas Jefferson expected of his ten-year-old daughter, Martha "Patsy" Jefferson, I have included the following letter in which he put her on a schedule. This is his idea of "industry" for a ten-year-old girl.

As you can see, Jefferson set high standards for his young daughter—standards that are perhaps a little too high for us today. But we can still learn from them. Research and common sense agree that children "learn up" to our expectations of them.

Dear Patsy,

After four days' journey, I arrived here without any accident, and in as good health as when I left Philadelphia. The conviction that you would be more improved in the situation I have placed you than if still with me, has solaced me on my parting with you, which my love for you has rendered a difficult thing. The acquirements which I hope you will make under the tutors I have provided for you will render you more worthy of my love; and if they cannot increase it, they will prevent its diminution. Consider the good lady who has taken you under her roof, who has undertaken to see that you perform all your exercises, and to admonish you in all those wanderings from what is right or what is clever, to which your inexperience would expose you; consider her, I say, as your mother, as the only person to whom, since the loss with which Heaven has pleased to afflict you, you can now look up; and that her displeasure or disapprobation, on any occasion, will be an immense misfortune, which should you be so unhappy as to incur by any unguarded act, think no concession too much to regain her good will. With respect to the distribution of your time, the following is what I should approve:

From 8 to 10, practice music.
From 10 to 1, dance one day and draw another.
From 1 to 2, draw on the day you dance, and write a letter next day.
From 3 to 4, read French.
From 4 to 5, exercise yourself in music.
From 5 till bed-time, read English, write, etc.

Communicate this plan to Mrs. Hopkinson, and if she approves of it, pursue it. As long as Mrs. Trist remains in Philadelphia, cultivate her affection. She has been a valuable friend to you, and her good sense and good heart make her valued by all who know her, and by nobody on earth more than me. I expect you will write me by every post. Inform me what books you read, what tunes you learn, and enclose me your best copy of every lesson in drawing. Write also one letter a week either to your Aunt Eppes, your Aunt Skipwith, your Aunt Carr, or the little lady from whom I now enclose a letter, and always put the letter you so write under cover to me. Take care that you never spell a word wrong. Always before you write a word, consider how it is spelt, and, if you do not remember it, turn to a dictionary. It produces great praise to a lady to spell well. I have placed my happiness on seeing you good and accomplished; and no distress this world can now bring on me would equal that of your disappointing my hopes. If you love me, then strive to be good under every situation and to all living creatures, and to acquire those accomplishments which I have put in your power, and which will go far towards ensuring you the warmest love of your affectionate father.

P.S. Keep my letters and read them at times, that you may always have present in your mind those things which will endear you to me.

∞

Alexander Hamilton's
"Rules for Mr. Philip Hamilton," 1800

PHILIP HAMILTON was the oldest child of Alexander and Elizabeth Hamilton. He was extremely bright and a favorite of his parents.

Hamilton set this regimen for his son, who had recently graduated from college and was studying law. But even these rules weren't enough to save Philip from being killed in a gun duel with a man who had once given a speech critical of his father. And like son, like father, about three years later, Alexander Hamilton himself died in a gun duel over political differences with Aaron Burr.

Compared to Patsy Jefferson's, this is a more reasonable schedule (and for an older person too).

From the first of April to the first of October he is to rise not later than six o'clock; the rest of the year not later than seven. If earlier, he will deserve commendation. Ten will be his hour of going to bed throughout the year.

From the time he is dressed, in the morning till nine o'clock (the time for breakfast excepted), he is to read law. At nine he goes to the office, and continues there until dinner time. He will be occupied partly in writing and partly in reading law.

After dinner he reads law at home till five o'clock. From this time till seven he disposes of his time as he pleases. From seven to ten he reads and studies whatever he pleases.

From twelve on Saturday he is at liberty to amuse himself.

On Sunday he will attend the morning church. The rest of the day may be applied to innocent recreations.

He must not depart from any of these rules without my permission.

∞

George Washington to George Washington Custis, January 7, 1798

GEORGE WASHINGTON'S adopted grandson, George Washington Custis, had recently dropped out of the College of New Jersey (now Princeton University) and returned home to Mount Vernon. Disappointed in his grandson's lack of discipline at school, Washington advised Custis that he should follow a "system" or schedule at Mount Vernon, which he devised for him in the following note. Much in the spirit of Franklin, Washington wrote to Custis that such a system "renders every thing more easy."

System in all things should be aimed at; for in execution, it renders every thing more easy.

If now and then, of a morning before breakfast, you are inclined, by way of change, to go out with a Gun, I shall not object to it; provided you return by the hour we usually set down to that meal.

From breakfast, until about an hour before Dinner (allowed for dressing, & preparing for it, that you may appear decent) I shall expect you will confine yourself to your studies; and diligently attend to them; endeavouring to make yourself master of whatever is recommended to, or required of you.

While the afternoons are short, and but little interval between rising from dinner and assembling for Tea, you may employ that time in walking, or any other recreation.

After Tea, if the Studies you are engaged in require it, you will, no doubt perceive the propriety & advantage of returning to them, until the hour of rest.

Rise early, that by habit it may become familiar—agreeable—healthy —and profitable. It may for a while, be irksome to do this; but that will wear off; and the practise will produce a rich harvest forever thereafter; whether in public, or private walks of Life.

Make it an invariable rule to be in place (unless extraordinary circumstances prevent it) at usual breakfasting, dining, and tea hours. It is [not] only disagreeable, but it is also very inconvenient, for servants to be running here, & there, and they know not where, to summon you to them, when their duties, and attendance, on the company who are seated, render it improper.

Saturday may be appropriated to riding to your Gun, or other proper amusements.

Time disposed of in this manner, makes ample provision for exercise & every useful, or necessary recreation; at the sametime that the hours allotted for study, *if really applied to it,* instead of running up & down stairs, & wasted in conversation with any one who will talk with you, will enable you to make considerable progress in whatsoever line is marked out for you: and that you may do it, is my sincere wish.

∞

Benjamin Franklin, "Advice to a Young Tradesman, Written by an Old One," 1748, *and* Autobiography

HERE'S SOME more good advice from Franklin on how to succeed in business. The ever shrewd Franklin advises here that it is essential to be not only industrious and frugal in reality but also to make sure one presents oneself in that way. His observation about creditors states a timeless truth. Franklin followed his own advice quite faithfully and ran his nearest competitor, Samuel Keimer, out of town, as the next entry from his *Autobiography* recounts.

Franklin, who was nearly penniless when he ran away from home as a young teenager and rose to become one of the most successful Americans, believed that in this country, the same path to success was open to other enterprising people. In his *Autobiography,* he ascribed "[t]o Industry and Frugality the early Easiness of his circumstances, and the Acquisition of His Fortune, with all that Knowledge which enabled him to be an Useful citizen, and obtained for him some Degree of Reputation among the Learned."

ADVICE TO A YOUNG TRADESMAN, WRITTEN BY AN OLD ONE

To my Friend A. B.
As you have desired it of me, I write the following Hints, which have been of Service to me, and may, if observed, be so to you.

Remember that TIME is Money. He that can earn Ten Shillings a Day by his Labour, and goes abroad, or sits idle one half of that Day, tho' he spends but Sixpence during his Diversion or Idleness, ought not to reckon That the only Expence; he has really spent or rather thrown away Five Shillings besides.

Remember that CREDIT is Money. If a Man lets his Money lie in my Hands after it is due, he gives me the Interest, or so much as I can make of it during that Time. This amounts to a considerable Sum where a Man has good and large Credit, and makes good Use of it.

Remember that Money is of a prolific generating Nature. Money can beget Money, and its Offspring can beget more, and so on. Five Shillings turn'd, is *Six:* Turn'd again, 'tis Seven and Three Pence; and so on 'til it becomes an Hundred Pound. The more there is of it, the more it produces every Turning, so that the Profits rise quicker and quicker. He that kills a breeding Sow, destroys all her Offspring to the thousandth Generation. He that murders a Crown, destroys all it might have produc'd, even Scores of Pounds. . . .

The most trifling Actions that affect a Man's Credit, are to be regarded. The Sound of your Hammer at Five in the Morning or Nine at Night, heard by a Creditor, makes him easy Six Months longer. But if he sees you at a Billiard Table, or hears your Voice in a Tavern, when you should be at Work, he sends for his Money the next Day. Finer Cloaths than he or his Wife wears, or greater Expence in any particular than he affords himself, shocks his Pride, and he duns you to humble you. Creditors are a kind of People, that have the sharpest Eyes and Ears, as well as the best Memories of any in the World. . . .

In short, the Way to Wealth, if you desire it, is as plain as the Way to Market. It depends chiefly on two Words, INDUSTRY and FRUGALITY; *i. e.* Waste neither Time nor Money, but make the best Use of both. He that gets all he can honestly, and saves all he gets (necessary Expences excepted) will certainly become RICH; If that Being who governs the World, to whom all should look for a Blessing on their Honest Endeavours, doth not in his wise Providence otherwise determine.

I began now gradually to pay off the debt I was under for the printing-house. In order to secure my credit and character as a tradesman, I took care not only to be in *reality* industrious and frugal, but to avoid all appearances to the contrary. I drest plainly; I was seen at no places of idle diversion. I never went out a fishing or shooting; a book, indeed, sometimes debauch'd me from my work, but that was seldom, snug, and gave no scandal; and, to show that I was not above my business, I sometimes brought home the paper I purchas'd at the stores thro' the streets on a wheelbarrow. Thus being esteem'd an industrious, thriving young man, and paying duly for what I bought, the merchants who imported stationery solicited my custom; others proposed supplying me with books, and I went on swimmingly. In the mean time, Keimer's credit and business declining daily, he was at last forc'd to sell his printing-house to satisfy his creditors. He went to Barbadoes, and there lived some years in very poor circumstances.

∞

Thomas Jefferson to Martha Jefferson, March 28, 1787

HERE IS Jefferson to Patsy again. She is now fourteen, the oldest of his children and a student in a convent in Paris when Jefferson, detecting a proclivity to idleness in his otherwise perfect daughter, exhorted her to be industrious. He stressed to Patsy the dangers of idleness, urging her to run from it "as you would from the precipice of a gulph." Jefferson told her that the "American character," as opposed to the European, would be one of self-reliance and independence, of finding "means within" ourselves. Industry was an important and necessary "habit" to inculcate for citizens in a country of such vast opportunities.

. . . *It* is your future happiness which interests me, and nothing can contribute more to it (moral rectitude always excepted) than the

contracting a habit of industry and activity. Of all the cankers of human happiness, none corrodes it with so silent, yet so baneful a tooth, as indolence. Body and mind both unemployed, our being becomes a burthen, and every object about us loathsome, even the dearest. Idleness begets ennui, ennui the hypochondria, and that a diseased body. No laborious person was ever yet hysterical. Exercise and application produce order in our affairs, health of body, chearfulness of mind, and these make us precious to our friends. It is while we are young that the habit of industry is formed. If not then, it never is afterwards. The fortune of our lives therefore depends on employing well the short period of youth. If at any moment, my dear, you catch yourself in idleness, start from it as you would from the precipice of a gulph. You are not however to consider yourself as unemployed while taking exercise. That is necessary for your health, and health is the first of all objects. For this reason if you leave your dancing master for the summer, you must increase your other exercise. I do not like your saying that you are unable to read the antient print of your Livy, but with the aid of your master. We are always equal to what we undertake with resolution. A little degree of this will enable you to decypher your Livy. If you always lean on your master, you will never be able to proceed without him. It is a part of the American character to consider nothing as desperate; to surmount every difficulty by resolution and contrivance. In Europe there are shops for every want. It's inhabitants therefore have no idea that their wants can be furnished otherwise. Remote from all other aid, we are obliged to invent and to execute; to find means within ourselves, and not to lean on others. Consider therefore the conquering your Livy as an exercise in the habit of surmounting difficulties, a habit which will be necessary to you in the country where you are to live, and without which you will be thought a very helpless animal, and less esteemed.

I do not doubt either your affection or dispositions. But great exertions are necessary, and you have little time left to make them. Be industrious then, my dear child. Think nothing unsurmountable by resolution and application, and you will be all that I wish you to be.

∞

Benjamin Franklin, "Information to Those Who Would Remove to America," September 1782

FRANKLIN SAYS here that bad examples are "more rare" in America, and this must comfort parents. Would he say the same today?

The almost general Mediocrity of Fortune that prevails in America obliging its People to follow some Business for subsistence, those Vices, that arise usually from Idleness, are in a great measure prevented. Industry and constant Employment are great preservatives of the Morals and Virtue of a Nation. Hence bad Examples to Youth are more rare in America which must be a comfortable Consideration to Parents. To this may be truly added, that serious Religion, under its various Denominations, is not only tolerated, but respected and practised. Atheism is unknown there; Infidelity rare and secret; so that persons may live to a great Age in that Country, without having their Piety shocked by meeting with either an Atheist or an Infidel. And the Divine Being seems to have manifested his Approbation of the mutual Forbearance and Kindness with which the different Sects treat each other, by the remarkable Prosperity with which He has been pleased to favour the whole Country.

∞

James Madison to William Bradford, November 9, 1772

WILLIAM BRADFORD (whom we've met in an earlier chapter) was Madison's fellow college classmate and good friend. Recent graduates of the College of New Jersey (now Princeton), Bradford and Madison had enjoyed their college days so much that they were now suffering a little from the post-graduation blues. Bradford was in Philadelphia, trying to figure out, as he put it, "what business I shall follow in my life." He told Madison ("Jemmy" to his friends) that he was in no hurry to figure this out. Madison wrote back to give him some affectionate advice to make sure his friend didn't languish for too long.

As you seem to require that I should be open and unreserved, (which is indeed the only proof of true friendship) I will venture to give you a word of advice, though it be more to convince you of my affection for you than from any apprehension of your needing it. Pray do not suffer those impertinent fops that abound in every city to divert you from your business and philosophical amusements. You may please them more by admitting them to the enjoyment of your company, but you will make them respect and admire you more by showing your indignation at their follies, and by keeping them at a becoming distance. I am luckily out of the way of such troubles, but I know you are surrounded with them; for they breed in towns and populous places as naturally as flies do in the shambles, because there they get food enough for their vanity and impertinence.

∞

"I Am Determined to Be Cool"
John Adams to Abigail Adams, July 1, 1774

IN JUNE 1774 John Adams was elected to be a Massachusetts delegate to the First Continental Congress. Adams was a thirty-nine-year-old lawyer, building a law practice, and father of four children. He viewed his election to the First Continental Congress with some trepidation. He was uncertain that he was up to the task—he worried about deficiencies in his education, social status, and political experience. He was also concerned about the financial security of his family. Though Adams had a large law practice, its future was far from certain. He also believed that he had spent his money "indiscreetly" on a few occasions: for books, a boat, a pew, and a house in Boston. How would his law practice and his family survive while he served his country in Philadelphia?

His duty to his country and to his family appeared to be in conflict. He wrote later to Abigail that "I am melancholly for the Public, and anxious for my Family, as for myself a Frock and Trowsers, an Hoe and Spade, would do for my Remaining Days. For God Sake make your children, *hardy, active,* and *industrious,* for Strength, Activity and Industry will be their only Resource and Dependence."

In this letter, John Adams shares his struggles with Abigail. His life and its travails echoes those of many others—as always, with Adams the echoes and travails are louder and deeper.

I am determined to be cool, if I can; I have suffered such Torments to my Mind, heretofore, as have almost overpowered my Constitution, without any Advantage: and now I will laugh and be easy if I can, let the Conflict of Parties, terminate as it will—let my own Estate and Interest suffer what it will. Nay whether I stand high or low in the Estimation of the World, so long as I keep a Conscience void of Offence towards God and Man. And thus I am determined by the Will of God, to do, let what will become of me or mine, my Country, or the World.

I shall arouse myself ere long I believe, and exert an Industry, a Frugality, a hard Labour, that will serve my family, if I cant serve my Country. I will not lie down and die in Dispair. If I cannot serve my Children by the Law, I will serve them by Agriculture, by Trade, by some Way, or other. I thank God I have a Head, an Heart and Hands which if once fully exerted alltogether, will succeed in the World as well as those of the mean spirited, low minded, fawning obsequious scoundrels who have long hoped, that my Integrity would be an Obstacle in my Way, and enable them to out strip me in the face.

But what I want in Comparison of them, of Villany and servility, I will make up in Industry and Capacity. If I dont they shall laugh and triumph.

I will not willingly see Blockheads, whom I have a Right to despise, elevated above me, and insolently triumphing over me. Nor shall Knavery, through any Negligence of mine, get the better of Honesty, nor Ignorance of Knowledge, nor Folly of Wisdom, nor Vice of Virtue.

I must intreat you, my dear Partner in all the Joys and Sorrows, Prosperity and Adversity of my Life, to take a Part with me in the Struggle. I pray God for your Health—intreat you to rouse your whole Attention to the Family, the stock, the Farm, the Dairy. Let every Article of Expence which can possibly be spared be retrench'd. Keep the Hands attentive to their Business, and [let] the most prudent Measures of every kind be adopted and pursued with Alacrity and Spirit.

I am &c.,   John Adams

∞

Benjamin Franklin, Poor Richard Improved or "The Way to Wealth," 1758

BENJAMIN FRANKLIN was twenty-six-years old when he wrote his first *Poor Richard's Almanack.* In his *Autobiography,* Franklin recounts that he filled his almanacks with "proverbial sentences, chiefly such as inculcating Industry and Frugality, as the means of procuring wealth and thereby securing virtue." His almanacks were extremely popular, and he sold more than ten thousand copies annually.

The following selection was the last *Poor Richard's Almanack.* By this time, Franklin was a very wealthy and successful man and had already retired from his printing business. Thus he could afford not to be so frugal, and he enjoyed spending his money on himself and others. But in this last almanack, Franklin culled together some of his best aphorisms on industry and frugality from past editions and put them in a speech by one of his created characters "Father Abraham." This essay was known as "The Way to Wealth."

The first part of "The Way to Wealth" focuses on the virtue of industry.

It would be thought a hard Government that should tax its People one-tenth Part of their *Time,* to be employed in its Service. But *Idleness* taxes many of us much more, if we reckon all that is spent in absolute *Sloth,* or doing of nothing, with that which is spent in idle Employments or Amusements, that amount to nothing. *Sloth,* by bringing on Diseases, absolutely shortens life. *Sloth, like Rust, consumes faster than Labour wears; while the used Key is always bright*, as *Poor Richard* says. *But dost thou love Life, then do not squander Time, for that's the stuff Life is made of*, as *Poor Richard* says. How much more than is necessary do we spend in sleep, forgetting that *The sleeping Fox catches no Poultry*, and that *There will be sleeping enough in the Grave*, as *Poor Richard* says.

If Time be of all Things the most precious, wasting Time must be, as *Poor Richard* says, *the greatest Prodigality;* since, as he elsewhere tells us, *Lost Time is never found again;* and *what we call Time enough, always proves little enough:* Let us then up and be doing, and doing to the Purpose; so by Diligence shall we do more with less Perplexity. *Sloth makes all Things difficult, but Industry all easy*, as *Poor Richard* says; and *He that riseth late must trot all Day, and shall scarce overtake his Business at Night;* while *Laziness travels so slowly, that Poverty soon overtakes him*, as we read in *Poor Richard*, who adds, *Drive thy Business, let not that drive thee;* and *Early to Bed, and early to rise, makes a Man healthy, wealthy, and wise.*

So what signifies *wishing* and *hoping* for better Times. We may make these Times better, if we bestir ourselves. *Industry need not wish*, as *Poor Richard* says, *and he that lives upon Hope will die fasting. There are no Gains without Pains; then Help Hands, for I have no Lands*, or if I have, they are smartly taxed. And as *Poor Richard* likewise observes, *He that hath a Trade hath an Estate; and he that hath a Calling, hath an Office of Profit and Honour;* but then the *Trade* must be worked at, and the *Calling* well followed, or neither the *Estate* nor the *Office* will enable us to pay our Taxes. If we are industrious, we shall never starve; for, as *Poor Richard* says, *At the working Man's House Hunger looks in, but dares not enter.* Nor will the Bailiff or the Constable enter, for *Industry pays Debts, while Despair encreaseth them*, says *Poor Richard.* What though you have found no Treasure, nor has any rich Relation left you a Legacy, *Diligence is the Mother of Good-luck* as *Poor Richard* says *and God gives all Things to Industry. Then plough deep, while Sluggards sleep, and you shall have Corn to sell and to keep*, says *Poor Dick.* Work while it is called To-day, for you know not how much you may be hindered To-morrow, which makes *Poor Richard* say, *One to-day is worth two To-morrows*, and farther, *Have you somewhat to do To-morrow, do it To-day.* If you were a Servant, would you not be ashamed that a good Master should catch you idle? Are you then your own Master, *be ashamed to catch yourself idle*, as *Poor Dick* says. When there is so much to be done for yourself, your family, your Country, and your gracious King, be up by Peep of Day; *Let not the Sun look down and say, Inglorious here he lies.* . . .

Methinks I hear some of you say, *Must a Man afford himself no Leisure?* I will tell thee, my friend, what *Poor Richard* says, *Employ thy Time well, if thou meanest to gain Leisure; and, since thou art not sure of a Minute, throw not away an Hour.* Leisure, is Time for doing something useful; this Leisure the diligent Man will obtain, but the lazy Man never; so that, as *Poor Richard* says *A Life of Leisure and a Life of Laziness are two Things.*

THE SECOND part of "The Way to Wealth" focuses on the benefits of Frugality.

So much for Industry, my Friends, and Attention to one's own Business; but to these we must add *Frugality,* if we would make our *Industry* more certainly successful. A Man may, if he knows not how to save as he gets, *keep his Nose all his Life to the Grindstone,* and die not worth a *Groat* at last. *A fat Kitchen makes a lean Will,* as *Poor Richard* says; and

> *Many Estates are spent in the Getting,*
> *Since Women for Tea forsook Spinning and Knitting,*
> *And Men for Punch forsook Hewing and Splitting.*

If you would be wealthy, says he, in another Almanack, *think of Saving as well as of Getting: The Indies have not made Spain rich, because her Outgoes are greater than her Incomes.*

Away then with your expensive Follies, and you will not then have so much Cause to complain of Hard Times, heavy Taxes, and chargeable Families; for, as *Poor Dick* says,

> *Women and Wine, Game and Deceit,*
> *Make the Wealth small and the Wants great.*

And farther, *What maintains one Vice, would bring up two Children.* You may think perhaps, that a *little* Tea, or a *little* Punch now and then, Diet a *little* more costly, Clothes a *little* finer, and a *little* Entertainment now and then, can be no *great* Matter; but remember what *Poor Richard* says, *Many a Little makes a Mickle;* and farther, Beware of little *Expences; A small Leak will sink a great Ship;* and again, *Who Dainties love, shall Beggars prove;* and moreover, *Fools make Feasts, and wise Men eat them.*

Here you are all got together at this Vendue of *Fineries* and *Knick-nacks*. You call them *Goods;* but if you do not take Care, they will prove *Evils* to some of you. You expect they will be sold *cheap,* and perhaps they may for less than they cost; but if you have no Occasion for them, they must be *dear* to you. Remember what *Poor Richard* says; *Buy what thou hast no Need of, and ere long thou shalt sell they Necessaries.* And again, *At a great Pennyworth pause a while:* He means, that perhaps the Cheapness is *apparent* only, and not *Real;* or the bargain, by straitening thee in thy Business, may do thee more Harm than Good. For in another Place he says, *Many have been ruined by buying good Pennyworths.* Again, *Poor Richard* says, 'tis *foolish to lay out Money in a Purchase of Repentance;* and yet this Folly is practised every Day at Vendues, for want of minding the Almanack. *Wise Men,* as *Poor Dick* says, *learn by others Harms, Fools scarcely by their own;* but *felix quem faciunt aliena pericula coutum.* Many a one, for the Sake of Finery on the Back, have gone with a hungry Belly, and half-starved their Families. *Silks and Sattins, Scarlet and Velvets,* as *Poor Richard* says, *put out the Kitchen Fire.*

These are not the *Necessaries* of Life; they can scarcely be called the *Conveniences;* and yet only because they look pretty, how many *want* to *have* them! The *artificial* Wants of Mankind thus become more numerous than the *Natural;* and, as *Poor Dick* says, *for one poor Person, there are an hundred indigent.* By these, and other Extravagancies, the Genteel are reduced to poverty, and forced to borrow of those whom they formerly despised, but who through Industry and Frugality have maintained their Standing; in which Case it appears plainly, that *A Ploughman on his Legs is higher than a Gentleman on his Knees,* as *Poor Richard* says. Perhaps they have had a small Estate left them, which they knew not the Getting of; they think, *'tis Day, and will never be Night;* that a little to be spent out of *so much,* is not worth minding; *a Child and a Fool,* as *Poor Richard* says, *imagine Twenty shillings and Twenty Years can never be spent* but, *always taking out of the Meal-tub, and never putting in, soon comes to the bottom;* as *Poor Dick* says, *When the Well's dry, they know the Worth of Water.* But this they might have known before, if they had taken his Advice; *If you would know the Value of Money, go and try to borrow some; for, he that goes a borrowing goes a sorrowing;* and indeed so does he that lends to such People, when he goes *to get it in again. Poor Dick* farther advises, and says,

> *Fond Pride of Dress is sure a very Curse;*
> *E'er Fancy you consult, consult your Purse.*

And again, *Pride is as loud a Beggar as Want, and a great deal more saucy.* When you have bought one fine Thing, you must buy ten more, that your Appearance may be all of a Piece; but *Poor Dick* says, *'Tis easier to suppress the first Desire, than to satisfy all that follow it.* And 'tis as truly Folly for the Poor to ape the Rich, as for the Frog to swell, in order to equal the ox.

> *Great Estates may venture more,*
> *But little Boats should keep near Shore.*

'Tis, however, a Folly soon punished; for *Pride that dines on Vanity, sups on Contempt,* as *Poor Richard* says. And in another Place, *Pride breakfasted with Plenty, dined with Poverty, and supped with Infamy.*

∞

Thomas Jefferson to Martha Jefferson, May 5 and May 21, 1787

J EFFERSON WROTE several more letters to his fourteen-year-old daughter telling her that industry is "the true secret, the grand recipe for felicity." By applying ourselves to our studies, our work, our hobbies, etc., we become self-reliant. Jefferson thought that if we equip ourselves with talents and skills, we will enjoy life to the fullest.

Jefferson tells Patsy that she should be "always doing." Jefferson's preoccupation with rooting out idleness in his daughter might seem strange to us children of the television age. Watching television—a passive activity—can be entertaining, but I think most of us would agree that it is not the most rewarding of activities for either the mind or body or soul and that much if it today is simply degrading. Whatever television is or is not, it is not "doing."

MAY 5, 1787

Determine never to be idle. No person will have occasion to complain of the want of time, who never loses any. It is wonderful how much may be done, if we are always doing. And that you may be always doing good, my dear, is the ardent prayer of yours affectionately.

MAY 21, 1787

I expect to be at Paris about the middle of next month. By that time we may begin to expect our dear Polly. It will be a circumstance of inexpressible comfort to me to have you both with me once more. The object most interesting to me for the residue of my life, will be to see you both developing daily those principles of virtue and goodness which will make you valuable to others and happy in yourselves, and acquiring those talents and that degree of science which will guard you at all times against ennui, the most dangerous poison of life. A mind always employed is always happy. This is the true secret, the grand recipe for felicity. The idle are the only wretched. In a world which furnishes so many emploiments which are useful, and so many which are amusing, it is our own fault if we ever know what ennui is, or if we are ever driven to the miserable resource of gaming, which corrupts our dispositions, and teaches us a habit of hostility against all mankind. We are now entering the port of Toulouse, where I quit my bark; and of course must conclude my letter. Be good and be industrious, and you will be what I shall most love in this world. Adieu my dear child. Yours affectionately.

∞

Benjamin Franklin, "Brave Men at Fires," 1733

BENJAMIN FRANKLIN and his fellow members of the Junto Club established Philadelphia's first voluntary fire company. Franklin also founded the first fire insurance company in America to protect homeowners and businessmen against fire losses.

The following selection demonstrates that industry is not just a virtue for purely selfish ends. Rather, as Franklin says in this entry, industry makes us "worthy" members of civil society, for it enables us to be of service to our neighbors.

TO THE PUBLISHER OF THE GAZETTE.

An experienc'd Writer, has said, there was never a great Man that was not an industrious Man, and I believe that there never was a good Man that was a lazy Man. . . .

The brave Men who at Fires are active and speedy with their best Advice and Example, or the Labour of their Hands, are uppermost in my

Thoughts. This kind of Industry seems to me a great Virtue. He that is afraid to leave a warm Bed, and to walk in the Dark, and to dawb or tear his Clothes or his Skin; He that makes no Difference between Virtue and Vice, and takes no Pleasure in Hospitality; and He that cares not who suffers, if he himself gains by it, or suffers not; will not any one of them, be industriously concern'd (if their own Dwellings are out of Danger) in preserving from devouring Flames either private or publick Buildings.

But how pleasing must it be to a thinking Man to observe, that not a Fire happens in this Town, but soon after it is seen and cry'd out, the Place is crowded by active Men of different Ages, Professions and Titles; who, as of one Mind and Rank, apply themselves with all Vigilance and Resolution, according to their Abilities, to the hard Work of conquering the increasing Fire. Some of the chiefest in Authority, and numbers of good Housekeepers, are ever ready, not only to direct but to labour, and are not seen to shun Parts or Places the most hazardous; and Others who having scarce a Coat in the World besides that on their Backs, will venture that, and their Limbs, in saving of Goods surrounded with Fire, and in rending off flaming Shingles. They do it not for Sake of Reward of Money or Fame: There is no Provision of either made for them. But they have a Reward in themselves, and they love one another. . . .

Ye Men of Courage, Industry, and Goodness, continue thus in well doing; and if you grow not ostentatious, it will be thought by every good Man who sees your Performances; here are brave Men, Men of Spirit and Humanity, good Citizens, or Neighbours, capable and worthy of civil Society, and the Enjoyment of a happy Government.

∞

Benjamin Franklin, Autobiography

AS FAMOUS as he was for his exhortations for thrift and industry, Franklin never believed that making money was our highest calling. In 1737, Franklin wrote in his *Poor Richard's Almanack:* "The noblest question in the world is *What Good may I do in it?*" And so, in 1740 Franklin applied his industry and skills toward the invention of a more efficient and economical stove. The "Franklin stove," as it became known, made everyday life much more comfortable for thousands of Americans who had, up to this point, put up with deficient heating mechanisms. Soon, nearly all homes in America (including Jefferson's Monticello) were heated by the superior Franklin stove. Franklin was offered a patent giving him sole rights to sell the stove for a fixed period of time, but he opted not to (even though he could have made a vast fortune) so that it could be more widely enjoyed by more Americans.

In order of time, I should have mentioned before, that having, in 1742, invented an open stove for the better warming of rooms, and at the same time saving fuel, as the fresh air admitted was warmed in entering, I made a present of the model to Mr. Robert Grace, one of my early friends, who, having an iron-furnace, found the casting of the plates for these stoves a profitable thing, as they were growing in demand. To promote that demand, I wrote and published a pamphlet, entitled *"An Account of the new-invented Pennsylvania Fireplaces; wherein their Construction and Manner of Operation is particularly explained; their Advantages above every other Method of warming Rooms demonstrated; and all Objections that have been raised against the Use of them answered and obviated,"* etc. This pamphlet had a good effect. Gov'r. Thomas was so pleas'd with the construction of this stove, as described in it, that he offered to give me a patent for the sole vending of them for a term of years; but I declin'd it from a principle which has ever weighed with me on such occasions, viz., *That, as we enjoy great advantages from the inventions of others, we should be glad of an opportunity to serve others by any invention of ours; and this we should do freely and generously.*

An ironmonger in London however, assuming a good deal of my pamphlet, and working it up into his own, and making some small changes in the machine, which rather hurt its operation, got a patent for it there, and made, as I was told, a little fortune by it. And this is not the only instance of patents taken out for my inventions by others, tho' not always with the same success, which I never contested, as having no desire of profiting by patents myself, and hating disputes. The use of these fireplaces in very many houses, both of this and the neighbouring colonies, has been, and is, a great saving of wood to the inhabitants.

∽

Benjamin Rush to William Claypoole, July 29, 1782

DR. BENJAMIN Rush was known for his compassion for the sick, for the poor, and for the suffering. Here he shows that although a doctor must be a good businessman, he does not have to be one without heart.

DR. BENJAMIN RUSH GIVES ADVICE TO A YOUNG PHYSICIAN

The following short directions to Dr. Claypoole were given as the parting advice of his old friend and master. If properly attended to, they will ensure him business and happiness in North Carolina.

1. Take care of the poor. By becoming faithful over a few, you will become a ruler over many. When you are called to visit a poor patient, imagine you hear a voice sounding in your ears, "Take care of him, and I will repay thee."

2. Go regularly to some place of worship. A physician cannot be a bigot. Worship with Mohamitans rather than stay at home on Sundays.

3. Never resent an affront offered to you by a *sick* man.

4. Avoid intimacies with your patients if possible, and visit them only in sickness.

5. Never *sue* a patient, but after a year's services get a bond from him if possible.

6. Receive as much pay as possible in goods or the produce of the country. Men have not half the attachment to these things that they have to money.

7. Acquire a habit of visiting your patients *regularly* at *one* certain hour.

8. Never dispute about a bill. Always make reductions rather than quarrel with an old and profitable patient.

9. Don't insert trifling advice or services in a bill. You can incorporate them with important matters such as a pleurisy or the reduction of a bone.

10. Never make light (to a patient) of *any* case.

11. Never appear in a hurry in a sickroom, nor talk of indifferent matters till you have examined and prescribed for your patient.

Yours sincerely,

∞

Thomas Jefferson to John Adams, December 10, 1819, and Adams to Jefferson, December 21, 1819

READING CICERO, the ancient Roman jurist, Jefferson began to reflect on the decline of the Roman Empire. With the decay of the Roman Empire in mind, he asked how a government under the control of a "demoralized and depraved" people can "continue good." How was it, he wondered, that the great statesmen of ancient Rome were unable to realize "one single day of free and rational government," something that Americans enjoy every day?

He posed these questions to Adams for some illumination. Below, Adams raises some questions of his own in response to Jefferson—and warns of the danger of a nation "thoroughly corrupted." In the midst of unimaginable material prosperity, we would do well to consider these words.

JEFFERSON TO ADAMS

I have been amusing myself latterly with reading the voluminous letters of Cicero. They certainly breathe the purest effusions of an exalted patriot, while the parricide Caesar is left in odious contrast. When the enthusiasm however kindled by Cicero's pen and principles, subsides into cool reflection, I ask myself, What was that government which the virtues of Cicero were so zealous to restore, and the ambition of Caesar to subvert? And if Caesar had been as virtuous as he was daring and sagacious, what could he, even in the plenitude of his usurped power have done to lead his fellow citizens into good government? I do not say to *restore it,* because they never had it, from the rape of the Sabines to the ravages of the Caesars. If their people indeed had been, like ours, enlightened, peaceable, and really free, the answer would be obvious. 'Restore independance to all your foreign conquests, relieve Italy from the government of the rabble of Rome, consult it as a nation entitled to self government, and do it's will.' But steeped in corruption vice and venality as the whole nation was, (and nobody had done more than Caesar to corrupt it) what could even Cicero, Cato, Brutus have done, had it been referred to them to establish a good government for their country? They had no ideas of government themselves but of their de-generate Senate, nor the people of liberty, but of the factious opposition of their tribunes. They had afterwards their Titusses, their Trajans and Antoninuses, who had the will to make them happy, and the power to mould their government into a good and permanent form. But it would seem as if they could not see their way clearly to do it. No government can continue good but under the controul of the people: and their peo-ple were so demoralised and depraved as to be incapable of exercising a wholsome controul. Their reformation then was to be taken up ab incunabulis ["from the beginning"]. Their minds were to be informed, by education, what is right and what wrong, to be encoraged in habits of virtue, and deterred from those of vice by the dread of punishments, proportioned indeed, but irremissible; in all cases, to follow truth as the only safe guide, and to eschew error which bewilders us in one false consequence after another in endless succession. These are the inculcations necessary to render the people a sure basis for the structure of order and good government. But this would have been an operation of a generation or two at least, within which period would have succeeded many Neros and Commoduses, who would have quashed the whole process. I confess then I can neither see what Cicero, Cato and Brutus, united and uncontrouled, could have devised to lead their people into good government, nor how this aenigma can be solved, nor how further shewn why it has been the fate of that delightful country never to have known to this day, and through a course of five and twenty hundred years, the history of which we possess one single day of free and rational government. Your intimacy with their history, antient, middle and modern, your familiarity with the improvements in the science of government at this time, will enable you , if any body, to go back with our principles and opinions to the times of Cicero, Cato, and Brutus, and tell us by what process these great and virtuous men could have led so unenlightened and vitiated a people into freedom and good government, et eris mihi magnus Apollo. Cura ut valeas, et tibi persuade carissimum te mihi esse ["and you will be great Apollo to me. Take care of your health and be assured that you are most dear to me"].

ADAMS TO JEFFERSON

Dear Sir

I must answer your great question of the 10th. in the words of Dalembert to his Correspondent, who asked him what is Matter—"Je vous avoue que Je n'en scais rien ["I confess that I know nothing about it"]."

In some part of my Life I read a great Work of a Scotchman on the Court of Augustus, in which with much learning, hard Study, and fatiguing labour, he undertook to prove that had Brutus and Cassius been conqueror, they would have restored virtue and liberty to Rome.

Mais Je n'en crois rien ["But I don't believe it"]. Have you ever found in history one single example of a Nation th[o]roughly Corrupted, that was afterwards restored to Virtue, and without Virtue, there can be no political Liberty. . . .

Will you tell me how to prevent riches from becoming the effects of temperance and industry? Will you tell me how to prevent riches from producing luxury? Will you tell me how to prevent luxury from producing effeminacy intoxication extravagance Vice and folly? When you will answer me these questions, I hope I may venture to answer yours. Yet all these ought not to discourage us from exertion, for with my friend Jeb, I believe no effort in favour of Virtue is lost, and all good Men ought to struggle both by their Council and Example.

Samuel Adams to John Scollay, December 30, 1780

SAMUEL ADAMS, second cousin of John Adams, lived by the same austere principles that he preached to others. As a young man, he had been inspired by the sermons of George Whitefield, the leading preacher of America's First Great Awakening, enjoining listeners to lead a life of piety and simplicity. Though Adams's father was a prosperous man who bequeathed to Sam his malt company, Adams displayed little skill or concern for making money. He wore the same old wig and shabby red suit and coat every day. When he was elected as a Massachusetts delegate to the First Continental Congress, his friends worried that he would make a bad impression and not be as influential as the better dressed delegates. Thus the men and women of Boston outfitted Adams with a new suit, a new wig and hat, six pairs of the best silk hose, six pairs of new shoes, and even gave him some spending money. Off he went, looking brand new.

Adams's austerity was not the general rule for most of the Founders, and Adams sometimes carried things a little too far. Still, the sentiments he expresses are not without foundation—in all our affluence, it's not a bad idea to be reminded every now and then that a republican form of government presupposes much more of its citizens than any other form of government. And the "more" it presupposes comes from the inside, not the outside.

Our Government, I perceive, is organizd on the Basis of the new Constitution. I am affraid there is more Pomp & Parade than is consistent with those sober Republican Principles, upon which the Framers of it thought they had founded it. Why should this new Œra be introducd with Entertainments expensive & tending to dissipate the Minds of the People? Does it become us to lead the People to such publick Diversions as promote Superfluity of Dress & Ornament, when it is as much as they

can bear to support the Expense of cloathing a naked Army? Will Vanity & Levity ever be the Stability of Government, either in States, in Cities, or what, let me hint to you is of the last Importance, in *Families?* Of what Kind are those Manners, by which, as we are truly informed in a late Speech, "not only the freedom but the very Existence of Republicks is greatly affected?' How fruitless is it, to recommend "the adapting the Laws in the most perfect Manner possible, to the Suppression of Idleness Dissipation & Extravagancy," if such Recommendations are counteracted by the Example of Men of Religion, Influence & publick Station? I meant to consider this Subject in the View of the mere Citizen. But I have mentiond the sacred Word *religion.* I confess, I am surprizd to hear, that some particular Persons have been so unguarded as to give their Countenance to such kind of Amusements. I wish Mr____would recollect his former Ideas when his Friend Whitfield thunderd in the Pulpit against Assemblies & Balls. I think he has disclaimd Diversions, in some Instances, which to me have always appeard innocent. Has he changd his Opinions, or has the Tendency of things alterd? Do certain Manners tend to quench the Spirit of Religion at one time & are they harmless at another? Are Morals so vague as to be sanctified or dispens'd with by the Authority of different Men? He does not believe this. But I will not be severe, for I love my Friend. Religion out of the Question for the present. It was asked in the Reign of Charles the 2d of England, How shall we turn the Minds of the People from an Attention to their Liberties? The Answer was, by making them extravagant, luxurious, effeminate.

∞

Noah Webster, "Advice to the Young," 1834

THE "love of finery," Webster points out, can be found in all peoples and all countries. Still, Webster believed that Americans live in a different kind of country, a country that depends on republican simplicity.

In your mode of living, be not ambitious of adopting every extravagant fashion. Many fashions are not only inconvenient and expensive, but inconsistent with good taste. The love of finery is of savage origin; the rude inhabitant of the forest delights to deck his person with pieces of shining metal, with painted feathers, and with some appendage dangling from the ears or nose. The same love of finery infects civilized men and women, more or less, in every country, and the body is adorned with brilliant gems and gaudy attire. But true taste demands great simplicity of dress. A well made person is one of the most beautiful of all God's works, and a simple neat dress, displays this person to the best advantage.

∞

George Washington to Bushrod Washington, January 15, 1783

ONE OF the wealthiest of the Founders, Washington took the time at the closing of the Revolutionary War to urge plain dress and discipline in his favorite nephew, Bushrod. One of Washington's biographers, Washington Irving, wrote that Washington wore a plain, brown "home-spun" suit to his first inauguration as president. When Lafayette sent

Washington the keys to the Bastille as a present, he sent a pair of simple silver shoe buckles to reciprocate. Certainly republicanism is modest dress. Yet, not all the founders agreed: John Hancock dressed like a peacock in Boston, while John Adams wore a silk suit with a sword dangling from the side to his inauguration.

As Washington says, expensive clothes do not make the man. Some great men dressed up, some down.

Dear Bushrod: You will be surprized perhaps at receiving a letter from me; but if the end is answered for which it is written, I shall not think my time miss-spent.

Your Father, who seems to entertain a very favorable opinion of your prudence, and I hope you merit it: in one or two of his letters to me, speaks of the difficulty he is under to make you remittances. Whether this arises from the scantiness of his funds, or the extensiveness of your demands, is matter of conjecture, with me. I hope it is not the latter, because common prudence, and every other consideration which ought to have weight in a reflecting mind is opposed to your requiring more than his conveniency and a regard to his other Children will enable him to pay; and because he holds up no idea in his Letter, which would support me in the conclusion. Yet when I take a view of the inexperience of Youth, the temptations in, and vices of Cities; and the distresses to which our Virginia Gentlemen are driven by an accumulation of Taxes and the want of a market; I am almost inclined to ascribe it, in part to both. Therefore, as a friend, I give you the following advice.

Let the object, which carried you to Philadelphia, be always before your Eyes; remember, that it is not the mere study of the Law, but to become eminent in the Profession of it which is to yield honor and profit; the first was your choice, let the second be your ambition, and that dissipation is incompatible with both. . . .

Do not conceive that fine Clothes make fine Men, any more than fine feathers make fine Birds. A plain genteel dress is more admired and obtains more credit than lace and embroidery in the Eyes of the judicious and sensible.

⧈

Thomas Jefferson to Martha Jefferson Randolph, January 5, 1808

JEFFERSON EXHORTED frugal living to his daughters, but for Jefferson himself, this precept did not translate into practice. It is well known that Jefferson died heavily in debt—at his death, his debt would be the equivalent of several million dollars today. Part of his financial woes was due to his indulgences in books, fine wines, and upkeep and remodeling of Monticello. However, some of his financial troubles can be traced to events beyond his control, i.e., the devaluation of the currency during the Revolutionary War; a debt he inherited from his father-in-law; a $20,000 defaulted loan he had co-signed for a friend; and simple bad luck at farming. Jefferson also believed that years of public service, which had taken him away from managing his farm, contributed to his plight.

Whatever the case, these debts "overwhelmed" Jefferson, who viewed them as "a deadly blast of all my peace of mind during my remaining days."

But I know nothing more important to inculcate into the minds of young people than the wisdom, the honor, and the blessed comfort of living within their income, to calculate in good time how much less pain will cost them the plainest stile of living which keeps them out of debt, than after a few years of splendor above their income, to have their property taken away for debt when they have a family growing up to maintain and provide for. Lessons enough are before their eyes, among their nearest acquaintances if they will but contemplate and bring the examples home to themselves. Still there is another evil against which we cannot guard, unthrifty marriages; because characters are not known until they are tried. But even here, a wife imbued with principles of prudence, may go far towards arresting or lessening the evils of an improvident management. In your moralising conversations with your children, I have no doubt you endeavor to warn them against the rocks on which they see so many shipwrecked. Altho we cannot expect that none of our posterity are to become the victims of imprudence or misfortune, yet we cannot but be particularly anxious to ward off the evil from those in present being, who having been brought up in our bosoms, cannot suffer without our own suffering equally.

❦

Benjamin Franklin, Autobiography

BENJAMIN FRANKLIN recalls in his *Autobiography* how he made it big. His success depended much on his own initiative and industry but also on his supportive wife. Here, Franklin shares a charming anecdote about his wife's introduction of "luxury" into their family. As we say in today's idiom, "It happens." This in many families is indeed the way of the world.

. . . *We* have an English proverb that says, "He that would thrive, must ask his wife." It was lucky for me that I had one as much disposed to industry and frugality as myself. She assisted me cheerfully in my business, folding and stitching pamphlets, tending shop, purchasing old linen rags for the paper-makers, etc., etc. We kept no idle servants, our table was plain and simple, our furniture of the cheapest. For instance, my breakfast was a long time bread and milk (no tea), and I ate it out of a twopenny earthen porringer, with a pewter spoon. But mark how luxury will enter families, and make a progress in spite of principle: being called one morning to breakfast, I found it in a china bowl, with a spoon of silver! They had been bought for me without my knowledge by my wife, and had cost her the enormous sum of three-and-twenty shillings, for which she had no other excuse or apology to make, but that she thought *her* husband deserved a silver spoon and china bowl as well as any of his neighbors. This was the first appearance of plate and china in our house, which afterward, in a course of years, as our wealth increased, augmented gradually to several hundred pounds in value.

∽

George Washington to George Washington Parke Custis, November 28, 1796

GEORGE WASHINGTON Parke Custis, Washington's adopted grandson, was not a very disciplined young man—in part because Martha and George were often indulgent parents. Washington struggled to set him on the right course. In this letter, Washington attempts to warn Custis, then fifteen years old, of the danger of forming bad habits, especially idleness. Washington appeals to Custis to discipline himself for his own happiness but also asks him to consider how much he will be pleased to see his grandson become a "useful member of society."

Dear Washington: In a few hasty lines, covering your sister's letter and a comb, on Saturday last, I promised to write more fully to you by the post of this day. I am now in the act of performing that promise.

The assurances you give me of applying diligently to your studies, and fulfilling those obligations which are enjoined by your Creator and due to his creatures, are highly pleasing and satisfactory to me. I rejoice in it on two accounts; first, as it is the sure means of laying the foundation of your own happiness, and rendering you, if it should please God to spare your life, a useful member of society hereafter; and secondly, that I may, if I live to enjoy the pleasure, reflect that I have been, in some degree, instrumental in effecting these purposes.

You are now extending into that stage of life when good or bad habits are formed. When the mind will be turned to things useful and praiseworthy, or to dissipation and vice. Fix on whichever it may, it will stick by you; for you know it has been said, and truly, "that as the twig is bent so it will grow." This, in a strong point of view, shows the propriety of letting your inexperience be directed by maturer advice, and in placing guard upon the avenues which lead to idleness and vice. The latter will approach like a thief, working upon your passions; encouraged, perhaps, by bad examples; the propensity to which will increase in proportion to the practice of it and your yielding. This admonition proceeds from the purest affection for you; but I do not mean by it, that you are to become a stoic, or to deprive yourself in the intervals of study of any recreations or manly exercise which reason approves.

∞

"To Be Useful Even After My Death," Benjamin Franklin's Philanthropy, 1790–1990

We began this chapter with Benjamin Franklin's humble entry into the city of Philadelphia. Franklin, who ran away from his home in Boston and arrived in Philadelphia in 1723 with only a few coins in his pocket, died a very wealthy man. At his death in 1790, he owned numerous properties in Philadelphia, a home in Boston, pasture lands outside Philadelphia, and land in Georgia, Nova Scotia, and elsewhere. When he died, his estate was worth over $250,000—by today's dollars, that would make him the equivalent of a multimillionaire, several times over.

Franklin never forgot the "kind loans" two friends gave him as a young man which, he noted, served as "the foundation of my fortune." To give others the start of their fortune—"to be useful even after my death if possible," as he put it in a codicil to his will—he bequeathed trust funds of 1,000 pounds each to his hometown of Boston and his adopted town of Philadelphia. Franklin instructed that loans were to be made "to such young married artificers, under the age of twenty-five years, as have served an apprenticeship in the said town, and faithfully fulfilled the duties required in their indentures, so as to obtain a good moral character from at least two respectable citizens who are willing to become their

sureties." Under Franklin's plan, loans would be given to young entre-
preneurs at 5 percent interest. It was his hope that the trust would "be
continually augmented by the interest" and would grow over the next
one hundred years, even two hundred years.

Franklin calculated that each fund would be worth one hundred and
thirty-one thousand pounds after one hundred years, at which time, he
instructed that one hundred thousand pounds of the fund be invested in
public works projects, such as roads, bridges, and in Philadelphia, making the Schuylkill River navigable. The remaining $31,000 would con-
tinue to be loaned at interest. At the end of two hundred years, Franklin
stipulated that the sum was to be divided between the town of Boston
and the state of Massachusetts; and similarly, between Philadelphia and
the state of Pennsylvania. He didn't leave any more explicit instructions,
"not presuming to carry my views farther."

In 1990, two hundred years after his death, the two trust funds were
worth 6.5 million dollars. And some of this money was designated to be
used as grants to help young people learn a trade or craft, young people
today, who, like Franklin in 1723, are eager to make good in life.

VI

JUSTICE

"I think I have observed that integrity *in the conduct of both the living and the dead takes a stronger hold of the human heart than any other virtue. It is placed before mercy by the name of* justice *in the Scriptures, and* just *men are in many parts of the inspired writings placed upon very high ground. It is right it should be so. The world stands in more need of justice than charity, and indeed it is the want of justice that renders charity everywhere so necessary."*

BENJAMIN RUSH TO JOHN ADAMS, SEPTEMBER 4, 1811

What is justice? Is it rule by the strong? by the wise? by the rich? by the poor? Or is justice rule by the majority? Is justice rooted in God's will? in history? in mere human convention? Or is justice rooted in Nature? There are, of course, no ready-made or simple answers to such questions, the most fundamental that any political community faces. But if the answer to the question "What is justice?" is not clear, the human striving for justice cannot be doubted. As James Madison wrote, "Justice is the end of government. It is the end of civil society. It ever has been, and ever will be pursued, until it be obtained, or until liberty be lost in the pursuit."

"To establish justice" is, according to the Preamble to the Constitution, one of the first priorities of forming these United States. But what exactly did the Founders intend to establish? What was *their* answer to the question of justice? Madison, Jefferson, Adams, and our other lawgivers were students of antiquity and the Enlightenment. They read widely, drawing upon sources of ancient and modern political thought, from Plato, Aristotle, Cicero, Bacon, Locke, Hume, Montesquieu, and many others to formulate an idea of justice.

As it happens, the Founders' answer was at once peculiarly American and universal. Our founding document, the Declaration of Independence defines justice as follows: "We hold these truths to be self evident: that all men are created equal; that they are endowed by their Creator with certain unalienable rights; that among these are life, liberty, and the pursuit of happiness; that to secure these rights, governments are insti- tuted among men, deriving their just powers from the consent of the governed." Justice as defined by the Founders requires the proper means —rule by the consent of the governed—in the service of the correct ends, the protection of man's unalienable (today we would say "inalien- able") rights to life, liberty, and the pursuit of happiness. Moreover, justice so defined was not conventional, that is, it was not based upon personal whim or human dictate. In the view of the Founders, rights were God-given and government by consent was rooted in "the Laws of Nature and of Nature's God," as the first paragraph of the Declaration of Independence states. As Lincoln would write of the Declaration, it is the repository of "an abstract truth, applicable to all men and all times." Jefferson noted that Americans could not be "insensible" that they were acting for all of mankind. But the Declaration of Independence is also peculiarly our truth, and especially applicable to us. Jefferson put it best when he said he intended it to be "an expression of the American mind."

Many of the letters and speeches of the Founders collected for this chapter might be taken as glosses and enlargements upon that "abstract truth." In the words of Madison, the rights for which the Americans fought were the "rights of human nature."

Consider, for example, the right of conscience. James Madison, Ameri- ca's—and perhaps the world's—greatest champion of religious freedom and toleration, thought the word "toleration" itself was too stingy, as it implied that one dominant religious sect was entitled to extend toleration to minority sects. Madison believed in the more "generous principle" of religious freedom: that "all men are equally entitled to the full and free exercise of [religion] according to the dictates of conscience; and there- fore no man or class of men ought, on account of religion to be invested with peculiar emoluments or privileges. For while religion, as Washing- ton wrote in his Farewell Address, was to be the main pillar supporting the American experiment, most of the Founders agreed that religious faith cannot be directed by outward force. True and saving faith, they argued, comes only by the gentle arts of persuasion acting on a free conscience.

But could this right be realized if the state and the church were one, as they then were in England and most of the world? The danger they foresaw was twofold: Just as men with political ambitions might make use of religion to usurp the rights of the people, so too men with religious

ambitions might make use of government to extend their spiritual king-
doms. Thus the Founders separated church from state in order to protect
the right of each individual to worship freely, without fear of persecution.
As Madison wrote, "Religion flourishes in greater purity without than
with the aid of government."

In addition to religious freedom, justice required, as the U.S. Constitution stipulates, that the U.S. government not confer titles of nobility upon
any individual. In America, justice might well give rise to a *natural*
aristocracy, as Jefferson put it, based on talent and virtue, but there
would be no aristocracy of birth or rank. In this spirit, the Constitution
stipulates that "no title of nobility shall be granted by the United States."

Another distinctive character of American justice, from the time of the
nation's founding, was the protection of private property. This was vitally
important to the Founders, in part because they viewed private property
as a protective "fence," as the philosopher John Locke called it, to a
person's liberty as well as his other rights. Madison, in *Federalist 10*,
argued that the first object of government was the "protection of the
different and unequal faculties of acquiring property" and the possessions that resulted from these faculties. Madison argued that property
would be best protected from the tyranny of the majority through a novel
approach designed to counteract the harmful effect of factions. That
effect, and the solution, are also discussed in Madison's *Federalist 10*,
portions of which I have included.

But the Founders were not blind apologists for the rampant pursuit of
property. Indeed they had an enlarged and elevated understanding of
property that went beyond mere material possessions.

Madison argued that property had two meanings. The first is obvious
enough—it applies to our material possessions. But property, in Madison's view, had "a larger and juster meaning" insofar as it applies to our
religious and political opinions, our discourse with others about such
matters, our safety and liberty, our faculties, our rights, and, most important, our consciences—"the most sacred of all property." Justice, said
Madison, was the protection of property, in both senses of the word.

Justice in America also means equality. Or as Lincoln summed it up:
"No man is good enough to govern another man, *without the other's
consent*." But, of course, America has not always lived up to that particular abstract truth. In fact, from its very beginning, it egregiously violated
the principle of equality. I am thinking in particular of America's original
sin of slavery. Some of the Founders were themselves slaveholders and
some defended slavery as a necessary evil. The principal author of the
Declaration of Independence, Thomas Jefferson, was himself a slave

owner. But there was also among them some strong and conscientious objectors to slavery—Alexander Hamilton, Benjamin Franklin, John Jay, Benjamin Rush, and John Adams, to name a few. The Founders—slaveholders and those who opposed slavery, and every point on the spectrum in between—all wrestled mightily with the question of slavery. The record is, of course, mixed; the Founders did not in their own time extend justice to all, but they put forward the great charter which would end slavery here forever, a charter that Lincoln drew from to support and justify the emancipation of all slaves. Surely nobody came closer to capturing the failure, and the profound achievement, of the Founders on this one issue than Martin Luther King, Jr. According to him, the Declaration of Independence was a "promissory note," written for future use, applicable to all times, peoples, and places.

American justice, as the Founders knew, offered the world something new. They realized that the eyes of mankind were upon them to see if it was possible to have a government without religious persecution, without artificial privilege, without titles, without arbitrary rule. One foreign observer from an aristocratic country worried that America may not have all the ornaments that come with a privileged class but was consoled by the fact that equality in America was more pleasing to God and thus more just, "and in its justice lies its greatness and beauty."

∞

"We Hold These Truths"
The Declaration of Independence, July 4, 1776

BEFORE THE delegates to the Second Continental Congress could vote on Richard Henry Lee's June 7th resolution for independence, a declaration of the reasons for separation from Great Britain was needed. Thomas Jefferson—then thirty-three—had scarcely spoken more than three sentences as a delegate to the Second Continental Congress. But John Adams knew Jefferson was less reserved, indeed eloquent, with the pen and encouraged him to write the Declaration of Independence. Jefferson wrote the draft of the Declaration of Independence on a small, fold-up writing desk in the parlor of a room he rented at a Philadelphia boardinghouse. It took Jefferson a little more than two weeks to finish the draft, which was then subjected to revision by his fellow delegates.

Jefferson later explained that the Declaration of Independence "was the fundamental act of union of these States." It certainly was that and much more. Lincoln, a great student of Jefferson, described the Declaration of Independence as our "ancient faith" and the "father of all moral principle" in America.

All freedom-loving people, from all corners of the earth, respond to the proclamation of the rights of human nature that Jefferson enshrined in the American mind and soul. Here is an excerpt:

IN CONGRESS, JULY 4, 1776
THE UNANIMOUS DECLARATION OF THE THIRTEEN
UNITED STATES OF AMERICA

When in the Course of human events, it becomes necessary for one people to dissolve the political bands which have connected them with another, and to assume among the Powers of the earth, the separate and equal station to which the Laws of Nature and of Nature's God entitle them, a decent respect to the opinions of mankind requires that they should declare the causes which impel them to the separation.

We hold these truths to be self-evident, that all men are created equal, that they are endowed by their Creator with certain unalienable Rights, that among these are Life, Liberty and the pursuit of Happiness. That to secure these rights, Governments are instituted among Men, deriving their just powers from the consent of the governed, That whenever any Form of Government becomes destructive of these ends, it is the Right of the People to alter or to abolish it, and to institute new Government, laying its foundation on such principles and organizing its powers in such form, as to them shall seem most likely to effect their Safety and Happiness. Prudence, indeed, will dictate that Governments long established should not be changed for light and transient causes; and accordingly all experience hath shown, that mankind are more disposed to suffer, while evils are sufferable, than to right themselves by abolishing the forms to which they are accustomed. But when a long train of abuses and usurpations, pursuing invariably the same Object evinces a design to reduce them under absolute Despotism, it is their right, it is their duty, to throw off such Government, and to provide new Guards for their future security.—Such has been the patient sufferance of these Colonies; and such is now the necessity which constrains them to alter their former Systems of Government. The history of the present King of Great Britain is a history of repeated injuries and usurpations, all having in direct object the establishment of an absolute Tyranny over these States. To prove this, let Facts be submitted to a candid world.

∞

"An Expression of the American Mind"
Thomas Jefferson to Henry Lee,
May 8, 1825

NEARLY FIFTY years after the fact, Jefferson explained to soldier and statesman Henry "Light-Horse Harry" Lee what he intended when he wrote the Declaration of Independence. Here is, arguably, the most consequential political document in the world described as just good old American common sense.

. . . *With* respect to our rights, and the acts of the British government contravening those rights, there was but one opinion on this side of the water. All American whigs thought alike on these subjects. When forced, therefore, to resort to arms for redress, an appeal to the tribunal of the world was deemed proper for our justification. This was the object of the Declaration of Independence. Not to find out new principles, or new arguments, never before thought of, not merely to say things which had never been said before; but to place before mankind the common sense of the subject, in terms so plain and firm as to command their assent, and to justify ourselves in the independent stand we are compelled to take. Neither aiming at originality of principle or sentiment, nor yet copied from any particular and previous writing, it was intended to be an expression of the American mind, and to give to that expression the proper tone and spirit called for by the occasion. All its authority rests then on the harmonizing sentiments of the day, whether expressed in conversation, in letters, printed essays, or in the elementary books of public right, as Aristotle, Cicero, Locke, Sidney, etc. . . .

∞

"Justice Is the End of Government"
James Madison, Federalist No. 51

THE FOUNDERS believed that it is not enough that government be democratic; they believed that government must also respect the rights and protect the liberties of the people. That is justice. This is Madison's classic statement of this position.

Justice is the end of government. It is the end of civil society. It ever has been, and ever will be pursued, until it be obtained, or until liberty be lost in the pursuit. In a society under the forms of which the stronger faction can readily unite and oppress the weaker, anarchy may as truly be said to reign, as in a state of nature where the weaker individual is not secured against the violence of the stronger: And as in the latter state even the stronger individuals are prompted by the uncertainy of their condition, to submit to a government which may protect the weak as well as themselves: So in the former state, will the more powerful factions or parties be gradually induced by a like motive, to wish for a government which will protect all parties, the weaker as well as the more powerful.

∞

George Mason, *Virginia Declaration of Rights, January 1776*

VIRGINIANS played a most decisive role in the founding of America—we often think of George Washington, Thomas Jefferson, James Madison, and Patrick Henry as the most prominent of her sons. But we shouldn't forget George Mason, a wealthy Virginia planter and self-educated lawyer, who wrote a Bill of Rights for the Virginia Constitution that served as a model for the Declaration of Independence and the Bill of Rights of the Constitution. Mason's Declaration of Rights not only stipulates the rights of free government but also the requirements of free government—that is, citizens with a "firm adherence to Justice, Moderation, Temperance, Frugality, and Virtue."

A declaration of rights made by the Representatives of the good people of Virginia, assembled in full and free Convention; which rights do pertain to them and their posterity, as the basis and foundation of Government.

That all men are by nature equally free and independent, and have certain inherent rights, of which, when they enter into a state of society, they cannot, by any compact, deprive or divest their posterity; namely, the enjoyment of life and liberty, with the means of acquiring and possessing property, and pursuing and obtaining happiness and safety.

That all power is vested in, and consequently derived from, the People; that magistrates are their trustees and servants, and at all times amenable to them.

That Government is, or ought to be, instituted for the common benefit, protection, and security of the people, nation, or community;—of all the various modes and forms of Government that is best which is capable of producing the greatest degree of happiness and safety, and is most effectually secured against the danger of mal-administration;—and that, whenever any Government shall be found inadequate or contrary to these purposes, a majority of the community hath an indubitable, unalienable, and indefeasible right, to reform, alter, or abolish it, in such manner as shall be judged most conducive to the publick weal.

That no man, or set of men, are entitled to exclusive or separate emoluments and privileges from the community, but in consideration of publick services; which, not being descendible, neither ought the offices of Magistrate, Legislator, or Judge, to be hereditary. . . .

That no free Government, or the blessing of liberty, can be preserved to any people but by a firm adherence to justice, moderation, temperance, frugality, and virtue, and by frequent recurrence to fundamental principles.

That Religion, or the duty which we owe to our *Creator,* and the manner of discharging it, can be directed only by reason and conviction, not by force or violence; and, therefore, all men are equally entitled to the free exercise of religion, according to the dictates of conscience; and that it is the mutual duty of all to practice Christian forbearance, love, and charity, towards each other.

∞

James Madison, *"The Greatest Trust Ever Confided to a Political Society," Address to the States, April 25, 1783*

MADISON BELIEVED that the future of free government depends upon America's success. Either the "rights of human nature" will be vindicated on the American stage or lost forever.

Let it be remembered finally that it has ever been the pride and boast of America, that the rights for which she contended were the rights of human nature. By the blessing of the Author of these rights on the means exerted for their defence, they have prevailed against all opposition and form the basis of thirteen independant States. No instance has heretofore occurred, nor can any instance be expected hereafter to occur, in which the unadulterated forms of Republican Government can pretend to so fair an opportunity of justifying themselves by their fruits. In this view the Citizens of the U.S. are responsible for the greatest trust ever confided to a Political Society. If justice, good faith, honor, gratitude & all the other Qualities which enoble the character of a nation, and fulfil the ends of Government, be the fruits of our establishments, the cause of liberty will acquire a dignity and lustre, which it has never yet enjoyed; and an example will be set which can not but have the most favorable influence on the rights of mankind. If on the other side, our Governments should be unfortunately blotted with the reverse of these cardinal and essential Virtues, the great cause which we have engaged to vindicate, will be dishonored & betrayed; the last & fairest experiment in favor of the rights of human nature will be turned against them; and their patrons & friends exposed to be insulted & silenced by the votaries of Tyranny and Usurpation.

By order of the United States in Congress assembled.

∞

"We Are Acting for All Mankind" Thomas Jefferson to Dr. Joseph Priestley, June 19, 1802

LIKE MADISON, Jefferson is well aware that he and others were acting not only for America but for the entire world as well. It is up to Americans to show the world that self-government is a viable alternative to the despotism and tyrannies of the past. If we succeed, the world will follow.

In the great work which has been effected in America, no individual has a right to take any great share to himself. Our people in a body are wise, because they are under the unrestrained and unperverted operation of their own understanding. Those whom they have assigned to the direction of their affairs, have stood with a pretty even front. If any one of them was withdrawn, many others entirely equal, have been ready to fill his place with as good abilities. A nation, composed of such materials, and free in all its members from distressing wants, furnishes hopeful implements for the interesting experiment of self-government; and we feel that we are acting under obligations not confined to the limits of our own society. It is impossible not to be sensible that we are acting for all mankind; that circumstances denied to others, but indulged to us, have imposed on us the duty of proving what is the degree of freedom and self-government in which a society may venture to leave its individual members. . . .

∞

"That Diabolical, Hell-conceived Principle of Persecution" James Madison to William Bradford, Jr., January 24, 1774

JAMES MADISON once told his good friend William Bradford, Jr., that he should "fall more in love with liberty." Madison's love affair with liberty went deep. He was a member of the Episcopalian Church, which happened to be the established church of Virginia. Yet, having witnessed the persecution and eventual imprisonment of a half-dozen Baptist preachers in Culpeper, Virginia, Madison, just out of Princeton College, wrote this letter to his good friend to share his outrage. While this sort of religious persecution might be common in the Old World, Madison was impatient with its presence in the colonies.

From an early age then, Madison dedicated his life to making America, in his words, an "asylum to the persecuted and oppressed of every nation and religion." Madison wrote the First Amendment guaranteeing religious liberty to all Americans.

. . . *I* have indeed as good an atmosphere at home as the climate will allow; but have nothing to brag of as the state and liberty of my country. Poverty and luxury prevail among all sorts; pride, ignorance, and knavery among the priesthood, and vice and wickedness among the laity. This is bad enough, but it is not the worst I have to tell you. That diabolical, hell-conceived principle of persecution rages among some; and to their eternal infamy, the clergy can furnish their quota of imps for such business. This vexes me the worst of anything whatever. There are at this time in the adjacent country not less than five or six well-meaning men in close jail for publishing their religious sentiments, which in the main are very orthodox. I have neither patience to hear, talk, or think of anything relative to this matter; for I have squabbled and scolded, abused and ridiculed, so long about it to little purpose, that I am without common patience. So I must beg you to pity me, and pray for liberty of conscience to all.

∞

Thomas Jefferson,
"A Bill for Establishing Religious Freedom"

I N 1779, Jefferson introduced this bill into the Virginia General Assembly, but it was not enacted until 1786 (see Madison's "A Memorial and Remonstrance," page 327). Upon reflection many years later in 1819, Madison wrote to Jefferson: "It was the universal opinion of the century preceding the last that civil government could not stand without the prop of a religious establishment, and that the Christian religion itself, would perish if not supported by a legal provision for its clergy. The experience of Virginia consciously corroborates the disproof of both opinions."

Jefferson was so proud of this bill that he listed it, along with his authorship of the Declaration of Independence and his establishment of the University of Virginia, on his tombstone.

Well aware that the opinions and belief of men depend not on their own will, but follow involuntarily the evidence proposed to their minds; that Almighty God hath created the mind free, *and manifested his supreme will that free it shall remain by making it altogether insusceptible of restraint;* that all attempts to influence it by temporal punishments, or burthens, or by civil incapacitations, tend only to beget habits of hypocrisy and meanness, and are a departure from the plan of the holy author of our religion, who being lord both of body and mind, yet chose not to propagate it by coercions on either, as was in his Almighty power to do, *but to extend it by its influence on reason alone* that the impious presumption of legislators and rulers, civil as well as ecclesiastical, who, being themselves but fallible and uninspired men, have assumed dominion over the faith of others, setting up their own opinions and modes of thinking as the only true and infallible, and as such endeavoring to impose them on others, hath established and maintained false religions over the greatest part of the world and through all time: That to compel a man to furnish contributions of money for the propagation of opinions which he disbelieves *and abhors,* is sinful and tyrannical: that even the forcing him to support this or that teacher of his own religious persuasion, is depriving him of the comfortable liberty of giving his contributions to the particular pastor whose morals he would make his pattern,

and whose powers he feels most persuasive to righteousness; and is withdrawing from the ministry those temporary rewards, which proceeding from an approbation of their personal conduct, are an additional incitement to earnest and unremitting labours for the instruction of mankind; that our civil rights have no dependance on our religious opinions, any more than our opinions in physics or geometry; that therefore the proscribing any citizen as unworthy the public confidence by laying upon him an incapacity of being called to offices of trust and emolument, unless he profess or renounce this or that religious opinion, is depriving him injuriously of those privileges and advantages to which, in common with his fellow citizens, he has a natural right; that it tends also to corrupt the principles of that *very* religion it is meant to encourage, by bribing, with a monopoly of worldly honours and emoluments, those who will externally profess and conform to it; that though indeed these are criminal who do not withstand such temptation, yet neither are those innocent who lay the bait in their way; *that the opinions of men are not the object of civil government, nor under its jurisdiction;* that to suffer the civil magistrate to intrude his powers into the field of opinion and to restrain the profession or propagation of principles on supposition of their ill tendency is a dangerous falacy, which at once destroys all religious liberty, because he being of course judge of that tendency will make his opinions the rule of judgment, and approve or condemn the sentiments of others only as they shall square with or differ from his own; that it is time enough for the rightful purposes of civil government for its officers to interfere when principles break out into overt acts against peace and good order; and finally, that truth is great and will prevail if left to herself; that she is the proper and sufficient antagonist to error, and has nothing to fear from the conflict unless by human interposition disarmed of her natural weapons, free argument and debate; errors ceasing to be dangerous when it is permitted freely to contradict them.

We the General Assembly of Virginia do enact that no man shall be compelled to frequent or support any religious worship, place, or ministry whatsoever, nor shall be enforced, restrained, molested, or burthened in his body or goods, nor shall otherwise suffer, on account of his religious opinions or belief; but that all men shall be free to profess, and by argument to maintain, their opinions in matters of religion, and that the same shall in no wise diminish, enlarge, or affect their civil capacities.

And though we well know that this assembly, elected by the people for the ordinary purposes of legislation only, have no power to restrain the acts of succeeding Assemblies, constituted with powers equal to our own, and that therefore to declare this act irrevocable would be of no effect in law; yet we are free to declare, and do declare, that the rights hereby asserted are of the natural rights of mankind, and that if any act shall be hereafter passed to repeal the present or to narrow its operation, such act will be an infringement of natural right.

∞

James Madison,
"A Memorial and Remonstrance,"
October 1785

IN 1784, Patrick Henry introduced an Assessment Bill in the Virginia General Assembly to tax Virginians to support the "teachers of the

Christian religion" of all sects. As George Washington, John Marshall, and Richard Henry Lee were some of the prominent supporters of the bill, it would likely have passed, but Madison and others were able to delay the vote. He took that time to write "A Memorial and Remonstrance" and mobilized public opinion, especially the Baptists, against the bill. When the legislature reconvened the assessment bill died without a vote. Madison had made the case for freedom of conscience so convincingly that Jefferson's Bill for Religious Liberty, that had first been proposed to the Virginia legislature in 1779, was finally passed instead.

This piece of work is a classic and influential statement on the importance and need for *independence* of religion. The duties of religion precede, and transcend, those of civil society. Here is an excerpt:

To the Honorable the General Assembly of the Commonwealth of Virginia:

We, the subscribers, citizens of the said Commonwealth, having taken into serious consideration, a Bill printed by order of the last Session of General Assembly, entitled "A Bill establishing a provision for Teachers of the Christian Religion," and conceiving that the same, if finally armed with the sanctions of a law, will be a dangerous abuse of power, are bound as faithful members of a free State, to remonstrate against it, and to declare the reasons by which we are determined. We remonstrate against the said Bill.

Because we hold it for a fundamental and undeniable truth, "that Religion or the duty which we owe to our Creator and the manner of discharging it, can be directed only by reason and conviction, not by force or violence." The Religion then of every man must be left to the conviction and conscience of every man: and it is the right of every man to exercise it as these may dicate. This right is in its nature an unalienable right. It is unalienable; because the opinions of men, depending only on the evidence contemplated by their own minds, cannot follow the dictates of other men: It is unalienable also; because what is here a right towards men, is a duty towards the Creator. It is the duty of every man to render to the Creator such homage, and such only, as he believes to be acceptable to him. This duty is precedent both in order of time and degree of obligation, to the claims of Civil Society. Before any man can be considered as a member of Civil Society, he must be considered as a subject of the Governor of the Universe: And if a member of Civil Society, who enters into any subordinate Association, must always do it with a reservation of his duty to the general authority; much more must every man who becomes a member of any particular Civil Society, do it with a saving of his allegiance to the Universal Sovereign. We maintain therefore that in matters of Religion, no man's right is abridged by the institution of Civil Society, and that Religion is wholly exempt from its cognizance. True it is, that no other rule exists, by which any question which may divide a Society, can be ultimately determined, but the will of the majority; but it is also true, that the majority may trespass on the rights of the minority.

Because the proposed establishment is a departure from that generous policy, which, offering an asylum to the persecuted and oppressed of every Nation and Religion, promised a lustre to our country, and an accession to the number of its citizens. What a melancholy mark is the Bill of sudden degeneracy? Instead of holding forth an asylum to the persecuted, it is itself a signal of persecution. It degrades from the equal rank of Citizens all those whose opinions in Religion do not bend to those of the Legislative authority. Distant as it may be, in its present form, from the Inquisition it differs from it only in degree. The one is the first step, the other the last in the career of intolerance. The magnanimous sufferer under this cruel scourge in foreign Regions, must view the Bill as a Beacon on our Coast, warning him to seek some other haven, where liberty and philanthropy in their due extent may offer a more certain repose from his troubles.

∞

George Washington to Colonel Benedict Arnold, September 14, 1775

IN A failed effort to enlist the help of French Canadians in the revolutionary cause, George Washington sent Colonel Benedict Arnold to Quebec on an expedition. The Continental Army had already exhibited signs of anti-Catholic sentiment; rumors that the Continental Army was planning to burn an effigy of the Pope abounded. Thus, Washington wrote the following letter and issued orders that all soldiers were to respect the rights of conscience of the largely Catholic inhabitants of Quebec. Here are morality, prudence, religion, and military strategy all combined.

It is ironic that Benedict Arnold was to carry out and enforce the order against imprudence and folly, since he was later to be guilty of much worse.

Sir: You are intrusted with a Command of the utmost Consequence to the Interest and Liberties of America. Upon your Conduct and Courage and that of the Officers and Soldiers detached on this Expedition, not only the Success of the present Enterprize, and your Honour, but the Safety and Welfare of the Whole Continent may depend. I charge you, therefore, and the Officers and Soldiers, under your Command, as you value your own Safety and Honour and the Favour and Esteem of your Country, that you consider yourselves, as marching, not through an Enemy's Country; but that of our Friends and Brethren, for such the Inhabitants of Canada, and the Indian Nations have approved themselves in this unhappy Contest between Great Britain and America. That you check by every Motive of Duty and Fear of Punishment, every Attempt to plunder or insult any of the Inhabitants of Canada. Should any American Soldier be so base and infamous as to injure any Canadian or Indian, in his Person or Property, I do most earnestly enjoin you to bring him to such severe and exemplary Punishment as the Enormity of the Crime may require. Should it extend to Death itself it will not be disproportional to its Guilt at such a Time and in such a Cause: But I hope and trust, that the brave Men who have voluntarily engaged in this Expedition, will be governed by far different Views, that Order, Discipline and Regularity of Behaviour will be as conspicuous, as their Courage and Valour. I also give it in Charge to you to avoid all Disrespect to or Contempt of the Religion of the Country and its Ceremonies. Prudence, Policy, and a true Christian Spirit, will lead us to look with Compassion upon their Errors without insulting them. While we are contending for our own Liberty, we should be very cautious of violating the Rights of Conscience in others, ever considering that God alone is the Judge of the Hearts of Men, and to him only in this Case, they are answerable. Upon the whole, Sir, I beg you to inculcate upon the Officers and Soldiers, the Necessity of preserving the strictest Order during their March through Canada; to represent to them the Shame, Disgrace and Ruin to themselves and Country, if they should by their Conduct, turn the Hearts of our Brethren in Canada against us. And on the other Hand, the Honours and Rewards which await them, if by their Prudence and good Behaviour, they conciliate the Affections of the Canadians and Indians, to the great Interests of America, and convert those favorable Dispositions they have shown into a lasting Union and Affection. Thus wishing you and the Officers and

Soldiers under your Command, all Honour, Safety and Success, I remain Sir, etc.

∾

George Washington to the Hebrew Congregation of Newport, Rhode Island, September 9, 1790

MEMBERS OF the Newport Hebrew Congregation wrote the president to congratulate Washington on his presidency and to "reflect on those days . . . of difficulty and danger, when the God of Israel, who delivered David from the peril of the sword, shielded [Washington's] head in the day of battle. . . ."

In his beautiful reply, Washington set forth the American principle of religious liberty: Here no one sect "tolerated" another—here we were all, Jews and Christians, equally Americans, and here "there shall be none to make him afraid." What a promise! How rarely, in the story of inhumanity and misery that is history, has this promise been realized.

Gentlemen, While I receive with much satisfaction, your Address replete with expressions of affection and esteem, I rejoice in the opportunity of assuring you, that I shall always retain a grateful remembrance of the cordial welcome I experienced in my visit to Newport, from all classes of citizens.

The reflection on the days of difficulty and danger which are past, is rendered the more sweet, from a consciousness that they are succeeded by days of uncommon prosperity and security. If we have wisdom to make the best use of the advantages with which we are now favored, we cannot fail, under the just administration of a good government, to become a great and a happy people.

The citizens of the United States of America, have a right to applaud themselves for having given to mankind examples of an enlarged and liberal policy—a policy worthy of imitation. ALL possess alike liberty of conscience, and immunities of citizenship. It is now no more that toleration is spoken of, as if it was by the indulgence of one class of people, that another enjoyed the exercise of their inherent natural rights. For happily the government of the United States, which gives to bigotry no sanction—to persecution no assistance, requires only that they who live under its protection should demean themselves as good citizens, in giving it on all occasions their effectual support.

It would be inconsistent with the frankness of my character not to avow, that I am pleased with your favorable opinion of my administration, and fervent wishes for my felicity. May the Children of the Stock of Abraham, who dwell in this land, continue to merit and enjoy the good-will of the other inhabitants; while every one shall sit in safety under his own vine and fig tree, and there shall be none to make him afraid. May the Father of all mercies scatter light and not darkness in our paths, and make us all in our several vocations useful here, and in his own due time and way everlastingly happy.

∞

George Washington, To the Roman Catholics in the United States of America, March 15, 1790

IT IS fitting that the first president, a Protestant, wrote letters to both Jews and Catholics assuring them of the same blessings in America and so to all of all faiths.

The prospect of national prosperity now before us is truly animating, and ought to excite the exertions of all good men to establish and secure the happiness of their country, in the permanent duration of its freedom and independence. America, under the smiles of a Divine Province, the protection of a good government, and the cultivation of manners, morals, and piety, cannot fail of attaining an uncommon degree of eminence, in literature, commerce, agriculture, improvements at home and respectability abroad.

As mankind become more liberal they will be more apt to allow that all those who conduct themselves as worthy members of the community are equally entitled to the protection of civil government. I hope ever to see America among the foremost nations in examples of justice and liberality. And I presume that your fellow-citizens will not forget the patriotic part which you took in the accomplishment of their Revolution, and the establishment of their government; or the important assistance which they received from a nation in which the Roman Catholic faith is professed.

I thank you, gentlemen, for your kind concern for me. While my life and my health shall continue, in whatever situation I may be, it shall be my constant endeavour to justify the favourable sentiments which you are pleased to express of my conduct. And may the members of your society in America, animated alone by the pure spirit of Christianity, and still conducting themselves as the faithful subjects of our free government, enjoying every temporal and spiritual felicity.

∞

George Washington to the Presbyterian Church General Assembly, May 26, 1789

THIS IS Washington's response to a letter from the General Assembly of Presbyterian Churches. Here, Washington reiterates the importance of freedom of conscience for all with the expectation (as in his more famous letter to the Hebrew Congregation) that all Americans conduct themselves virtuously as good citizens. In other words, freedom of conscience did not mean freedom from restraint and private and public morality.

While I reiterate the professions of my dependence upon Heaven as the source of all public and private blessings; I will observe that the general prevalence of piety, philanthropy, honesty, industry, and economy seems, in the ordinary course of human affairs, particularly necessary for advancing and confirming the happiness of our country. While all men within our territories are protected in worshipping the Deity according to the dictates of their consciences; it is rationally to be expected from them in return, that they will be emulous of evincing the sanctity of their professions by the innocence of their lives and the beneficence of their actions; for no man, who is profligate in his morals, or a bad member of the civil community, can possibly be a true Christian, or a credit to his own religious society.

I desire you to accept my acknowledgments for your laudable endeavours to render men sober, honest, and good Citizens, and the obedient subjects of a lawful government.

⬭

James Madison's Letters to Dr. Jacob de la Motta and Mordecai M. Noah

JACOB DE la Motta played an active role in building a synagogue in Savannah, Georgia. He gave an address at the dedication of the new synagogue, which he sent to James Madison and Thomas Jefferson. Mordecai M. Noah was a prominent Jewish diplomat, playwright, and journalist.

To both men, Madison gave classic expression to the American principle of toleration: "Equal laws, protecting equal rights" secure all that is good—the rights of conscience, a loyal citizenry, and goodwill among all.

TO DR DE LA MOTTA
MONTPELLIER, AUGUST 1820

Sir,—I have received your letter of the 7th instant, with the Discourse delivered at the Consecration of the Hebrew Synagogue at Savannah, for which you will please to accept my thanks.

The history of the Jews must forever be interesting. The modern part of it is, at the same time, so little generally known, that every ray of light on the subject has its value.

Among the features peculiar to the political system of the United States, is the perfect equality of rights which it secures to every religious sect. And it is particularly pleasing to observe in the good citizenship of such as have been most distrusted and oppressed elsewhere a happy illustration of the safety and success of this experiment of a just and benignant policy. Equal laws, protecting equal rights, are found, as they ought to be presumed, the best guarantee of loyalty and love of country; as well as best calculated to cherish that mutual respect and good will among citizens of every religious denomination which are necessary to social harmony, and most favorable to the advancement of truth. The account you give of the Jews of your congregation brings them fully within the scope of these observations.

TO M. M. NOAH
MONTPELLIER, MAY 15, 1818

Sir,—I have received your letter of the 6th, with the eloquent discourse delivered at the consecration of the Jewish Synagogue. Having ever regarded the freedom of religious opinions and worship as equally belonging to every sect, and the secure enjoyment of it as the best human provision for bringing all either into the same way of thinking, or into that mutual charity which is the only substitute, I observe with pleasure the view you give of the spirit in which your sect partake of the blessings offered by our Government and laws.

∞

James Madison, "A Property in Our Rights," National Gazette, *March 29, 1792*

IT IS well known, of course, that every American has a right to life, liberty, and *property*. But property meant more to the founders than a plot of land or a piece of merchandise. "In its larger and juster meaning," Madison explains, it embraces our opinions and especially our religious opinions. Ultimately, it is for the protection of these spiritual goods that humans institute government.

This term [property] in its particular application means "that domination which one man claims and exercises over the external things of the world, in exclusion of every other individual."

In its larger and juster meaning, it embraces every thing to which a man may attach a value and have a right; and *which leaves to every one else the like advantage.*

In the former sense, a man's land, or merchandize, or money is called his property.

In the latter sense, a man has property in his opinions and the free communication of them.

He has a property of peculiar value in his religious opinions, and in the profession and practice dictated by them.

He has property very dear to him in the safety and liberty of his person.

He has an equal property in the free use of his faculties and free choice of the objects on which to employ them.

In a word, as a man is said to have a right to his property, he may be equally said to have a property in his rights.

Where an excess of power prevails, property of no sort is duly respected. No man is safe in his opinions, his person, his faculties or his possessions.

Where there is an excess of liberty, the effect is the same, tho' from an opposite cause.

Government is instituted to protect property of every sort; as well that which lies in the various rights of individuals, as that which the term particularly expresses. This being the end of government, that alone is a *just* government, which *impartially* secures to every man, whatever is his *own*. . . .

Conscience is the most sacred of all property; other property depending in part on positive law, the exercise of that, being a natural and inalienable right. To guard a man's house as his castle, to pay public and enforce private debts with the most exact faith, can give no title to invade a man's conscience which is more sacred than his castle. . . .

If there be a government then which prides itself on maintaining the inviolability of property; which provides that none shall be taken *directly* even for public use without indemnification to the owner, and yet *directly* violates the property which individuals have in their opinions, their religion, their persons, and their faculties; nay more, which *indirectly* violates their property, in their actual possessions, in the labor that acquires their daily subsistence, and in the hallowed remnant of time which ought to relieve their fatigues and soothe their cares, the inference will have been anticipated, that such a government is not a pattern for the United States.

If the United States mean to obtain or deserve the full praise due to wise and just governments, they will equally respect the rights of property, and the property in rights.

∞

James Madison to James Monroe, October 5, 1786

JAMES MADISON shares some reflections on the problem of majority tyranny in this letter to his friend James Monroe.

. . . *There* is no maxim in my opinion which is more liable to be misapplied, and which therefore more needs elucidation than the current one that the interest of the majority is the political standard of right and wrong. Taking the word "interest" as synonomous with "Ultimate happiness," in which sense it is qualified with every necessary moral ingredient, the proposition is no doubt true. But taking it in the popular sense, as referring to immediate augmentation of property and wealth, nothing can be more false. In the latter sense it would be the interest of the majority in every community to despoil & enslave the minority of individuals; and in a federal community to make a similar sacrifice of the minority of the component States. In fact it is only reestablishing under another name and a more spe[c]ious form, force as the measure of right. . . .

∞

James Madison, Federalist No. 10, *November 22, 1787*

THE ANTI-FEDERALISTS, who opposed the Constitution, thought that the country was too vast and the population too large to sustain a republican form of government. The French philosopher Montesquieu had taught that republics thrive in small territories with a basically homogeneous population, with citizens holding similar opinions and sentiments. As Brutus, the pen name of one of the leading Anti-Federalists, wrote, "History furnishes no example of a free republic, any thing like the extent of the United States."

In an original and enduring contribution to modern political science, Madison argued in *Federalist 10* that an extended republic was not only possible but desirable. According to Madison, size and diversity were strengths, not weaknesses, in that they solved the problem of factionalism. In a large republic there would be a diversity of interests, ensuring that the permanent oppression of one class of citizens by another would not happen. Everyone, at some time or another, would be in the minority, given the wide range of interests possible in such a large and diverse nation.

Among the numerous advantages promised by a well constructed Union, none deserves to be more accurately developed than its tendency to break and control the violence of faction. The friend of popular governments, never finds himself so much alarmed for their character and fate, as when he contemplates their propensity to this dangerous vice. He will not fail therefore to set a due value on any plan which, without violating the principles to which he is attached, provides a proper cure for it. The instability, injustice and confusion introduced into the public councils, have in truth been the mortal diseases under which popular governments have every where perished.

By a faction I understand a number of citizens, whether amounting to a majority or minority of the whole, who are united and actuated by some common impulse of passion, or of interest, adverse to the rights of other citizens, or to the permanent and aggregate interests of the community.

There are two methods of curing the mischiefs of faction: the one, by removing its causes; the other, by controling its effects.

There are again two methods of removing the causes of faction: the one by destroying the liberty which is essential to its existence; the other, by giving to every citizen the same opinions, the same passions, and the same interests.

It could never be more truly said than of the first remedy, that it is worse than the disease. Liberty is to faction, what air is to fire, an aliment without which it instantly expires. But it could not be a less folly to abolish liberty, which is essential to political life, because it nourishes faction, than it would be to wish the annihilation of air, which is essential to animal life, because it imparts to fire its destructive agency.

The second expedient is an impracticable, as the first would be unwise. As long as the reason of man continues fallible, and he is at liberty to exercise it, different opinions will be formed. As long as the connection subsists between his reason and his self-love, his opinions and his passions will have a reciprocal influence on each other; and the former will be objects to which the latter will attach themselves. The diversity in the faculties of men from which the rights of property originate, is not less an insuperable obstacle to a uniformity of interests. The protection of these faculties is the first object of Government. From the protection of different and unequal faculties of acquiring property, the possession of different degrees and kinds of property immediately results: and from the influence of these on the sentiments and views of the respective proprietors, ensues a division of the society into different interests and parties. . . .

When a majority is included in a faction, the form of popular government on the other hand enables it to sacrifice to its ruling passion or interest, both the public good and the rights of other citizens. To secure the public good, and private rights, against the danger of such a faction, and at the same time to preserve the spirit and the form of popular government, is then the great object to which our enquiries are directed: Let me add that it is the great desideratum, by which alone this form of government can be rescued from the opprobrium under which it has so long labored, and be recommended to the esteem and adoption of mankind. . . .

A Republic, by which I mean a Government in which the scheme of representation takes place, opens a different prospect, and promises the cure for which we are seeking. Let us examine the points in which it varies from pure Democracy, and we shall comprehend both the nature of the cure, and the efficacy which it must derive from the Union.

The . . . point of difference is, the greater number of citizens and extent of territory which may be brought within the compass of Republican, than of Democratic Government; and it is this circumstance principally which renders factious combinations less to be dreaded in the former, than in the latter. The smaller the society, the fewer probably will be the distinct parties and interests composing it; the fewer the distinct parties and interests, the more frequently will a majority be found of the same party; and the smaller the number of individuals composing a majority, and the smaller the compass within which they are placed, the more easily will they concert and execute their plans of oppression. Extend the sphere, and you take in a greater variety of parties and interests; you make it less probable that a majority of the whole will have a common motive to invade the rights of other citizens; or if such a common motive exists, it will be more difficult for all who feel it to discover their own stength, and to act in unison with each other. Besides other impediments, it may be remarked, that where there is a consciousness of unjust or dishonorable purposes, communication is always checked by distrust, in proportion to the number whose concurrence is necessary. . . .

In the extent and proper structure of the Union, therefore, we behold a Republican remedy for the diseases most incident to Republican Government. And according to the degree of pleasure and pride, we feel in being Republicans, ought to be our zeal in cherishing the spirit, and supporting the character of Federalists.

∞

Thomas Jefferson to James Madison,
October 28, 1785

JEFFERSON WAS in aristocratic France and saw firsthand how the concentration of wealth and land in a few hands led to "numberless instances of wretchedness." In his letter to Madison, Jefferson acknowledged that it would be "impracticable" to expect an equal division of property. But Jefferson believed that America could provide a more equitable division of land, one that would encourage and reward hard work and industry.

Dear Sir,—Seven o'clock, and retired to my fireside, I have determined to enter into conversation with you. . . .

As soon as I had got clear of the town I fell in with a poor woman walking at the same rate with myself and going the same course. Wishing to know the condition of the laboring poor I entered into conversation with her, which I began by enquiries for the path which would lead me into the mountain: and thence proceeded to enquiries into her vocation, condition and circumstances. She told me she was a day laborer at 8 sous or 4d. sterling the day: that she had two children to maintain, and to pay a rent of 30 livres for her house (which would consume the hire of 75 days), that often she could get no employment and of course was without bread. As we had walked together near a mile and she had so far served me as a guide, I gave her, on parting, 24 sous. She burst into tears of a gratitude which I could perceive was unfeigned because she was unable to utter a word. She had probably never before received so great an aid. This little *attendrissement,* with the solitude of my walk, led me into a train of reflections on that unequal division of property which occasions the numberless instances of wretchedness which I had observed in this country and is to be observed all over Europe.

The property of this country is absolutely concentred in a very few hands, having revenues of from half a million of guineas a year downwards. These employ the flower of the country as servants, some of them having as many as 200 domestics, not laboring. They employ also a great number of manufacturers and tradesmen, and lastly the class of laboring husbandmen. But after all there comes the most numerous of all classes, that is, the poor who cannot find work. I asked myself what could be the reason so many should be permitted to beg who are willing to work, in a country where there is a very considerable proportion of uncultivated lands? These lands are undisturbed only for the sake of game. It should seem then that it must be because of the enormous wealth of the proprietors which places them above attention to the increase of their revenues by permitting these lands to be labored. I am conscious that an equal division of property is impracticable, but the consequences of this enormous inequality producing so much misery to the bulk of mankind, legislators cannot invent too many devices for subdividing property, only taking care to let their subdivisions go hand in hand with the natural affections of the human mind. The descent of property of every kind therefore to all the children, or to all the brothers and sisters, or other relations in equal degree, is a politic measure and a practicable one. Another means of silently lessening the inequality of property is to exempt all from taxation below a certain point, and to tax the higher portions or property in geometrical progression as they rise. Whenever there are in any country uncultivated lands and unemployed poor, it is clear that the laws of property have been so far extended as to violate natural right. The earth is given as a common stock for man to labor and live on. If for the encouragement of industry we allow it to be appropriated, we must take care that other employment be provided to those excluded from the appropriation. If we do not, the fundamental right to labor the earth returns to the unemployed. It is too soon yet in our country to say that every man who cannot find employment, but who can find uncultivated land, shall be at liberty to cultivate it, paying a moderate rent. But it is not too soon to provide by every possible means that as few as possible shall be without a little portion of land. The small landholders are the most precious part of a state.

∞

"A Government Truly Republican"
Thomas Jefferson, Autobiography

AFTER COMPLETING the Declaration of Independence, Jefferson turned his attention to revising the laws of his home state of Virginia to bring them into accord with the principles of the American Revolution. Out of the fifty-one bills he had drafted, Jefferson singled out the following four as the most important to a republican form of government: the bill for the abolition of primogeniture (a law that gave the first born son the right of inheritance); the bill for abolition of entail (the old English custom of limiting the inheritance of property not merely to a single heir but to a succession of heirs); the bill for religious liberty; and the bill for a more general diffusion of knowledge. These bills reflect the fundamentals of republican government—equality, freedom of religion, and enlightenment.

I considered 4 of these bills, passed or reported, as forming a system by which every fibre would be eradicated of antient or future aristocracy; and a foundation laid for a government truly republican. The repeal of the laws of entail would prevent the accumulation and perpetuation of wealth in select families, and preserve the soil of the country from being daily more & more absorbed in Mortmain. The abolition of primogeniture, and equal partition of inheritances removed the feudal and unnatural distinctons which made one member of every family rich, and all the rest poor, substituting equal partition, the best of all Agrarian laws. The restoration of the rights of conscience relieved the people from taxation for the support of a religion not theirs; for the establishment was truly of the religion of the rich, the dissenting sects being entirely composed of the less wealthy people; and these, by the bill for a general education, would be qualified to understand their rights, to maintain them, and to exercise with intelligence their parts in self-government; and all this would be effected without the violation of a single natural right of any one individual citizen.

❦

Thomas Jefferson to James Madison, September 6, 1789, and Madison to Jefferson, February 4, 1790

JEFFERSON ENTERED into a philosophical exchange with his friend Madison on the question of "[w]hether one generation of men has a right to bind another." The letter in large part reflected Jefferson's interest in transforming the feudal society of France, where he was serving as a diplomatic minister, to a truly democratic one. But Jefferson told Madison that his thoughts might have some practical application in

America as well. Jefferson held the unusual idea that all debts—a matter of some personal interest perhaps to him given the state of his finances —be cancelled every nineteen years, that being his estimate of the length of a generation. Among other things, Jefferson also believed that each new generation should write its own constitution. He shared these philosophical speculations with Madison, who was serving in Congress, and suggested that in his official capacity in Congress he might find them worthy of legislation. Madison, rather gently and politely, pointed out not only the philosophical weakness of this but also the practical impossibility, given the fact that "generations" had the distressing characteristic of being born at all times. Further, Madison stressed that a "descent of obligations" passed from one generation to the next and these obligations ensured political stability and fostered reverence for the law.

Despite their fundamental disagreement on this issue, Jefferson and Madison remained the steadiest of friends. Here are some excerpts from their famous exchange.

JEFFERSON TO MADISON

Dear Sir

I sit down to write to you without knowing by what occasion I shall send my letter. I do it because a subject comes into my head which I would wish to develope a little more than is practicable in the hurry of the moment of making up general dispatches.

The question Whether one generation of men has a right to bind another, seems never to have been started either on this or our side of the water. Yet it is a question of such consequences as not only to merit decision, but place also, among the fundamental principles of every government. The course of reflection in which we are immersed here on the elementary principles of society has presented this question to my mind; and that no such obligaton can be so transmitted I think very capable of proof.—I set out on this ground, which I suppose to be self evident, *'that the earth belongs in usufruct to the living'*: that the dead have neither powers nor rights over it. The portion occupied by any individual ceases to be his when himself ceases to be, and reverts to the society. If the society has formed no rules for the appropriation of it's lands in severality, it will be taken by the first occupants. These will generally be the wife and children of the decendent. If they have formed rules of appropriation, those rules may give it to the wife and children, or to some one of them, or to the legatee of the deceased. So they may give it to his creditor. But the child, the legatee, or creditor takes it, not by any natural right, but by a law of the society of which they are members, and to which they are subject. Then no man can, by *natural right,* oblige the lands he occupied, or the persons who succeed him in that occupation, to the paiment of debts contracted by him. For if he could, he might, during his own life, eat up the usufruct of the lands for several generations to come, and then the lands would belong to the dead, and not to the living, which would be the reverse of our principle. . . .

I suppose that the received opinion, that the public debts of one generation devolve on the next, has been suggested by our seeing habitually in private life that he who succeeds to lands is required to pay the debts of his ancestor or testator: without considering that this requisition is municipal only, not moral; flowing from the will of the society, which has found it convenient to appropriate lands, become vacant by the death of their occupant, on the condition of a paiment of his debts: but that between society and society, or generation and generation, there is no municipal obligation, no umpire but the law of nature. We seem not to have perceived that, by the law of nature, one generation is to another as one independant nation to another.

. . . On similar ground it may be proved that no society can make a perpetual constitution, or even a perpetual law. The earth belongs always to the living generation. They may manage it then, and what proceeds from it, as they please, during their usufruct. They are masters too of their own persons, and consequently may govern them as they please. But persons and property make the sum of the objects of government. The constitution and the laws of their predecessors [are] extinguished then in their natural course with those who gave them being. This could preserve that being till it ceased to be itself, and no longer. Every constitution then, and every law, naturally expires at the end of 19 years. If it be enforced longer, it is an act of force, and not of right.—It may be said that the succeeding generation exercising in fact the power of repeal, this leaves them as free as if the constitution or law had been expressly limited to 19 years only.

. . . Turn this subject in your mind, my dear Sir, and particularly as to the power of contracting debts; and develope it with that perspicuity and cogent logic so peculiarly yours. Your station in the councils of our country gives you an opportunity of producing it to public consideration, of forcing it into discussion. At first blush it may be rallied, as a theoretical speculation: but examination will prove it to be solid and salutary.

Dear Sir

Your favor of the 9th day of Jany. inclosing one of Sept. last did not get to hand till a few days ago. The idea which the latter evolves is a great one, and suggests many interesting reflections to legislators; particularly when contracting and providing for public debts. Whether it can be received in the extent your reasonings give it, is a question which I ought to turn more in my thoughts than I have yet been able to do, before I should be justified in making up a full opinion on it. My first thoughts though coinciding with many of yours, lead me to view the doctrine as not in *all* respects compatible with the course of human affairs. I will endeavor to sketch the grounds of my skepticism.

"As the earth belongs to the living, not to the dead, a living generation can bind itself only: In every society the will of the majority binds the whole: According to the laws of mortality, a majority of those ripe at any moment for the exercise of their will do not live beyond nineteen years: To that term then is limited the validity of *every* act of the Society; Nor within that limitation, can any declaration of the public will be valid which is not *express.*" This I understand to be the outline of the argument.

The acts of a political society may be divided into three classes.

1. The fundamental Constitution of the Government.

2. Laws involving stipulations which render them irrevocable at the will of the Legislature.

3. Laws involving no such irrevocable quality.

However applicable in Theory the doctrine may be to a Constitution, it seems liable in practice to some very powerful objections. Would not a Government so often revised become too mutable to retain those prejudices in its favor which antiquity inspires, and which are perhaps a salutary aid to the most rational Government in the most enlightened age? Would not such a periodical revision engender pernicious factions that might not otherwise come into existence? Would not, in fine, a Government depending for its existence beyond a fixed date, on some positive and authentic intervention of the Society itself, be too subject to the casualty and consequences of an actual interregnum?

In the 2d. class, exceptions at least to the doctrine seem to be *requisite* both in Theory and practice:

If the earth be the gift of nature to the living their title can extend to the earth in its natural State only. The *improvements* made by the dead form a charge against the living who take the benefit of them. This charge can no otherwise be satisfyed than by executing the will of the dead accompanying the improvements.

Debts may be incurred for purposes which interest the unborn, as well as the living: such are debts for repelling a conquest, the evils of which descend through many generations. Debts may even be incurred principally for the benefit of posterity: such perhaps is the present debt of the U. States, which far exceeds any burdens which the present generation could well apprehend for itself. The term of 19 years might not be sufficient for discharging the debts in either of these cases.

There seems then to be a foundation in the nature of things, in the relation which one generation bears to another, for the *descent* of obligations from one to another. Equity requires it. Mutual good is promoted by it. All that is indispensable in adjusting the account between the dead and the living is to see that the debits against the latter do not exceed the advances made by the former. Few of the incumbrances entailed on nations would bear a liquidation even on this principle.

∽

"No Title of Nobility"
Constitution, Article 1, Section 9, and
James Madison, Congress, May 11, 1789

VICE-PRESIDENT John Adams and others had supported giving a title to President George Washington, such as "His Highness the President of the United States and Protector of the Rights of the Same." The thought was that such titles would add dignity to the new and untried form of government. For his suggestion, many in the House of Representatives conferred the title "His Rotundity" to Adams.

James Madison, serving in the First Congress, disagreed with Adams not because titles are dangerous to liberty but because "they are not very reconcilable with the nature of our Government, or the genius of the people." This was the same sentiment that was earlier enshrined in the Constitution in art. 1, sec. 9. America was to be a republic.

U.S. CONSTITUTION, ART. 1, SEC. 9

No Title of Nobility shall be granted by the United States: And no Person holding any Office of Profit or Trust under them, shall, without the Consent of the Congress, accept of any present, Emolument, Office, or Title, of any kind whatever, from any King, Prince, or foreign State.

IN CONGRESS, MAY 11, 1789

I do not conceive titles to be so pregnant with danger as some gentlemen apprehend. I believe a President of the United States, clothed with all the powers given in the Constitution, would not be a dangerous person to the liberties of America, if you were to load him with all the titles of Europe or Asia. We have seen superb and august titles given, without conferring power and influence, or without even obtaining respect. One of the most impotent sovereigns in Europe has assumed a title as high as human invention can devise; for example, what words can imply a greater magnitude of power and strength than that of High Mightiness? This title seems to border almost upon impiety; it is assuming the preeminence and omnipotence of the Deity; yet this title, and many others cast in the same mould, have obtained a long time in Europe, but have they conferred power? Does experience sanction such an opinion? Look at the Republic I have alluded to, and say if their present state warrants the idea?

I am not afraid of titles, because I fear the danger of any power they could confer, but I am against them because they are not very reconcilable with the nature of our Government or the genius of the people. Even if they were proper in themselves, they are not so at this juncture of time. But my strongest objection is founded in principle; instead of increasing, they diminish the true dignity and importance of a Republic, and would in particular, on this occasion, diminish the true dignity of the first magistrate himself. If we give titles, we must either borrow or invent them. If we have recourse to the fertile fields of luxuriant fancy, and deck out an airy being of our own creation, it is a great chance but its fantastic properties would render the empty phantom ridiculous and absurd. If we borrow, the servile imitation will be odious, not to say ridiculous also; we must copy from the pompous sovereigns of the East, or follow the inferior potentates of Europe; in either case, the splendid tinsel or gorgeous robe would disgrace the manly shoulders of our chief. The more truly honourable shall we be, by showing a total neglect and disregard to things of this nature; the more simple, the more Republican we are in our manners, the more rational dignity we shall acquire.

∽

"The World's Best Hope," Thomas Jefferson, First Inaugural Address, March 4, 1801

HERE, PRESIDENT Jefferson outlines the basic "principles" of American government and the ones that will shape his administration. In this speech, Jefferson called these principles the "creed of our political faith," making America "the world's best hope."

Several interesting questions are explicit or implicit in this address: Can man govern himself? Can he govern others? If we are demanding of those who govern us, should we not be at least equally demanding of ourselves for the conduct of our self-government?

. . . *Sometimes* it is said that man can not be trusted with the government of himself. Can he, then, be trusted with the government of others? Or have we found angels in the forms of kings to govern him? Let history answer this question.

Let us, then, with courage and confidence pursue our own Federal and Republican principles, our attachment to union and representative government. Kindly separated by nature and a wide ocean from the exterminating havoc of one quarter of the globe: too high-minded to endure the degradations of the others; possessing a chosen country, with room enough for our descendants to the thousandth and thousandth generation; entertaining a due sense of our equal right to the use of our own faculties, to the acquisitions of our own industry, to honor and confidence from our fellow-citizens, resulting not from birth, but from our actions and their sense of them; enlightened by a benign religion, professed, indeed, and practiced in various forms, yet all of them inculcating honesty, truth, temperance, gratitude, and the love of man; acknowledging and adoring an overruling Providence, which by all its dispensations proves that it delights in the happiness of man here and his greater happiness hereafter—with all these blessings, what more is necessary to make us a happy and a prosperous people? Still one thing more, fellow-citizens—a wise and frugal Government, which shall restrain men from injuring one another, shall leave them otherwise free to regulate their own pursuits of industry and improvement, and shall not take from the mouth of labor the bread it has earned. This is the sum of good government, and this is necessary to close the circle of our felicities.

About to enter, fellow-citizens, on the exercise of duties which comprehend everything dear and valuable to you, it is proper you should understand what I deem the essential principles of our Government, and consequently those which ought to shape its Administration I will compress them within the narrowest compass they will bear, stating the general principle, but not all its limitations. Equal and exact justice to all men, of whatever state or persuasion, religious or political, peace, commerce, and honest friendship, with all nations—entangling alliances with none; the support of the state governments in all their rights, as the most competent administrations for our domestic concerns and the surest bulwarks against anti-republican tendencies; the preservation of the general government in its whole constitutional vigor, as the sheet anchor of our peace at home and safety abroad; a jealous care of the right of election by the people—a mild and safe corrective of abuses which are lopped by the sword of the revolution where peaceable remedies are unprovided; absolute acquiescence in the decisions of the majority—the vital principle of republics, from which there is no appeal but to force, the vital principle and immediate parent of despotism; a well-disciplined militia—our best reliance in peace and for the first moments of war, till regulars may relieve them; the supremacy of the civil over the military authority; economy in the public expense, that labor may be lightly burdened; the honest payment of our debts and sacred preservation of the public faith, encouragement of agriculture, and of commerce as its handmaid; the diffusion of information and the arraignment of all abuses at the bar of public reason; freedom of religion; freedom of the press; freedom of person under the protection of the *habeas corpus;* and trial by juries impartially selected—these principles form the bright constellation which has gone before us, and guided our steps through an age of revolution and reformation. The wisdom of our sages and the blood of our heroes have been devoted to their attainment. They should be the creed of our political faith—the text of civil instruction—the touchstone by which to try the services of those we trust; and should we wander from them in moments of error or alarm, let us hasten to retrace our steps and to regain the road which alone leads to peace, liberty, and safety.

∞

James Madison, Federalist No. 57

UNDER THE plan for the House of Representatives, the Anti-Federalists thought that only the wealthy or most prominent citizens would be able to garner the recognition necessary to win office in such large districts. The result would be that the House of Representatives would consist of the elite, who would not resemble the electorate.

Here James Madison addresses their concerns by pointing out that there are no property, religious, or class qualifications for voters or candidates. The only qualification for elected officials is "the esteem and confidence of his country." The House of Representatives, Madison believed, would truly reflect the great body of the electorate.

He was equally concerned, however, that government represent settled and wise opinion, a role Madison envisioned for the Senate.

To the People of the State of New York:

The *third* charge against the House of Representatives is, that it will be taken from that class of citizens which will have least sympathy with the mass of the people, and be most likely to aim at an ambitious sacrifice of the many to the aggrandizement of the few.

The aim of every political constitution is, or ought to be, first to obtain for rulers men who possess most wisdom to discern, and most virtue to pursue, the common good of the society; and in the next place, to take the most effectual precautions for keeping them virtuous whilst they continue to hold their public trust. The elective mode of obtaining rulers is the characteristic policy of republican government. The means relied on in this form of government for preventing their degeneracy are numerous and various. The most effectual one, is such a limitation of the term of appointments as will maintain a proper responsibility to the people.

Let me now ask what circumstance there is in the constitution of the House of Representatives that violates the principles of republican government, or favors the elevation of the few on the ruins of the many? Let me ask whether every circumstance is not, on the contrary, strictly conformable to these principles, and scrupulously impartial to the rights and pretensions of every class and description of citizens?

Who are to be the electors of the federal representatives? Not the rich, more than the poor; not the learned, more than the ignorant; not the haughty heirs of distinguished names, more than the humble sons of obscurity and unpropitious fortune. The electors are to be the great body of the people of the United States. They are to be the same who exercise the right in every State of electing the corresponding branch of the legislature of the State.

Who are to be the objects of popular choice? Every citizen whose merit may recommend him to the esteem and confidence of his country. No qualification of wealth, of birth, of religious faith, or of civil profession is permitted to fetter the judgement or disappoint the inclination of the people.

∞

"I Tremble for My Country"
The Founders on Slavery, 1773–1826

THERE IS no getting around the fact that many of the Founders held slaves. It is also true that most of the Founders—even those who held slaves—struggled and agonized over the existence of an institution so at odds with the principles of American justice. We often look back at the Founders and accuse them of hypocrisy; it is easy to regard ourselves as morally superior to them. But in pointing out their hypocrisy, we are not discovering anything that the Founders themselves were not aware of. Many, such as the slave holder Patrick Henry, admitted that there was no rationale for defending this institution, save for the "inconvenience of living here without them." Most of the Founders knew, in the words of Madison, that slavery was "evil" and the "blot" on "our Republican character."

The delegates to the Constitutional Convention in 1787 recognized this in their debate over what to do about slavery. In art. 1, sec. 2 of the Constitution, slaves are referred to as "three-fifths" of a person. This was a compromise reached with the slave holders of the South, who wanted to count slaves as full persons in order to have more representation, and ultimately more power, in Congress. The three-fifths clause of the Constitution prevented the slave interest from dominating the legislative process. In addition, art. 1, sec. 9 of the Constitution gave Congress power to end the slave trade in 1808. And finally, an important change was made to art. 4, sec. 2, which contains the fugitive-slave clause. The clause had originally described persons "legally" held in bondage. But members of the Convention objected to the word "legally," as it might give the impression of the Constitution's "favoring the idea that slavery was legal in a moral view."* Instead, "under the Laws thereof" was used. Nowhere can the word "slavery" be found in the Constitution—and this was deliberate. Most of the delegates hoped that the document would put the institution of slavery on the path of eventual extinction, and that there would be a time when former slaves would enjoy full rights under the Constitution. Former slave Frederick Douglass, who had once been a great critic of the Constitution, became one of its strongest defenders, and called it "a glorious liberty document" which he "found to contain principles and purposes, entirely hostile to the existence of slavery." †

It is difficult for us living in twentieth-century America to understand why the Founders' love of liberty did not move them to give immediate freedom to the slaves. But as difficult as it is to imagine, we must recall how entrenched the institution of slavery was, how deep prejudice ran, and the hostility and fear between the two races. Many citizens viewed slaves as subhuman, as property. No one, no matter how obtuse, could be insensible to the slaves' anger and resentment at being denied justice. The prevalent fear was that the two races could not live in harmony with each other. How could former masters begin to treat "property" as full citizens and respect the full rights of freed slaves? And was it possible for former slaves simply to forgive their tormentors for the great evil inflicted upon them and their families? This was the quandary; this was what made Jefferson "tremble" for his country.

Many have observed that the founding did not solve the problem of slavery, but actually created it. That is, the sentiments of the revolution raised America's consciousness and created a great anti-slavery movement—in the 1780s, the abolitionist movement began. It was only after the revolution that the northern states began abolishing slavery, beginning with Pennsylvania in 1780. By the early nineteenth century, slavery had disappeared from all northern states. It would later take a Civil War (and 600,000 lives lost in that war) in the nineteenth century and a civil rights movement in the twentieth century to right the wrongs of this

---

* Farrand, *The Records of the Federal Convention*, vol. 2, p. 628.
† Douglass, "The Meaning of July Fourth for the Negro," July 5, 1852.

evil. The Founders' struggles with the existence of slavery should be considered in this light. What follows are some of the Founders' thoughts.

THOMAS JEFFERSON, *NOTES ON THE STATE OF VIRGINIA*, QUERY XVIII, 1787

And can the liberties of a nation be thought secure when we have removed their only firm basis, a conviction in the minds of the people that these liberties are of the gift of God? That they are not to be violated but with his wrath? Indeed I tremble for my country when I reflect that God is just: that his justice cannot sleep for ever: that considering numbers, nature and natural means only, a revolution of the wheel of fortune, an exchange of situation, is among possible events: that it may become probable by supernatural interference! The Almighty has no attribute which can take side with us in such a contest.—But it is impossible to be temperate and to pursue this subject through the various considerations of policy, of morals, of history natural and civil. We must be contented to hope they will force their way into every one's mind. I think a change already perceptible, since the origin of the present revolution. The spirit of the master is abating, that of the slave rising from the dust, his condition mollifying, the way I hope preparing, under the auspices of heaven, for a total emancipation, and that this is disposed, in the order of events, to be with the consent of the masters, rather than by their extirpation.

JOHN JAY TO R. LUSHINGTON, NEW YORK, MARCH 15, 1786

It is much to be wished that slavery may be abolished. The honour of the States, as well as justice and humanity, in my opinion, loudly call upon them to emancipate these unhappy people. To contend for our own liberty, and to deny that blessing to others, involves an inconsistency not to be excused.

Whatever may be the issue of the endeavours of restrictions with which narrow policy opposes the extension of Divine benevolence. It is pleasant, my Lord, to dream of these things, and I often enjoy that pleasure; but though, like some of our other dreams, we may wish to see them realized, yet the passions and prejudices of mankind forbid us to expect it.

THOMAS PAINE TO BENJAMIN RUSH, MARCH 16, 1790

I wish most anxiously to see my much loved America—it is the Country from whence all reformations must originally spring—I despair of seeing an Abolition of the infernal trafic in Negroes—we must push that matter further on your side the water—I wish that a few well instructed Negroes could be sent among their Brethren in Bondage, for until they are enabled to take their own part nothing will be done—

∞

Declaration of Independence, Draft, Thomas Jefferson, 1776

IN 1775, the population in America was 2.5 million. About one-fifth of all Americans were black, and nearly all of them were slaves living in the South. In Virginia, slaves were half the population, while in South Carolina, slaves outnumbered white inhabitants, constituting two-thirds of the population.* At the time that Jefferson declared that all men were free and equal, about half a million were not.

Jefferson attempted to protest the wrongs of slavery in our founding document, the Declaration of Independence. John Adams believed that the passages condemning slavery were the best parts of the Declaration. Yet the Southern states strongly opposed Jefferson's position and would not vote for independence so long as it was included. It was stricken from the final draft.

He [George III] has waged cruel war against human nature itself, violating it's most sacred rights of life and liberty in the persons of a distant people who never offended him, captivating & carrying them into slavery in another hemisphere, or to incur miserable death in their transportation thither. This piratical warfare, the opprobrium of INFIDEL powers, is the warfare of the CHRISTIAN king of Great Britain. Determined to keep open a market where MEN should be bought & sold, he has prostituted his negative for suppressing every legislative attempt to prohibit or to restrain this execrable commerce. And that this assemblage of

* Statistics cited in Bernard Bailyn, *The Great Republic: A History of the American People*, vol. 1, p. 164.

horrors might want no fact of distinguished die, he is now exciting those very people to rise in arms among us, and to purchase that liberty of which he has deprived them, by murdering the people on whom he also obtruded them: thus paying off former crimes committed against the LIBERTIES of one people, with crimes which he urges them to commit against the LIVES of another.

∽

"I Will Not, I Cannot Justify It"
Patrick Henry to Robert Pleasants,
January 18, 1773

SO WHAT was the appeal of slavery? Here's one of the Southerners, a great one. In this strikingly honest self-assessment by Patrick Henry we discover a well-worn excuse of the great and not so great—not actively seeking evil but just "being drawn along," ironically, from the man known forever by his words, "Give me liberty, or give me death."

Is it not amazing that at a time when the rights of humanity are defined and understood with precision, in a country, above all others, fond of liberty, that in such an age and in such a country we find men professing a religion the most humane, mild, gentle and generous, adopting a principle as repugnant to humanity as it is inconsistent with the Bible, and destructive to liberty? Every thinking, honest man rejects it in speculation; how few in practice from conscientious motives!

Would anyone believe I am the master of slaves of my own purchase! I am drawn along by the general inconvenience of living here without them. I will not, I cannot justify it. However culpable my conduct, I will so far pay my devoir to virtue as to own the excellence and rectitude of her precepts, and lament my want of conformity to them.

I believe a time will come when an opportunity will be offered to abolish this lamentable evil. Everything we do is to improve it, if it happens in our day; if not, let us transmit to our descendants, together with our slaves, a pity for their unhappy lot and an abhorrence of slavery. If we cannot reduce this wished-for reformation to practice, let us treat the unhappy victims with lenity. It is the furthest advance we can make toward justice. It is a debt we owe to the purity of our religion, to show that it is at variance with that law which warrants slavery.

I know not when to stop. I could say many things on the subject, a serious view of which gives a gloomy perspective to future times.

∞

Alexander Hamilton to John Jay,
March 14, 1779

ALEXANDER HAMILTON wrote the following letter endorsing a plan to enlist the slaves of South Carolina in the Continental Army and, in return, giving them their freedom. The plan was the idea of his best friend, John Laurens, who presented it before Congress, which did not adopt it.

Col. Laurens, who will have the honor of delivering you this letter, is on his way to South Carolina, on a project, which I think, in the present situation of affairs there, is a very good one and deserves every kind of support and encouragement. This is to raise two three or four batalions of negroes; with the assistance of the government of that state, by contributions from the owners in proportion to the number they possess. If you should think proper to enter upon the subject with him, he will give you a detail of his plan. He wishes to have it recommended by Congress to the state; and, as an inducement, that they would engage to take those batalions into Continental pay.

I foresee that this project will have to combat much opposition from prejudice and self-interest. The contempt we have been taught to entertain for the blacks, makes us fancy many things that are founded neither in reason nor experience; and an unwillingness to part with property of so valuable a kind will furnish a thousand arguments to show the impracticability or pernicious tendency of a scheme which requires such a sacrifice. But it should be considered, that if we do not make use of them in this way, the enemy probably will; and that the best way to counteract the temptations they will hold out will be to offer them ourselves. An essential part of the plan is to give them their freedom with their muskets. This will secure their fidelity, animate their courage, and I believe will have a good influence upon those who remain, by opening a door to their emancipation. This circumstance, I confess, has no small weight in inducing me to wish the success of the project; for the dictates of humanity and true policy equally interest me in favour of this unfortunate class of men.

∞

James Madison, Federalist No. 38 *and* No. 42

AT THE Constitutional Convention of 1787, Southern delegates threatened to withdraw from the plan for union. Compromises had to be made—as Madison wrote, "[g]reat as the evil is, a dismemberment of the union would be worse." Madison here defends the Constitution—which allowed banning the slave trade in 1808—as putting the institution of slavery on the path of eventual extermination. The words "slavery" and "slave" were deliberately left out of the Constitution. Madison was correct that the "illicit practice" of slavery would end, although it took Abraham Lincoln and a Civil War to accomplish that end.

Is the importation of slaves permitted by the new Constitution for twenty years? By the old, it is permitted for ever.

It were doubtless to be wished that the power of prohibiting the importation of slaves, had not been postponed until the year 1808, or rather that it had been suffered to have immediate operation. But it is not difficult to account either for this restriction on the general government, or for the manner in which the whole clause is expressed. It ought to be considered as a great point gained in favor of humanity, that a period of twenty years may terminate for ever within these States, a traffic which has so long and so loudly upbraided the barbarism of modern policy; that within that period it will receive a considerable discouragement from the fœderal Government, and may be totally abolished by a concurrence of the few States which continue the unnatural traffic, in the prohibitory example which has been given by so great a majority of the Union. Happy would it be for the unfortunate Africans, if an equal prospect lay before them, of being redeemed from the oppressions of their European brethren! Attempts have been made to pervert this clause into an objection against the Constitution, by representing it on one side as a criminal toleration of an illicit practice, and on another, as calculated to prevent voluntary and beneficial emigrations from Europe to America. I mention these misconstructions, not with a view to give them an answer, for they deserve none; but as specimens of the manner and spirit in which some have thought fit to conduct their opposition to the proposed government.

∞

Northwest Ordinance, July 13, 1787

THE NORTHWEST Ordinance outlawed the spread of slavery in the new territories. It demonstrated that the Founders fundamentally wanted to restrict slavery and that Congress had the power to do it. When they were given the chance to restrict slavery, they did.

ARTICLE VI (NORTHWEST ORDINANCE)

"*There* shall be neither slavery nor involuntary servitude in the said territory, otherwise than in the punishment of crimes, whereof the party shall have been duly convicted: *Provided always,* That any person escaping into the same, from whom labor or service is lawfully claimed in any one of the original States, such fugitive may be lawfully reclaimed, and conveyed to the person claiming his or her labor or service as aforesaid."

⚮

". . . *Brethren and Members of One Great Family"* Benjamin Rush, *Commonplace Book,* June 18, 1792, and August 22, 1793

BENJAMIN RUSH was a strong opponent of slavery and a strong advocate for the brotherhood of man. Here he shares in his Commonplace Book some thoughts about ways of bringing together the races. The first place for desegregation was naturally in God's house, and Rush found that at funerals and at churches the conventional barriers separating black from white disappeared.

June 18. This day I attended the funeral of Wm. Gray's wife, a black woman, with about 50 more white persons and two Episcopal Clergymen. The white attendants were chiefly the neighbours of the deceased. The sight was a new one in Philadelphia, for hitherto (a few cases excepted) the negroes alone attended each other's funerals. By this event it is to be hoped the partition wall which divided the Blacks from the Whites will be still further broken down and a way prepared for their union as brethren and members of one great family.

August 22. Attended a dinner a mile below the tower in 2nd Street to celebrate the raising of the roof of the African Church. About 100 white persons, chiefly carpenters, dined at one table, who were waited upon by Africans. Afterward about 50 black people sat down at the same table, who were waited upon by white people. Never did I see people more happy. Some of them shed tears of joy. A old black man took Mr. Nicholson by the hand and said to him, "May you live long, and when you die, may you not die eternally." I gave them two toasts, viz: "Peace on earth and good will to man," and, "May African Churches everywhere soon succeed African bondage." The last was received with three cheers.

∞

George Washington,
Last Will and Testament, July 9, 1799

WASHINGTON WAS one of the few prominent Founders who freed his slaves at his death. He not only freed them but also provided for their education and established a trust fund to help them in their freedom. This trust fund continued to support his former slaves and their descendants well into the nineteenth century.

Item Upon the decease [of] my wife, it is my Will and desire th[at] all the Slaves which I hold in *[my] own right,* shall receive their free[dom.] To emancipate them during [her] life, would, tho' earnestly wish[ed by] me, be attended with such insu[perab]le difficulties on account of thei[r interm]ixture by Marriages with the [Dow]er Negroes, as to excite the most pa[i]nful sensations, if not disagreeabl[e c]onsequences from the latter, while [both] descriptions are in the occupancy [of] the same Proprietor; it not being [in] my power, under the tenure by whic[h t]he Dower Negroes are held, to man[umi]t them. And whereas among [thos]e who will receive freedom ac[cor]ding to this devise, there may b[e so]me, who from old age or bodily infi[rm]ities, and others who on account of [thei]r infancy, that will be unable to [su]pport themselves; it is [my] Will a[nd de]sire that all who [come under the first] and second descrip[tion shall be comfor]tably cloathed and [fed by my heirs while] they live; and [3] that such of the latter description as have no parents living, or if living are unable, or unwilling to provide for them, shall be bound by the Court until they shall arrive at the age of twenty five years; and in cases where no record can be produced, whereby their ages can be ascertained, the judgment of the Court upon its own view of the subject, shall be adequate and final. The Negroes thus bound, are (by their Masters or Mistresses) to be taught to read and write; and to be brought up to some useful occupation, agreeably to the Laws of the Commonwealth of Virginia, providing for the support of Orphan and other poor Children. And I do hereby expressly forbid the Sale, or transportation out of the said Commonwealth, of any Slave I may die possessed of, under any pretence whatsoever. And I do moreover most pointedly, and most solemnly enjoin it upon my Executors hereafter named, or the Survivors of them, to see that this [cl]ause respecting Slaves, and every part thereof be

religiously fulfilled at the Epoch at which it is directed to take place; without evasion, neglect or delay, after the Crops which may then be on the ground are harvested, particularly as it respects [4] the aged and infirm; Seeing that a regular and permanent fund be established for their Support so long as there are subjects requiring it; not trusting to the uncertain provision to be made by individuals.

∞

Jefferson's Last Letter,
Thomas Jefferson to Roger C. Weightman,
June 24, 1826

THIS WAS Jefferson's last letter, declining an invitation to travel to Washington, D.C., to attend a celebration commemorating the fiftieth anniversary of American independence. Jefferson was too ill to attend, but he found the right words, as usual, to express the significance of the occasion. Fifty years after writing the Declaration of Independence, Jefferson could say: "All eyes are opened, or opening, to the rights of man."

Respected Sir,—The kind invitation I receive from you, on the part of the citizens of the city of Washington, to be present with them at their celebration on the fiftieth anniversary of American Independence, as one of the surviving signers of an instrument pregnant with our own, and the fate of the world, is most flattering . . . I should, indeed, with peculiar delight, have met and exchanged there congratulations personally with the small band, the remnant of that host of worthies, who joined with us on that day, in the bold and doubtful election we were to make for our country, between submission or the sword; and to have enjoyed with them the consolatory fact, that our fellow citizens, after half a century of experience and prosperity, continue to approve the choice we made. May it be to the world, what I believe it will be, (to some parts sooner, to others later, but finally to all,) the signal of arousing men to burst the chains under which monkish ignorance and superstition had persuaded them to bind themselves, and to assume the blessings and security of self-government. That form which we have substituted, restores the free right to the unbounded exercise of reason and freedom of opinion. All eyes are opened, or opening, to the rights of man. The general spread of the light of science has already laid open to every view the palpable truth, that the mass of mankind has not been born with saddles on their backs, nor a favored few booted and spurred, ready to ride them legitimately, by the grace of God.

VII

*P*IETY

"*Of* all the dispositions and habits which lead to political prosperity, religion and morality are indispensable supports. In vain would that man claim the tribute of patriotism, who should labour to subvert these great pillars of human happiness, these firmest props of the duties of men and citizens."

So declared George Washington to his friends and fellow citizens in his famous Farewell Address of 1796. Here was something new: a revolutionary, a warrior for the rights of man, reminding his countrymen that their experiment in republican government would come to no good without religion. For the first time in human history, then, a group of brave men and women dared to show the world that a country could be dedicated to the rights of man without abandoning religion in the process . . . a difficult task, as the French Revolution would show in a few years' time. Free government was not to be led by men and women free of religion. It was the view of the Founders that if the American experiment was to succeed, a reliance upon God was necessary. But if the world had never before seen anything like this, such an ideal was nothing new to Washington, who throughout his long and storied career expressed again and again his faith that he could "trace the finger of Providence through those dark and mysterious events" that gave rise to the United States of America. He believed that America was part of the divine plan of superintending providence.

America has always been seen by foreign observers as well as by Americans themselves as a land blessed by Divine Providence. Tocqueville would describe the voyage of the Puritans (America's first immigrants) as "the scattering of the seed of a great people which God with

His own hands is planting on a predestined shore." Borrowing a line from the Scriptures, Thomas Hutchinson, an early historian, wrote that God brought a vine into the wilderness of New England, and caused it to take root, and it filled the land. John Jay, one of the authors of the *Federalist Papers,* saw the "design of Providence" in the birth of America. A young John Adams wrote in his diary that "America was designed by Providence for the theatre, on which man was to make his true figure, on which science, virtue, liberty, happiness, and glory were to exist in peace." Adams also noted that he had considered the "settlement of America with reverence and wonder, as the opening of a grand scheme and design in Providence for the illumination of the ignorant, and the emancipation of the slavish part of mankind all over the earth." And it was John Winthrop, the first governor of Massachusetts, who earlier famously declared America "a city upon a hill," provided, that is, that "we shall [not] deal falsely with our God in this work we have undertaken, and so cause him to withdraw his present help from us."

Thus America, in the eyes of many of the Founders, was a "New Israel." American exceptionalism—what made this country truly unique —was not its long history or established cultural traditions, for we had neither. What made this country different from all others was a prevalent belief that God played a direct and active hand in founding a people. Like the Jerusalem of old, America's "New Jerusalem" was to become God's promised land to the oppressed—an example to all humankind. In short, without God's blessing, many of the Founders, especially Washington, believed that this country would never have come into being.

But how could Americans continue to merit God's grace? The Founders had different answers to this question. George Washington believed that it was incumbent on the American people to show gratitude, both publicly and privately, to the "Great Author of every public and private good." James Madison observed that we owe our first allegiance to the ruler of the Universe. Benjamin Franklin suggested that "doing good to men is the only service of God in our power; and to imitate his beneficence is to glorify him." By worshiping and conducting ourselves in such ways that are pleasing to God, we would ensure that the American experiment would continue to thrive.

And for most of our history we have remained a religious people. From the very first moment that Americans officially declared themselves before the world to be one people, they appealed to the "Creator" and the "Laws of Nature and of Nature's God." From the brave pilgrims who left their homeland in pursuit of religious liberty to the courageous men and women who struggled to win the Revolutionary War, the first Americans never abandoned their faith in God as a provider of instruction and sustenance.

One of my favorite—and surprising—examples of this rock-solid faith involves Benjamin Franklin, easily the most irreverent of the Founders. At the Constitutional Convention of 1787, the delegates reached an impasse, threatening an end to their efforts to construct a more secure union. Franklin's solution was to ask his fellow delegates to pray for "the assistance of Heaven." As John Adams would later put it, "Our Constitution was made only for a moral and religious people. It is wholly inadequate to the government of any other."

And so at other times in our history, from the struggle to overcome the institution of slavery in the nineteenth century to the civil-rights crusade in our own century to times of war in both centuries, America has drawn deeply from the wellsprings of religious faith.

But if there was a "Biblical fragrance" to America, as Tocqueville thought, it was not to be a theocracy. If our first duty as citizens is to worship the ruler of the universe, as Madison taught, and if religion is the first of our political institutions, as Tocqueville observed, this worship had to be given freely, and this religion had to be cultivated by private supports.

In America, unlike any other country of the time, the Founders envisioned a land where people of all faiths could worship God without fear of persecution. The freedom to worship would, in turn, cultivate the piety and virtue necessary for the success of self-government. Washington noted that it would be folly to believe that national morality could be sustained without the support and guidance of religion. And although the Founders provided the widest scope for religious liberty, they presupposed that the principles of the Judeo-Christian tradition would be enshrined in the hearts of all citizens. These religious principles, Benjamin Rush argued, should be encouraged for they "promote the happiness of society and the safety and well being of civil government."

But let me end this introduction with the words of Thomas Jefferson, who rivaled Franklin in his religious heterodoxy. In his *Notes on the State of Virginia,* the man, accused by many of being an atheist, demanded of the American people: ". . . can the liberties of a nation be thought secure when we have removed their only firm basis, a conviction in the minds of the people that these liberties are of the gift of God?"

∽

George Washington, "Farewell Address"

WASHINGTON HAD firmly made up his mind that he would not seek a third term. In his second presidential term, Washington had presided over divisive issues: his refusal to allow the United States to become involved with the French Revolution; his signing of the Jay Treaty which patched things up with Great Britain; and the development (against his wishes) of political parties, headed by rivals Jefferson and Hamilton. His critics wasted no time attacking him. He was ready to leave.

Washington worried about the stability of this young nation. Was it going to go the way of all republics before it, that is, toward despotic rule? And implicitly, could the nation develop a government steered by law, not by the force of Washington's or any other great man's reputation? In the Farewell Address, famous for Washington's advice in matters of foreign policy, it should not be overlooked that Washington also focused on the importance of domestic policy. Later, Jefferson made the Farewell Address, for "conveying political lessons of peculiar value," required reading for the students at the University of Virginia. Washington's last official address to the American people reminds them that national strength and stability rests on the pillars of private morality, most especially religion. The word he uses to describe the role of religion and morality in America is not "optional" or "desirable" or "helpful"; it is "indispensable."

. . . *Of* all the dispositions and habits which lead to political prosperity, Religion and morality are indispensable supports. In vain would that man claim the tribute of Patriotism, who should labour to subvert these great Pillars of human happiness, these firmest props of the duties of Men and citizens. The mere Politician, equally with the pious man ought to respect and to cherish them. A volume could not trace all their connections with private and public felicity. Let it simply be asked where is the security for property, for reputation, for life, if the sense of religious obligation desert the oaths, which are the instruments of investigation in Courts of Justice? And let us with caution indulge the supposition, that morality can be maintained without religion. Whatever may be conceded to the influence of refined education on minds of peculiar structure, reason and experience both forbid us to expect that National morality can prevail in exclusion of religious principle.

'Tis substantially true, that virtue or morality is a necessary spring of popular government. The rule indeed extends with more or less force to every species of free Government. Who that is a sincere friend to it, can look with indifference upon attempts to shake the foundation of the fabric.

Promote then as an object of primary importance, Institutions for the general diffusion of knowledge. In proportion as the structure of a government gives force to public opinion, it is essential that public opinion should be enlightened. . . .

Observe good faith and justice towds. all Nations. Cultivate peace and harmony with all. Religion and morality enjoin this conduct; and can it be that good policy does not equally enjoin it? It will be worthy of a free, enlightened, and, at no distant period, a great Nation, to give to mankind the magnanimous and too novel example of a People always guided by an exalted justice and benevolence. Who can doubt that in the course of time and things the fruits of such a plan would richly repay any temporary advantages wch. might be lost by a steady adherence to it? Can it be, that Providence has not connected the permanent felicity of a Nation with its virtue? The experiment, at least, is recommended by every sentiment which ennobles human Nature. Alas! is it rendered impossible by its vices?

<hr />

John Adams, "To the Officers of the First Brigade of the Third Division of the Militia of Massachusetts," October 11, 1798

CAN THERE be any doubt that the American experiment depends on the piety of its citizens? Not according to President John Adams.

While our country remains untainted with the principles and manners which are now producing desolation in so many parts of the world; while she continues sincere, and incapable of insidious and impious policy, we shall have the strongest reason to rejoice in the local destination assigned us by Providence. But should the people of America once become capable of that deep simulation towards one another, and towards foreign nations, which assumes the language of justice and moderation while it is practicing iniquity and extravagance, and displays in the most captivating manner the charming pictures of candor, frankness, and sincerity, while it is rioting in rapine and insolence, this country will be the most miserable habitation in the world; because we have no government armed with power capable of contending with human passions unbridled by morality and religion. Avarice, ambition, revenge, or gallantry, would break the strongest cords of our Constitution as a whale goes through a net. Our Constitution was made only for a moral and religious people. It is wholly inadequate to the government of any other.

∞

Benjamin Franklin, "Doctrine to Be Preached," 1731

AT THE age of nineteen, Benjamin Franklin committed what he would later refer to as "another erratum" in his life, by writing and publishing *A Dissertation on Liberty and Necessity, Pleasure and Pain*. In the *Dissertation*, Franklin argued for the doctrine of necessity: Because God is all-powerful and good, and because all things happen from his will, there is no distinction between virtue and vice. (For example, if one happens to be a thief, there is nothing one can do about it for it is the will of God.)

A couple of years after publishing this work, Franklin came to regret it. He realized that under its influence, he behaved badly and that his acquaintances who accepted "the doctrine of necessity" were bad influences on him. Here was life and experience altering belief. Thus he wrote "Articles of Belief and Acts of Religion," a doctrine or creed that served him for the rest of his life. Although as an adult he was never a member of a particular religious sect, Franklin believed that it was important to live one's life by a moral or religious creed.

That there is one God Father of the Universe.

That he is infinitely good, Powerful and wise.

That he is omnipresent.

That he ought to be worshipped, by Adoration Prayer and Thanksgiving both in publick and private.

That he loves such of his Creatures as love and do good to others; and will reward them either in this World or hereafter.

That Men's Minds do not die with their Bodies, but are made more happy or miserable after this Life according to their Actions.

That Virtuous Men ought to league together to strengthen the Interest of Virtue, in the World: and so strengthen themselves in Virtue.

That Knowledge and Learning is to be cultivated, and Ignorance dissipated.

That none but the Virtuous are wise.

That Man's Perfection is in Virtue.

∽

John Adams to Zabdiel Adams, June 21, 1776

HERE JOHN Adams in a letter to his cousin Zabdiel Adams, gives voice to his own internal "exchanges" and makes clear his sense of the only sensible resolution thereof.

Who would not wish to exchange the angry Contentions of the Forum, for the peaceful Contemplations of the Closet. Where Contemplations prune their ruffled Wings and the free Soul looks down to pitty Kings? Who would not Exchange the discordant Scenes of Envy, Pride, Vanity, Malice, Revenge, for the sweet Consolations of Philosophy, the serene Composure of the Passions, the divine Enjoyments of Christian Charity, and Benevolence?

Statesmen my dear Sir, may plan and speculate for Liberty, but it is Religion and Morality alone, which can establish the Principles upon which Freedom can securely stand.... The only foundation of a free Constitution, is pure Virtue, and if this cannot be inspired into our People, in a greater Measure, than they have it now, They may change their Rulers, and the forms of Government, but they will not obtain a lasting Liberty.—They will only exchange Tyrants and Tyrannies.—You cannot therefore be more pleasantly, or usefully employed than in the Way of your Profession, pulling down the Strong Holds of Satan. This is not Cant, but the real sentiment of my Heart.—Remember me with much respect, to your worthy family, and to all Friends.

∞

Washington's Prayer at Valley Forge, 1777

FRANKLIN DELANO Roosevelt observed that for the eight years of the Revolutionary War, "every winter was a Valley Forge. Throughout the thirteen states there existed fifth columnists—and selfish men, jealous men, fearful men, who proclaimed that Washington's cause was hopeless, and that he should ask for a negotiated peace." Roosevelt observed that "Washington's conduct in those hard times has provided the model for all Americans ever since—a model of moral stamina." *

Prayer and faith sustained Washington through his many trials. Though some have disputed the accuracy of Washington biographer Mason Weems's depiction of Washington's praying at Valley Forge, many of Washington's fellow officers, such as Alexander Hamilton, reported that they often saw General Washington at prayer. Thus I thought this a wonderful account worthy of inclusion.

In the winter of '77, while Washington, with the American army lay encamped at Valley Forge, a certain good old FRIEND, of the respectable family and name of Potts, if I mistake not, had occasion to pass through the woods near head-quarters. Treading his way along the venerable grove, suddenly he heard the sound of a human voice, which as he advanced increased on his ear, and at length became like the voice of one speaking much in earnest. As he approached the spot with a cautious step, whom should he behold, in a dark natural bower of ancient oaks, but the commander in chief of the American armies on his knees at prayer! Motionless with surprise, friend Potts continued on the place till the general, having ended his devotions, arose, and, with a countenance of angel serenity, retired to headquarters: friend Potts then went home, and on entering his parlour called out to his wife, "Sarah, my dear! Sarah! All's well! all's well! George Washington will yet prevail!"

"What's the matter, Isaac?" replied she; "thee seems moved."

"Well, if I seem moved, 'tis no more than what I am. I have this day seen what I never expected. Thee knows that I always thought the sword and the gospel utterly inconsistent; and that no man could be a soldier and a christian at the same time. But George Washington has this day convinced me of my mistake."

* Fireside Chat, February 23, 1942.

He then related what he had seen, and concluded with this prophetical remark—"If George Washington be not a man of God, I am greatly deceived—and still more shall I be deceived if God do not, through him, work out a great salvation for America."

When he was told that the British troops at Lexington, on the memorable 19th of April, 1775, had fired on and killed several of the Americans, he replied, *"I grieve for the death of my countrymen, but rejoice that the British are still so determined to keep God on our side,"* alluding to that noble sentiment which he has since so happily expressed; viz. *"The smiles of Heaven can never be expected on a nation that disregards the eternal rules of order and right, which Heaven itself has ordained."*

—From Mason Weems, *Life of Washington*

∞

Benjamin Franklin to Elizabeth Hubbart, February 22, 1756

THIS LETTER addresses the death of Franklin's favorite brother, John. He died of bladder disease, from which he suffered for many years.

Elizabeth Hubbart was John Franklin's young stepdaughter. This letter was later and frequently reprinted so as to give consolation to mourners.

Again, these people knew death well and were determined to know God better—for in that way was "real life."

Dear child,

I condole with you, we have lost a most dear and valuable relation, but it is the will of God and Nature that these mortal bodies be laid aside, when the soul is to enter into real life; 'tis rather an embrio state, a preparation for living; a man is not completely born until he be dead: Why then should we grieve that a new child is born among the immortals? A new member added to their happy society? We are spirits. That bodies should be lent us, while they can afford us pleasure, assist us in acquiring knowledge, or doing good to our fellow creatures, is a kind and benevolent act of God—when they become unfit for these purposes and afford us pain instead of pleasure—instead of an aid, become an incumbrance and answer none of the intentions for which they were given, it is equally kind and benevolent that a way is provided by which we may get rid of them. Death is that way. We ourselves prudently choose a partial death. In some cases a mangled painful limb, which cannot be restored, we willingly cut off—He who plucks out a tooth, parts with it freely since the pain goes with it, and he that quits the whole body, parts at once with all pains and possibilities of pains and diseases it was liable to, or capable of making him suffer.

Our friend and we are invited abroad on a party of pleasure—that is to last forever—His chair was first ready and he is gone before us—we could not all conveniently start together, and why should you and I be grieved at this, since we are soon to follow, and we know where to find him. Adieu,

❧

Mercy Warren, History of the Rise, Progress, and Termination of the American Revolution

IN 1805, Mercy Warren published a three-volume history of the American Revolution. In concluding her history, Warren reflected on the decline of republican virtue or, as she put it, "the relaxation of manners" since the Revolution. The excerpt following contains those thoughts and her advice that to sustain the work of the revolutionaries, Americans must sustain their moral and religious character.

Nothing seemed to be wanting to the United States but a continuance of their union and virtue. It was their interest to cherish true, genuine republican virtue, in politics; and in religion, a strict adherence to a sublime code of morals, which has never been equalled by the sages of ancient time, nor can ever be abolished by the sophistical reasonings of modern philosophers. Possessed of this palladium, America might bid defiance both to foreign and domestic intrigue, and stand on an eminence that would command their veneration of nations, and the respect of their monarchs; but a defalcation from these principles may leave the sapless vine of liberty to droop, or to be rooted out by the hand that had been stretched out to nourish it.

The world might reasonably have expected, from the circumstances connected with the first settlement of the American colonies, which was in consequence of their attachment to the religion of their fathers, united with a spirit of independence relative to civil government, that there would have been no observable dereliction of those honorable principles, for many ages to come. From the sobriety of their manners, their simple habits, their attention to the education and moral conduct of their children, they had the highest reason to hope, that it might have been long, very long, before the faith of their religion was shaken, or their principles corrupted, either by the manners, opinions, or habits of foreigners, bred in the courts of despotism, or the schools of licentiousness.

This hope shall not yet be relinquished. There has indeed been some relaxation of manners, and the appearance of a change in public opinion not contemplated when revolutionary scenes first shook the western world. But it must be acknowledged, that the religious and moral character of Americans yet stands on a higher grade of excellence and purity, than that of most other nations. It has been observed, that "a violation of manners has destroyed more states than the infraction of laws." It is necessary for every *American,* with becoming energy to endeavour to stop the dissemination of principles evidently destructive of the cause for which they have bled. It must be the combined virtue of the rulers and of the people to do this, and to rescue and save their civil and religious rights from the outstretched arm of tyranny, which may appear under any mode or form of government.

∞

Benjamin Rush, "On Slavekeeping," 1773

BENJAMIN RUSH shows that ministers of faith have a first duty to show their congregants the sins of slavery, writing that they should "neglect not the weightier laws of justice and humanity." As Rush says, the Bible —from the Hebrew Bible to the New Testament—makes it plain that God, as Jefferson would later put it, "has no attribute which can take sides with" Americans who support the existence of slavery. Religion is the law of a free people.

Ye men of sense and virtue—Ye advocates for American liberty, rouse up and espouse the cause of humanity and general liberty. Bear a testimony against a vice which degrades human nature, and dissolves that universal tie of benevolence which should connect all the children of men together in one great family.—The plant of liberty is of so tender a nature, that it cannot thrive long in the neighbourhood of slavery. Remember the eyes of all Europe are fixed upon you, to preserve an asylum for freedom in this country, after the last pillars of it are fallen in every other quarter of the globe.

But chiefly—ye ministers of the gospel, whose dominion over the principles and actions of men is so universally acknowledged and felt,— Ye who estimate the worth of your fellow creatures by their immortality, and therefore must look upon all mankind as equal;—let your zeal keep pace with your opportunities to put a stop to slavery. While you inforce the duties of "tithe and cummin," neglect not the weightier laws of justice and humanity. Slavery is an Hydra sin, and includes in it every violation of the precepts of the Law and the Gospel. In vain will you command your flocks to offer up the incense of faith and charity, while they continue to mingle the sweat and blood of Negro slaves with their sacrifices. —If the blood of Abel cried aloud for vengeance;—If, under the Jewish dispensation, cities of refuge could not screen the deliberate murderer— if even manslaughter required sacrifices to expiate it,—and if a single murder so seldom escapes with impunity in any civilized country, what may you not say against that trade, or those manufactures—or laws, which destroy the lives of so many thousands of our fellow-creatures every year?—If in the Old Testament "God swears by his holiness, and by the excellency of Jacob, that the earth shall tremble, and every one mourn that dwelleth therein for the iniquity of those who oppress the poor and crush the needy," "who buy the poor with silver, and the needy with a pair of shoes," what judgments may you not denounce upon those who continue to perpetrate these crimes, after the more full discovery which God has made of the law of equity in the New Testament. Put them in mind of the rod which was held over them a few years ago in the Stamp and Revenue Acts. Remember that national crimes require national punishments, and without declaring what punishment awaits this evil, you may venture to assure them, that it cannot pass with impunity, unless God shall cease to be just or merciful.

∞

John Adams to Thomas Jefferson, June 28, 1813

ADAMS LOOKS back at the founding of America, observing that the principles of American liberty and the general principles of Christianity mutually reinforce each other.

The general *Principles,* on which the Fathers Atchieved Independence, were the only Principles in which that beautiful Assembly of young Gentlemen could Unite, and these Principles only could be intended by them in their Address, or by me in my Answer. And what were these *general Principles?* I answer, the general Principles of Christianity, in which all those Sects were United: And the *general Principles* of English and American Liberty, in which all those young Men United, and which had United all Parties in America, in Majorities sufficient to assert and maintain her Independence.

Now I will avow, that I then believed, and now believe, that those general Principles of Christianity, are as eternal and immutable, as the Existence and Attributes of God; and that those Principles of Liberty, are as unalterable as human Nature and our terrestrial, mundane System. I could therefore safely say, consistently with all my then and present Information, that I believed they would never make Discoveries in contradiction to these *general Principles*. In favour of these *general Principles* in Phylosophy, Religion and Government, I could fill Sheets of quotations from Frederick of Prussia, from Hume, Gibbon, Bolingbroke, Reausseau and Voltaire, as well as Neuton and Locke: not to mention thousands of Divines and Philosophers of inferiour Fame.

∞

"To Walk Humbly with Thy God"
George Washington, Circular Address to the States, June 8, 1783

FROM TIME to time during the Revolutionary War, Washington sent "circulars"—official and nearly identical letters and reports—to the governors of each of the colonies to update them on the progress of the war. This was his last circular, announcing his retirement from the military.

But this letter is about much more than simply stepping down from his command. Though the war was over, the work of building a nation, or establishing America's national character, had just begun. In this address, Washington observed that, though a nation could have hardly come into being at a more auspicious time, Americans still must make a "choice" and work hard to determine whether this nation will be a success.

This Circular Address acknowledges America's special origin at the confluence of the tides of history and heroism—an origin that seems to us, in retrospect, to be inevitable but was both contingent and circumstantial.

In America's effort to establish a national character, God's blessings must be acknowledged—He has given much to the inhabitants of this land. As free creatures of His, they must now, like Adam and Eve, determine their own fate and worthiness in their garden paradise. Wash-

ington gives credit "above all" to "the pure and benign light of Revelation," for preparing America to be a "display of human greatness and
felicity." In the last paragraph Washington paraphrases Micah 6:8, which
reads: "He hath showed thee, O man, what *is* good; and what doth the
Lord require of thee, but to do justly, and to love mercy, and to walk
humbly with thy God?"

The Citizens of America, placed in the most enviable condition, as
the sole Lords and Proprietors of a vast Tract of Continent, comprehending all the various soils and climates of the World, and abounding with all
the necessaries and conveniences of life, are now by the late satisfactory
pacification, acknowledged to be possessed of absolute freedom and
Independency; They are, from this period, to be considered as the Actors
on a most conspicuous Theatre, which seems to be peculiarly designated
by Providence for the display of human greatness and felicity; Here, they
are not only surrounded with every thing which can contribute to the
completion of private and domestic enjoyment, but Heaven has crowned
all its other blessings, by giving a fairer oppertunity for political happiness, than any other Nation has ever been favored with. Nothing
can illustrate these observations more forcibly, than a recollection of
the happy conjuncture of times and circumstances, under which our
Republic assumed its rank among the Nations; The foundation of our
Empire was not laid in the gloomy age of Ignorance and Superstition,
but at an Epocha when the rights of mankind were better understood
and more clearly defined, than at any former period, the researches of
the human mind, after social happiness, have been carried to a great
extent, the Treasures of knowledge, acquired by the labours of Philosophers, Sages and Legislatures, through a long succession of years, are
laid open for our use, and their collected wisdom may be happily applied
in the Establishment of our forms of Government; the free cultivation of
Letters, the unbounded extension of Commerce, the progressive refinement of Manners, the growing liberality of sentiment, and above all, the
pure and benign light of Revelation, have had a meliorating influence on
mankind and increased the blessings of Society. At this auspicious period, the United States came into existence as a Nation, and if their
Citizens should not be completely free and happy, the fault will be
intirely their own.

I now make it my earnest prayer, that God would have you, and the
State over which you preside, in his holy protection, that he would
incline the hearts of the Citizens to cultivate a spirit of subordination and
obedience to Government, to entertain a brotherly affection and love for

one another, for their fellow Citizens of the United States at large, and particularly for their brethren who have served in the Field, and finally, that he would most graciously be pleased to dispose us all, to do Justice, to love mercy, and to demean ourselves with that Charity, humility and pacific temper of mind, which were the Characteristicks of the Divine Author of our blessed Religion, and without an humble imitation of whose example in these things, we can never hope to be a happy Nation.

***

Benjamin Rush, Commonplace Book, May 27, 1790

IN THIS brief reflection to himself in his *Commonplace Book,* Rush reminds Christians to look for the face of Jesus in all human beings.

ON SOLITUDE

The powers of the human mind appear to be arranged in a certain order like the strata of earth. They are thrown out of their order by the fall of man. The moral powers appear to have occupied the highest and first place. They recover it in solitude, and after sleep, hence the advantage of solitary punishments, and of consulting our morning pillow in cases where there is a doubt of what is right, or duty. The first thoughts in a morning if followed seldom deceive or mislead us. They are generally seasoned by the moral powers.

In Macbeth a lady is restrained from the murder of a king by his resemblance of her father as he slept. Should not all men be restrained from acts of violence and even of unkindness against their fellow men by observing in them something which resembles the Saviour of the World? If nothing else certainly, a human figure?

***

"So Help Me God," George Washington, First Inaugural Address, April 30, 1789

ON APRIL 14, 1789, Washington was notified by an old friend that he had been unanimously elected to the presidency. Before leaving for

New York to assume the office of president, Washington wrote one of the few emotional entries in his diary: "About ten o'clock I bade adieu to Mount Vernon, to private life and to domestic felicity, and with a mind oppressed with more anxious and painful sensations than I have words to express set out for New York with the best disposition to render service to my country in obedience to its call but with less hope of answering its expectations."

If Washington entered the office of presidency with diffidence and doubts, it was because he was deeply aware of the enormous task ahead of him and the impact it would have on generations to come. Before the eyes of mankind, Washington would lead the experiment of self-government.

According to Washington Irving, on the day of his inauguration, Washington wore a homespun suit of brown cloth, put his hand on the Bible held by James Otis, and repeated the oath of office. Irving wrote that upon concluding the oath, "Mr. Otis would have raised the Bible to [Washington's] lips but he bowed down reverently and kissed it." Washington also added "so help me God" to the official presidential oath of office, and every president since has followed his example.

In the excerpt below, Washington gave thanks to the Almighty for the blessings America had received during the Revolution and Constitution making, and asked for His continued support. Unlike many contemporary speeches where God and Providence are part of a string of mentions, in our first president's first address, the presence of Providence suffuses the entire speech as it suffuses creation.

Fellow-Citizens of the Senate and the House of Representatives. . . . Such being the impressions under which I have, in obedience to the public summons, repaired to the present station; it would be peculiarly improper to omit in this first official Act, my fervent supplications to that Almighty Being who rules over the Universe, who presides in the Councils of Nations, and whose providential aids can supply every human defect, that his benediction may consecrate to the liberties and happiness of the People of the United States, a Government instituted by themselves for these essential purposes: and may enable every instrument employed in its administration to execute with success, the functions allotted to his charge. In tendering this homage to the Great Author of every public and private good, I assure myself that it expresses your sentiments not less than my own; nor those of my fellow-citizens at large, less than either. No People can be bound to acknowledge and adore the invisible hand, which conducts the Affairs of men more than the People of the United States. Every step, by which they have advanced to the character of an independent nation, seems to have been distinguished by some token of providential agency. And in the important revolution just accomplished in the system of their United Government, the tranquil deliberations and voluntary consent of so many distinct communities, from which the event has resulted, cannot be compared with the means by which most Governments have been established, without some return of pious gratitude along with an humble anticipation of the future blessings which the past seem to presage. These reflections, arising out of the present crisis, have forced themselves too strongly on my mind to be suppressed. You will join with me I trust in thinking, that there are none under the influence of which, the proceedings of a new and free Government can more auspiciously commence. . . . In these honorable qualifications, I behold the surest pledges . . . that the foundations of our National policy will be laid in the pure and immutable principles of private morality; and the pre-eminence of a free Government, be exemplified by all the attributes which can win the affections of its Citizens, and command the respect of the world.

I dwell on this prospect with every satisfaction which an ardent love for my Country can inspire: since there is no truth more thoroughly established, than that there exists in the oeconomy and course of nature, an indissoluble union between virtue and happiness, between duty and advantage, between the genuine maxims of an honest and magnanimous policy, and the solid rewards of public prosperity and felicity: Since we ought to be no less persuaded that the propitious smiles of Heaven, can never be expected on a nation that disregards the eternal rules of order and right, which Heaven itself has ordained: And since the preservation of the sacred fire of liberty, and the destiny of the Republican model of Government, are justly considered as *deeply,* perhaps as *finally* staked, on the experiment entrusted to the hands of the American people.

Having thus imparted to you my sentiments, as they have been awakened by the occasion which brings us together, I shall take my present leave; but not without resorting once more to the benign parent of the human race, in humble supplication that since he has been pleased to favour the American people, with opportunities for deliberating in perfect tranquility, and dispositions for deciding with unparellelled unanimity on a form of Government, for the security of their Union, and the advancement of their happiness; so his divine blessing may be equally *conspicuous* in the enlarged views, the temperate consultations, and the wise measures on which the success of this Government must depend.

∾

Northwest Ordinance; Article 3, July 13, 1787

THE NORTHWEST Ordinance, originally drafted by Thomas Jefferson, was enacted by the Congress under the Articles of Confederation. The significance of the Northwest Ordinance was that, unlike Great Britain, which refused to allow a colony to become a full-fledged member of its commonwealth, the Northwest Ordinance provided the means by which a territory could eventually apply for statehood and become part of the United States, not just a colony of it. In addition, the Northwest Ordinance, as noted earlier, outlawed slavery in the territories.

The territory stretching to the Mississippi was a wilderness populated by Indians. Eager settlers were ready to go forth, but it was important that they regulate their conduct with the Indians and among themselves. Thus the ordinance stipulated trial by jury, freedom of conscience, education and the importance of religion, morality, and justice. Again note the word used to modify religion's place in the territories of America—"necessary."

Religion, morality, and knowledge being necessary to good government and the happiness of mankind, schools and the means of education shall forever by encouraged. The utmost good faith shall always be observed towards the Indians; their lands and property shall never be taken from them without their consent; and in their property, rights, and liberty they never shall be invaded or disturbed unless in just and lawful wars authorized by Congress; but laws founded in justice and humanity shall, from time to time, be made, for preventing wrongs being done to them and for preserving peace and friendship with them.

∾

The Question of Representation: Benjamin Franklin's Invocation for Prayer at the Constitutional Convention, June 28, 1787

FOR TEN weeks delegates to the Constitutional Convention bitterly debated the question of representation. At issue was whether representation was to be based on the population of each state or if each state would be given one vote. Delegates from the small states supported the New Jersey Plan, which proposed one vote per state and a one-house Confederation Congress; delegates from the larger states supported the Virginia Plan, which based representation in both houses on population.

The debate over which plan to adopt became very heated and threatened to dissolve the Convention. Historians have called this period the "critical juncture" in the Convention. Tempers flared, impatience and frustration grew, so much so that on June 28, Franklin, the oldest delegate there at eighty-one, invoked the aid of the Almighty.

The delegates never acted on Franklin's motion for prayer for several reasons: the problem of maintaining the secrecy vital to the proceedings of the convention; the panic this might provoke among the public sensing the desperation of the delegates; and the fact that the convention had no money to pay a clergyman.

But Franklin's motion, at least for a short while, brought calm to the proceedings, and by mid-July a compromise was reached. And while it might have seemed odd for the perhaps least reverent Founder of them all to suggest prayer, historians agree that his motion was sincere, and that in his saying "God governs in the affairs of men," in that company, he was not alone in his belief.

The small progress we have made after 4 or five weeks close attendance & continual reasonings with each other—our different sentiments on almost every question, several of the last producing as many noes as ays, is methinks a melancholy proof of the imperfection of the Human Understanding. We indeed seem to *feel* our own want of political wisdom, since we have been running about in search of it. We have gone back to ancient history for models of Government, and examined the different forms of those Republics which having been formed with the seeds of their own dissolution now no longer exist. And we have viewed Modern States all round Europe, but find none of their Constitutions suitable to our circumstances.

In this situation of this Assembly, groping as it were in the dark to find political truth, and scarce able to distinguish it when presented to us, how has it happened, Sir, that we have not hitherto once thought of humbly applying to the Father of lights to illuminate our understandings? In the beginning of the Contest with G. Britain, when we were sensible of danger we had daily prayer in this room for the divine protection.—

Our prayers, Sir, were heard, and they were graciously answered. All of us who were engaged in the struggle must have observed frequent instances of a Superintending providence in our favor. To that kind providence we owe this happy opportunity of consulting in peace on the means of establishing our future national felicity. And have we now forgotten that powerful friend? or do we imagine that we no longer need his assistance? I have lived, Sir, a long time, and the longer I live, the more convincing proofs I see of this truth—*that God governs in the affairs of men*. And if a sparrow cannot fall to the ground without his notice, is it probable that an empire can rise without his aid? We have been assured, Sir, in the sacred writings, that "except the Lord build the House they labour in vain that build it." I firmly believe this; and I also believe that without his concurring aid we shall succeed in this political building no better than the Builders of Babel: We shall be divided by our little partial local interests; our projects will be confounded, and we ourselves shall become a reproach and bye word down to future ages. And what is worse, mankind may hereafter from this unfortunate instance, despair of establishing Governments by Human Wisdom and leave it to chance, war and conquest.

I therefore beg leave to move—that henceforth prayers imploring the assistance of Heaven, and its blessings on our deliberations, be held in this Assembly every morning before we proceed to business, and that one or more of the Clergy of this City be requested to officiate in that service.

∞

John Adams, Inaugural Address, March 4, 1797

THOUGH IT is recorded that the audience for John Adams's inaugural address was so saddened by the departure of President Washington that many were moved to tears, they were also privileged to hear the second President's stirring affirmation of the connection between religion and the success of the American experiment.

If a resolution to do justice as far as may depend upon me, at all times and to all nations, and maintain peace, friendship, and benevolence with all the world; if an unshaken confidence in the honor, spirit, and resources of the American people, on which I have so often hazarded my all and never been deceived; if elevated ideas of the high destinies of this country and of my own duties toward it, founded on a knowledge of the moral principles and intellectual improvements of the people deeply engraven on my mind in early life, and not obscured but exalted by experience and age; and, with humble reverence, I feel it to be my duty to add, if a veneration for the religion of a people who profess and call themselves Christians, and a fixed resolution to consider a decent respect for Christianity among the best recommendations for the public service, can enable me in any degree to comply with your wishes, it shall be my strenuous endeavor that this sagacious injunction of the two Houses shall not be without effect.

With this great example before me, with the sense and spirit, the faith and honor, the duty and interest, of the same American people pledged to support the Constitution of the United States, I entertain no doubt of its continuance in all its energy, and my mind is prepared without hesitation to lay myself under the most solemn obligations to support it to the utmost of my power.

And may that Being who is supreme over all, the Patron of Order, the Fountain of Justice, and the Protector in all ages of the world of virtuous liberty, continue His blessing upon this nation and its Government and give it all possible success and duration consistent with the ends of His providence.

∞

George Washington, Thanksgiving Proclamation, New York, October 3, 1789

OUR FIRST Thanksgiving was, of course, held by the Pilgrims in the fall of 1621. Washington's Thanksgiving Proclamation was our first national Thanksgiving. Abraham Lincoln in 1863 made it an annual national holiday to be celebrated on the last Thursday of November. Originally it was a day of thanks and prayer and supplication and request for divine blessing. A few helpings of those would go nicely and wouldn't hurt with the stuffing and gravy of today.

Whereas it is the duty of all Nations to acknowledge the providence of Almighty God, to obey his will, to be grateful for his benefits, and humbly to implore his protection and favor, and Whereas both Houses of Congress have by their joint Committee requested me "to recommend to the People of the United States a day of public thanks-giving and prayer to be observed by acknowledging with grateful hearts the many signal favors of Almighty God, especially by affording them an opportunity peaceably to establish a form of government for their safety and happiness."

Now therefore I do recommend and assign Thursday the 26th, day of November next to be devoted by the People of these States to the service of that great and glorious Being, who is the beneficent Author of all the good that was, that is, or that will be. That we may then all unite in rendering unto him our sincere and humble thanks, for his kind care and protection of the People of this country previous to their becoming a Nation, for the signal and manifold mercies, and the favorable interpositions of his providence, which we experienced in the course and conclusion of the late war, for the great degree of tranquillity, union, and plenty, which we have since enjoyed, for the peaceable and rational manner in which we have been enabled to establish constitutions of government for our safety and happiness, and particularly the national One now lately instituted, for the civil and religious liberty with which we are blessed, and the means we have of acquiring and diffusing useful knowledge and in general for all the great and various favors which he hath been pleased to confer upon us.

And also that we may then unite in most humbly offering our prayers and supplications to the great Lord and Ruler of Nations and beseech him to pardon our national and other transgressions, to enable us all, whether in public or private stations, to perform our several and relative duties properly and punctually, to render our national government a blessing to all the People, by constantly being a government of wise, just and constitutional laws, discreetly and faithfully executed and obeyed, to protect and guide all Sovereigns and Nations (especially such as have shown kindness unto us) and to bless them with good government, peace, and concord. To promote the knowledge and practice of true religion and virtue, and the encrease of science among them and Us, and generally to grant unto all Mankind such a degree of temporal prosperity as he alone knows to be best.

∞

Benjamin Franklin to George Whitefield, July 6, 1749

THOUGH NOT an especially religious man (or regular churchgoer, as Sundays for Franklin were days for studying), Franklin took a keen liking to Whitefield, the leading preacher of the "Great Awakening" in America in the 1740s.

In his *Autobiography,* Franklin notes: "Multitudes of all sects and denominations that attended his [Whitefield's] sermons were enormous, and it was matter of speculation to me, who was one of the number, to observe the extraordinary influence of his oratory on his hearers, and how much they admired and respected him, notwithstanding his common abuse of them by assuring them that they were naturally half beasts and half devils. It was wonderful to see the change soon made in the manners of our inhabitants. From being thoughtless or indifferent about religion, it seemed as if all the world were growing religious, so that one could not walk through the town in an evening without hearing psalms sung in different families of every street."

Franklin helped to spread the word by printing Whitefield's sermons in his paper. He also gave him lodgings in the rooms above his printing shop. When other preachers in town, who were jealous of Whitefield's popularity, refused to give him a pulpit from which to speak, Franklin played a role in financing a new building "expressly for the use of any preacher of any religious persuasion who might desire to say something to the people at Philadelphia; the design in building not being to accommodate a particular sect, but the inhabitants in general; so that even if the Mufti of Constantinople were to send a missionary to preach Mohammadeanism to us, he would find a pulpit at his service."

His own individualistic approach to faith did not get in the way of his appreciation of the beneficial and important works of a good preacher. In this letter to the famous preacher, Franklin expresses his support for the religious enterprise—as a method of inculcating morality among the "lower ranks" and "the grandees." In Franklin's time enlightenment and religion were believed to be on the same side, as they should be in our day as well.

. . . *I* am glad to hear that you have frequent opportunities of preaching among the great. If you can gain them to a good and exemplary life, wonderful changes will follow in the manners of the lower ranks; for, *ad Exemplum Regis, etc.* On this principle Confucius, the famous eastern reformer, proceeded. When he saw his country sunk in vice, and wickedness of all kinds triumphant, he applied himself first to the grandees; and having by his doctrine won them to the cause of virtue, the commons followed in multitudes. The mode has a wonderful influence on mankind; and there are numbers that perhaps fear less the being in Hell, than out of the fashion! Our more western reformations began with the ignorant mob; and when numbers of them were gained, interest and party-views drew in the wise and great. Where both methods can be used, reformations are like to be more speedy. O that some method could be found to make them lasting! He that shall discover that, will, in my opinion, deserve more, ten thousand times, than the inventor of the longtitude.

My wife and family join in the most cordial salutations to you and good Mrs. Whitefield, I am, dear Sir, your very affectionate friend, and most obliged humble servant,

∞

George Washington, General Orders, New York, July 9, 1776

THIS IS George Washington's response to news of the passage of the Declaration of Independence. He was elated by the news, hoping it might give the troops a clearer sense of purpose by finally shutting the door on any hopes or speculation of reconciliation with Great Britain.

According to Washington Irving, his biographer, Washington's somber statement was aimed at discouraging irresponsible behavior by jubilant soldiers. Hearing the news of the passage of the Declaration of Independence, New York crowds had pulled down a statue of King George and had broken it up in order to convert the materials into bullets for ammunition. Washington learned that some of his soldiers might have taken part in this. As Washington Irving records, "Washington censured it in general orders, as having much the appearance of a riot and a want of discipline, and the army was forbidden to indulge in any irregularities of the kind. It was his constant effort to inspire his countrymen in arms with his own elevated idea of the cause in which they were engaged, and to make them feel that it was no ordinary warfare, admitting of vulgar passions and perturbations." *

Washington was consistent; he had the gift of always being himself, with eyes on the important things. St. Augustine writes of the "ordo amorum"—the order of the loves. General Washington seemed to have them always right.

The Hon. Continental Congress having been pleased to allow a Chaplain to each Regiment, with the pay of Thirty-three Dollars and one third pr month—The Colonels or commanding officers of each regiment are directed to procure Chaplains accordingly; persons of good Characters and exemplary lives—To see that all inferior officers and soldiers pay them a suitable respect and attend carefully upon religious exercises. The blessing and protection of Heaven are at all times necessary but especially so in times of public distress and danger—The General hopes and trusts, that every officer and man, will endeavour so to live, and act, as becomes a Christian Soldier defending the dearest Rights and Liberties of his country.

∞

Benjamin Franklin to Mary Stevenson, June 11, 1760

IN 1757, Franklin went with his son to England, where he rented rooms from Mrs. Margaret Stevenson, a widow. Franklin became especially good friends with her daughter, Mary, a highly intelligent girl. In fact, he became a father figure to the young girl, who shared his interest in the scientific experiments and questions of the day. Not surprisingly, he encouraged her to pursue these studies. But in this entry, Franklin,

* Weems, *Life of Washington*, vol. 2, p. 258.

the scientist, tells her of our more important duties. Knowledge of nature is not as important as knowledge and performance of our duties to God, to family, and to friends.

Franklin's is a more calm and ordered view than Adams's (at least Adams as a young man). As we will see later, what for Adams is a struggle and a temptation is for Franklin a category in the order of creation to be known and appreciated.

DEAR POLLY,

There is, however, a prudent Moderation to be used in Studies of this kind. The Knowledge of Nature may be ornamental, and it may be useful, but if to attain an Eminence in that, we neglect the Knowledge and Practice of essential Duties, we deserve Reprehension. For there is no Rank in Natural Knowledge of equal Dignity and Importance with that of being a good Parent, a good Child, a good Husband, or Wife, a good Neighbour or Friend, a good Subject or Citizen, that is, in short, a good Christian. Nicholas Gimcrack, therefore, who neglected the Care of his Family, to pursue Butterflies, was a just Object of Ridicule, and we must give him up as fair Game to the Satyrist.

. . . Adieu, my dear Friend, and believe me ever Yours affectionately

∽

Abigail Adams to John Adams, October 9, 1775

AN EPIDEMIC had hit the town of Braintree, Massachusetts, home of Abigail and John Adams—an epidemic that killed John Adams's brother and struck John and Abigail's young son, Tommy. Abigail was exhausted and weak without her husband, who was in Philadelphia serving in the Continental Congress. In August, Abigail had sent to John a "bill of mortality" listing the eight neighbors who had just died that week, along with others. Elizabeth Smith, Abigail's mother, who came to help her daughter, was stricken herself and, after suffering for a couple of weeks, died under Abigail's care. Abigail was almost "ready to faint under this severe and heavy stroke."

As the following letter demonstrates, Abigail Adams was restored by her faith in God and never doubted His divine goodness. America's Founders lived with death in their midst, at their hearth on a regular basis. Such adversity did not provoke them to doubt or to curse God but, rather, to thank Him for the blessings left to them. These people had much reason "to murmur at providence" but did not.

But the heavy stroke which most of all distresses me is my dear Mother. I cannot overcome my too selfish sorrow, all her tenderness towards me, her care and anxiety for my welfare at all times, her watchfulness over my infant years, her advice and instruction in maturer age; all, all indear her memory to me, and highten my sorrow for her loss. At the same time I know a patient submission is my duty. I will strive to obtain it! But the lenient hand of time alone can blunt the keen Edg of Sorrow. He who deignd to weep over a departed Friend, will surely forgive a sorrow which at all times desires to be bounded and restrained, by a firm Belief that a Being of infinite wisdom and unbounded Goodness, will carve out my portion in tender mercy towards me! Yea tho he slay me I will trust in him said holy Job. What tho his corrective Hand hath been streatched against me; I will not murmer. Tho earthly comforts are taken away I will not repine, he who gave them has surely a right to limit their duration, and has continued them to me much longer than I deserved. I might have been striped of my children as many others have been. I might o! forbid it Heaven, I might have been left a solitary widow.

Still I have many blessing[s] left, many comforts to be thankfull for, and rejoice in. I am not left to mourn as one without hope.

My dear parent knew in whom she had Believed, and from the first attack of the distemper she was perswaded it would prove fatal to her. A solemnity possess'd her soul, nor could you force a smile from her till she dyed. The voilence of her disease soon weakened her so that she was unable to converse, but whenever she could speak, she testified her willingness to leave the world and an intire resignation to the Divine Will. She retaind her senses to the last moment of her Existance, and departed the World with an easy tranquility, trusting in the merits of a Redeamer. Her passage to immortality was marked with a placid smile upon her countanance, nor was there to be seen scarcely a vestage of the king of Terrors.

> "The sweet remembrance of the just
> Shall flourish when they sleep in Dust."

Tis by soothing Grief that it can be healed.

"Give Sorrow words.
The Grief that cannot speak
Whispers the o'er fraught heart and bids it Break."

∞

George Washington, General Orders, May 15, 1776

ON MAY 5, 1776, George Washington wrote to Congress that [t]he designs of the enemy are too much behind the curtain for me to form any accurate opinion of their plan of operations fore the summer's campaign. We are left to wander, therefore, in the field of conjecture."

Waiting in New York for the British General Howe and his troops to return from Halifax, Washington issued the order on May 15 for prayer, fasting, and humble supplication to the Lord for His continued blessings. Soon Washington was to face one of his greatest military challenges. Without the guiding hand of Providence, it is hard to explain how a ragtag army, many of its soldiers barefoot and without uniforms, was able to defeat the most seasoned and highly trained military force in the world. Looking back, we can see that the American cause for liberty should have probably ended right then and there in New York, where American troops were outnumbered and outgunned nearly three to one by the British troops and armada. At the battle of Brooklyn Heights, the American troops lost more than 1,000 men. The British were on the verge of capturing all our troops and bringing the rebellion to an early close. But the British, for some reason, delayed the final siege. Then, rain and fog miraculously set in, providing cover for the American troops to evacuate Long Island undetected across the river, filled with British ships, into Manhattan. The divine hand of providence seemed to be at work, answering the supplications of Washington and his troops.

In war, in peace, in deliberation, on rising, on going to bed, our greatest president called on and renewed his faith.

The Continental Congress having ordered, Friday the 17th. Instant to be observed as a day of "fasting, humiliation and prayer, humbly to supplicate the mercy of Almighty God, that it would please him to pardon all our manifold sins and transgressions, and to prosper the Arms of the United Colonies, and finally, establish the peace and freedom of America, upon a solid and lasting foundation"—The General commands all officers, and soldiers, to pay strict obedience to the Orders of the Continental Congress, and by their unfeigned, and pious observance of their religious duties, incline the Lord, and Giver of Victory, to prosper our arms.

The regiment of Artillery to be mustered, Sunday morning, at eight o'clock, upon the Common, where the Commissary General of Musters will attend.

∞

John Adams, Diary, August 14, 1796

ADAMS WAS serving his second term as vice-president during this time. With Congress in recess, Adams returned to his farm in Quincy for the summer. This much-needed break from the tumults of politics in Philadelphia allowed Adams to resume writing more regularly in his *Diary.*

One great advantage of the Christian religion is that it brings the great principle of the law of nature and nations—Love your neighbor as yourself, and do to others as you would that others should do to you,— to the knowledge, belief, and veneration of the whole people. Children, servants, women, and men, are all professors in the science of public and private morality. No other institution for education, no kind of political discipline, could diffuse this kind of necessary information, so universally among all ranks and descriptions of citizens. The duties and rights of the man and the citizen are thus taught from early infancy to every creature. The sanctions of a future life are thus added to the observance of civil and political, as well as domestic and private duties. Prudence, justice, temperance, and fortitude, are thus taught to be the means and conditions of future as well as present happiness.

∞

Alexander Hamilton to Elizabeth Hamilton, July 1804

THESE TWO letters were written as Hamilton prepared for a duel against Aaron Burr.

Burr had run for president against Thomas Jefferson, and though Hamilton was a bitter rival of Jefferson, he supported Jefferson rather than Burr. Burr then set his sights on becoming governor of New York and possibly leading a secessionist movement in New York, breaking up the Union and building a strong Northern confederacy. Hamilton attacked Burr and his plan in the press. As a result, Burr was defeated. Enraged, Burr challenged Hamilton to a duel. Though Hamilton did not believe in dueling (he lost his son Philip to a duel), he believed that the code of honor did not give him any out.

In these letters, one gets the sense that Hamilton never intended to shoot at Burr and had a premonition that he was to die.

For most of his life, Hamilton was not what one would call a traditional Christian. But historians have shown that later in life, he had a conversion of sorts, and these letters extolling his wife to "fly to the bosom of God and be comforted" show that he believed in the promise of a "better world." Indeed, on his deathbed he made several requests that he receive a last Communion, which he eventually did.

To Mrs. Hamilton, July 10, 1804

This letter, my dear Eliza, will not be delivered to you, unless I shall first have terminated my earthly career, to begin, as I humbly hope, from redeeming grace and divine mercy, a happy immortality. If it had been possible for me to have avoided the interview, my love for you and my precious children would have been alone a decisive motive. But it was not possible, without sacrifices which would have rendered me unworthy of your esteem. I need not tell you of the pangs I feel from the idea of quitting you, and exposing you to the anguish I know you would feel. Nor could I dwell on the topic, lest it should unman me. The consolations of religion, my beloved, can alone support you; and these you have a right to enjoy. Fly to the bosom of your God, and be comforted. With my last idea I shall cherish the sweet hope of meeting you in a better world. Adieu, best of wives—best of women. Embrace all my darling children for me.

To Mrs. Hamilton, Tuesday evening, ten o'clock

This is my second letter. The scruples of a Christian have determined me to expose my own life to any extent, rather than subject myself to the guilt of taking the life of another. This much increases my hazards, and redoubles my pangs for you. But you had rather I should die innocent than live guilty. Heaven can preserve me, and I humbly hope will; but, in the contrary event, I charge you to remember that you are a Christian. God's will be done! The will of a merciful God must be good. Once more, Adieu, my darling, darling wife.

∞

Noah Webster, "Advice to the Young" from Value of the Bible and Excellence of the Christian Religion, *1834*

TODAY, NOAH Webster is perhaps best remembered for his spellers and dictionaries. But Webster called his revision of the King James Bible "the most important undertaking" of his life. Almost all American homes had at least one book in the house—the Bible. Webster wanted to make the Bible more accessible to Americans by correcting the grammar and geographical mistakes and by updating archaisms. In 1833, Webster published a revised edition of the King James Bible. The selection below was taken from *Value of the Bible and Excellence of the Christian Religion,* which was written as a companion piece to Webster's edition of the Bible.

Here is a good case made for the benefits that accrue to anyone in reading the Bible. For believers it is evident why they should read. But to gain knowledge of the human heart and the "characters of men" no book surpasses. Also, Webster advises entrusting government to good men, to men who will rule in the fear of God. This seemingly obvious and uncontroversial piece of advice now seems to some antiquated and irrelevant. Many people now believe such considerations actually do not matter at all. Too bad. Such cavalier dismissals put the people at peril.

When you become entitled to exercise the right of voting for public officers, let it be impressed on your mind that God commands you to choose for rulers, *just men who will rule in the fear of God.* The preservation of a republican government depends on the faithful discharge of this duty; if the citizens neglect their duty, and place unprincipled men in office, the government will soon be corrupted; laws will be made, not for the public good, so much as for selfish or local purposes; corrupt or incompetent men will be appointed to execute the laws; the public revenues will be squandered on unworthy men; and the rights of the citizens will be violated or disregarded. If a republican government fails to secure public prosperity and happiness, it must be because the citizens neglect the divine commands, and elect bad men to make and administer the laws. Intriguing men can never be safely trusted.

For a knowledge of the human heart, and the characters of men, it is customary to resort to the writings of Shakespeare, and of other dramatic authors, and to biography, novels, tales, and fictitious narratives. But whatever amusement may be derived from such writings, they are not the best authorities for a knowledge of mankind. The most perfect maxims and examples for regulating your social conduct and domestic economy, as well as the best rules of morality and religion, are to be found in the Bible. The history of the Jews presents the true character of man in all its forms. All the traits of human character, good and bad; all the passions of the human heart; all the principles which guide and misguide men in society, are depicted in that short history, with an artless simplicity that has no parallel in modern writings. As to maxims of wisdom or prudence, the Proverbs of Solomon furnish a complete system, and sufficient, if carefully observed, to make any man wise, prosperous, and happy. The observation, that "a soft answer turneth away wrath," if strictly observed by men, would prevent half the broils and contentions that inflict wretchedness on society and families.

But were we assured that there is to be no future life, and that men are to perish at death like the beasts of the field; the moral principles and precepts contained in the scriptures ought to form the basis of all our civil constitutions and laws. These principles and precepts have truth, immutable truth, for their foundation; and they are adapted to the wants of men in every condition of life. They are the best principles and precepts, because they are exactly adapted to secure the practice of universal justice and kindness among men; and of course to prevent crimes, war, and disorders in society. No human laws dictated by different principles from those in the gospel, can ever secure these objects. All the miseries and evils which men suffer from vice, crime, ambition, injustice, oppression, slavery, and war, proceed from their despising or neglecting the precepts contained in the Bible.

As the means of temporal happiness then the Christian religion ought to be received, and maintained with firm and cordial support. It is the real source of all genuine republican principles. It teaches the equality of men as to rights and duties; and while it forbids all oppression, it commands due subordination to law and rulers. It requires the young to yield obedience to their parents, and enjoins upon men the duty and selecting their rulers from their fellow citizens of mature age, sound wisdom, and real religion—"men who fear God and hate covetousness." The ecclesiastical establishments of Europe, which serve to support tyrannical governments, are not the Christian religion, but abuses and corruptions of it. The religion of Christ and his apostles, in its primitive simplicity and purity, unencumbered with the trappings of power and the pomp of ceremonies, is the surest basis of a republican government.

Never cease then to give to religion, to its institutions, and to its ministers, your strenuous support. The clergy in this country are not possessed of rank and wealth; they depend for their influence on their talents and learning, on their private virtues and public services. They are the firm supporters of law and good order, the friends of peace, the expounders and teachers of Christian doctrines, the instructors of youth, the promoters of benevolence, of charity, and of all useful improvements. During the war of the revolution, the clergy were generally friendly to the cause of the country. The present generation can hardly have a tolerable idea of the influence of the New-England clergy, in sustaining the patriotic exertions of the people, under the appalling discouragements of the war. The writer remembers their good offices with gratitude. Those men therefore who attempt to impair the influence of that respectable order, in this country, attempt to undermine the best supports of religion; and those who destroy the influence and authority of the christian religion, sap the foundations of public order, of liberty, and of republican government.

For instruction then in social, religious, and civil duties, resort to the scriptures for the best precepts and most excellent examples for imitation. The example of unhesitating faith and obedience in Abraham, when he promptly prepared to offer his son Isaac, as a burnt offering, at the command of God, is a perfect model of that trust in God which becomes dependent beings. The history of Joseph furnishes one of the most charming examples of fraternal affection, and of filial duty and respect for a venerable father, ever exhibited in human life. Christ and his apostles presented, in their lives, the most perfect example of disinterested benevolence, unaffected kindness, humility, patience in adversity, forgiveness of injuries, love to God, and to all mankind. If men would universally cultivate these religious affections and virtuous dispositions, with as much diligence as they cultivate human science and refinement of manners, the world would soon become a terrestrial paradise.

∞

Benjamin Franklin to Jane Mecom, July 28, 1743

BENJAMIN FRANKLIN'S father had seventeen children. Franklin was the youngest boy, and his sister Jane Franklin the youngest girl and his favorite sibling. Though they maintained a long and interesting correspondence throughout their lives, they were sharply divided on the matter of religion. While Jane remained a devout Congregationalist, Franklin did not. On one occasion, Jane wrote a letter to her brother in which she accused him of being "against worshipping of God" and advised him that good works alone were not enough to get to heaven.

Though it is true that Franklin cared more about good works than traditional modes of worship, he did not entirely neglect the latter. In the following letter, Franklin assures his sister that he too believes it is important to worship God and to this effect has written his own articles of faith. (Along the way, he encourages his sister to be tolerant of those like himself who differ with her in matters of faith: "I would only have you make me the small allowances that I extend to you," he writes.)

Dearest Sister Jenny

I took your Admonition very kindly, and was far from being offended at you for it. If I say any thing about it to you, 'tis only to rectify some wrong Opinions you seem to have entertain'd of me, and that I do only because they give you some Uneasiness, which I am unwilling to be the Occasion of. You express yourself as if you thought I was against Worshipping of God, and believed Good Works would merit Heaven; which are both Fancies of your own, I think, without Foundation. I am so far from thinking that God is not to be worshipped, that I have compos'd and wrote a whole Book of Devotions for my own Use: And I imagine there are few, if any, in the World, so weake as to imagine, that the little Good we can do here, can *merit* so vast a Reward hereafter. There are some Things in your New England Doctrines and Worship, which I do not agree with, but I do not therefore condemn them, or desire to shake your Belief or Practice of them. We may dislike things that are nevertheless right in themselves. I would only have you make me the same Allowances, and have a better Opinion both of Morality and your Brother.

∞

George Washington to Samuel Langdon, September 28, 1789

IN THIS letter, Washington succinctly captures the feeling, prevalent in the new nation, that God played a decisive role in the founding of a new people.

. . . *The* man must be bad indeed who can look upon the events of the American Revolution without feeling the warmest gratitude towards the great Author of the Universe whose divine interposition was so frequently manifested in our behalf. And it is my earnest prayer that we may so conduct ourselves as to merit a continuance of those blessings with which we have hitherto been favored. I am etc.

∞

Benjamin Franklin, Appeal for the Hospital, August 8 and August 15, 1751

FRANKLIN was involved in founding the first hospital in America and many other charitable projects in Philadelphia that relieved the suffering of the poor and the sick. Franklin notes that it is by exercising the virtue of charity that "most of all recommends us to the Deity" and believes that if we take care of the neediest among us, God will take care of us.

Post obitum benefacta manent, æternaque Virtus
Non metuit Stygiis, nec rapiatur Aquis.

"After death good deeds remain, eternally:
Virtue fears not the Styx and is not carried away by its waters."

I was sick, and ye visited me.   Matth. xxv.

. . . But tho' every Animal that hath Life is liable to Death, Man, of all other Creatures, has the greatest Number of *Diseases* to his Share; whether they are the Effects of our Intemperance and Vice, or are given us, that we may have a greater Opportunity of exercising towards each other that Virtue, which most of all recommends us to the Deity, I mean CHARITY.

The great Author of our Faith, whose Life should be the constant Object of our Imitation, as far as it is not inimitable, always shew'd the greatest Compassion and regard for the SICK; he disdain'd not to visit and minister Comfort and Health to the meanest of the People; and he frequently inculcated the same Disposition in his Doctrine and Precepts to his Disciples. For this one Thing, (in that beautiful Parable of the Traveller wounded by Thieves) the *Samaritan* (who was esteemed no better than a *Heretick,* or an *Infidel* by the *Orthodox* of those Times) is preferred to the *Priest* and the *Levite;* because he did not, like them, pass by, regardless of the Distress of his Brother Mortal; but when he came to the Place where the half-dead Traveller lay, *he had Compassion on him, and went to him, and bound up his Wounds, pouring in Oil and Wine, and set him on his own Beast, and brought him to an Inn, and took Care of him.*—*Dives,* also, the rich Man, is represented as being excluded from the Happiness of Heaven, because he fared sumptuously every Day, and had Plenty of all Things, and yet neglected to comfort and assist his poor Neighbour, who was helpless and *full of Sores,* and might perhaps have been revived and restored with small Care, *by the Crumbs that fell from his Table, or, as we say, with his loose Corns.*—*I was sick, and ye Visited me,* is one of the Terms of Admission into Bliss, and the Contrary, a Cause of Exclusion: That is, as our Saviour himself explains it, *Ye have visited, or ye have not visited, assisted and comforted those who stood in need of it, even tho' they were the least, or meanest of Mankind.* This Branch of *Charity* seems essential to the true Spirit of Christianity; and should be extended to all in general, whether Deserving or Undeserving, as far as our Power reaches. Of the ten Lepers who were cleansed, *nine* seem to have been much more unworthy than the *tenth,* yet in respect to the Cure of their Disease, they equally shared the Goodness of God. And the great Physician in sending forth his Disciples, always gave them a particular Charge, *that into whatsoever City they entered, they should heal* ALL *the Sick,* without Distinction.

When the good *Samaritan* left his Patient at the Inn, *he gave Money to the Host, and said,* TAKE CARE OF HIM, *and what thou spendest more, I will repay thee.* We are in this World mutual Hosts to each other; the Circumstances and Fortunes of Men and Families are continually changing; in the course of a few Years we have seen the Rich become Poor, and the Poor Rich; the Children of the Wealthy languishing in Want and Misery, and those of their Servants lifted into Estates, and abounding in the good Things of this Life. Since then, our present State, how prosperous soever, hath no Stability, but what depends on the good Providence of God, how careful should we be not to *harden our Hearts* against the Distresses of our Fellow Creatures, lest He who owns and governs all, should punish our Inhumanity, deprived us of a Stewardship in which we have so unworthily behaved, *laugh at our Calamity and mock when our Fear cometh.* Methinks when Objects of Charity, and Opportunities of relieving them, present themselves, we should hear the Voice of this *Samaritan,* as if it were the Voice of God sounding in our Ears, TAKE CARE OF THEM, *and whatever thou spendest, I will repay thee.*

—*The Pennsylvania Gazette,* August 8, 1751

(A continuation of same subject one week later)

. . . It is hoped therefore, that whoever will maturely consider the inestimable Blessings that are connected to a proper Execution of the present Hospital Scheme in this City, can never be so void of Humanity and the essential Duties of Religion as to turn a deaf Ear to the numberless Cries of the Poor and Needy, and refuse for their Assistance, a little of that Superfluity, which a bountiful Providence has so liberally bestowed on them.

The Pennsylvania Gazette, August 15, 1751

∞

John Adams, Diary, *February 16 and May 28, 1756*

A RECENT graduate of Harvard University, and unsure if he wanted to pursue the study of law or theology, Adams took a job in 1755 as schoolmaster in Worcester, Massachusetts. Of course, the young and ambitious Adams was thinking of bigger things outside of his small classroom. Adams brooded a lot during his three years as schoolmaster and recorded his broodings in his diary. Well aware that vanity was his "cardinal vice and cardinal folly," he freely confessed his weaknesses, in turmoil that his worldly ambitions overwhelmed the Biblical teachings for humility.

Students who read Adams will discover that the Founders were not stodgy, serene, entirely cerebral, and purely spiritual beings. Here is the hard, self-doubting, suffering mind and soul trying to figure out what it's all about. The question of meaning is often fought out with difficulty in men's souls. For some men, like Washington, God's presence is a constant comfort and source of repose—they are God's serene souls. For others God's presence often feels like accusation and judgment. For much of his life that was Adams's predilection and he found himself often "wrestling with angels." Here is God's tortured soul.

February 16, 1756

Oh! that I could wear out of my mind every mean and base affectation, conquer my natural Pride and Self Conceit, expect no more defference from my fellows than I deserve, acquire that meekness, and humility, which are the sure marks and Characters of a great and generous Soul, and subdue every unworthy Passion and treat all men as I wish to be treated by all. How happy should I then be, in the favour and good will of all honest men, and the sure prospect of a happy immortality!

May 1756

Drank Tea at Mr. Putnams.—What is the proper Business of Mankind in this Life? We came into the World naked and destitute of all the Conveniences and necessaries of Life. And if we were not provided for, and nourished by our Parents or others should inevitably perish as soon as born. We increase in strength of Body and mind by slow and insensible Degrees. 1/3 of our Time is consumed in sleep, and 3/4 of the remainder, is spent in procuring a mere animal sustenance. And if we live to the Age of three score and Ten and then set down to make an estimate in our minds of the Happiness we have enjoyed and the Misery we have suffered, We shall find I am apt to think, that the overbalance of Happiness is quite inconsiderable. We shall find that we have been through the greatest Part of our Lives pursuing Shadows, and empty but glittering Phantoms rather than substances. We shall find that we have applied our whole Vigour, all our Faculties, in the Pursuit of Honour, or Wealth, or Learning or some other such delusive Trifle, instead of the real and everlasting Excellences of Piety and Virtue. Habits of Contemplating the Deity and his transcendent Excellences, and correspondent Habits of complacency in and Dependence upon him, Habits of Reverence and Gratitude, to God, and Habits of Love and Compassion to our fellow men and Habits of Temperance, Recollection and self Government will afford us a real and substantial Pleasure. We may then exult in a Consciousness of the Favour of God, and the Prospect of everlasting Felicity.

∞

Benjamin Franklin to Joseph Huey, June 6, 1753

FRANKLIN'S PLEA that faith produce more good works seems right. It is a fair request.

The Faith you mention has doubtless its use in the World. I do not desire to see it diminished, nor would I endeavor to lessen it in any Man. But I wish it were more productive of Good Works than I have generally seen it: I mean real good Works, Works of Kindness, Charity, Mercy, and Publick Spirit; not Holiday-keeping, Sermon-Reading or Hearing, performing Church Ceremonies, or making long Prayers, fill'd with Flatteries and Compliments, despis'd even by wise Men, and much less capable of pleasing the Deity. The Worship of God is a Duty, the hearing and reading of Sermons may be useful; but if Men rest in Hearing and Praying, as too many do, it is as if a Tree should value itself on being water'd and putting forth Leaves, tho' it never produc'd any Fruit.

Your great Master tho't much less of these outward Appearances and Professions than many of his modern Disciples. He prefer'd the Doers of the World to the meer Hearers; the Son that seemingly refus'd to obey his Father and yet perform'd his Commands, to him that profess'd his Readiness but neglected the Works; the heretical but charitable Samaritan, to the uncharitable tho' orthodox Priest and sanctified Levite: and those who gave Food to the hungry, Drink to the Thirsty, Raiment to the Naked, Entertainment to the Stranger, and Relief to the Sick, &c. tho' they never heard of his Name, he declares shall in the last Day be accepted, when those who cry Lord, Lord; who value themselves on their Faith tho' great enough to perform Miracles but have neglected good Works shall be rejected. He profess'd that he came not to call the Righteous but

Sinners to Repentance, which imply'd his modest Opinion that there were some in his Time so good that they need not hear even him for Improvement; but now a days we have scarce a little Parson, that does not think it the Duty of every Man within his Reach to sit under his petty Ministrations, and that whoever omits them offends God. I wish to such more Humility, and to you Health and Happiness, being Your Friend and Servant

∞

James Wilson, "The Laws of Nature," 1790

JAMES WILSON came to America from Scotland in 1765 in order to study law. He signed the Declaration of Independence and the Constitution and later became a justice on the U.S. Supreme Court. Benjamin Rush described his mind as a "blaze of light . . . He rendered great and essential services to his country in every stage of the Revolution."

Wilson's sophisticated legal mind did not neglect the duties of a higher law. He believed that the law of God was the "supreme" law in the land and the basis of all moral obligations.

Having thus stated the question—what is the efficient cause of moral obligation?—I give it this answer—the will of God. This is the supreme law. His just and full right of imposing laws, and our duty in obeying them, are the sources of our moral obligations. If I am asked—why do you obey the will of God? I answer—because it is my duty to do so. If I am asked again—how do you know this to be your duty? I answer again—because I am told so by my moral sense or conscience. If I am asked a third time—how do you know that you ought to do that, of which your conscience enjoins the performance? I can only say, I *feel* that such is my duty. Here investigation must stop; reasoning can go no farther. The science of morals, as well as other sciences, is founded on truths, that cannot be discovered or proved by reasoning. Reason is confined to the investigation of unknown truths by the means of such as are known. We cannot, therefore, begin to reason, till we are furnished, otherwise than by reason, with some truths, on which we can found our arguments. Even in mathematics, we must be provided with axioms perceived intuitively to be true, before our demonstrations can com-

mence. Morality, like mathematics, has its intuitive truths, without which we cannot make a single step in our reasonings upon the subject. Such an intuitive truth is that, with which we just now closed our investigation. If a person was not possessed of the feeling before mentioned; it would not be in the power of arguments, to give him any conception of the distinction between right and wrong. These terms would be to him equally unintelligible, as the term *color* to one who was born and has continued blind. But that there is, in human nature, such a moral principle, has been felt and acknowledged in all ages and nations.

Now that we have stated and answered the first question; let us proceed to the consideration of the second—how shall we, in particular instances, learn the dictates of our duty, and make, with accuracy, the proper distinction between right and wrong; in other words, how shall we, in particular cases, discover the will of God? We discover it by our conscience, by our reason, and by the Holy Scriptures. The law of nature and the law of revelation are both divine; they flow, though in different channels, from the same adorable source. It is, indeed, preposterous to separate them from each other. The object of both is—to discover the will of God—and both are necessary for the accomplishment of that end.

∽

Benjamin Franklin to Ezra Stiles, *March 9, 1790*

EZRA STILES was president of Yale and an old friend of Franklin's. Stiles wrote a letter to Franklin requesting a confidential account of his religious views. Here is Franklin's reply—candid and authentic. This is about as "unreligious" as any of the Founders got.

You desire to know something of my Religion. It is the first time I have been questioned upon it. But I cannot take your Curiosity amiss, and shall endeavour in a few Words to gratify it. Here is my Creed. I believe in one God, Creator of the Universe. That he governs it by his Providence. That he ought to be worshipped. That the most acceptable Service we render to him is doing good to his other Children. That the soul of Man is immortal, and will be treated with Justice in another Life respecting its Conduct in this. These I take to be the fundamental Principles of all sound Religion, and I regard them as you do in whatever Sect I meet with them.

As to Jesus of Nazareth, my Opinion of whom you particularly desire, I think the System of Morals and his Religion, as he left them to us, the best the World ever saw or is likely to see; but I apprehend it has received various corrupting Changes, and I have, with most of the present Dissenters in England, some Doubts as to his Divinity; tho' it is a question I do not dogmatize upon, having never studied it, and think it needless to busy myself with it now, when I expect soon an Opportunity of knowing the Truth with less Trouble. I see no harm, however, in its being believed, if that Belief has the good Consequence, as probably it has, of making his Doctrines more respected and better observed; especially as I do not perceive, that the Supreme takes it amiss, by distinguishing the Unbelievers in his Government of the World with any peculiar Marks of his Displeasure.

I shall only add, respecting myself, that, having experienced the Goodness of that Being in conducting me prosperously thro' a long life, I have no doubt of its Continuance in the next, though without the smallest Conceit of meriting such Goodness. . . .

❧

John Adams to Benjamin Rush, July 19, 1812

JOHN ADAMS and Benjamin Rush carried on a lively correspondence, especially during the years of 1805-1813. Their letters were full of reminiscences of their revolutionary days. They also discussed their views on philosophical, moral, and religious questions of the day.

In the month of March last I was called to the house in another part of town which was built by my father, in which he lived and died and from which I buried him; and in the chamber in which I was born I could not forbear to weep over the remains of a beautiful child of my son Thomas that died of the whooping cough. Why was I preserved 3/4 of a century, and that rose cropped in the bud? I, almost dead at top and in all my limbs and wholly useless to myself and the world? Great Teacher, tell me.

What has preserved this race of Adamses in all their ramifications, in such numbers, health, peace, comfort, and mediocrity? I believe it is religion, without which they would have been rakes, fops, sots, gamblers, starved with hunger, frozen with cold, scalped by Indians, &c., &c., &c., been melted away and disappeared. . . .

❧

John Adams to Benjamin Rush, February 2, 1807

LIKE NOAH Webster's piece, here is another straightforward argument for reading the Bible.

The Bible contains the most profound philosophy, the most perfect morality, and the most refined policy, that ever was conceived upon earth. It is the most republican book in the world, and therefore I will still revere it. The curses against fornication and adultery, and the prohibition of every wanton glance or libidinous ogle at a woman, I believe to be the only system that ever did or ever will preserve a republic in the world. There is a paradox for you. But if I don't make it out, you may say if you please that I am an enthusiast. I say then that national morality never was and never can be preserved without the utmost purity and chastity in women; and without national morality a republican govern- ment cannot be maintained. Therefore, my dear Fellow Citizens of Amer- ica, you must ask leave of your wives and daughters to preserve your republic. I believe I shall write a book upon this topic before I die, and if I could articulate a word, I don't know but I would go into the pulpit and preach upon it. I should be very learned: ransack Greece and Rome and Judea and France and England and Holland, &c.

John Adams to Thomas Jefferson, December 3, 1813

THE CORRESPONDENCE between Adams and Jefferson is among the most famous exchange of letters in America. In these letters, many historians have noted, we find the thoughts, ideas, and feelings of the founding. Many have argued that these two men were not only ad- dressing each other but also future generations of Americans.

One of the more popular topics that these two men discussed was religion. Here again a tribute to the persuasiveness of George Whitefield, the leading preacher of America's First Great Awakening, whom we saw earlier in this chapter.

I know of no Philosopher, or Theologian, or Moralist ancient or modern more profound; more infallible than Whitefield, if the Anecdote that I have heard be true.

He began; "Father Abraham"! with his hands and Eyes gracefully di- rected to the Heavens as I have more than once seen him; "Father Abraham," "who have you there with you"? ["]have you Catholicks?" No. "Have you Protestants". No. "Have you Churchmen". No. "Have you Dissenters". No. "Have you Presbyterians"? No. "Quakers?" No. ["]Ana- baptists"? No. "Who have you then?" "Are you alone"? No.

"My Brethren,! You have the Answer to all these questions in the Words of My Text, "He who feareth God and worketh Righteousness, shall be accepted of him.""

Thomas Jefferson to Miles King, September 26, 1814

J E F F E R S O N   D E E P L Y cherished the liberty of conscience of all individuals and hoped that others would respect his as well. In this letter, he looks forward to an eternal brotherhood of man, where divisions caused by differences of religious creeds are finally overcome.

Sir,—I duly received your letter of August 20th, and I thank you for it, because I believe it was written with kind intentions, and a personal concern for my future happiness. Whether the particular revelation which you suppose to have been made to yourself were real or imaginary, your reason alone is the competent judge. For dispute as long as we will on religious tenets, our reason at last must ultimately decide, as it is the only oracle which God has given us to determine between what really comes from Him and the phantasms of a disordered or deluded imagination. When He means to make a personal revelation, He carries conviction of its authenticity to the reason He has bestowed as the umpire of truth. You believe you have been favored with such a special communication. Your reason, not mine, is to judge of this; and if it shall be His pleasure to favor me with a like admonition, I shall obey it with the same fidelity with which I would obey His known will in all cases. Hitherto I have been under the guidance of that portion of reason which He has thought proper to deal out to me. I have followed it faithfully in all important cases, to such a degree at least as leaves me without uneasiness; and if on minor occasions I have erred from its dictates, I have trust in Him who made us what we are, and know it was not His plan to make us always unerring. He has formed us moral agents. Not that, in the perfection of His state, He can feel pain or pleasure in anything we may do; He is far above our power; but that we may promote the happiness of those with whom He has placed us in society, by acting honestly towards all, benevolently to those who fall within our way, respecting sacredly their rights, bodily and mental, and cherishing especially their freedom of conscience, as we value our own. I must ever believe that religion substantially good which produces an honest life, and we have been authorized by One whom you and I equally respect, to judge of the tree by its fruit. Our particular principles of religion are a subject of accountability to our God alone. I inquire after no man's, and trouble none with mine; nor is it given to us in this life to know whether yours or mine, our friends or our foes, are exactly the right. Nay, we have heard it said that there is not a Quaker or a Baptist, a Presbyterian or an Episcopalian, a Catholic or a Protestant in heaven; that, on entering that gate, we leave those badges of schisms behind, and find ourselves united in those principles only in which God has united us all. Let us not be uneasy then about the different roads we may pursue, as believing them the shortest, to that our last abode; but, following the guidance of a good conscience, let us be happy in the hope that by these different paths we shall all meet in the end. And that you and I may there meet and embrace, is my earnest prayer. And with this assurance I salute you with brotherly esteem and respect.

∞

Thomas Jefferson to John Adams, January 11, 1817

HERE IS a typical subject matter often discussed in the correspondence between Jefferson and Adams—religion. Jefferson shares some of his lifelong reflections on religious faith, emphasizing the importance of freedom of conscience.

. . . *The* result of your 50. or 60. years of religious reading in the four words 'be just and good' is that in which all our enquiries must end; as the riddles of all the priesthoods end in four more 'ubi panis, ibi deus ["where there is bread, there is God"].' What all agree in is probably right; what no two agree in most probably wrong. One of our fan-colouring biographers, who paints small men as very great, enquired of me lately, with real affection too, whether he might consider as authentic, the change in my religion much spoken of in some circles. Now this supposed that they knew what had been my religion before, taking for it the word of their priests, whom I certainly never made the confidants of my creed. My answer was 'say nothing of my religion. It is known to my god and myself alone. Its evidence before the world is to be sought in my life. If that has been *honest and dutiful to society,* the religion which has regulated it cannot be a bad one.' Affectionately Adieu.

Benjamin Rush,
"Of the Mode of Education Proper in a Republic," 1798

IN 1776, Benjamin Franklin proposed the following motto as the national seal for the United States: "Rebellion to Tyrants Is Obedience to God." Here, Benjamin Rush shows why this is true—how the principles of liberty and equality in America are best sustained by an education in religion.

I proceed in the next place, to enquire, what mode of education we shall adopt so as to secure to the state all the advantages that are to be derived from the proper instruction of youth; and here I beg leave to remark, that the only foundation for a useful education in a republic is to be laid in Religion. Without this there can be no virtue, and without virtue there can be no liberty, and liberty is the object and life of all republican governments.

Such is my veneration for every religion that reveals the attributes of the Deity, or a future state of rewards and punishments, that I had rather see the opinions of Confucius or Mahomed inculcated upon our youth, than see them grow up wholly devoid of a system of religious principles. But the religion I mean to recommend in this place is that of the New Testament.

It is foreign to my purpose to hint at the arguments which establish the truth of the Christian revelation. My only business is to declare, that all its doctrines and precepts are calculated to promote the happiness of society, and the safety and well being of civil government. A Christian cannot fail of being a republican. The history of the creation of man, and of the relation of our species to each other by birth, which is recorded in the Old Testament, is the best refutation that can be given to the divine right of kings, and the strongest argument that can be used in favor of the original and natural equality of all mankind. A Christian, I say again, cannot fail of being a republican, for every precept of the Gospel inculcates those degrees of humility, self-denial, and brotherly kindness, which are directly opposed to the pride of monarchy and the pageantry of a court. A Christian cannot fail of being useful to the republic, for his religion teacheth him, that no man "liveth to himself." And lastly, a Christian cannot fail of being wholly inoffensive, for his religion teacheth him, in all things to do to others what he would wish, in like circumstances, they should do to him.

∞

Thomas Jefferson to Thomas Jefferson Smith, February 21, 1825

A FRIEND asked Jefferson to give some advice to his young son, named after Jefferson, Thomas Jefferson Smith. Jefferson wrote a letter that was to be shown to Smith when he was old enough to appreciate it.

I think the litany of brief exhortations—"few words" is spectacular. In our age, all could be taken to heart with profit, especially "Murmur not at the ways of Providence." We live in a time of complaint from many who have much—perhaps too much.

This letter will, to you, be as one from the dead. The writer will be in the grave before you can weigh its counsels. Your affectionate and excellent father has requested that I would address to you something which might possibly have a favorable influence on the course of life you have to run; and I too, as a namesake, feel an interest in that course. Few words will be necessary, with good dispositions on your part. Adore God. Reverence and cherish your parents. Love your neighbor as yourself, and your country more than yourself. Be just. Be true. Murmur not at the ways of Providence. So shall the life into which you have entered, be the portal to one of eternal and ineffable bliss. And if to the dead it is permitted to care for the things of this world, every action of your life will be under my regard. Farewell.

SOURCES

Adams, Charles Francis. *The Letters of Mrs. Adams.* 2 vols. Boston: Charles C. Little and James Brown, 1841.

Adams, Charles Francis. *The Works of John Adams.* 10 vols. Boston: Little, Brown & Co., 1850–1856.

Andrews, James DeWitt, ed. *The Works of James Wilson.* 2 vols. Chicago: Callaghan and Company, 1896.

Baldwin, James. *The Story of Liberty.* American Book Company, 1919.

Bowen, Catherine Drinker. *Miracle at Philadelphia.* Boston: Little, Brown & Company, 1986.

Brandes, Paul, ed. *John Hancock's Life and Speeches: A Personalized Vision of the American Revolution 1763–1793.* Lanham, MD: Scarecrow Press, 1996.

Brookhiser, Richard. *Founding Father: Rediscovering George Washington.* New York: The Free Press, 1996.

Brubaker, Abram. *The Spirit of America.* Garden City, New York: Doubleday, Page & Co., 1920.

Burstein, Andrew. *The Inner Jefferson: Portrait of a Grieving Optimist.* Charles Hesville: University of Virginia Press.

Butterfield, L.H., ed. *Adams Family Correspondence.* 6 vols. Cambridge, Mass.: Belknap Press of Harvard University, 1963.

Butterfield, L.H., ed. *The Book of Abigail and John: Selected Letters of the Adams Family 1762–1784.* Cambridge, Mass.: Harvard University Press, 1975.

Butterfield, L.H., ed. *Diary and Autobiography of John Adams.* 4 vols. Cambridge, Mass.: Belknap Press of Harvard University, 1961.

Butterfield, L.H., ed. *Letters of Benjamin Rush.* 2 vols. Princeton, N.J.: Princeton University Press, 1951.

Butterfield, L.H., ed. *My Dearest Julia: The Love Letters of Dr. Benjamin Rush to Julia Stockton.* New York: N. Watson Academic Publications, 1979.

Cappon, Lester, ed. *The Adams-Jefferson Letters: The Complete Correspondence Between Thomas Jefferson and Abigail and John Adams.* Chapel Hill: University of North Carolina Press for The Institute of Early American History and Culture at Williamsburg, Virginia, 1987.

Cushing, Harry Alonzo, ed. *The Writings of Samuel Adams.* 4 vols. New York: G.P. Putnam's Sons, 1904–1908.

Dwight, Nathaniel. *The Lives of the Signers of the Declaration of Independence.* New York: A.S. Barnes & Company, 1876.

Farmer, Lydia Hoyt. *The Life of Lafayette, the Knight of Liberty in Two Worlds and Two Centuries.* New York: T.Y. Crowell & Co., 1888.

Farrand, Max, ed. *The Records of the Federal Convention of 1787*. Rev. ed., 4 vols. New Haven and London: Yale University Press, 1937.

Fitzpatrick, John C. *The Writings of George Washington from the Original Manuscript Sources, 1745–1799*. 39 vols. Washington, D.C.: Government Printing Office, 1931–1944.

Ford, Paul Leceister, ed. *The Works of Thomas Jefferson*. 12 vols. New York and London: G.P. Putnam's Sons, 1904–1905.

Frost, John. *Lives of the Heroes of the American Revolution*. Boston: Phillips & Samson, 1848.

Grant, Ruth W. and Nathan Tarcov, eds. *John Locke: Some Thoughts Concerning Education and of the Conduct of the Understanding*. Indianapolis: Hackett Publishing Company, Inc., 1996.

Hart, Ann Clark, ed. *Abraham Clark: Signer of the Declaration of Independence*. San Francisco: The Pioneer Press, 1923.

Holland, Rupert Sargent. *Lafayette for Young Americans*. George W. Jacobs & Co, 1922.

Hunt, Gaillard, ed. *The Writings of James Madison*. 9 vols. New York: G.P. Putnam's Sons, 1900–1910.

Irving, Washington, *Life of George Washington*. 3 vols. New York: G.P. Putnam & Co., 1855.

Johnston, Henry P. *The Correspondence and Public Papers of John Jay*. 4 vols. New York and London: G.P. Putnam's Sons, 1890–1893.

Koch, Andrienne. *Jefferson and Madison: The Great Collaboration*. New York: Oxford University Press, 1964.

Labaree, Leonard W. *The Papers of Benjamin Franklin*. 27 vols. New Haven: Yale University Press, 1959.

Langguth, A.J. *Patriots: The Men Who Started the American Revolution*. New York: Simon & Schuster, 1988.

Lipscomb, Andrew A. and Albert Ellery Bergh. *The Writings of Thomas Jefferson*. 20 vols. Washington, D.C.: Thomas Jefferson Memorial Association, 1905.

Lodge, Henry Cabot. *The Works of Alexander Hamilton*. 12 vols. New York, London: G.P. Putnam's Sons, The Knickerbocker Press, 1904.

Mitchell, Stewart. *New Letters of Abigail Adams, 1788–1801*. Boston: Houghton Mifflin, 1947.

Morris, Anne Cary. *Diary and Letters of Gouverneur Morris*. New York: Charles Scribner's Sons, 1898.

Nicolay, Helen. *The Boys Life of Thomas Jefferson*. New York: D. Appleton-Century Co., 1933.

Padover, Saul, ed. *The Complete Madison: His Basic Writings*. Millwood, New York: Kraus Reprint Co., 1973.

Padover, Saul, ed. *The Mind of Alexander Hamilton*. New York: Harper, 1958.

Paine, Thomas. *The Complete Political Works of Thomas Paine*. 2 vols. New York: Peter Eckler, Publisher, 1891.

Peterson, Merill D. *The Portable Thomas Jefferson*. New York: Viking Press, 1975.

Randall, Henry S. *The Life of Thomas Jefferson*. 3 vols. Freeport, N.Y.: Books for Libraries Press, 1857.

Randolph, Sarah N. *The Domestic Life of Thomas Jefferson*. New York: Harper & Brothers, Publishers, Franlin Square, 1871.

Rives, William C. *History of the Life and Times of James Madison.* 3 vols. Freeport, N.Y.: Books for Libraries Press, 1859–1868, reprinted 1970.

Rowland, Kate Mason. *The Life of George Mason.* New York: G.P. Putnam's Sons, 1892.

Runes, Dagobert D., ed. *The Selected Writings of Benjamin Rush.* New York: Philosophical Library, 1947.

Rutland, Robert A. *James Madison: The Founding Father.* New York: Macmillan Publishing Company, 1987.

Smith, Richard Norton. *Patriarch: George Washington and the New American Nation.* Boston: Houghton Mifflin Company, 1993.

Smyth, Albert Henry, ed. *The Writings of Benjamin Franklin.* 10 vols. New York: Macmillan Co., 1905–1907.

Stevenson, Burton. *Great Americans As Seen By the Poets.* Philadelphia, London: J.B. Lippincott Company, 1933.

Storing, Herbert J., ed. *The Complete Anti-Federalist.* 7 vols. Chicago: University of Chicago Press, 1981.

Tappan, Eva March. *American Hero Stories.* Boston: Houghton, Mifflin & Co., 1906.

Webster, Noah. *A Collection of Essays and Fugitiv Writings on Moral, Historical, Political and Literary Subjects.* Boston, 1790. Reprint, Delmar, N.Y.: Scholars's Facsimiles & Reprints, 1977.

Webster, Noah. *Value of the Bible and Excellence of the Christian Religion: For the Use of Families and Schools.* San Francisco: Foundation for American Christian Education, 1988.

Weems, Mason. *A History of the Life and Death, Virtues and Exploits of General George Washington.* New York: Grosset & Dunlap Publishing, 1927.

Wilson, Woodrow. *George Washington.* New York: Harper & Brothers, 1896.

Wirt, William. *Sketches of the Life and Character of Patrick Henry.* New York, 1859.

INDEX

Page numbers in *italics* refer to authorship of documents.

PERMISSIONS

For permission to reprint copyrighted material, grateful acknowledgment is made to the following publishers:

Thomas Jefferson to John Adams: November 13, 1818, January 21, 1812, October 12, 1823, March 25, 1826, and December 10, 1819; Thomas Jefferson to Abigail Adams: September 25, 1785 and June 13, 1804; Abigail Adams to Thomas Jefferson: June 6, 1785, May 20, 1804; John Adams to Thomas Jefferson: January 1, 1812, December 21, 1819, June 28, 1813, and December 3, 1813, reprinted from *The Adams–Jefferson Letters, Vol. I and II,* edited by Lester J. Cappon. Copyright © renewed 1987 by Stanley B. Cappon. Used by permission of the publisher.

Abigail Adams to Mary Cranch: January 5, 1790, reprinted from *New Letters of Abigail Adams: 1788–1801.* Copyright 1974 by Houghton-Mifflin. Used courtesy of the publisher.

"Thomas Jefferson and Benjamin Franklin at the Second Continental Congress," reprinted from *The Boys Life of Thomas Jefferson* by Helen Nicolay. Copyright 1905, 1906, by the Century Co., Copyright renewed 1933 by Helen Nicolay. Used by permission of Dutton Signet, a division of Penguin Books USA Inc.

Benjamin Rush to Julia Rush: November 15, 1775, and June 11, 1812, reprinted from *My Dearest Julia: The Love Letters of Dr. Benjamin Rush to Julia Stockton.* Copyright 1979 by N. Watson Academic Publications. Used by permission of the publisher.

Abigail Adams to John Adams: June 18, 1775, August 11, 1763, September 12, 1763, May 9, 1764, March 31, 1776, and December 23, 1782; John Adams to Abigail Smith Adams: July 7, 1775, October 4, 1762, February 14, 1763, August 1763, May 7, 1764, September 30, 1764, April 14, 1776, October 29, 1775, and July 1, 1774, reprinted from *The Book of Abigail and John: Selected Letters of the Adams Family, 1762–1884,* edited by L.H. Butterfield, March Friedlaender, and Mary-Jo Kline. Copyright © 1975 by the Massachusetts Historical Society. Used by permission of Harvard University Press.

Abigail Adams to John Adams: October 9, 1775, and John Adams to Abigail Smith: 1762–1765 from Vol I; John Quincy Adams to John Adams: March 16, 1780, and March 17, 1780; Abigail Adams to John Quincy Adams: June 1778, from Vol. III; Abigail Adams to John Adams: June 17, 1782, and January 21, 1781, from Vol. IV; Abigail Adams to John Adams: October 25, 1775, from Vol. V; and Abigail Adams to Mary Cranch: February 20, 1785, from Vol. VI. All reprinted from *The Adams Family Correspondence,* edited by L.H. Butterfield. 6 vols. Copyright 1963 by Belknap Press of Harvard University Press. Used by permission of the publisher.

John Adams, *Diary:* February 16, 1756, May 1756, and August 14, 1796, reprinted from Volumes I and III of *Diary and Autobiography of John Adams.* Copyright 1961 by Belknap Press of Harvard University Press. Used by permission of the publisher.

"George Washington and Gouverneur Morris at the Constitutional Convention," reprinted from *The Records of the Federal Convention of 1787,* Volume III, edited by Max Farrand. Copyright © 1911, 1937, renewed 1966 by Yale University Press. Used by permission of the publisher.

Benjamin Franklin's "Rules for Making Oneself a Disagreeable Companion" and "Doctrine to Be Preached," reprinted from Volume I, *The Papers of Benjamin Franklin,* edited by Leonard Labaree. Copyright 1959 by Yale University Press. Used by permission of the publisher.

Picture Credits:
ARCHIVE PHOTOS: 23, 74, 99, 215, 235, 252, 263, 306. CORBIS-BETTMANN: 37, 47, 52, 106, 122, 140, 143, 163, 177, 192, 269, 286, 302, 311, 320, 325, 355, 363, 373, 406. CULVER PICTURES INC: 65. UPI/CORBIS-BETTMANN: 360

LaVergne, TN USA
16 September 2010
197217LV00006B/1/P